SRA Reading Mastery

Signature Edition

Language Arts
Presentation Book B
Grade 1

Siegfried Engelmann
Jean Osborn
Karen Lou Seitz Davis

McGraw Hill SRA

Columbus, OH

SRAonline.com

 SRA

Send all inquiries to this address:
SRA/McGraw-Hill
4400 Easton Commons
Columbus, OH 43219

ISBN: 978-0-07-612485-5
MHID: 0-07-612485-1

5 6 7 8 9 RMN 13 12 11

The *McGraw·Hill* Companies

Table of Contents

Scope and Sequence *at the back of the book*

Objectives

- Identify an object by stated criteria. (Exercise 1)
- Discriminate between true and false statements and generate true and false statements. (Exercise 2)
- Given a complex sentence, answer questions involving who, what, where, when and why. (Exercise 3)
- Replace a word in a sentence with an opposite and generate statements with opposites. (Exercise 4)
- Answer questions involving previously learned calendar facts. (Exercise 5)
- **Write three sentences about story characters.** (Exercise 6)
- Follow coloring rules involving classes and subclasses. (Exercise 7)
- Complete an analogy involving class. (Exercise 8)

EXERCISE 1 Descriptions

1. You're going to figure out what object I'm thinking of.
2. Listen: I'm thinking of a vehicle that has wheels. Name some vehicles that I could be thinking of. (Call on individual children.)
3. Listen: The vehicle with wheels I'm thinking of makes a lot of noise.
- Could I be thinking of a train? (Signal.) *Yes.* How do you know? (Call on a child. Idea: *It's a vehicle with wheels that makes a lot of noise.*)
4. (Repeat step 3 until firm.)
5. Everybody, could I be thinking of an airplane? (Signal.) *Yes.*
- How do you know? (Call on a child. Idea: *It's a vehicle with wheels that makes a lot of noise.*)
- Everybody, could I be thinking of a bicycle? (Signal.) *No.*
- How do you know? (Call on a child. Idea: *It doesn't make a lot of noise.*)
- Everybody, could I be thinking of a motorcycle? (Signal.) *Yes.*
- How do you know? (Call on a child. Idea: *It's a vehicle with wheels that makes a lot of noise.*)
6. (Repeat step 5 until firm.)
7. Listen: The object I'm thinking of flies in the air.
- Could I be thinking of a train? (Signal.) *No.*
- How do you know? (Call on a child. Idea: *It doesn't fly in the air.*)

- Everybody, could I be thinking of an airplane? (Signal.) *Yes.*
- How do you know? (Call on a child. Idea: *It's a vehicle with wheels that makes a lot of noise and flies in the air.*)
8. Yes, I was thinking of an airplane.

EXERCISE 2 True—False

1. I'm going to say statements. Some of these statements are true and some are false. You tell me about each statement.
2. A shirt is a building. True or false? (Signal.) *False.*
- You find an airplane in a dentist's office. True or false? (Signal.) *False.*
- A table is an animal. True or false? (Signal.) *False.*
- You go to school to learn. True or false? (Signal.) *True.*
- A flower is not a container. True or false? (Signal.) *True.*
3. (Repeat step 2 until firm.)
4. Your turn. Make up a statement about a table that is true. (Call on three children. Praise each acceptable statement and have the group repeat it. Then say:) Everybody, that statement is . . . (Signal.) *true.*
5. Your turn. Now make up a statement about a table that is false. (Call on three children. Praise each acceptable statement and have the group repeat it. Then say:) Everybody, that statement is . . . (Signal.) *false.*

EXERCISE 3 Who—What—Where—When—Why

1. I'm going to say sentences that answer questions. One of the questions is why.
2. Listen: We sat next to the road because we were tired. Say the sentence. Get ready. (Signal.) *We sat next to the road because we were tired.*
- Who sat next to the road? (Signal.) *We did.*
- Where did we sit? (Signal.) *Next to the road.*
- Why did we sit next to the road? (Signal.) *Because we were tired.*
3. Everybody, say the whole sentence. Get ready. (Signal.) *We sat next to the road because we were tired.*
- Which word tells who? (Signal.) *We.*
- Which words tell where? (Signal.) *Next to the road.*
- Which words tell why? (Signal.) *Because we were tired.*
4. (Repeat step 3 until firm.)
5. Listen: Tomorrow, Mr. Brantly will go to Texas. Say the sentence. Get ready. (Signal.) *Tomorrow, Mr. Brantly will go to Texas.*
- Who will go to Texas? (Signal.) *Mr. Brantly.*
- When will Mr. Brantly go to Texas? (Signal.) *Tomorrow.*
- Where will Mr. Brantly go tomorrow? (Signal.) *To Texas.*
- What will Mr. Brantly do tomorrow? (Signal.) *Go to Texas.*
6. Everybody, say the whole sentence. Get ready. (Signal.) *Tomorrow, Mr. Brantly will go to Texas.*
- Which words tell who? (Signal.) *Mr. Brantly.*
- Which words tell where? (Signal.) *To Texas.*
- Which word tells when? (Signal.) *Tomorrow.*

EXERCISE 4 Opposites

1. You're going to make up statements that have the opposite word.
2. What's the opposite of pushing? (Signal.) *Pulling.*
- What's the opposite of shiny? (Signal.) *Dull.*
- What's the opposite of safe? (Signal.) *Dangerous.*
- What's the opposite of early? (Signal.) *Late.*
- What's the opposite of before? (Signal.) *After.*
- What's the opposite of start? (Signal.) *Finish.*

3. You're going to make up statements that have the opposite word.
4. Listen: The children played before school. Say that statement. Get ready. (Signal.) *The children played before school.*
- Now say a statement that tells the opposite about when the children played. Get ready. (Signal.) *The children played after school.*
5. Listen: She cooked the vegetables before she set the table. Say that statement. Get ready. (Signal.) *She cooked the vegetables before she set the table.*
- Now say a statement that tells the opposite about when she cooked the vegetables. Get ready. (Signal.) *She cooked the vegetables after she set the table.*
6. Listen: A crowd gathered at the finish line. Say that statement. Get ready. (Signal.) *A crowd gathered at the finish line.*
- Now say a statement that tells the opposite about where the crowd gathered. Get ready. (Signal.) *A crowd gathered at the starting line.*
7. Listen: The road was safe. Say that statement. Get ready. (Signal.) *The road was safe.*
- Now say a statement that tells the opposite about the road. Get ready. (Signal.) *The road was dangerous.*
8. Listen: The water was shallow. Say that statement. Get ready. (Signal.) *The water was shallow.*
- Now say a statement that tells the opposite about the water. Get ready. (Signal.) *The water was deep.*

EXERCISE 5 Calendar Facts

1. You learned calendar facts.
- Everybody, how many days are in a week? (Signal.) *Seven.*
- Everybody, say the days of the week. Get ready. (Signal.) *Sunday, Monday, Tuesday, Wednesday, Thursday, Friday, Saturday.*
2. How many weeks are in a year? (Signal.) *52.*
- Say the fact. Get ready. (Signal.) *There are 52 weeks in a year.*
3. How many days are in a year? (Signal.) *365.*
- Say the fact. Get ready. (Signal.) *There are 365 days in a year.*

4. How many seasons are in a year?
   (Signal.) *Four.*
• Name the four seasons. Get ready. (Signal.)
   Winter, spring, summer, fall.
5. How many months are in a year? (Signal.) *12.*
• Everybody, say the months. Get ready.
   (Signal.) *January, February, March, April,*
   May, June, July, August, September,
   October, November, December.
6. (Repeat step 5 until firm.)
7. What day of the week is it today? (Signal.)
• What day of the week will it be tomorrow?
   (Signal.)
• What's today's date? (Signal.)

WORKBOOK

EXERCISE 6 **Sentence Construction**

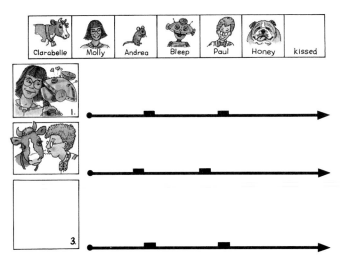

1. Everybody, find Lesson 61 in your
   workbook. Write your name at the top of
   the page. ✔
• You're going to make up sentences, but
   you're not going to use cutouts. You're
   just going to write the correct words. The
   words that you'll use are in the boxes at
   the top of the page. All the boxes except
   one have a picture.
2. Everybody, touch the first box. ✔
   Who is that? (Signal.) *Clarabelle.*
   And her name is written below.
• Touch the next box. ✔
   Who is that? (Signal.) *Molly.*
• Touch the next box. ✔
   Who is that? (Signal.) *Andrea.*

• Touch the next box. ✔
   Who is that? (Signal.) *Bleep.*
• Touch the next box. ✔
   Who is that? (Signal.) *Paul.*
• Touch the next box. ✔
   Who is that? (Signal.) *Honey.*
• Touch the last box. ✔
   That box just has a word. I'll tell you that
   word: **kissed.** What word? (Signal.) *Kissed.*
• That's what the characters did in pictures
   1 and 2.
• There is no picture for 3. I guess you'll just
   have to make a picture for 3 when we're all
   done.
3. Everybody, touch picture 1 by the top
   arrow. ✔
• Who did the kissing in that picture?
   (Signal.) *Bleep.*
• Who did Bleep kiss in that picture?
   (Signal.) *Molly.*
4. Everybody, say a sentence that tells what
   Bleep did in picture 1. (Signal.) *Bleep*
   kissed Molly.
• (Repeat step 4 until firm.)
5. Let's do the sentence the slow way. What's
   the first word in the sentence?
   (Signal.) *Bleep.*
• What's the next word in the sentence?
   (Signal.) *Kissed.*
• What's the last word in the sentence?
   (Signal.) *Molly.*
• (Repeat step 5 until firm.)
6. Your turn: Write the first sentence. Remember,
   Bleep's name starts with a capital **B.** Molly's
   name starts with a capital **M.** Write your
   sentence on arrow 1. Raise your hand when
   you're finished.
   (Observe children and give feedback.)
7. Now you're going to make up a sentence
   for picture 2.
• Everybody, who did the kissing in that
   picture? (Signal.) *Paul.*
• Who did Paul kiss? (Signal.) *Clarabelle.*
8. Everybody, say a sentence that tells what
   Paul did in picture 2. (Signal.) *Paul*
   kissed Clarabelle.
• (Repeat step 8 until firm.)
9. Your turn: Write the sentence for picture 2.
   Raise your hand when you're finished.
   (Observe children and give feedback.)

10. There is no picture 3. So here's what you'll do: First you'll make up a sentence that tells what your picture will show. You can write a sentence that uses any of the characters in the boxes. But don't write a sentence we've already done. Write your sentence. Raise your hand when you're finished.
(Observe children and give feedback.)

11. I'm going to call on several children to read their sentence for picture 3.
   • (Call on a child to read sentence 3. Repeat with several children. Praise original sentences that take the form: _____ *kissed* _____.)
   • (Repeat step 11 with several children.)

12. Let's make sure you can read all of your sentences.
   • (Call on several children:) Read all three sentences you wrote.
   • (Praise children who read appropriate sentences in correct order.)

13. Later, you'll have to draw a picture for sentence 3. Remember, your picture will show what your sentence says. (Call on several children:) What will your picture show?
   • (Praise those children whose response tells about their sentence.)

14. I'll show you some of the better pictures later.

EXERCISE 7 Classification

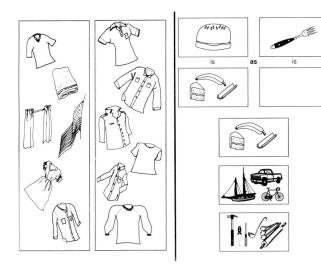

EXERCISE 8 Analogies

1. Everybody, find the next page in your workbook. ✔
   • (Hold up workbook. Point to first half.) These two pictures show two classes. One class has **one** kind of thing in it, the other class has **more** kinds of things in it.
   • Touch the picture that shows only **one** kind of thing. ✔
   • What kind of thing is that in the picture? (Signal.) *Shirts.*

2. Touch the picture that shows **more** than one kind of thing. ✔
   • Raise your hand if you can figure out the name of the class shown in that picture. ✔
   • Everybody, what's the name of that class? (Signal.) *Things made of cloth.*
   • Everybody, circle the picture that shows **more** kinds of things. ✔

3. Everybody, touch the picture that shows **one** kind of thing. ✔
   • Each shirt in that picture should be blue and white. What colors? (Signal.) *Blue and white.*
   • Mark a shirt in that picture. ✔

4. Touch the picture that shows **more** kinds of things. Each shirt in that picture should be red and black. What colors? (Signal.) *Red and black.*
   • Mark a shirt in that picture. ✔

EXERCISE 8 Analogies

1. (Hold up workbook. Point to second half.)
   • These pictures show something and the class it is in.

2. Touch the bun. ✔

3. The picture that's right below the bun shows what class it is in. Everybody, what class? (Signal.) *Food.*
   • Yes, that picture shows that a bun is food.

4. Touch the picture of the fork. ✔
   • One of the pictures below shows what class the fork is in. Touch the picture that shows what class a fork is in. ✔
   • Everybody, what class is it in? (Signal.) *Tools.*

5. Listen: A bun is food **as** a fork is a tool.
   • Tell me about a bun. Get ready. (Signal.) *A bun is food.*
   • Tell me about a fork. Get ready. (Signal.) *A fork is a tool.*
   • Draw a line from the fork to the class it is in. (Observe children and give feedback.)

Objectives

- Generate statements involving "can do" and "cannot do." (Exercise 1)
- Identify an object by stated criteria. (Exercise 2)
- Given a complex sentence, answer questions involving who, what, where, when and why. (Exercise 3)
- Replace a word in a sentence with an opposite and generate statement with opposites. (Exercise 4)
- Answer questions involving previously learned calendar facts. (Exercise 5)
- **Make up an ending to a story based on familiar story grammar.** (Exercise 6)
- Answer questions and make a picture consistent with the details of a story. (Exercise 7)
- Identify cardinal directions on a map. (Exercise 8)
- Complete an analogy involving class. (Exercise 9)

EXERCISE 1   Can Do

1. I'm going to ask questions about a woman and a wagon.
2. Everybody, can a woman write with a wagon? (Signal.) *No.*
- Say the statement. Get ready. (Signal.) *A woman cannot write with a wagon.*
3. Everybody, can a woman pull a wagon? (Signal.) *Yes.*
- Say the statement. Get ready. (Signal.) *A woman can pull a wagon.*
4. (Call on a child.)
- Your turn. Make up another statement that tells something a woman can do with a wagon. (After the child makes the statement, call on the group.) Say that statement about what a woman can do with a wagon. Get ready. (Signal.) *The group repeats the child's statement.*
5. (Call on another child.)
- Your turn. Now make a statement that tells something a woman cannot do with a wagon. (After the child makes the statement, call on the group.) Say that statement about what a woman cannot do with a wagon. Get ready. (Signal.) *The group repeats the child's statement.*
6. (Repeat steps 4 and 5 until firm.)

EXERCISE 2   Description

1. Get ready to play detective and find out what object I'm thinking of. I'll give you two clues.
2. (Hold up one finger.) It's an animal. (Hold up two fingers.) It lives on a farm.
3. Say the two things we know about the object.
- (Hold up one finger.) *It's an animal.*
- (Hold up two fingers.) *It lives on a farm.*
4. (Repeat step 3 until firm.)
5. Those clues don't tell you enough to find the right animal. They could tell you about a lot of animals. See how many animals you can name that live on a farm.
- (Call on individual children. The group is to name at least three animals that live on a farm, such as *a pig, a cow,* and *a chicken.*)
6. Here's another clue for finding the right object. Listen: It lays eggs.
- Everybody, say that. Get ready. (Signal.) *It lays eggs.*
7. Now here are the three things we know about the object.
- (Hold up one finger.) It's an animal.
- (Hold up two fingers.) It lives on a farm.
- (Hold up three fingers.) It lays eggs.
8. Everybody, say all the things we know. Get ready.
- (Hold up one finger.) *It's an animal.*
- (Hold up two fingers.) *It lives on a farm.*
- (Hold up three fingers.) *It lays eggs.*
9. Everybody, tell me what animal I am thinking of. (Pause.) Get ready. (Signal.) *A chicken.*

EXERCISE 3   Who—What—Where—When—Why

1. I'm going to say sentences that answer questions. One of the questions is why.
2. Listen: Yesterday, Liz stayed at home so she could help her mother. Everybody, say that statement. Get ready. (Signal.) *Yesterday, Liz stayed at home so she could help her mother.*
3. Listen: Who stayed at home? (Signal.) *Liz.*
- What did Liz do? (Signal.) *Stayed at home.*
- When did Liz stay at home? (Signal.) *Yesterday.*
- Why did Liz stay home? (Signal.) *To help her mother.*
- Where did Liz stay? (Signal.) *At home.*
4. Say the whole sentence again. Get ready. (Signal.) *Yesterday, Liz stayed at home so she could help her mother.*
- Which word tells who stayed at home? (Signal.) *Liz.*
- Which words tell where Liz stayed? (Signal.) *At home.*
- Which word tells when she stayed at home? (Signal.) *Yesterday.*
- Which words tell why she stayed at home? (Signal.) *To help her mother.*
- Which words tell who she helped? (Signal.) *Her mother.*

EXERCISE 4   Opposites

1. Here are some new opposites.
2. Listen: The opposite of under is over.
- What's the opposite of under? (Signal.) *Over.*
- What's the opposite of over? (Signal.) *Under.*
3. Listen: The opposite of wild is tame.
- What's the opposite of wild? (Signal.) *Tame.*
- What's the opposite of tame? (Signal.) *Wild.*
4. You're going to make up statements that have the opposite word.
5. Listen: The fox was wild. Say that statement. Get ready. (Signal.) *The fox was wild.*
- Now say a statement that tells the opposite about the fox. Get ready. (Signal.) *The fox was tame.*
6. Listen: The bird flew under the bridge. Say that statement. Get ready. (Signal.) *The bird flew under the bridge.*
- Now say a statement that tells the opposite about where the bird flew. Get ready. (Signal.) *The bird flew over the bridge.*

7. Listen: The girls finished before the boys finished. Say the statement. Get ready. (Signal.) *The girls finished before the boys finished.*
- Now say a statement that tells the opposite about when the girls finished. Get ready. (Signal.) *The girls finished after the boys finished.*
8. Listen: The leather was rough. Say that statement. Get ready. (Signal.) *The leather was rough.*
- Now say a statement that tells the opposite about the leather. Get ready. (Signal.) *The leather was smooth.*

EXERCISE 5   Calendar Facts

1. You learned calendar facts.
- Everybody, how many days are in a week? (Signal.) *Seven.*
- Everybody, say the days of the week. Get ready. (Signal.) *Sunday, Monday, Tuesday, Wednesday, Thursday, Friday, Saturday.*
2. How many weeks are in a year? (Signal.) *52.*
- Say the fact. Get ready. (Signal.) *There are 52 weeks in a year.*
3. How many days are in a year? (Signal.) *365.*
- Say the fact. Get ready. (Signal.) *There are 365 days in a year.*
4. How many seasons are in a year? (Signal.) *Four.*
- Name the four seasons. Get ready. (Signal.) *Winter, spring, summer, fall.*
5. How many months are in a year? (Signal.) *12.*
- Everybody, say the months. Get ready. (Signal.) *January, February, March, April, May, June, July, August, September, October, November, December.*
6. What day of the week is it today? (Signal.)
- What day of the week will it be tomorrow? (Signal.)
- What's today's date? (Signal.)

EXERCISE 6   Clarabelle And The Purple Plums

Story Completion

1. This is a new story about Paul and Clarabelle, but the whole ending is missing. Maybe you can figure out the ending if you remember how Clarabelle thinks and what she does.
- Here's the story:

One day, Paul painted his ladder pink and purple. He took a lot of time painting it. When he was done, he said, "That's perfectly perfect." The ladder had pink rungs and purple rungs. The sides of the ladder were also pink and purple. Paul said, "Now this ladder is perfect for picking purple plums." So he put the ladder against his purple plum tree and picked plenty of purple plums. When he had all the plums he could carry, he took them inside.

Well, Paul didn't know it, but Clarabelle was watching him. She saw him go up that ladder and pick those plums, and she said to herself, "I would like to do that, too."

So while Paul was inside the house, Clarabelle went over to Paul's pink-and-purple ladder. She started to climb, higher, higher and higher until she had almost reached a tree branch that was loaded with purple plums. And then . . .

2. Uh-oh. That's as far as the story goes. It doesn't tell the ending. It doesn't tell what happened to the ladder and Clarabelle. It doesn't tell what Paul did. Raise your hand when you can help me out with a good ending for this story. ✔

• (After hands are raised, say:) I'll say the part of the story just before it stops. Then I'll call on somebody to complete the whole story. Remember, you have to tell what happened to the ladder and Clarabelle and what Paul did.

• Listen:

While Paul was inside the house, Clarabelle went over to Paul's pink-and-purple ladder. She started to climb, higher, higher and higher until she had almost reached a tree branch that was loaded with purple plums. And then . . .

• (Call on several children:) Tell your ending to the story. (Praise endings that express these ideas: *The ladder broke. Clarabelle landed on the ground and Paul yelled at Clarabelle.* Or *The ladder broke. Clarabelle fell to the ground. She was covered with purple paint so Paul said, "That cow looks terrible, but I know how to fix her."*)

WORKBOOK

EXERCISE 7 Story Details

1. Everybody, find Lesson 62 in your workbook. Write your name at the top of the page. ✔

• The picture shows Clarabelle on the ground with a lot of pieces of wood lying around.

• Where did those pieces of wood come from? (Call on a child. Idea: *The broken ladder.*)

• Everybody, who is that standing in the background? (Signal.) *Paul.*

• What do you think he's saying to Clarabelle? (Call on a child. Idea: *"What were you doing on my ladder?"*)

• Where was Clarabelle just before this picture took place? (Call on a child. Idea: *On the ladder.*)

• Yes, Clarabelle was on the ladder just before the ladder fell apart.

• Look at Paul's expression. He looks very mad. He looks perturbed.

2. Later you can fix up the picture. Remember the color of the rungs and the sides of the ladder. And remember the color of those things that are in the tree.

EXERCISE 8 Map Reading

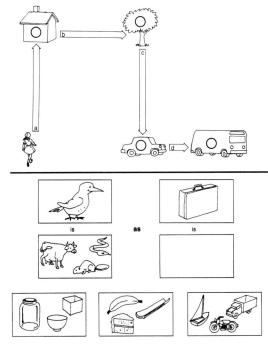

1. Everybody, find the next page in your workbook. (Hold up workbook. Point to top half.) Find the arrows. ✔
- The arrows show where the girl went. Touch the girl. ✔
2. The arrow shows which direction she went first. Touch arrow **A.** ✔
- Raise your hand when you know which direction that arrow is pointing. ✔
- Everybody, which direction? (Signal.) *North.*
- Yes, she went **north** to get to the house. Which direction did she go? (Signal.) *North.*
- So write **N** in the circle in the house. **N** stands for **north.** ✔
3. Touch the house. ✔
- The arrow that goes from the house shows where she went next. Touch arrow **B.** ✔
- Raise your hand when you know which direction that arrow is pointing. ✔
- Everybody, which direction? (Signal.) *East.*
- Yes, she went **east** from the house to get to the tree. Which direction did she go? (Signal.) *East.*
- So write **E** in the circle in the tree. **E** stands for **east.** ✔
4. Touch the tree. ✔
- Touch arrow **C.** ✔
- Raise your hand when you know which direction the arrow is pointing. ✔
- Everybody, which direction is that arrow pointing? (Signal.) *South.*
- Yes, she went **south** from the tree to get to the car. Which direction did she go? (Signal.) *South.*

- So write **S** in the circle on the car. **S** stands for **south.** ✔
5. Touch arrow **D.** ✔
- Raise your hand when you know the direction the arrow is pointing. ✔
- Everybody, which direction is that arrow pointing? (Signal.) *East.*
- Write **E** on the bus. **E** stands for **east.** ✔
6. Let's go over those arrows again.
- Touch arrow **A.** ✔
Everybody, which direction is that arrow pointing? (Signal.) *North.*
- Touch arrow **B.** ✔
Everybody, which direction is that arrow pointing? (Signal.) *East.*
- Touch arrow **C.** ✔
Everybody, which direction is that arrow pointing? (Signal.) *South.*
- Touch arrow **D.** ✔
Everybody, which direction is that arrow pointing? (Signal.) *East.*

EXERCISE 9 Analogies

1. (Hold up workbook. Point to bottom half.) These pictures show something and the class it is in.
2. Touch the bird. ✔
3. The picture that's right below the bird shows what class it is in. Everybody, what class? (Signal.) *Animals.*
- Yes, so those pictures show that a bird is an animal.
4. Touch the picture of the suitcase. ✔
- One of the pictures below shows what class the suitcase is in. Touch the picture that shows what class a suitcase is in. ✔
- Everybody, what class is it in? (Signal.) *Containers.*
5. Listen: A bird is an animal **as** a suitcase is a container.
- Tell me about a bird. Get ready. (Signal.) *A bird is an animal.*
- Tell me about a suitcase. Get ready. (Signal.) *A suitcase is a container.*
- Draw a line from the suitcase to the class it is in. (Observe children and give feedback.)

Objectives

- Generate statements to describe actions using present, past and future tense and "to" and "from." (Exercise 1)
- Name things that a statement does NOT tell. (Exercise 2)
- Identify an object by stated criteria. (Exercise 3)
- Name common opposites. (Exercise 4)
- Given a calendar, identify the day and date for "today" and "tomorrow" and one week from today. (Exercise 5)
- **Cooperatively generate an ending to a story.** (Exercise 6)
- Follow coloring rules involving classes and subclasses. (Exercise 7)
- Follow coloring rules involving parts of a whole. (Exercise 8)

EXERCISE 1 Actions

1. (Sit down.) Here's the first action game.
2. Listen: We will stand up. Everybody, say that. Get ready. (Signal.) *We will stand up.*
3. What are we going to do? (Signal.) *Stand up.*
4. Are we standing up now? (Signal.) *No.*
- Will we stand up? (Signal.) *Yes.*
5. Everybody, let's do it. (Signal.) (Stand up with the children.)
- What are we doing now? (Signal.) *Standing up.*
6. What were we doing before we stood up? (Signal.) *Sitting down.*
- Sit down. ✔
7. (Repeat steps 2 through 6 until firm.)
8. Look at me. Everybody, I'm going to move my finger from something to something else. See if you can tell me how my finger moves.
- My turn. (Place your finger on your head.) Watch. (Move it to your elbow.) I did it.
9. Your turn. Where did my finger move from? (Signal.) *Your head.*
- Where did my finger move to? (Signal.) *Your elbow.*
10. Everybody, how did I move my finger? (Signal.) *From your head to your elbow.*
11. Again. How did I move my finger? (Signal.) *From your head to your elbow.*
12. (Repeat step 11 until firm.)
13. Everybody, say the whole thing about how I moved my finger. Get ready. (Signal.) *You moved your finger from your head to your elbow.*
14. (Repeat step 13 until firm.)

EXERCISE 2 Statements

1. Listen to this statement. The boy is throwing the ball.
- Everybody, say the statement. Get ready. (Signal.) *The boy is throwing the ball.*
2. Does that statement tell what the boy will do tomorrow? (Signal.) *No.*
- Does that statement tell who the boy is throwing the ball to? (Signal.) *No.*
- Does that statement tell if the boy is wearing sneakers? (Signal.) *No.*
- Does that statement tell if the boy is smiling? (Signal.) *No.*
- Does that statement tell what the boy is doing now? (Signal.) *Yes.*
3. The boy is throwing the ball. Everybody, say the statement again. Get ready. (Signal.) *The boy is throwing the ball.*
4. Here's one thing that statement does not tell us. It doesn't tell what kind of ball the boy is throwing. Your turn to name two more things the statement does not tell us. (Call on individual children. Repeat both correct responses.)
5. You have named two things the statement does not tell us.
- Everybody, name the first thing. Get ready. (Hold up one finger.) (The group repeats the first response.)
- Everybody, name the second thing. Get ready. (Hold up two fingers.) (The group repeats the second response.)
6. (Repeat step 5 until firm.)

EXERCISE 3 Descriptions

1. You're going to figure out what object I'm thinking of.
2. Listen: I'm thinking of a piece of furniture that is made of wood. Name some furniture I could be thinking of. (Call on individual children.)
3. Listen: The wooden furniture I'm thinking of is found in a classroom.
- Could I be thinking of a desk? (Signal.) *Yes.*
- How do you know? (Call on a child. Idea: *It's wooden furniture found in a classroom.*)
4. (Repeat step 3 until firm.)
5. Everybody, could I be thinking of a bookcase? (Signal.) *Yes.*
- How do you know? (Call on a child. Idea: *It's wooden furniture found in a classroom.*)
- Everybody, could I be thinking of a picnic table? (Signal.) *No.*
- How do you know? (Call on a child. Idea: *It's not found in a classroom.*)
6. (Repeat step 5 until firm.)
7. Listen: The furniture I'm thinking of is used to hold books.
- Could I be thinking of a bookcase? (Signal.) *Yes.*
- How do you know? (Call on a child. Idea: *It's wooden furniture found in a classroom used to hold books.*)
- Everybody, could I be thinking of a wooden picture frame? (Signal.) *No.*
- How do you know? (Call on a child. Idea: *It's not used to hold books.*)
8. (Repeat step 7 until firm.)
9. Yes, I was thinking of a bookcase.

EXERCISE 4 Opposites

1. We're going to play a word game.
2. Everybody, think of a pool that is the opposite of shallow.
- What's the opposite of shallow? (Signal.) *Deep.*
- So a pool that is the opposite of shallow is . . . (Signal.) *deep.*

3. Everybody, think of a team who is doing the opposite of winning.
- What's the opposite of winning? (Signal.) *Losing.*
- So a team that is doing the opposite of winning is . . . (Signal.) *losing.*
4. Everybody, think of a window that is the opposite of shut.
- What's the opposite of shut? (Signal.) *Open.*
- So a window that is the opposite of shut is . . . (Signal.) *open.*
5. Everybody, think of a stick that is the opposite of rough.
- What's the opposite of rough? (Signal.) *Smooth.*
- So a stick that is the opposite of rough is . . . (Signal.) *smooth.*

EXERCISE 5 Calendar

1. (Present calendar.)
- We're going to talk about today, tomorrow, and one week from today.
2. Tell me the day of the week it is today. Get ready. (Signal.)
- Tell me the day of the week it will be tomorrow. Get ready. (Signal.)
- Tell me the day of the week it will be one week from today. Get ready. (Signal.)
3. (Repeat step 2 until firm.)
4. Now the dates.
- Tell me today's date. Get ready. (Signal.)
- Look at the calendar. ✔
- Tell me the date it will be one week from today. Get ready. (Signal.)
5. Once more.
- Listen: Tell me today's date. Get ready. (Signal.)
- Tell me tomorrow's date. Get ready. (Signal.)
- Tell me the date it will be one week from today. Get ready. (Signal.)
6. (Repeat step 5 until firm.)

EXERCISE 6   Rolla Slows Down

Story Completion

1. Everybody, open your workbook to Lesson 63. Write your name at the top of the page. ✔

- We're going to do a new story about Rolla, but the whole ending is missing. I guess you might be able to figure out the ending if you remember how Rolla thinks and what she does.

- Here's the story:

    Rolla was happy. The other horses in the merry-go-round were happy.

    The mothers were happy and all the kids were happy. But then one day, Rolla looked at the horse right in front of her and she said to herself, "That horse is too close to me. I would like to be farther away from that number eight."

- So what do you think she did? (Call on a child. Idea: *She tried to slow down.*)

    Well, when Rolla tried to slow down, all the other horses slowed down, too.

    And the music slowed down. And the mothers started to complain. One of them said, "This is not a merry-go-round. This is almost a merry-stand-still."

    Another one said, "Yes, and that music sounds like a dying cow."

    And the kids didn't want to go on the merry-go-round. They said, "Why just sit on a horse that is hardly going up and down and is moving around slower than a turtle?"

    Rolla had to work hard to slow down and all the other horses were saying, "Rolla, what are you doing? When you slow down, we have to slow down."

    But Rolla kept slowing down and slowing down. At the end of the day, she was very tired, but the number eight horse was just as close to her as it was at the beginning of the day.

    When the merry-go-round stopped that night, the other horses said, "Rolla, why are you keeping us from going at a good speed?"

    She had a great big tear in her eye. "Because," she said, "I'm number one and I shouldn't be so close to number eight. I want to be farther away from number eight."

    So the horses got together and talked and argued, and after a while horse number four said, "Rolla, if you couldn't see horse number eight, would you feel satisfied?"

    "Of course," she said. "If I couldn't see him right in front of me, then I would feel like number one."

    So the horses said, "Well, we have a plan that will fix things up so you can't see the horse in front of you."

    So here's what the horses did . . .

2. Uh-oh. That's as far as the story goes. It doesn't tell the ending. It doesn't tell what the horses did or what Rolla did after the other horses fixed things up. It doesn't tell how things were at the end of the story—how the mothers felt and how the kids felt. The story just stops right there. There are different things the horses may have done.

3. So let's work in teams. Each team will figure out how the horses fixed things up so Rolla would not see the horse in front of her. When your team gets a plan, tell it to me. If it's a good one, you can fix up your picture to show that plan. Then we'll have children from different teams tell the whole ending to the story.

- (Divide class into four teams.)
- Here's the rule for each team: Each team has to agree on **one** solution. So talk it over quietly and raise your hand when your team has a solution. I'll come around and you can whisper the solution to me.
- (For each acceptable solution, for example: *Blindfold Rolla; Put a divider between Rolla and horse 8; Disguise horse 8 as another animal; Put dark glasses on Rolla,* tell the team to fix up their pictures to show that solution.)
4. (After pictures are completed, say:) Now I'll say the part of the story just before it stops. Then I'll call on individual children to complete the whole story. Remember, you have to tell what the horses did and what happened afterwards—how the children liked it, how the mothers liked it and how Rolla liked it.
- Here's the part just before the story stops:

The horses got together, and after a while, horse number four said, "Rolla, if you couldn't see horse number eight, would you feel satisfied?"

"Of course," she said. "If I couldn't see him right in front of me, then I would feel like number one."

So the horses said, "Well, we have a plan that will fix things up so you can't see the horse in front of you."

So here's what the horses did . . .

5. (Call on a child:) Tell your team's ending to the story. (Praise ending that solves the problem and that tells how Rolla, the other horses, the mothers and the children felt.) (Repeat step 5 with several children.)

EXERCISE 7 Classification

1. Everybody, find the next page in your workbook. (Hold up workbook. Point to first half.) These two pictures show two classes. One class has **one** kind of thing in it, the other class has **more** kinds of things in it.
- Touch the picture that shows only one kind of thing. ✔
- What kind of thing is that in the picture? (Signal.) *Motorcycle.*
2. Touch the picture that shows **more** than one kind of thing. ✔
- Raise your hand if you can figure out the name of the class shown in that picture. ✔
- Everybody, what's the name of that class? (Signal.) *Vehicles.*
- Everybody, circle the picture that shows **more** kinds of things. ✔
3. Everybody, touch the picture that shows **one** kind of thing. ✔
- Each motorcycle in that picture should be blue and black. What colors? (Signal.) *Blue and black.*
- Mark a motorcycle in that picture. ✔
5. Touch the picture that shows **more** kinds of things.
- Each motorcycle in that picture should be green and blue. What colors? (Signal.) *Green and blue.*
- Mark a motorcycle in that picture. ✔

EXERCISE 8   Part—Whole

1. (Hold up workbook. Point to second half.)
   Now look at the window. ✔
2. Here's a coloring rule for the window.
   Listen: Color the panes orange. What's the
   rule? (Signal.) *Color the panes orange.*
   • Mark the panes. ✔
3. Here's another coloring rule for the window.
   Listen: Color the lock green. What's the
   rule? (Signal.) *Color the lock green.*
   • Mark the lock. ✔

4. Here's another coloring rule for the window.
   Listen: Color the handle brown. What's the
   rule? (Signal.) *Color the handle brown.*
   • Mark the handle. ✔
5. Part of the window is missing. What part is
   missing? (Signal.) *The frame.*
   • Yes, the frame. Before you color the
   window, you're going to follow the dots
   and make the frame.
6. Here's the coloring rule for the frame.
   Listen: Color the frame red. What's the
   rule? (Signal.) *Color the frame red.*
   • Mark the frame. ✔

Objectives

- Name classes and subclasses. (Exercise 1)
- Name common opposites. (Exercise 2)
- Identify an object by stated criteria. (Exercise 3)
- Apply narrowing criteria to guess a mystery object. (Exercise 4)
- Given a calendar, identify the day and date for "today" and "tomorrow" and one week from today. (Exercise 5)
- Write three sentences about story characters. (Exercise 6)

EXERCISE 1 Classification

1. We're going to talk about classes.
2. The class of building tools is made up of many kinds of tools. I'll name some kinds of tools in the class of building tools.
- Listen: screwdrivers, hammers, axes. You name some kinds of tools in the class of building tools. (Call on individual children. Praise reasonable answers such as *saws, hammers,* and *wrenches.*)
3. Think about this. If we took all screwdrivers from the class of building tools, would there be any building tools left? (Signal.) *Yes.*
4. Name some kinds of building tools that would be left. (Call on individual children. Praise all reasonable answers: that is, any kind of building tools except screwdrivers.)
5. Yes, if we took all the screwdrivers from the class of building tools, there would still be building tools left. So which class is bigger, the class of screwdrivers or the class of building tools? (Signal.) *The class of building tools.*
- Tell me how you know. Get ready. (Signal.) *The class of building tools has more kinds of things in it.*
6. (Repeat step 5 until firm.)
7. Think big. Tell me which class is bigger, the class of tools or the class of building tools. Get ready. (Signal.) *The class of tools.*
- Tell me how you know. Get ready. (Signal). *The class of tools has more kinds of things in it.*
8. (Repeat step 7 until firm.)

EXERCISE 2 Opposites

1. We're going to play a word game.
2. Everybody, think of a clown who is doing the opposite of laughing.
- A clown who is doing the opposite of laughing is . . . (Signal.) *crying.*
3. Everybody, think of a rock that is the opposite of smooth.
- A rock that is the opposite of smooth is . . . (Signal.) *rough.*
4. Everybody, think of a hole that is the opposite of deep.
- A hole that is the opposite of deep is . . . (Signal.) *shallow.*
5. Everybody, think of a rope that is the opposite of long.
- A rope that is the opposite of long is . . . (Signal.) *short.*
6. Think of a window that is the opposite of shut.
- A window that is the opposite of shut is . . . (Signal.) *open.*

EXERCISE 3 Description

1. You're going to figure out what object I'm thinking of.
2. Listen: I'm thinking of a container made of metal. Name some containers I could be thinking of. (Call on individual children.)
3. Listen: The metal container I'm thinking of is found in the kitchen.
- Could I be thinking of a table? (Signal.) *No.*
- How do you know? (Call on a child. Idea: *It's not a metal container.*)
4. (Repeat step 3 until firm.)

5. Everybody, could I be thinking of a frying pan? (Signal.) *Yes.*
- How do you know? (Call on a child. Idea: *It's a metal container found in the kitchen.*)
- Everybody, could I be thinking of a can of gasoline? (Signal.) *No.*
- How do you know? (Call on a child. Idea: *It's not found in the kitchen.*)
- Everybody, could I be thinking of a metal dish pan? (Signal.) *Yes.*
- How do you know? (Call on a child. Idea: *It's a metal container found in the kitchen.*)
6. (Repeat step 5 until firm.)
7. Listen: The object I'm thinking of is used to cook food.
- Could I be thinking of a dish pan? (Signal.) *No.*
- How do you know? (Call on a child. Idea: *It's not used to cook food.*)
- Everybody, could I be thinking of a frying pan? (Signal.) *Yes.*
- How do you know? (Call on a child. Idea: *It's a metal container found in the kitchen that's used to cook food.*)
8. Yes, I was thinking of a frying pan.

EXERCISE 4   Description

1. Get ready to play detective and find out what object I'm thinking of. I'll give you two clues.
2. (Hold up one finger.) It's an animal.
(Hold up two fingers.) It's long and skinny.
3. Say the two things we know about the object. Get ready.
- (Hold up one finger.) *It's an animal.*
- (Hold up two fingers.) *It's long and skinny.*
4. Those clues don't tell you enough to find the right animal. They could tell you about a lot of animals. See how many animals you can name that are long and skinny. (Call on individual children. The group is to name at least three animals that are long and skinny, such as *a snake, an alligator,* and *a worm.*)

5. Here's another clue for finding the right object. Listen: It has eyes but no legs.
- Everybody, say that. Get ready. (Signal.) *It has eyes but no legs.*
6. Now here are the three things we know about the object.
- (Hold up one finger.) It's an animal.
- (Hold up two fingers.) It's long and skinny.
- (Hold up three fingers.) It has eyes but no legs.
7. Everybody, say all the things we know. Get ready.
- (Hold up one finger.) *It's an animal.*
- (Hold up two fingers.) *It's long and skinny.*
- (Hold up three fingers. Signal.) *It has eyes but no legs.*
8. Everybody, tell me what animal I am thinking of. (Pause.) Get ready. (Signal.) *A snake.* Yes, a snake.
- (Accept eel.)

EXERCISE 5   Calendar

1. (Present calendar.)
- We're going to talk about today, tomorrow, and one week from today.
2. Tell me the day of the week it is today. Get ready. (Signal.)
- Tell me the day of the week it will be tomorrow. Get ready. (Signal.)
- Tell me the day of the week it will be one week from today. Get ready. (Signal.)
3. (Repeat step 2 until firm.)
4. Now the dates.
- Tell me today's date. Get ready. (Signal.)
- Look at the calendar. ✔
- Tell me the date it will be one week from today. Get ready. (Signal.)
5. Once more.
- Listen: Tell me today's date. Get ready. (Signal.)
- Tell me tomorrow's date. Get ready. (Signal.)
- Tell me the date it will be one week from today. Get ready. (Signal.)
6. (Repeat step 5 until firm.)

EXERCISE 6 Sentence Construction

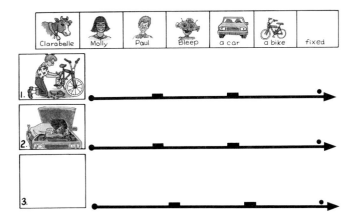

1. Everybody, open your workbook to Lesson 64. Write your name at the top of the page. ✔
- You're going to make up sentences again, but you're not going to use cutouts. You're just going to write the correct words. The words that you'll use are in the boxes at the top of the page. All the boxes except one have a picture.

2. Everybody, touch the first box. ✔ Who is that? (Signal.) *Clarabelle.* And her name is written below.
- Touch the next box. ✔ Who is that? (Signal.) *Molly.*
- Touch the next box. ✔ Who is that? (Signal.) *Paul.*
- Touch the next box. ✔ Who is that? (Signal.) *Bleep.*
- Touch the next box. ✔ What is that? (Signal.) *A car.*
- Touch the next box. ✔ What is that? (Signal.) *A bike.*
- Touch the last box. ✔ That box just has a word. I'll tell you that word: **fixed.** What word? (Signal.) *Fixed.*
- That's what the characters did in pictures 1 and 2.
- There is no picture for 3. I guess you'll just have to make a picture for 3 when we're all done.

3. Everybody, touch picture 1 by the top arrow. ✔
- Who is in that picture? (Signal.) *Paul.*
- What did Paul fix? (Signal.) *A bike.*

4. Everybody, say a sentence that tells what Paul did in picture 1. (Signal.) *Paul fixed a bike.*
- (Repeat step 4 until firm.)

5. Let's do the sentence the slow way. What's the first word in the sentence? (Signal.) *Paul.*
- What's the next word in the sentence? (Signal.) *Fixed.*
- What are the last words in the sentence? (Signal.) *A bike.*
- (Repeat step 5 until firm.)

6. Your turn: Write the first sentence. Remember, Paul's name starts with a capital **P.** Write your sentence on arrow 1. Raise your hand when you're finished. (Observe children and give feedback.)

7. Now you're going to make up a sentence for picture 2.
- Everybody, who is in that picture? (Signal.) *Molly.*
- What did Molly fix? (Signal.) *A car.*

8. Everybody, say a sentence that tells what Molly did in picture 2. (Signal.) *Molly fixed a car.*
- (Repeat step 8 until firm.)

9. Your turn: Write the sentence for picture 2. Raise your hand when you're finished. (Observe children and give feedback.)

10. There is no picture 3. So here's what you'll do: First you'll make up a sentence that tells what the picture will show. You can write a sentence that uses any of the characters in the boxes. But don't write a sentence we've already done. Write your sentence. Raise your hand when you're finished. (Observe children and give feedback.)

11. I'm going to call on several children to read their sentence for picture 3.
- (Call on a child to read sentence 3. Repeat with several children. Praise original sentences that take the form: *(Name) fixed _____.)*

12. Let's make sure you can read all of your sentences.
- (Call on several children:) Read all three sentences you wrote.
- (Praise children who read appropriate sentences in correct order.)

13. Later, you'll have to draw a picture for sentence 3. Remember, your picture will show what your sentence says.
- (Call on several children:) What will your picture show?
- (Praise those children whose response tells about their sentence.)

14. I'll show some of the better pictures later.

LESSON 65

EXERCISE 1   Opposites

1. We're going to play a word game.
2. Everybody, think of a box that is the opposite of shut. A box that is the opposite of shut is . . . (Signal.) *open.*
- A pan that is the opposite of shallow is . . . (Signal.) *deep.*
- A turtle that is the opposite of fast is . . . (Signal.) *slow.*
- A rug that is the opposite of rough is . . . (Signal.) *smooth.*
- A raincoat that is the opposite of wet is . . . (Signal.) *dry.*

EXERCISE 2   Statements

1. Listen to this statement. The man is driving. Everybody, say the statement. Get ready. (Signal.) *The man is driving.*
2. Does that statement tell you if the man is tall? (Signal.) *No.*
- Does that statement tell you what the man is doing now? (Signal.) *Yes.*
- Does that statement tell you what the man is driving? (Signal.) *No.*
- Does that statement tell you if the man is wearing a hat? (Signal.) *No.*
- Does that statement tell you what the man did yesterday? (Signal.) *No.*
3. The man is driving. Everybody, say that again. Get ready. (Signal.) *The man is driving.*
4. Your turn to name two things the statement does not tell you. (Call on individual children. Repeat both correct responses.)

5. You have named two things the statement does not tell us.
- Name the first thing. (Hold up one finger.) (The children give the first response.)
- Name the second thing. (Hold up two fingers.) (The children give the second response.)
6. (Repeat step 5 until firm.)

EXERCISE 3   Description

Note: The children are not to memorize the "funny" name in this task or in subsequent description tasks that involve a "funny" name.

1. I'm going to tell you about an object you know. But I'm going to call it a funny name. See if you can figure out what object I'm going to call a slup.
2. (Hold up one finger.)
   A slup is an animal. Say that. (Signal.) *A slup is an animal.*
- (Hold up two fingers.)
   A slup says moo. Say that. (Signal.) *A slup says moo.*
3. Everybody, say the things you know about a slup. Get ready.
- (Hold up one finger.) *A slup is an animal.*
- (Hold up two fingers.) *A slup says moo.*
4. (Repeat steps 2 and 3 until firm.)

5. Everybody, tell me the kind of animal I am calling a slup. (Pause.) Get ready. (Signal.) *A cow.*
6. I couldn't fool you. It's really a cow. How do you know a slup is a cow? (Call on a child. Idea: *It's an animal. It says moo.*)
7. How would you like to have a slup as a pet in your house? (Children respond.)

EXERCISE 4   Classification

1. Today we're going to talk about mashed potatoes. We can put mashed potatoes into three different classes. See how many classes you can name, starting with the smallest class.
2. Everybody, what's the smallest class for mashed potatoes? (Signal.) *Mashed potatoes.*
• What's the next bigger class? (Signal.) *Potatoes.*
• What's a bigger class? (Signal.) *Food.*
• (Accept any other correct responses, but use: *mashed potatoes, potatoes, food.*)
3. (Repeat step 2 until firm.)
4. What is one kind of object you would find in all those classes? (Signal.) *Mashed potatoes.*
5. Think of these classes: mashed potatoes, potatoes, food.
6. Would you find a French fry in all those classes? (Signal.) *No.*
• Name two of those classes you would find a French fry in. (Pause.) Get ready. (Tap 2 times.) *Potatoes. Food.*
7. Would you find a carrot in all those classes? (Signal.) *No.*
• Name the class you would find a carrot in. (Pause.) Get ready. (Signal.) *Food.*
8. (Repeat steps 5 through 7 until firm.)

EXERCISE 5   Calendar

1. (Present calendar.)
• We're going to talk about today, tomorrow, and one week from today.
2. Tell me the day of the week it is today. Get ready. (Signal.)
• Tell me the day of the week it will be tomorrow. Get ready. (Signal.)
• Tell me the day of the week it will be one week from today. Get ready. (Signal.)
3. (Repeat step 2 until firm.)

4. Now the dates.
• Tell me today's date. Get ready. (Signal.)
• Look at the calendar. ✔
• Tell me the date it will be one week from today. Get ready. (Signal.)
5. Once more.
• Listen: Tell me today's date. Get ready. (Signal.)
• Tell me tomorrow's date. Get ready. (Signal.)
• Tell me the date it will be one week from today. Get ready. (Signal.)
6. (Repeat step 5 until firm.)

EXERCISE 6   Analogies

1. You're going to make up sentences that are like the sentence I start with.
2. Listen: Your shoe is for some part of your body. What part? (Signal.) *Your foot.* Yes, your shoe is for your foot.
• Everybody, say that. Get ready. (Signal.) *Your shoe is for your foot.*
3. Your glove is for . . . (Signal.) *your hand.*
• Say the statement about your glove. Get ready. (Signal.) *Your glove is for your hand.*
4. Your shoe is for . . . (Signal.) *your foot.*
• Say the statement about your shoe. Get ready. (Signal.) *Your shoe is for your foot.*
5. Your hat is for . . . (Signal.) *your head.*
• Say the statement about your hat. Get ready. (Signal.) *Your hat is for your head.*
6. Your belt is for . . . (Signal.) *your waist.*
• Say the statement about your belt. Get ready. (Signal.) *Your belt is for your waist.*

EXERCISE 7   Bleep Learns The Months Of The Year *Part 1*

Storytelling

• Here's a new story about Molly and Bleep:

Molly was getting ready to go on a vacation with Mrs. Anderson. They planned to take a trip to the mountains and camp out. Bleep was supposed to stay at home and look after things there.

Molly was gathering up all the things she would take with her on the trip. She had flashlights and batteries. She had swimming suits and sunglasses. She had hiking shoes and lawn chairs. As she gathered up all the things she planned to take with her, she talked to Bleep. She said, "Now, remember to water all my plants next Monday."

"Okay, baby," Bleep said. "You want water, you got water."

"And, oh yes," Molly said. "Remember to feed the goldfish every day."

"Okay, baby," Bleep said. "You want fish food, you got fish food."

Molly suddenly stopped. "I almost forgot about the painters," she said. "You'll have to show them where the paint is. They'll be here on the first of July."

Bleep said, "Blurp."

"Why did you say, 'blurp'?" Molly asked.

Bleep said, "I don't remember."

Oh no, here we go again. But this time, Molly had a pretty good idea of what Bleep's problem was.

What do you think it was? (Call on a child. Idea: *Bleep didn't remember all the months of the year.*)

Molly decided to make sure she knew what Bleep's problem was. She said, "Bleep, what month was it that Mrs. Anderson and I went to the wrecking yard?"

Bleep said, "March."

Molly said, "And what month comes after March?"

Bleep said, "April, of course."

Molly said, "And what month comes after April?"

Bleep said, "May, of course."

Then Molly said, "And what month comes after May?"

Bleep said, "June, of course."

Molly said, "And what month comes after June?"

Bleep said, "Blurp, of course."

So Molly knew that Bleep knew some of the months, but he had trouble with July. She said, "Bleep, say the first three months of the year."

Bleep said, "January, February and March."

"Very good," Molly said. "Now say the three months that come after March."

Bleep said, "April, May and June."

"Very good," Molly said. "Now say the three months that come after June."

Bleep said, "Blurp, Blurp and Blurp."

"Not too good," Molly said. Then she asked, "Do you want to try the **last** three months of the year?"

Bleep said, "Okay, baby. Blurp, Blurp and December."

Well, now Molly knew Bleep's problem. He could say the **first** three months of the year—January, February and March. He could say the **next** three months—April, May and June. But after **June,** the only month he knew was the very last month of the year—December.

So Molly told Bleep, "I don't have much time to teach you about the months because I'm leaving on my vacation soon. But if you work hard, maybe you can learn all of the months before I go."

Bleep said, "Okay, baby."

And so Molly wrote the names of the months on cards for Bleep. Then she practiced saying the months with him. Each time she would start with January. And Bleep would say, "January, February, March." Then he'd say, "April, May, June."

But you know what he said after June.

• Everybody, what did Bleep say after June? (Signal.) *Blurp.* (Or *Blurp, Blurp, Blurp.*)

WORKBOOK

EXERCISE 8 Writing The Months Of The Year

1. Everybody, find Lesson 65 in your workbook. Write your name at the top of the page. ✔
• These are the months that Bleep worked on.
• I'll read the months on the first arrow: January, February, March. Your turn: Read those months. (Signal.) *January, February, March.*
• I'll read the months on the next arrow: April, May, June. Your turn: Read those months. (Signal.) *April, May, June.*
• Bleep could say those first six months perfectly. Who thinks they can say them like this: **January, February, March** (pause) **April, May, June?** (Call on several children. Praise children who say the first six months in order.)
• Some of you are as smart as Bleep.
2. Let's say all those months together, starting with **January.** Get ready. (Signal.) *January, February, March, April, May, June.*
• (Repeat step 2 until firm.)
3. Look at the picture of Bleep saying the months. ✔
• The only months he's saying are January and February.
4. Your turn: Write the rest of the months that are missing, starting with **March.** Remember to start each month with a capital letter. Raise your hand when you're finished.
(Observe children and give feedback.)

5. I'll read what Bleep should be saying **now.** Follow along: January, February, March, April, May, June, Blurp.
• Raise your hand if you wrote in all the correct months. ✔
6. Everybody, is "Blurp" really the month after **June?** (Signal.) *No.*
• Listen: After Molly worked with Bleep a while, he knew the month that really comes after June. If you know that month, raise your hand. ✔
• Everybody with your hand raised: What month comes after June? (Signal.) *July.*
• Right, I'll show you how to write **July.** (Write on the board:)

July

7. Now you can cross out the word "Blurp" and write the correct month above it. Do it. ✔
• Now your picture should show what Bleep could say after practicing with Molly a while.
8. Everybody, say the months the way Bleep could do it after Molly worked with him. Get ready. (Signal.) *January, February, March, April, May, June, July.*

EXERCISE 9

Map Reading

1. Everybody, find the next page in your workbook. ✔
• (Hold up workbook. Point to first half.) Find the arrows. ✔

- The arrows show where the farmer went. Touch the farmer. ✔
2. The arrow shows which direction he went first. Touch arrow **A.** ✔
- Raise your hand when you know which direction that arrow is pointing. ✔
- Everybody, which direction? (Signal.) *West.*
- Yes, he went **west** to get to the barn. Which direction did he go? (Signal.) *West.*
- So you'll write **W** in the circle on the barn.
3. Touch arrow **B.** ✔
- Raise your hand when you know which direction that arrow is pointing. ✔
- Everybody, which direction? (Signal.) *South.*
- So you'll write **S** on the tractor to show that the farmer went **south** from the barn to the tractor.
4. Touch arrow **C.** ✔
- Raise your hand when you know which direction the arrow is pointing. ✔
- Everybody, which direction is that arrow pointing? (Signal.) *East.*
- Yes, he went **east** to go from the tractor to the horse. So you'll write **E** on the horse to show that the farmer went **east** to get to the horse.
5. Touch arrow **D.** ✔
- Raise your hand when you know the direction of that arrow. ✔
- Everybody, which direction is that arrow pointing? (Signal.) *North.*
- So you'll write **N** on the pig to show that the farmer went north to get to the pig.
6. Let's go over those arrows again.
- Touch arrow **A.** ✔
- Which direction is that arrow pointing? (Signal.) *West.*
- So what letter will you write on the barn? (Signal.) *W.*

- Touch arrow **B.** ✔
- Which direction is that arrow pointing? (Signal.) *South.*
- So what letter will you write on the tractor? (Signal.) *S.*
- Touch arrow **C.** ✔
- Which direction is that arrow pointing? (Signal.) *East.*
- So what letter will you write on the horse? (Signal.) *E.*
- Touch arrow **D.** ✔
- Which direction is that arrow pointing? (Signal.) *North.*
- So what letter will you write on the pig? (Signal.) *N.*
7. Write the letters to show which direction the farmer went. Pencils down when you're finished.
(Observe children and give feedback.)

EXERCISE 10   **Materials**

1. (Hold up workbook. Point to second half.)
2. Here's a coloring rule for this picture. If an object is made of wood, color it brown or black. What's the rule? (Signal.) *If an object is made of wood, color it brown or black.*
3. (Repeat step 2 until firm.)
4. Mark the objects made of wood.
5. Here's another coloring rule for this picture. If an object is made of metal, color it purple. What's the rule? (Signal.) *If an object is made of metal, color it purple.*
6. (Repeat step 5 until firm.)
7. Make a purple mark on one of the objects made of metal.
8. Here's one more thing to do. Part of the pencil is missing. What part is missing? (Signal.) *The eraser.*
- Yes, the eraser. Before you color the pencil, follow the dots with your pencil to make the eraser.

Objectives

- Identify an object by stated criteria. (Exercise 1)
- Complete verbal analogies. (Exercise 2)
- Replace a word in a sentence with an opposite. (Exercise 3)
- Given a calendar, identify the day and date for "today" and "tomorrow" and one week from today. (Exercise 4)
- Answer questions about a new story. (Exercise 5)
- Complete a picture by cutting and pasting words to show a familiar character saying the months of the year. (Exercise 6)

EXERCISE 1 **Description**

1. You're going to figure out what object I'm thinking of.
2. Listen: I'm thinking of a tool made of metal. Name some of the objects I could be thinking of. (Call on individual children.)
3. Listen: The metal tool I'm thinking of is used for cutting.
- Could I be thinking of a knife? (Signal.) *Yes.*
- How do you know? (Call on a child. Idea: *It's a metal tool used for cutting.*)
4. (Repeat step 3 until firm.)
5. Everybody, could I be thinking of a pair of scissors? (Signal.) *Yes.*
- How do you know? (Call on a child. Idea: *It's a metal tool used for cutting.*)
- Everybody, could I be thinking of a piece of paper? (Signal.) *No.*
- How do you know? (Call on a child. Idea: *It's not a metal tool used for cutting.*)
6. (Repeat step 5 until firm.)
7. Listen: The object I'm thinking of has two handles and two blades.
- Could I be thinking of a pair of scissors? (Signal.) *Yes.*
- How do you know? (Call on a child. Idea: *It's a metal tool used for cutting that has two handles and two blades.*)
- Everybody, could I be thinking of a knife? (Signal.) *No.*
- How do you know? (Call on a child. Idea: *It doesn't have two handles and two blades.*)
8. (Repeat step 7 until firm.)
9. Yes, I was thinking of a pair of scissors.

EXERCISE 2 **Analogies**

1. You're going to make up sentences that are like the sentence I start with.
2. Listen: A dog makes the sound ruff. What sound does a dog make? (Signal.) *Ruff.* Yes, a dog makes the sound ruff.
- Everybody, say that. Get ready. (Signal.) *A dog makes the sound ruff.*
3. A cow makes the sound . . . (Signal.) *moo.*
- Say the statement about a cow. Get ready. (Signal.) *A cow makes the sound moo.*
4. A cat makes the sound . . . (Signal.) *meow.*
- Say the statement about a cat. Get ready. (Signal.) *A cat makes the sound meow.*
5. A frog makes the sound . . . (Signal.) *ribbit.*
- Say the statement about a frog. Get ready. (Signal.) *A frog makes the sound ribbit.*
6. A rooster makes the sound . . . (Signal.) *cock-a-doodle-doo.*
- Say the statement about a rooster. Get ready. (Signal.) *A rooster makes the sound cock-a-doodle-doo.*
7. A cow makes the sound . . . (Signal.) *moo.*
- Say the statement about a cow. Get ready. (Signal.) *A cow makes the sound moo.*

EXERCISE 3 Opposites

1. Listen: The opposite of throwing something is catching something.
- What's the opposite of throwing something? (Signal.) *Catching something.*
- What's the opposite of catching something? (Signal.) *Throwing something.*
- What's the opposite of asleep? (Signal.) *Awake.*
- What's the opposite of raw? (Signal.) *Cooked.*
- What's the opposite of safe? (Signal.) *Dangerous.*
- What's the opposite of early? (Signal.) *Late.*
- What's the opposite of before? (Signal.) *After.*
- What's the opposite of finishing something? (Signal.) *Starting something.*

2. You're going to make up statements that have the opposite word.
- Listen: The children read books after recess. Say that statement. Get ready. (Signal.) *The children read books after recess.*
- Now say a statement that tells the opposite about when the children read books. Get ready. (Signal.) *The children read books before recess.*

3. Listen: Ricky will throw the football. Say the statement. Get ready. (Signal.) *Ricky will throw the football.*
- Now say a statement that tells the opposite about what Ricky will do. Get ready. (Signal.) *Ricky will catch the football.*

4. Listen: He painted the fence after he painted the garage. Say the statement. Get ready. (Signal.) *He painted the fence after he painted the garage.*
- Now say a statement that tells the opposite about when he painted the garage. Get ready. (Signal.) *He painted the fence before he painted the garage.*

5. Listen: We couldn't wait for the movie to start. Say the statement. Get ready. (Signal.) *We couldn't wait for the movie to start.*
- Now say a statement that tells the opposite about what we couldn't wait for. Get ready. (Signal.) *We couldn't wait for the movie to finish.*

EXERCISE 4 Calendar

1. (Present calendar.)
- We're going to talk about today, tomorrow, and one week from today.
2. Tell me the day of the week it is today. Get ready. (Signal.)
- Tell me the day of the week it will be tomorrow. Get ready. (Signal.)
- Tell me the day of the week it will be one week from today. Get ready. (Signal.)
3. (Repeat step 2 until firm.)
4. Now the dates.
- Tell me today's date. Get ready. (Signal.)
- Look at the calendar. ✔
- Tell me the date it will be one week from today. Get ready. (Signal.)
5. Once more.
- Listen: Tell me today's date. Get ready. (Signal.)
- Tell me tomorrow's date. Get ready. (Signal.)
- Tell me the date it will be one week from today. Get ready. (Signal.)
6. (Repeat step 5 until firm.)

EXERCISE 5 Bleep Learns The Months Of The Year *Part 2*

Storytelling

1. Here's the last story about Molly and Bleep.

Molly was getting ready to go on a vacation with Mrs. Anderson. They planned to take a trip to the mountains and camp out. Bleep was supposed to stay at home and look after things there.

Molly was gathering up all the things she would take with her on the trip. She had flashlights and batteries. She had swimming suits and sunglasses. She had hiking shoes and lawn chairs. As she gathered up all the things she planned to take with her, she talked to Bleep. She said, "Now, remember to water all my plants next Monday."

"Okay, baby," Bleep said. "You want water, you got water."

"And, oh yes," Molly said. "Remember to feed the goldfish every day."

"Okay, baby," Bleep said. "You want fish food, you got fish food."

Molly suddenly stopped. "I almost forgot about the painters," she said. "You'll have to show them where the paint is. They'll be here on the first of July."

Bleep said, "Blurp."

"Why did you say, 'blurp'?" Molly asked.

Bleep said, "I don't remember."

Oh no, here we go again. But this time, Molly had a pretty good idea of what Bleep's problem was.

Molly decided to make sure she knew what Bleep's problem was. She said, "Bleep, what month was it that Mrs. Anderson and I went to the wrecking yard?"

Bleep said, "March."

Molly said, "And what month comes after March?"

- Everybody, what did Bleep say? (Signal.) *April, of course.* Yes.

Bleep said, "April, of course."

Molly said, "And what month comes after April?"

- Everybody, what did Bleep say? (Signal.) *May, of course.* Yes.

Bleep said, "May, of course."

Then Molly said, "And what month comes after May?"

- Everybody, what did Bleep say? (Signal.) *June, of course.* Right.

Bleep said, "June, of course."

Molly said, "And what month comes after June?"

- Everybody, what did Bleep say? (Signal.) *Blurp, of course.* Yes.

Bleep said, "Blurp, of course."

So Molly knew that Bleep knew some of the months, but he had trouble with July. She said, "Bleep, say the first three months of the year."

- Everybody, what did Bleep say? (Signal.) *January, February and March.* Yes.

Bleep said, "January, February and March."

"Very good," Molly said. "Now say the three months that come after March."

- Everybody, what did Bleep say? (Signal.) *April, May and June.* Yes.

Bleep said, "April, May and June."

"Very good," Molly said. "Now say the three months that come after June."

- Everybody, what did Bleep say? (Signal.) *Blurp, Blurp and Blurp.* Right.

Bleep said, "Blurp, Blurp and Blurp."

"Not too good," Molly said. Then she asked, "Do you want to try the **last** three months of the year?"

Bleep said, "Okay, baby. Blurp, Blurp and December."

Well, now Molly knew Bleep's problem. He could say the **first** three months of the year—January, February and March. He could say the **next** three months—April, May and June. But after **June,** the only month he knew was the very last month of the year.

- Everybody, what month is that? (Signal.) *December.* Right. Bleep knew December.

So Molly told Bleep, "I don't have much time to teach you about the months because I'm leaving on my vacation soon. But if you work hard, maybe you can learn all of the months before I go."

Bleep said, "Okay, baby."

And so Molly wrote the names of all the months on cards for Bleep. Then she practiced saying the months with Bleep. Each time she would start with January. And Bleep would say, "January, February, March." Then he'd say, "April, May, June."

But you know what he said after June.

After a while, Bleep could say: July, August, September.

- Everybody, say those three months. (Signal.) *July, August, September.*

And after another while, Bleep could say the last three months: October, November, December.

- Everybody, say those three months. (Signal.) *October, November, December.*

So pretty soon Bleep knew all **twelve** months.

- Let's see who knows the months as well as Bleep.
2. Everybody, say the first three months. (Signal.) *January, February, March.*

- Say the next three months. (Signal.) *April, May, June.*
- Say the next three months. (Signal.) *July, August, September.*
- Say the last three months. (Signal.) *October, November, December.*
- (Repeat step 2 until firm.)
3. I think we have some children who can say the twelve months as well as Bleep.

EXERCISE 6 Ordering The Months Of The Year

September			
March	June	February	May
November	January	April	July
October	August	December	

1. Everybody, open your workbook to Lesson 66. Write your name at the top of the page. ✔
- The picture is supposed to show Bleep saying all the months, but there are no words for what he's saying. The names of the months are at the bottom of the page, but they are all out of order. You'll have to put them where they belong.
- Your turn: Cut out each name. Do it fast. Raise your hand when you're finished. (Observe children and give feedback.)

2. Now you're going to put the months in the calendar.
- Listen: Say the first three months. (Signal.) *January, February, March.*
- (Write on the board:)

    January   February   March

- Find the cards for January, February and March. Then put them in the top row. Don't paste them in place. Just put them where they belong. Raise your hand when you're finished.
    (Observe children and give feedback.)
3. Now you have January, February and March.
- Say the next three months. (Signal.) *April, May, June.*
- (Write to show:)

    January   February   March
    April   May   June

- Find the cards for April, May and June. Then put them in the second row. Raise your hand when you're finished.
    (Observe children and give feedback.)
4. You have the cards for January, February, March, April, May and June.
- Say the next three months. (Signal.) *July, August, September.*
- (Write to show:)

    January   February   March
    April   May   June
    July   August   September

- Find the cards for July, August and September. Put them in the third row. Raise your hand when you're finished.
    (Observe children and give feedback.)
5. You have the cards for January, February, March, April, May, June, July, August and September.
- Say the last three months. (Signal.) *October, November, December.*
- See if you can put the last three months in place: October, November and December. Raise your hand when you're finished.
    (Observe children and give feedback.)
- (Write to show:)

    January   February   March
    April   May   June
    July   August   September
    October   November   December

- Who got it right? ✔
- Good for you.
6. Your turn: Paste all the months in place. Then say them to yourself, because you want to be able to say them as well as Bleep does. Raise your hand when you're finished.
    (Observe children and give feedback.)

Objectives

- Replace a word in a sentence with an opposite. (Exercise 1)
- Identify an object based on its characteristics. (Exercise 2)
- Given a calendar, identify the day and date for "today" and "tomorrow" and one week from today. (Exercise 3)
- Name things that a statement does NOT tell. (Exercise 4)
- Complete verbal analogies. (Exercise 5)
- **Relate a familiar story grammar to a picture that indicates the sequence of events for a new story.** (Exercise 6)
- Put on a play to show a new story. (Exercise 7)

EXERCISE 1 Opposites

1. Here are some new opposites.
2. Listen: The opposite of in front of is in back of.
- What's the opposite of in front of? (Signal.) *In back of.*
- What's the opposite of in back of? (Signal.) *In front of.*
3. Let's review. Listen: What's the opposite of wild? (Signal.) *Tame.*
4. You're going to make up statements that have the opposite word.
5. Listen: The hawk was in back of the mouse. Say the statement. Get ready. (Signal.) *The hawk was in back of the mouse.*
- Now say a statement that tells the opposite about where the hawk was. Get ready (Signal.) *The hawk was in front of the mouse.*
6. Listen: I held my hand over the table. Say the statement. Get ready. (Signal.) *I held my hand over the table.*
- Now say a statement that tells the opposite about where I held my hand. Get ready. (Signal.) *I held my hand under the table.*
7. Listen: The children got to school late. Say the statement. Get ready. (Signal.) *The children got to school late.*
- Now say a statement that tells the opposite about when the children got to school. Get ready. (Signal.) *The children got to school early.*
8. Listen: We were tired before lunchtime. Say the statement. Get ready. (Signal.) *We were tired before lunchtime.*
- Now say a statement that tells the opposite about when we were tired. Get ready. (Signal.) *We were tired after lunchtime.*

9. Listen: Kim likes to catch baseballs. Say the statement. Get ready. (Signal.) *Kim likes to catch baseballs.*
- Now say a statement that tells the opposite about what Kim likes. Get ready. (Signal.) *Kim likes to throw baseballs.*

EXERCISE 2 Description

Note: The children are not to memorize the "funny" name in this task.

1. I'm going to tell you about an object you know. But I'm going to call it a funny name. See if you can figure out what object I'm thinking about.
2. (Hold up one finger.) A tunk is a tool. Say that. (Signal.) *A tunk is a tool.*
- (Hold up two fingers.) A tunk is used to pound nails. Say that. (Signal.) *A tunk is used to pound nails.*
3. Everybody, say the things you know about a tunk. Get ready.
- (Hold up one finger.) *A tunk is a tool.*
- (Hold up two fingers.) *A tunk is used to pound nails.*
4. (Repeat steps 2 and 3 until firm.)
5. Everybody, tell me the kind of tool I am calling a tunk. (Pause.) Get ready. (Signal.) *A hammer.*
6. I couldn't fool you. It's really a hammer. How do you know a tunk is a hammer? (Call on a child. Idea: *It's a tool. It's used to pound nails.*)
7. How would you like to eat with a tunk? (Children respond.)

EXERCISE 3 Calendar

1. (Present calendar.)
- We're going to talk about today, tomorrow, and one week from today.
2. Tell me the day of the week it is today. Get ready. (Signal.)
- Tell me the day of the week it will be tomorrow. Get ready. (Signal.)
- Tell me the day of the week it will be one week from today. Get ready. (Signal.)
3. (Repeat step 2 until firm.)
4. Now the dates.
- Tell me today's date. Get ready. (Signal.)
- Look at the calendar. ✔
- Tell me the date it will be one week from today. Get ready. (Signal.)
5. Once more.
- Listen: Tell me today's date. Get ready. (Signal.)
- Tell me tomorrow's date. Get ready. (Signal.)
- Tell me the date it will be one week from today. Get ready. (Signal.)
6. (Repeat step 5 until firm.)

EXERCISE 4 Statements

1. Listen to this statement. They are flying kites. Everybody, say that statement. Get ready. (Signal.) *They are flying kites.*
2. Does that statement tell you if they are girls? (Signal.) *No.*
- Does that statement tell you if they are wearing coats? (Signal.) *No.*
- Does that statement tell you what they are doing now? (Signal.) *Yes.*
- Does that statement tell you what they will be doing tomorrow? (Signal.) *No.*
- Does that statement tell you if the kites are big? (Signal.) *No.*
3. They are flying kites. Everybody, say that statement again. Get ready. (Signal.) *They are flying kites.*
4. Name three things the statement does not tell you. (Call on individual children.) (Repeat all three correct responses.)

EXERCISE 5 Analogies

1. You're going to make up sentences that are like the sentence I start with.
2. Listen: People live in a building. What building? (Call on a child. Accept other responses but use: *a house.*) Yes, people live in a house.

- Say the statement. Get ready. (Signal.) *People live in a house.*
3. People buy raw food in a . . . (Signal.) *store.*
- Say the statement about where people buy raw food. Get ready. (Signal.) *People buy raw food in a store.*
4. People live in a . . . (Signal.) *house.*
- Say the statement about where people live. Get ready. (Signal.) *People live in a house.*
5. People learn new things in a . . . (Signal.) *school.*
- Say the statement about where people learn new things. Get ready. (Signal.) *People learn new things in a school.*
6. People keep their car in a . . . (Signal.) *garage.*
- Say the statement about where people keep their car. Get ready. (Signal.) *People keep their car in a garage.*
7. People buy raw food in a . . . (Signal.) *store.*
- Say the statement about where people buy raw food. Get ready. (Signal.) *People buy raw food in a store.*

WORKBOOK

EXERCISE 6 Sequence Story

The Bragging Rats Have a Jumping Contest

1. Everybody, open your workbook to Lesson 67. Write your name at the top of the page. ✔
- This picture shows another story about the bragging rats.

2. Everybody, touch number 1. ✔
- You can see the bragging rats arguing about something. And you can see the wise old rat telling them to do something.
- Touch number 2. ✔
- That's where the bragging rats go next. That's a place that shows how far you can jump. It's a long-jump pit.
- Touch number 3. ✔
- You know who that is. That little black rat is going to do something after the bragging rats go to number 2.

3. I can't read you this story about the bragging rats because somebody forgot to write it down again.
- Listen: Don't say anything. But see if you can figure out what the bragging rats are arguing about this time and how the wise old rat is telling them to settle their argument. That's what you'll have to tell at number 1. Then you'll tell what the bragging rats did at number 2 to settle the argument. Then you'll have to tell something about number 3.

4. Raise your hand if you think you can tell the whole story. Remember, first tell everything that happened at number 1, then tell what happened at number 2 and then tell about the little black rat at number 3.
- (Call on a child to tell the story. Repeat with several children. Praise stories that cover the following ideas at the appropriate number: (1) The bragging rats were arguing about who could jump the farthest. The wise old rat told them how to settle the argument: Go to the long-jump pit and see who jumps the farthest. (2) The bragging rats jumped, but not very far. (3) The little black rat jumped farther than either bragging rat and won the contest.)

5. Later, you'll color the picture.

EXERCISE 7   Bragging Rats Have a Jumping Contest

Putting On a Play

1. (Either put chalk marks or strips on the floor to simulate a long-jump pit or go outside.)
- Let's act out this story.
- (Identify children to play the parts of the two bragging rats, the wise old rat and the little black rat.)
- (Identify the simulated long-jump pit. Say:) Pretend this is the long-jump pit.
- (Point to one end of the long-jump pit. Say:) And this is the starting end.

2. We'll start out with the bragging rats arguing. So I want to hear a good argument. I want to hear those bragging rats telling about how far they can jump. They don't always tell the truth, do they?
- So they could say things like, "I can jump so far that I could . . ." and then you'll have to tell something amazing.
- After they argue a while, the wise old rat has to step in and tell them to stop arguing. Then he'll tell them how to settle their argument.
- And the bragging rats will take turns trying to jump farther than each other. Neither will jump very far.
- But then, it's the little black rat's turn. And I'll bet that those bragging rats will not be very happy when they see how far that little black rat can jump.

3. Here we go. Are the bragging rats ready to give us a good argument? Go.
- (Prompt each bragging rat to tell a couple of lies. Then prompt the wise old rat to intervene. Praise good acting.)

Objectives

- Name common opposites. (Exercise 1)
- Generate statements involving "can do" and "cannot do." (Exercise 2)
- Name common opposites. (Exercise 3)
- Given a calendar, identify the day and date for "today" and "tomorrow" and one week from today. (Exercise 4)
- Complete verbal analogies. (Exercise 5)
- Listen to a familiar story. (Exercise 6)
- Complete a picture by copying the words to show a familiar character saying the months of the year. (Exercise 7)
- Follow the coloring rules for classes and subclasses. (Exercise 8)
- Complete analogies involving class. (Exercise 9)

EXERCISE 1 **Opposites**

1. We're going to play a word game.
2. Everybody, think of a game that is the opposite of difficult.
- A game that is the opposite of difficult is . . . (Signal.) *easy.*
3. Everybody, think of a floor that is the opposite of smooth.
- A floor that is the opposite of smooth is . . . (Signal.) *rough.*
4. Everybody, think of a jar that is the opposite of open.
- A jar that is the opposite of open is . . . (Signal.) *shut.*
5. Everybody, think of a clown who is doing the opposite of crying.
- A clown who is doing the opposite of crying is . . . (Signal.) *laughing.*
6. Everybody, think of a bathtub that is the opposite of deep.
- A bathtub that is the opposite of deep is . . . (Signal.) *shallow.*

EXERCISE 2 **Can Do**

1. I'm going to ask questions about a woman and a paper bag.
2. Everybody, can a woman play music on a paper bag? (Signal.) *No.*
- Say the statement. Get ready. (Signal.) *A woman cannot play music on a paper bag.*
3. Everybody, can a woman tear a paper bag? (Signal.) *Yes.*
- Say the statement. Get ready. (Signal.) *A woman can tear a paper bag.*

4. (Call on a child.)
Your turn. Make up another statement that tells something a woman can do with a paper bag. (After the child makes the statement, call on the group.)
- Say the statement about what a woman can do with a paper bag. Get ready. (Signal.) (The group repeats the child's statement.)
- (Repeat until firm.)
5. (Call on another child.)
- Your turn. Now make up a statement that tells something a woman cannot do with a paper bag. (After the child makes the statement, call on the group.)
- Say the statement about what a woman cannot do with a paper bag. (Signal.) (The group repeats the child's statement.)
- (Repeat until firm.)
- (Repeat steps 4 and 5 until firm.)

EXERCISE 3 **Opposites**

1. Listen: the opposite of throwing something is catching something.
- What's the opposite of throwing something? (Signal.) *Catching something.*
- What's the opposite of catching something? (Signal.) *Throwing something.*
2. What's the opposite of asleep? (Signal.) *Awake.*
3. What's the opposite of raw? (Signal.) *Cooked.*

EXERCISE 4 Calendar

1. (Present calendar.)
• We're going to talk about today, tomorrow, and one week from today.
2. Tell me the day of the week it is today. Get ready. (Signal.)
• Tell me the day of the week it will be tomorrow. Get ready. (Signal.)
• Tell me the day of the week it will be one week from today. Get ready. (Signal.)
3. (Repeat step 2 until firm.)
4. Now the dates.
• Tell me today's date. Get ready. (Signal.)
• Look at the calendar. ✔
• Tell me the date it will be one week from today. Get ready. (Signal.)
5. Once more.
• Listen: Tell me today's date. Get ready. (Signal.)
• Tell me tomorrow's date. Get ready. (Signal.)
• Tell me the date it will be one week from today. Get ready. (Signal.)
6. (Repeat step 5 until firm.)

EXERCISE 5 Analogies

1. You're going to make up sentences that are like the sentence I start with.
2. Listen: A magazine is made of some material. What material? (Signal.) *Paper.* Yes, a magazine is made of paper.
• Everybody, say the statement. Get ready. (Signal.) *A magazine is made of paper.*
3. What material is a window made of? (Signal.) *Glass.*
• Say the statement about a window. Get ready. (Signal.) *A window is made of glass.*
4. What material is a towel made of? (Signal.) *Cloth.*
• Say the statement about a towel. Get ready. (Signal.) *A towel is made of cloth.*
5. What material is a coin made of? (Signal.) *Metal.*
• Say the statement about a coin. Get ready. (Signal.) *A coin is made of metal.*
6. What material is a board made of? (Signal.) *Wood.*
• Say the statement about a board. Get ready. (Signal.) *A board is made of wood.*
7. We'll talk about the same things, but we'll use a different type of statement.

8. Listen: A window is to glass. Say the statement. Get ready. (Signal.) *A window is to glass.*
9. Listen: A coin is to metal. Say the statement. Get ready. (Signal.) *A coin is to metal.*
10. Listen: A towel is to cloth. Say the statement. Get ready. (Signal.) *A towel is to cloth.*
11. Listen: A magazine is to paper. Say the statement. Get ready. (Signal.) *A magazine is to paper.*

EXERCISE 6 Bleep Learns The Months Of The Year

Review

1. Here's the last story about Molly and Bleep.

Molly was getting ready to go on a vacation with Mrs. Anderson. They planned to take a trip to the mountains and camp out. Bleep was supposed to stay at home and look after things there.

Molly was gathering up all the things she would take with her on the trip. She had flashlights and batteries. She had swimming suits and sunglasses. She had hiking shoes and lawn chairs. As she gathered up all the things she planned to take with her, she talked to Bleep. She said, "Now, remember to water all my plants next Monday."

"Okay, baby," Bleep said. "You want water, you got water."

"And, oh, yes," Molly said. "Remember to feed the goldfish every day."

"Okay, baby," Bleep said. "You want fish food, you got fish food."

Molly suddenly stopped. "I almost forgot about the painters," she said. "You'll have to show them where the paint is. They'll be here on the first of July."

Bleep said, "Blurp."

"Why did you say, 'blurp'?" Molly asked.

Bleep said, "I don't remember."

Oh, no, here we go again. But this time, Molly had a pretty good idea of what Bleep's problem was.

Molly decided to make sure she knew what Bleep's problem was. She said, "Bleep, what month was it that Mrs. Anderson and I went to the wrecking yard?"

Bleep said, "March."

Molly said, "And what month comes after March?"

Bleep said, "April, of course."

Molly said, "And what month comes after April?"

Bleep said, "May, of course."

Then Molly said, "And what month comes after May?"

Bleep said, "June, of course."

Molly said, "And what month comes after June?"

Bleep said, "Blurp, of course."

So Molly knew that Bleep knew some of the months, but he had trouble with July. She said, "Bleep, say the first three months of the year."

Bleep said, "January, February and March."

"Very good," Molly said. "Now say the three months that come after March."

Bleep said, "April, May and June."

"Very good," Molly said. "Now say the three months that come after June."

Bleep said, "Blurp, Blurp and blurp."

"Not too good," Molly said. Then she asked, "Do you want to try the **last** three months of the year?"

Bleep said, "Okay, baby. Blurp, Blurp and December."

Well, now Molly knew Bleep's problem. He could say the **first** three months of the year—January, February and March. He could say the **next** three months—April, May and June. But after June, the only month he knew was the very last month of the year—December.

So Molly told Bleep, "I don't have much time to teach you about the months because I'm leaving on my vacation soon. But if you work hard, maybe you can learn all of the months before I go."

Bleep said, "Okay, baby."

And so Molly wrote the names of all the months on cards for Bleep. Then she practiced saying the months with him. Each time she would start with January. And Bleep would say, "January, February, March." Then he'd say, "April, May, June."

But you know what he said after June.

After a while, Bleep could say: July, August, September.

And after another while, Bleep could say the last three months: October, November, December.

So, pretty soon Bleep knew all the months.

2. Let's see who knows the months as well as Bleep.
3. Everybody, say the first three months. (Signal.) *January, February, March.*
* Say the next three months. (Signal.) *April, May, June.*
* Say the next three months. (Signal.) *July, August, September.*
* Say the last three months. (Signal.) *October, November, December.*
* (Repeat step 3 until firm.)

EXERCISE 7 Writing The Months Of The Year

1. (Write on the board:)

March	February	January
May	April	June
September	July	August
October	December	November

   - I wrote all the months but not in the right order. I'm going to see if I can trick you.
2. Everybody, open your workbook to Lesson 68. Write your name at the top of the page. ✔
   - The picture is supposed to show Bleep saying all the months. But you'll have to write them.
   - Listen: Say the first three months. (Signal.) *January, February, March.*
   - (Underline the top row of names on the board.) Those names are in this row. See if you can write them where they belong. Write the **first** three months. Raise your hand when you're finished.
     (Observe children and give feedback.)
   - (Change top row to show:)

        January   February   March

   - Here's what you should have for the top row. Raise your hand if you got it right. ✔

3. The first three months are **January, February, March.**
   - Everybody, what are the next three months? (Signal.) *April, May, June.*
   - (Underline the second row.) Here they are, but they're in the wrong order. Write the names for the second row where they belong. Raise your hand when you're finished.
     (Observe children and give feedback.)
   - (Change the second row to show:)

        April   May   June

   - Here's what you should have for the second row. Raise your hand if you got it right. ✔
4. Those three months are **April, May, June.** Everybody, say the **next** three months. (Signal.) *July, August, September.*
   - (Underline the third row.)
   - Here they are. Write the names for the third row where they belong. Raise your hand when you're finished.
     (Observe children and give feedback.)
   - (Change the third row to show:)

        July   August   September

   - Here's what you should have for the third row. Raise your hand if you got it right. ✔
5. Those three months are **July, August, September.**
   - Everybody, say the **last** three months. (Signal.) *October, November, December.*
   - (Underline the last row.) Here they are. Write the names for the last row where they belong. Raise your hand when you're finished.
     (Observe children and give feedback.)
   - (Change the last row to show:)

        October   November   December

   - Here's what you should have for the last row. Raise your hand if you got it right. ✔
6. If you **really** remember all the months of the year, we'll put on a play next time.

EXERCISE 8 Classification

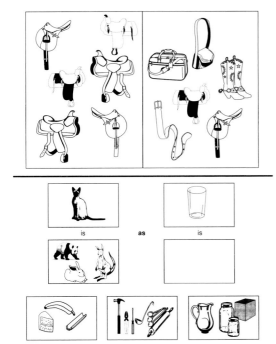

1. Everybody, find the next page in your workbook. ✔
- (Hold up workbook. Point to top half.)
- These boxed pictures show two classes. One class has **one** kind of thing in it, the other class has **more** kinds of things in it.
- Touch the picture that shows only **one** kind of thing. ✔
- What kind of thing is that in the picture? (Signal.) *Saddles.*
2. Touch the picture that shows **more** than one kind of thing. ✔
- Raise your hand if you can figure out the name of the class shown in that picture. ✔
- Everybody, what's the name of that class? (Signal.) *Things made of leather.*
- Everybody, circle the picture that shows **more** kinds of things. ✔

3. Everybody, touch the picture that shows **one** kind of thing. ✔
- The saddles in that picture should be brown. What color? (Signal.) *Brown.*
- Mark a saddle in that picture. ✔
4. Touch the picture that shows **more** kinds of things. The saddles in that picture should be black. What color? (Signal.) *Black.*
- Mark a saddle in that picture. ✔

EXERCISE 9 Analogies

1. (Hold up workbook. Point to bottom half.)
- These pictures show something and the class it is in.
2. Touch the cat. ✔
3. The picture that's right below the cat shows what class it is in. Everybody, what class? (Signal.) *Animals.*
4. Touch the picture of the glass. ✔
- One of the pictures below shows what class the glass is in. Touch the picture that shows what class a glass is in. ✔
- Everybody, what class is it in? (Signal.) *Containers.*
5. Listen: A cat is to animals as a glass is to containers.
- Tell me about a cat. Get ready. (Signal.) *A cat is to animals.*
- Tell me about a glass. Get ready. (Signal.) *A glass is to containers.*
6. Draw a line from the glass to the class it is in. (Observe children and give feedback.)

Objectives

- **Generate statements to describe actions involving "before."** (Exercise 1)
- Generate statements involving "can do" and "cannot do." (Exercise 2)
- Given a calendar, identify the day and date for "today" and "tomorrow" and one week from today. (Exercise 3)
- Replace a word in a sentence with an opposite. (Exercise 4)
- Identify an object based on its characteristics. (Exercise 5)
- Construct a verbal analogy and **repeat the definition of analogy.** (Exercise 6)
- Put on a play to show a familiar story. (Exercise 7)
- Make a picture consistent with details of a story. (Exercise 8)

EXERCISE 1   Actions

1. Here's the first action game.
2. Watch me. (Touch your knee. Keep touching it.) What am I doing? (Signal.) *Touching your knee.*
3. (Stop touching your knee. Touch your head and keep touching it.) What am I doing now? (Signal.) *Touching your head.*
4. What did I do **before** I touched my head? (Signal.) *Touched your knee.*
- Say the whole thing about what I did before I touched my head. Get ready. (Signal.) *Before you touched your head, you touched your knee.*
5. What am I doing now? (Signal.) *Touching your head.*
- Say the whole thing about what I am doing. Get ready. (Signal.) *You are touching your head.*

EXERCISE 2   Can Do

1. I'm going to ask questions about a man and an envelope.
2. Everybody, can a man write on an envelope? (Signal.) *Yes.*
- Say the statement. Get ready. (Signal.) *A man can write on an envelope.*
3. Everybody, can a man sleep in an envelope? (Signal.) *No.*
- Say the statement. Get ready. (Signal.) *A man cannot sleep in an envelope.*
4. (Call on a child.)
- Your turn. Now make up another statement that tells something a man can do with an envelope. (After the child makes the statement, call on the group.)
- Say the statement about what the man can do with an envelope. Get ready. (Signal.) (The group repeats the child's statement.)
- (Repeat until firm.)
5. (Call on another child.) Your turn. Now make up a statement that tells something a man cannot do with an envelope. (After the child makes the statement, call on the group.)
- Say the statement about what a man cannot do with an envelope. Get ready. (Signal.) (The group repeats the child's statement.)
- (Repeat until firm.)

EXERCISE 3   Calendar

1. (Present calendar.)
- We're going to talk about today, tomorrow, and one week from today.
2. Tell me the day of the week it is today. Get ready. (Signal.)
- Tell me the day of the week it will be tomorrow. Get ready. (Signal.)
- Tell me the day of the week it will be one week from today. Get ready. (Signal.)
3. (Repeat step 2 until firm.)
4. Now the dates.
- Tell me today's date. Get ready. (Signal.)
- Look at the calendar. ✔
- Tell me the date it will be one week from today. Get ready. (Signal.)
5. Once more.
- Listen: Tell me today's date. Get ready. (Signal.)
- Tell me tomorrow's date. Get ready. (Signal.)
- Tell me the date it will be one week from today. Get ready. (Signal.)
6. (Repeat step 5 until firm.)

EXERCISE 4 Opposites

1. Here are some opposites.
2. What's the opposite of safe? (Signal.) *Dangerous.*
3. What's the opposite of early? (Signal.) *Late.*
4. What's the opposite of before? (Signal.) *After.*
5. What's the opposite of finishing something? (Signal.) *Starting something.*
6. You're going to make up statements that have the opposite word.
7. Listen: The children read books after recess.
   - Say the statement. Get ready. (Signal.) *The children read books after recess.*
   - Now say a statement that tells the opposite about when the children read books. Get ready. (Signal.) *The children read books before recess.*
8. Listen: The mountain was dangerous.
   - Say the statement. Get ready. (Signal.) *The mountain was dangerous.*
   - Now say a statement that tells the opposite about the mountain. Get ready. (Signal.) *The mountain was safe.*
9. Listen: He painted the fence after he painted the garage.
   - Say the statement. Get ready. (Signal.) *He painted the fence after he painted the garage.*
   - Now say a statement that tells the opposite about when he painted the fence. Get ready. (Signal.) *He painted the fence before he painted the garage.*
10. Listen: We couldn't wait for the race to start.
    - Say the statement. Get ready. (Signal.) *We couldn't wait for the race to start.*
    - Now say a statement that tells the opposite about what we couldn't wait for. Get ready. (Signal.) *We couldn't wait for the race to finish.*

EXERCISE 5 Description

Note: The children are not to memorize the "funny" name in this task.

1. I'm going to tell you about an object you know. But I'm going to call it a funny name. See if you can figure out what object I'm talking about.
2. (Hold up one finger.)
   - Grum is food. Say that. (Signal.) *Grum is food.*
   - (Hold up two fingers.)
   - Grum is cold. Say that. (Signal.) *Grum is cold.*
   - (Hold up three fingers.)
   - You can eat grum from a cone. Say that. (Signal.) *You can eat grum from a cone.*
3. Everybody, say all the things you know about grum. Get ready.
   - (Hold up one finger.) *Grum is food.*
   - (Hold up two fingers.) *Grum is cold.*
   - (Hold up three fingers.) *You can eat grum from a cone.*
4. (Repeat steps 2 and 3 until firm.)
5. Everybody, tell me what grum is. (Pause.) Get ready. (Signal.) *Ice cream.*
6. I couldn't fool you. It's really ice cream. How do you know grum is ice cream? (Call on a child. Idea: *It's food. It's cold. You can eat it from a cone.*)
7. How would you like to sit on grum? (Accept reasonable responses.)

EXERCISE 6 Analogies

1. We're going to make up an **analogy.** What are we going to make up? (Signal.) *An analogy.*
- An analogy tells the way things are the same and the way they're different.
2. We're going to make up an **analogy** that tells how animals move.
- What is the analogy going to tell? (Signal.) *How animals move.*
3. Here are the animals we're going to use in the analogy: A bird and a fish. Which animals? (Signal.) *A bird and a fish.*
4. Name the first animal. Get ready. (Signal.) *A bird.* Yes, a bird.
- Tell me how that animal moves. Get ready. (Signal.) *It flies.*
5. Here's the first part of the analogy. Listen: A bird is to flying. Say the first part of the analogy. Get ready. (Signal.) *A bird is to flying.* Yes, a bird is to flying.
6. The second animal is a fish.
- Tell me how that animal moves. Get ready. (Signal.) *It swims.*
7. Here's the second part of the analogy. Listen: A fish is to swimming. Say the second part of the analogy. Get ready. (Signal.) *A fish is to swimming.* Yes, a fish is to swimming.
8. (Repeat steps 3 through 7 until firm.)
9. My turn. I'm going to say the whole analogy. First I'm going to tell how a bird moves, and then I'm going to tell how a fish moves. Listen: A bird is to flying as a fish is to swimming.
10. Let's say the analogy together. Get ready. *A bird is to flying **as** a fish is to swimming.*
11. All by yourselves. Say the analogy that tells how a bird moves and how a fish moves. Get ready. (Signal.) *A bird is to flying **as** a fish is to swimming.*
12. (Repeat step 11 until firm.)

EXERCISE 7 Putting On a Play

Bleep Learns The Months Of The Year

1. We're going to do a play for part of the story about Molly and Bleep. We'll need somebody to play the part of Molly and somebody to play the part of Bleep.
- (Identify children to play the two parts.)
2. I'll read part of the story. I'll tell the story a little differently than I did before. So Molly and Bleep will really have to remember the story and listen well. Then Molly will have to say the things that Molly says in the story and Bleep will have to say the things that Bleep says in the story. Here we go:

Molly was getting ready to go on a vacation with Mrs. Anderson. They planned to take a trip to the mountains and camp out. Bleep was supposed to stay at home and look after things there.

Molly was gathering up all the things she would take with her on the trip. She had flashlights and batteries. She had swimming suits and sunglasses. She had hiking shoes and lawn chairs. As she gathered up all the things she planned to take with her, she talked to Bleep. She said, "Now remember to water all my plants next Monday."

"Okay, baby," Bleep said. "You want water, you got water."

- Let's act out that part. Molly, tell Bleep what he needs to do next Monday. Bleep, remember what you say. Go Molly. (Idea: Molly tells Bleep, *"Now remember to water all my plants next Monday."* Bleep says, *"Okay, baby. You want water, you got water."*)

- Listen to the next part:

  "And, oh yes," Molly said. "Remember to feed the goldfish every day."

  "Okay, baby," Bleep said. "You want fish food, you got fish food."

- Let's do that part. Go Molly.
  (Idea: Molly tells Bleep, *"And, oh yes. Remember to feed the goldfish every day."* Bleep says, *"Okay, baby. You want fish food, you got fish food."*)
- Listen to the next part:

  Molly suddenly stopped. "I almost forgot about the painters," she said. "You'll have to show them where the paint is. They'll be here on the first of July."

  Bleep said, "Blurp."

  "Why did you say, 'blurp'?" Molly asked.

  Bleep said, "I don't remember."

- Let's act out that part. Go Molly.
  (Idea: Molly tells Bleep, *"I almost forgot about the painters. You'll have to show them where the paint is. They'll be here on the first of July."* Bleep says, *"Blurp."* Molly says, *"Why did you say, 'blurp'?"* Bleep says, *"I don't remember."*)

  Molly asked Bleep a lot of questions to discover his problem. She finally asked him to say the first three months and he answered.

- Molly, ask him the first three months, and Bleep, answer.
  (Idea: Molly says, *"What are the first three months?"* Bleep says, *"January, February, March."*)
- Listen:

  Then Molly asked about the next three months and Bleep answered.

- Molly, do it, and Bleep, answer.
  (Idea: Molly says, *"What are the next three months?"* Bleep says, *"April, May, June."*)
- Listen:

  Then Molly asked about the next three months and Bleep answered.

- Molly, do it, and Bleep, answer.
  (Idea: Molly says, *"What are the next three months?"* Bleep says, *"Blurp, Blurp, and Blurp."*)

  Finally, Molly asked about the last three months and Bleep answered.

- Molly, do it, and Bleep, answer.
  (Idea: Molly says, *"What are the last three months?"* Bleep says, *"Blurp, Blurp and December."*)
- Listen:

  Molly worked with Bleep and after a while she could ask about the months and he could say all of them right.

- Ask Bleep about the months, Molly. Start with the first three months, then the next three months, the next three months and the last three months. We'll see how smart Bleep was at the end of the story. (Idea: Molly asks Bleep about each three months and he responds correctly.)
3. Did Molly and Bleep do a pretty good job? (Children respond.)
- Did our Bleep know his months pretty well at the end of the story? (Children respond.)
- (Praise children for a good performance.)

EXERCISE 8 Story Details

1. Everybody, open your workbook to Lesson 69. Write your name at the top of the page. ✔
- This picture shows Molly and Bleep at the same time.
2. Touch the picture of Molly. ✔
- Where is Molly in this picture? (Call on a child. Idea: *Camping.*)
- Where is Bleep? (Call on a child. Idea: *By the garage at home.*)
- Some of the things shown in Molly's picture are things she gathered to take on her trip. I'll tell you one thing she gathered: lawn chairs. She's sitting in a lawn chair.
- Listen: Four other things in Molly's picture are things she gathered to take with her on the trip. All those things should be red.
- Put a red mark on everything that was named in the story. But don't put a red mark on Molly or Mrs. Anderson. And don't do anything to Bleep's picture. Just do Molly's picture. Raise your hand when you've marked all five things that are named in the story. Don't mark anything that was **not** named in the story. (Observe children and give feedback.)

- (Call on a child:) Name the five things in the picture of Molly that should be red. (Idea: *Lawn chair, hiking shoes, sunglasses, flashlight, swimming suit.*)
3. Everybody, touch the picture of Bleep. ✔
- This picture shows what Bleep was doing at the same time Molly was sitting in her lawn chair in the mountains.
- What was Bleep doing? (Call on a child. Idea: *Showing the painters where the paint was.*)
- Bleep was showing the painters where the paint was. So you know what month it must be. Everybody, what month? (Signal.) *July.*
- You're going to write **July** in the box at the top of Bleep's picture.
- (Write on the board:)

July

- Write **July** in the box. Raise your hand when you're finished. (Observe children and give feedback.)
4. I'll read what the painter is saying to Bleep. I'm not going to tell you what Bleep says. And I don't want anybody to say the answer out loud. The painter is saying, "We'll start painting right away."
- Raise your hand if you know what Bleep would say back to the painter. ✔
- (Write on the board:)

Okay, baby.

- Here's what Bleep said. Everybody, what did he say? (Signal.) *Okay, baby.*
5. You can write that in the picture. Then color the things in Molly's part and Bleep's part of the picture.

Objectives

- Construct a verbal analogy. (Exercise 1)
- Name things that a statement does NOT tell. (Exercise 2)
- Replace a word in a sentence with an opposite. (Exercise 3)
- Given a calendar, identify the day and date for "today" and "tomorrow" and one week from today. (Exercise 4)
- Demonstrate relationship between "or" alternatives and the word "maybe." (Exercise 5)
- Match unique utterances to the familiar story character who would speak them. (Exercise 6)
- Follow coloring rules involving classes and subclasses. (Exercise 7)
- **Complete an analogy involving use.** (Exercise 9)

EXERCISE 1   Analogies

1. We're going to make up an analogy that tells where vehicles go.
2. What is the analogy going to tell? (Signal.) *Where vehicles go.*
3. Here are the vehicles we're going to use in the analogy: a boat and an airplane. Which vehicles? (Signal.) *A boat and an airplane.*
4. Name the first vehicle. Get ready. (Signal.) *A boat.* Yes, a boat.
- Tell me where that vehicle goes. Get ready. (Signal.) *In water.*
5. Here's the first part of the analogy. Listen: A boat is to water. What's the first part of the analogy? (Signal.) *A boat is to water.* Yes, a boat is to water.
6. The second vehicle is an airplane. Tell me where that vehicle goes. Get ready. (Signal.) *In air.*
7. Here's the second part of the analogy. Listen: An airplane is to air. What's the second part of the analogy? (Signal.) *An airplane is to air.* Yes, an airplane is to air.
8. (Repeat steps 3 through 7 until firm.)
9. My turn. I'm going to say the whole analogy. First I'm going to tell where a boat goes, and then I'm going to tell where an airplane goes. Listen: A boat is to water **as** an airplane is to air.
10. Let's say the analogy together. Get ready. *A boat is to water **as** an airplane is to air.*
11. All by yourselves. Say the analogy that tells where a boat goes and where an airplane goes. Get ready. (Signal.) *A boat is to water as an airplane is to air.*
12. (Repeat step 11 until firm.)

EXERCISE 2   Statements

1. Listen to this statement. The girl will sit in a swing. Everybody, say the statement. Get ready. (Signal.) *The girl will sit in a swing.*
2. Does that statement tell if the girl is wearing a dress? (Signal.) *No.*
- Does that statement tell what the girl is doing now? (Signal.) *No.*
- Does that statement tell what the girl did yesterday? (Signal.) *No.*
- Does that statement tell if the girl is skinny? (Signal.) *No.*
- Does that statement tell what the girl will do? (Signal.) *Yes.*
3. The girl will sit in a swing. Everybody, say the statement again. Get ready. (Signal.) *The girl will sit in a swing.*
4. Your turn to name two things the statement does not tell you. (Call on individual children.)
- (Repeat both correct responses.)
5. You have named two things the statement does not tell us.
- Name the first thing. Get ready. (Hold up one finger.) (The children give the first response.)
- Name the second thing. Get ready. (Hold up two fingers.) (The children give the second response.)
6. (Repeat step 5 until firm.)

EXERCISE 3   Opposites

1. Let's review.
2. Listen: The opposite of in front of is in back of.
- What's the opposite of in front of? (Signal.) *In back of.*

- What's the opposite of in back of? (Signal.) *In front of.*
- Listen: What's the opposite of wild? (Signal.) *Tame.*
- What's the opposite of over? (Signal.) *Under.*
- What's the opposite of after? (Signal.) *Before.*

3. You're going to make up statements that have the opposite word.
4. Listen: The hawk was in back of the mouse.
- Say the statement. Get ready. (Signal.) *The hawk was in back of the mouse.*
- Now say a statement that tells the opposite about where the hawk was. Get ready. (Signal.) *The hawk was in front of the mouse.*
5. Listen: I held my hand over the table.
- Say the statement. Get ready. (Signal.) *I held my hand over the table.*
- Now say a statement that tells the opposite about where I held my hand. Get ready. (Signal.) *I held my hand under the table.*
6. Listen: The children got to school late.
- Say the statement. Get ready. (Signal.) *The children got to school late.*
- Now say a statement that tells the opposite about when the children got to school. Get ready. (Signal.) *The children got to school early.*
7. Listen: We were tired before lunchtime.
- Say the statement. Get ready. (Signal.) *We were tired before lunchtime.*
- Now say a statement that tells the opposite about when we were tired. Get ready. (Signal.) *We were tired after lunchtime.*

EXERCISE 4 Calendar

1. (Present calendar.)
- We're going to talk about today, tomorrow, and one week from today.
2. Tell me the day of the week it is today. Get ready. (Signal.)
- Tell me the day of the week it will be tomorrow. Get ready. (Signal.)
- Tell me the day of the week it will be one week from today. Get ready. (Signal.)
3. (Repeat step 2 until firm.)

4. Now the dates.
- Tell me today's date. Get ready. (Signal.)
- Look at the calendar. ✔
- Tell me the date it will be one week from today. Get ready. (Signal.)
5. Once more.
- Listen: Tell me today's date. Get ready. (Signal.)
- Tell me tomorrow's date. Get ready. (Signal.)
- Tell me the date it will be one week from today. Get ready. (Signal.)
6. (Repeat step 5 until firm.)

EXERCISE 5 Actions

1. Here's the first action game. I'm going to do something. See if you can figure out what I'm going to do.
2. Listen: I'm going to stamp my foot or clap or wave.
- What am I going to do? (Signal.) *Stamp your foot or clap or wave.*
3. Yes, I'm going to stamp my foot or clap or wave.
- Am I going to walk? (Signal.) *No.*
- Am I going to wave? (Signal.) *Maybe.*
- Am I going to stamp my foot? (Signal.) *Maybe.*
- Am I going to clap? (Signal.) *Maybe.*
4. Here I go. (Stamp your foot.)
- Did I stamp my foot? (Signal.) *Yes.*
- Did I wave? (Signal.) *No.*
- Did I clap? (Signal.) *No.*
5. What did I do? (Signal.) *Stamped your foot.*
6. Here's the next game.
7. Everybody, you're going to touch your nose and touch your knee at the same time. Get ready. (Signal.) ✔
- What are you doing? (Signal.) *Touching my nose and touching my knee.*
8. Say the whole thing. Get ready. (Signal.) *I am touching my nose and touching my knee.*
9. Everybody, you're going to hold up your thumb and hold up your feet. Get ready. (Signal.) ✔
- What are you doing? (Signal.) *Holding up my thumb and holding up my feet.*
10. Say the whole thing. Get ready. (Signal.) *I am holding up my thumb and holding up my feet.*
11. Hands and feet down.

EXERCISE 6 Extrapolation

What Characters Say

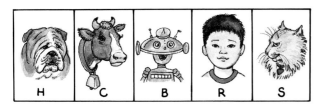

1. _____
2. _____
3. _____
4. _____
5. _____

1. Everybody, open your workbook to Lesson 70. Write your name at the top of the page. ✔
• These are pictures of characters from some stories you've heard. Each picture has a letter under it. The letter is the initial of the character in the picture.
2. Touch the first picture. ✔
• Who is in that picture? (Signal.) *Honey.*
• What letter is under that picture? (Signal.) *H.* **H** is the first letter in the word **Honey.**
3. Who is in the next picture? (Signal.) *Clarabelle.*
• What letter is under Clarabelle? (Signal.) *C.* **C** is the first letter in her name.
4. Who is in the next picture? (Signal.) *Bleep.*
• What letter is under Bleep? (Signal.) *B.* **B** is the first letter in Bleep's name.
5. Who is in the next picture? (Signal.) *Roger.*
• What letter is under Roger? (Signal.) *R.* **R** is the first letter in Roger's name.
6. Who is in the last picture? (Signal.) *Sweetie.*
• What letter is under Sweetie? (Signal.) *S.* **S** is the first letter in Sweetie's name.

7. Here's the game we'll play: I'll say five different things. For each thing I say, you're going to write the letter for the character who would say that. You're not going to say anything out loud. You'll just find the right picture and write the letter for that character.
8. Everybody, touch number 1 and keep touching it. ✔
• Listen and don't say anything. Here's the statement for number 1: "I'd love to go roller-skating just like those children are doing."
• Find the character who would say that. Write the letter for that character on line 1. Raise your hand when you're finished. (Observe children and give feedback.)
9. Everybody, which character would love to go roller-skating just like the children? (Signal.) *Clarabelle.*
• So what letter did you write for number 1? (Signal.) *C.*
• (Write on the board:)

1.   C

• Here's what you should have for number 1. Raise your hand if you got it right. ✔
10. Everybody, touch number 2. ✔
• Listen and don't say anything. Here's the statement for number 2: "Look at those little chicks. Yum, yum."
• Find the character who would say that. Write the letter for that character on line 2. Raise your hand when you're finished. (Observe children and give feedback.)
11. Everybody, which character would say, "Look at those little chicks. Yum, yum"? (Signal.) *Sweetie.*
• So what letter did you write for number 2? (Signal.) *S.*
• (Write to show:)

1.	C
2.	S

• Here's what you should have for number 2. Raise your hand if you got it right. ✔

12. Everybody, touch number 3. ✔
- Listen and don't say anything. Here's the statement for number 3: "When I sat down, my hat was right over there; but now, I don't know where it is."
- Find the character who would say that. Write the letter for that character on line 3. Raise your hand when you're finished. (Observe children and give feedback.)
13. Everybody, which character would have trouble finding a hat? (Signal.) *Roger.*
- So what letter did you write for number 3? (Signal.) *R.*
- (Write to show:)

1.	C
2.	S
3.	R

Here's what you should have for number 3. Raise your hand if you got it right. ✔

14. Everybody, touch number 4. ✔
- Listen and don't say anything. Here's the statement for number 4: "If that cat doesn't behave, I'll have to give him a little nip somewhere."
- Find the character who would say that. Write the letter for that character on line 4. Raise your hand when you're finished. (Observe children and give feedback.)
15. Everybody, which character would give a cat a little nip? (Signal.) *Honey.*
- So what letter did you write for number 4? (Signal.) *H.*
- (Write to show:)

1.	C
2.	S
3.	R
4.	H

- Here's what you should have for number 4. Raise your hand if you got it right. ✔
16. Everybody, touch number 5. ✔
- Listen and don't say anything. Here's the statement for number 5: "Okay, baby."
- Find the character who would say that. Write the letter for that character on line 5. Raise your hand when you're finished. (Observe children and give feedback.)

17. Everybody, which character would say "Okay, baby"? (Signal.) *Bleep.*
- So what letter did you write for number 5? (Signal.) *B.*
- (Write to show:)

1.	C
2.	S
3.	R
4.	H
5.	B

- Here's what you should have for number 5. Raise your hand if you got it right. ✔
18. Raise your hand if you got everything right. ✔ Wow. You really know the characters we've read about.

EXERCISE 7   Classification

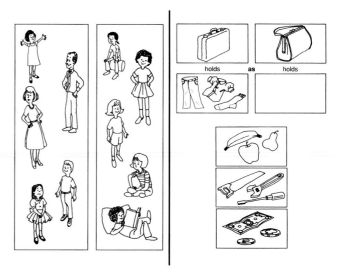

1. Everybody, find the next page in your workbook. ✔
- (Hold up workbook. Point to first half.)
- Touch the picture that shows only **one** kind of thing. ✔
- What kind of thing is that in the picture? (Signal.) *Girls.*
2. Touch the picture that shows **more** than one kind of thing. ✔
- Raise your hand if you can figure out the name of the class shown in that picture. ✔
- Everybody, what's the name of that class? (Signal.) *People.*
- Everybody, circle the picture that shows **more** kinds of things. ✔

3. Everybody, touch the picture that shows **one** kind of thing. ✔
- Each girl in that picture should be wearing red and purple clothing. What colors? (Signal.) *Red and purple.*
- Mark a girl in that picture. ✔
4. Touch the picture that shows **more** kinds of things. The girls in that picture should be wearing yellow clothing. What color? (Signal.) *Yellow.*
- Mark a girl in that picture. ✔

EXERCISE 8 Analogies

1. (Hold up workbook. Point to second half.) These pictures show something and what it holds.
2. Touch the suitcase. ✔
- The picture that's right below shows what it holds. Everybody, what does a suitcase hold? (Signal.) *Clothes.*

3. Touch the picture of the purse. ✔
- One of the pictures below shows what it holds. Touch the picture that shows what a purse holds. ✔
- Everybody, what does a purse hold? (Signal.) *Money.*
4. Tell me about a suitcase. Get ready. (Signal.) *A suitcase holds clothes.*
- Tell me about a purse. Get ready. (Signal.) *A purse holds money.*
- Listen: A suitcase holds clothes **as** a purse holds money.
5. Say the whole analogy about a suitcase and a purse. Get ready. (Signal.) *A suitcase holds clothes as a purse holds money.*
6. (Repeat step 5 until firm.)
7. Draw a line from the purse to what it holds. (Observe children and give feedback.)

Objectives

- Construct a verbal analogy involving material. (Exercise 1)
- Given a calendar, identify the day and date for "today" and "tomorrow" and one week from today. (Exercise 2)
- Identify an object that fits stated criteria. (Exercise 3)
- Identify an object based on its characteristics. (Exercise 4)
- Name members of a class and subclass and **identify the bigger class.** (Exercise 5)
- Relate a familiar story grammar to a picture that indicates the sequence of events for a new story. (Exercise 6)
- Identify cardinal directions on a map. (Exercise 7)
- Follow coloring rules involving materials. (Exercise 8)

EXERCISE 1 Analogies

1. We're going to make up an analogy that tells what the containers are made of.
2. What is the analogy going to tell? (Signal.) *What containers are made of.*
3. Here are the containers we're going to use in the analogy: a bag and a bottle.
- Which containers? (Signal.) *A bag and a bottle.*
4. Name the first container. Get ready. (Signal.) *A bag.* Yes, a bag.
- Tell what the container is made of. Get ready. (Signal.) *Paper.*
5. Here's the first part of the analogy. Listen: A bag is to paper. What's the first part of the analogy? (Signal.) *A bag is to paper.* Yes, a bag is to paper.
6. Now name the second container. Get ready. (Signal.) *A bottle.*
- Tell me what that container is made of. Get ready. (Signal.) *Plastic.*
7. Here's the second part of the analogy. A bottle is to plastic. What's the second part of the analogy? (Signal.) *A bottle is to plastic.* Yes, a bottle is to plastic.
8. (Repeat steps 3 through 7 until firm.)

9. Now you're going to say the whole analogy. First you're going to tell what a bag is made of, and then you're going to tell what a bottle is made of.
10. Say the analogy that tells what a bag is made of and what a bottle is made of. Get ready. (Signal.) *A bag is to paper as a bottle is to plastic.*
11. (Repeat steps 9 and 10 until firm.)

EXERCISE 2 Calendar

1. (Present calendar.)
- We're going to talk about today, tomorrow, and one week from today.
2. Tell me the day of the week it is today. Get ready. (Signal.)
- Tell me the day of the week it will be tomorrow. Get ready. (Signal.)
- Tell me the day of the week it will be one week from today. Get ready. (Signal.)
3. (Repeat step 2 until firm.)
4. Now the dates.
- Tell me today's date. Get ready. (Signal.)
- Look at the calendar. ✔
- Tell me the date it will be one week from today. Get ready. (Signal.)
5. Once more.
- Listen: Tell me today's date. Get ready. (Signal.)
- Tell me tomorrow's date. Get ready. (Signal.)
- Tell me the date it will be one week from today. Get ready. (Signal.)
6. (Repeat step 5 until firm.)

EXERCISE 3   Description

1. Get ready to play detective and find out what object I'm thinking of. I'll give you two clues.
2. (Hold up one finger.) It's a container.
- (Hold up two fingers.) You can put garbage in it.
3. Say the two things we know about the object. Get ready.
- (Hold up one finger.) *It's a container.*
- (Hold up two fingers) *You can put garbage in it.*
4. (Repeat step 3 until firm.)
5. Those clues don't tell you enough to find the right container. They could tell you about a lot of containers. See how many containers you can name that you can put garbage in. (Call on individual children. The group is to name at least three containers that you can put garbage in, such as *a bag, a wastebasket,* and *a bucket.*)
6. Here's another clue for finding the right object. Listen: It's made of paper. Everybody, say that. Get ready. (Signal.) *It's made of paper.*
7. Now here are the three things we know about the object.
- (Hold up one finger.) It's a container.
- (Hold up two fingers.) You can put garbage in it.
- (Hold up three fingers.) It's made of paper.
8. Everybody, say all the things we know. Get ready.
- (Hold up one finger.) *It's a container.*
- (Hold up two fingers.) *You can put garbage in it.*
- (Hold up three fingers.) *It's made of paper.*
9. Everybody, tell me what container I am thinking of. (Pause.) Get ready. (Signal.) *A paper bag.* Yes, a paper bag.

EXERCISE 4   Description

> *Note:* The children are not to memorize the "funny" name in this task.

1. I'm going to tell you about an object you know. But I'm going to call it a funny name. See if you can figure out what object I'm talking about.
2. (Hold up one finger.) An atbit is a building. Say that. (Signal.) *An atbit is a building.*
- (Hold up two fingers.) An atbit is made of wood. Say that. (Signal.) *An atbit is made of wood.*
- (Hold up three fingers.) You find an atbit on a farm. Say that. (Signal.) *You find an atbit on a farm.*
3. Everybody, let's say all the things you know about an atbit. Get ready.
- (Hold up one finger.) *An atbit is a building.*
- (Hold up two fingers.) *An atbit is made of wood.*
- (Hold up three fingers.) *You find an atbit on a farm.*
4. (Repeat steps 2 and 3 until firm.)
5. Everybody, tell me what an atbit is. (Pause.) Get ready. (Signal.) *A barn.*
6. I couldn't fool you. It's really a barn. How do you know an atbit is a barn? (Call on a child. Idea: *It's a building. It's made of wood. You find it on a farm.*)
7. How would you like to eat an atbit for breakfast? (Children respond.)

EXERCISE 5   Classification

1. We're going to talk about classes.
2. If we took all young girls from the class of people, would there be any kinds of people left? (Signal.) *Yes.*
3. Name some kinds of people that would be left. (Call on individual children. Praise appropriate responses.)

4. The class of young girls is made up of many kinds of girls. I'll name some kinds of girls in the class of young girls. Listen: Five-year-old girls, seven-year-old girls. You name some kinds of girls in the class of young girls. (Call on individual children. Praise reasonable answers, such as *three-year-old girls, four-year-old girls, six-year-old girls*.)

5. Think about this. If we took all the five-year-old girls from the class of young girls, would there be any young girls left? (Signal.) *Yes.*

6. Name some kinds of young girls that would be left. (Call on individual children. Praise all acceptable answers: any kind of young girl except five-year-old girls.)

7. Yes, if we took all the five-year-old girls from the class of young girls, there would still be young girls left. So which class is bigger, the class of five-year-old girls or the class of young girls? (Signal.) *The class of young girls.*

• How do you know? (Signal.) *The class of young girls has more kinds of girls in it.*

8. Think big. Which class is bigger, the class of people or the class of young girls? (Pause.) Get ready. (Signal.) *The class of people.*

9. Think big. Which class is bigger, the class of young girls or the class of five-year-old girls? (Pause.) Get ready. (Signal.) *The class of young girls.*

WORKBOOK

EXERCISE 6 **The Bragging Rats Race**

Sequencing

1. Everybody, open your workbook to Lesson 71. Write your name at the top of the page. ✔

• These are pictures that show the first story about the bragging rats. The pictures are in order. That means that the **first** picture shows something that happened at the **beginning** of the story. The **next** picture shows something that happened **next** in the story. The very **last** picture shows something that happened at the **end** of the story.

2. Everybody, touch picture 1. ✔
   What's happening in that picture? (Call on several children. Ideas: *The bragging rats are arguing about who is the fastest runner and The wise old rat is telling the bragging rats that he has an idea.*)

3. Everybody, touch picture 2. ✔

• What's happening in that picture? (Call on several children. Idea: *The bragging rats are lined up ready to race to the pond and back.*)

4. Everybody, touch picture 3. ✔

• What's happening in that picture? (Call on several children. Idea: *The rat with the yellow teeth is stepping on the long tail of the gray rat.*)

5. Everybody, touch picture 4. ✔

• What's happening in that picture? (Call on several children. Ideas: *The bragging rats are arguing in the pond and the others are laughing.*)

6. You can use these pictures to tell the **whole** story about the bragging rats. You have to start out by telling **why** the bragging rats are arguing in the first place. Then tell the things that happened in each picture. Raise your hand if you think you can tell the whole story. Remember, you have to tell the beginning and then tell about each picture. (Call on several children to tell the story. Instruct the other children to follow along or raise their hand if they hear a problem. Praise stories that tell what happens in each picture.)

7. Later you can color the pictures. Maybe you can tell the story to somebody in your family. I bet they will think it's a silly story. Maybe you can tell it to me before you go home today.

EXERCISE 7 Map Reading

1. Everybody, find the next page in your workbook. ✔
- (Hold up workbook. Point to first half.)
- The arrows show where the dog went. Touch the dog. ✔
2. You'll follow the arrows and tell me what the dog chased. The arrow that goes from the dog shows which direction it went first. Touch the arrow. ✔
- Raise your hand when you know which direction that arrow is pointing. ✔
- Everybody, which direction? (Signal.) *North.*
- Yes, the dog went **north** to chase the cat. Which direction did he go? (Signal.) *North.*
- So what letter will you write in the circle on the cat? (Signal.) *N.*
3. Touch the arrow that goes from the cat. ✔
- Raise your hand when you know which direction that arrow is pointing. ✔
- Everybody, which direction? (Signal.) *West.*
- So what letter will you write on the rabbit? (Signal.) *W.*

4. Touch the arrow that goes from the rabbit. ✔
- Raise your hand when you know which direction the arrow is pointing. ✔
- Everybody, which direction is that arrow pointing? (Signal.) *South.*
- So what letter will you write on the frog? (Signal.) *S.*
5. Touch the arrow that goes from the frog. ✔
- Raise your hand when you know the direction of that arrow. ✔
- Everybody, which direction is that arrow pointing? (Signal.) *West.*
- So what letter will you write on the mouse? (Signal.) *W.*
6. Write the letters to show which direction the dog went. Pencils down when you're finished. (Observe children and give feedback.)

EXERCISE 8 Materials

1. (Hold up workbook. Point to second half.)
2. Here's a coloring rule for this picture. If an object is made of wood, color it brown or orange. What's the rule? (Signal.) *If an object is made of wood, color it brown or orange.*
3. (Repeat step 2 until firm.)
4. Mark two objects made of wood. ✔
5. Here's another coloring rule for this picture. If an object is made of cloth, color it yellow. What's the rule? (Signal.) *If an object is made of cloth, color it yellow.*
6. (Repeat step 5 until firm.)
7. Make a yellow mark on one of the objects made of cloth. ✔
8. Here's one more thing to do. Part of the shirt is missing. What part is missing? (Signal.) *The sleeve.*
- Yes, the sleeve. Before you color the shirt, follow the dots and make the sleeve.

Objectives

- Construct a verbal analogy. (Exercise 1)
- Name common opposites. (Exercise 2)
- Given a calendar, identify the day and date for "today" and "tomorrow" and one week from today. (Exercise 3)
- Identify an object based on its characteristics. (Exercise 4)
- **Given two statements, tell which one tells more about what happened and why it tells more.** (Exercise 5)
- Given a common noun, answer questions involving "can do." (Exercise 6)
- Match unique utterances to the familiar story character who would speak them. (Exercise 7)
- Follow coloring rules involving classes and subclasses. (Exercise 8)
- Follow coloring rules involving materials. (Exercise 9)

EXERCISE 1 Analogies

1. Now we're going to make up an analogy that tells what animals say.
2. What is the analogy going to tell? (Signal.) *What animals say.*
3. Here are the animals we're going to use in the analogy: a cat and a frog. Which animals? (Signal.) *A cat and a frog.*
4. Name the first animal. Get ready. (Signal.) *A cat.* Yes, a cat.
- Tell me what that animal says. (Signal.) *Meow.*
5. Here's the first part of the analogy. Listen: A cat is to meowing. Say the first part. Get ready. (Signal.) *A cat is to meowing.* Yes, a cat is to meowing.
6. Now name the second animal. Get ready. (Signal.) *A frog.*
- Tell me what that animal says. Get ready. (Signal.) *Ribbit.*
7. Here's the second part of the analogy. Listen: A frog is to ribbiting. What's the second part of the analogy? (Signal.) *A frog is to ribbiting.* Yes, a frog is to ribbiting.
8. (Repeat steps 4 through 7 until firm.)
9. Get ready to say the whole analogy with me. First tell what a cat says, and then tell what a frog says. Say the analogy. Get ready. (Signal.) (Respond with the children.) *A cat is to meowing as a frog is to ribbiting.*
10. All by yourselves. Say the analogy that tells what a cat says and what a frog says. Get ready. (Signal.) *A cat is to meowing as a frog is to ribbiting.*
11. (Repeat step 10 until firm.)

EXERCISE 2 Opposites

1. We're going to play a word game.
2. Everybody, think of a class that is the opposite of noisy.
- A class that is the opposite of noisy is . . . (Signal.) *quiet.*
3. Everybody, think of a playground that is the opposite of dangerous.
- A playground that is the opposite of dangerous is . . . (Signal.) *safe.*
4. Everybody, think of a floor that is the opposite of shiny.
- A floor that is the opposite of shiny is . . . (Signal.) *dull.*
5. Everybody, think of a truck that is doing the opposite of pulling.
- A truck that is doing the opposite of pulling is . . . (Signal.) *pushing.*
6. Everybody, think of a shelf that is the opposite of narrow.
- A shelf that is the opposite of narrow is . . . (Signal.) *wide.*

EXERCISE 3 Calendar

1. (Present calendar.)
- We're going to talk about today, tomorrow, and one week from today.
2. Tell me the day of the week it is today. Get ready. (Signal.)
- Tell me the day of the week it will be tomorrow. Get ready. (Signal.)
- Tell me the day of the week it will be one week from today. Get ready. (Signal.)
3. (Repeat step 2 until firm.)

4. Now the dates.
- Tell me today's date. Get ready. (Signal.)
- Look at the calendar. ✔
- Tell me the date it will be one week from today. Get ready. (Signal.)

5. Once more.
- Listen: Tell me today's date. Get ready. (Signal.)
- Tell me tomorrow's date. Get ready. (Signal.)
- Tell me the date it will be one week from today. Get ready. (Signal.)

6. (Repeat step 5 until firm.)

EXERCISE 4   Description

1. I'm going to tell you about an object you know. But I'm going to call it a funny name. See if you can figure out what object I'm thinking about.

2. (Hold up one finger.)
- A mank is a vehicle. Say that. (Signal.) *A mank is a vehicle.*
- (Hold up two fingers.)
- A mank holds a lot of people. Say that. (Signal.) *A mank holds a lot of people.*
- (Hold up three fingers.)
- You can ride a mank to school. Say that. (Signal.) *You can ride a mank to school.*

3. Everybody, say all the things you know about a mank. Get ready.
- (Hold up one finger.) *A mank is a vehicle.*
- (Hold up two fingers.) *A mank holds a lot of people.*
- (Hold up three fingers.) *You can ride a mank to school.*

4. (Repeat steps 2 and 3 until firm.)

5. Everybody, what kind of vehicle am I calling a mank? (Pause.) Get ready. (Signal.) *A bus.*

6. I couldn't fool you. It's really a bus. How do you know a mank is a bus? (Call on a child. Idea: *It's a vehicle. It holds a lot of people. You can ride it to school.*)

7. How would you like to ride a mank to the zoo? (Children respond.)

EXERCISE 5   Why—When—Where

1. I'm going to say two statements. One statement tells more about what happened.

2. Here's the first statement: The bees chased a bear. Everybody, say that statement. Get ready. (Signal.) *The bees chased a bear.*

3. Here's the second statement: The bees chased a bear in the woods. Everybody, say that statement. Get ready. (Signal.) *The bees chased a bear in the woods.*

4. Listen to the statements again.
- (Hold up one finger.) The bees chased a bear.
- (Hold up two fingers.) The bees chased a bear in the woods.

5. Everybody, say the statement that tells more. (Pause.) Get ready. (Signal.) *The bees chased a bear in the woods.*

6. That statement tells more than the other statement. Does it tell **where, why,** or **when** the bees chased a bear? (Pause.) (Signal.) *Where.*
- Yes, it tells where the bees chased a bear.

7. Listen to that statement again.
- The bees chased a bear in the woods. Where did the bees chase a bear? (Signal.) *In the woods.*

8. I'm going to say two more statements. One statement tells more about what happened.

9. Here's the first statement: The spider made a web to catch flies. Everybody, say that statement. Get ready. (Signal.) *The spider made a web to catch flies.*

10. Here's the second statement: The spider made a web. Everybody, say the statement. Get ready. (Signal.) *The spider made a web.*

11. Listen to the statements again.
- (Hold up one finger.) The spider made a web to catch flies.
- (Hold up two fingers.) The spider made a web.

12. Everybody, say the statement that tells more. (Pause.) Get ready. (Signal.) *The spider made a web to catch flies.*

13. That statement tells more than the other statement. Does it tell **where, why,** or **when** the spider made a web? (Pause.) Get ready. (Signal.) *Why.*
- Yes, it tells why the spider made a web.

14. Listen to that statement again.
- The spider made a web to catch flies.
- Why did the spider make a web? (Signal.) *To catch flies.*

EXERCISE 6　Can Do

1. Everybody, I'm going to call on individual children to name things we can do with a suitcase.
2. (Call on a child.)
- What's one thing we can do with a suitcase? (After the child gives a correct response, call on the group.) Let's all say the whole thing. Get ready. (Signal.) (The group repeats the child's response.)
3. (Call on another child.)
- What's another thing we can do with a suitcase? (After the child gives a correct response, call on the group.) Let's all name those things we can do with a suitcase.
- What's the first thing?
  (Hold up one finger.) (The group repeats the first response.)
- What's the second thing?
  (Hold up two fingers.) (The group repeats the second response.)
4. (Call on another child.)
- What's another thing we can do with a suitcase? (After the child gives a correct response, call on the group.)
- Let's all name those things we can do with a suitcase.
- What's the first thing?
  (Hold up one finger.) (The group repeats the first response.)
- What's the second thing?
  (Hold up two fingers.) (The group repeats the second response.)
- What's the third thing?
  (Hold up three fingers.) (The group repeats the third response.)
5. Now I'm going to call on individual children to name things we cannot do with a suitcase.
6. (Call on another child.)
- What's one thing we cannot do with a suitcase? (After the child gives a correct response, call on the group.) Let's all say the whole thing. Get ready. (Signal.) (The group repeats the child's response.)
7. (Call on another child.)
- What's another thing we cannot do with a suitcase? (After the child responds, call on the group.) Let's all name those things we cannot do with a suitcase.
- What's the first thing?
  (Hold up one finger.) (The group repeats the first response.)

- What's the second thing?
  (Hold up two fingers.) (The group repeats the second response.)
8. (Call on another child.)
- What's another thing we cannot do with a suitcase? (After the child gives a correct response, call on the group.) Let's all name those things we cannot do with a suitcase.
- What's the first thing?
- (Hold up one finger.) (The group repeats the first response.)
- What's the second thing?
  (Hold up two fingers.) (The group repeats the second response.)
- What's the third thing?
  (Hold up three fingers.) (The group repeats the third response.)

WORKBOOK

EXERCISE 7　Extrapolation

What Characters Say

1.＿＿＿＿＿＿
2.＿＿＿＿＿＿
3.＿＿＿＿＿＿
4.＿＿＿＿＿＿
5.＿＿＿＿＿＿

1. Everybody, open your workbook to Lesson 72. Write your name at the top of the page. ✔
- These are pictures of characters from some stories you've heard. Each picture has a letter under it. The letter is the initial of the character in the picture.
2. Touch the first picture. ✔
- Who is in that picture? (Signal.) *A bragging rat.*

- What letter is under that picture? (Signal.) *B.*
- **B** is the first letter in the words **Bragging Rat.**
- Who is in the next picture? (Signal.) *Sweetie.*
- What letter is under Sweetie? (Signal.) *S.*
- **S** is the first letter in **Sweetie's** name.
- Who is in the next picture? (Signal.) *Roxie.*
- What letter is under Roxie? (Signal.) *R.*
- **R** is the first letter in **Roxie's** name.
- Who is in the last picture? (Signal.) *Molly Mix-up.*
- What letter is under Molly Mix-up? (Signal.) *M.*
- **M** is the first letter in **Molly's** name.
3. Here's the game we'll play. I'll say five different things. For each thing I'll say, you're going to write the letter for the character who would say that. You're not going to say anything out loud. You'll just find the right picture and write the letter for that character.
4. Everybody, touch number 1. ✔
- Listen and don't say anything. Here's the statement for number 1: "Look at those wonderful orange rocks. I'd love to take them home."
- Find the character who would say that. Write the letter for that character on line 1. Raise your hand when you're finished. **(Observe children and give feedback.)**
- Everybody, which character would love to take some orange rocks home? (Signal.) *Roxie.*
- So what letter did you write for number 1? (Signal.) *R.*
- (Write on the board:)

1.	R

- Here's what you should have for number 1. Raise your hand if you got it right. ✔
5. Everybody, touch number 2. ✔
- Listen and don't say anything. Here's the statement for number 2: "From here, that fish looks pretty small and helpless, but let me tell you, that fish can really bite."
- Find the character who would say that. Write the letter for that character on line 2. Raise your hand when you're finished. **(Observe children and give feedback.)**
- Everybody, which character would say, "From here, that fish looks pretty small and helpless, but let me tell you, that fish can really bite"? (Signal.) *Sweetie.*

- So what letter did you write for number 2? (Signal.) *S.*
- (Write to show:)

1.	R
2.	**S**

- Here's what you should have for number 2. Raise your hand if you got it right. ✔
6. Everybody, touch number 3. ✔
- Listen and don't say anything. Here's the statement for number 3: "One of these days, I'm going to invent something that is perfect."
- Find the character who would say that. Write the letter for that character on line 3. Raise your hand when you're finished. **(Observe children and give feedback.)**
- Everybody, which character would want to invent something that is perfect? (Signal.) *Molly Mix-up.*
- So what letter did you write for number 3? (Signal.) *M.*
- (Write to show:)

1.	R
2.	S
3.	**M**

- Here's what you should have for number 3. Raise your hand if you got it right. ✔
7. Everybody, touch number 4. ✔
- Listen and don't say anything. Here's the statement for number 4: "I could get out of that maze so fast that I would be out of that maze before you even knew I went into the maze."
- Find the character who would say that. Write the letter for that character on line 4. Raise your hand when you're finished. **(Observe children and give feedback.)**
- Everybody, which character would tell lies like that? (Signal.) *The bragging rat.*
- So what letter did you write for number 4? (Signal.) *B.*
- (Write to show:)

1.	R
2.	S
3.	M
4.	**B**

- Here's what you should have for number 4. Raise your hand if you got it right. ✔
8. Everybody, touch number 5.
- Listen and don't say anything. Here's the statement for number 5: "I don't know why I can't keep them in my room. They are beautiful."
- Find the character who would say that. Write the letter for that character on line 5. Raise your hand when you're finished. (Observe children and give feedback.)
- Everybody, which character would want to keep some beautiful things in a room? (Signal.) *Roxie.*
- So what letter did you write for number 5? (Signal.) *R.*
- What beautiful things do you think Roxie was talking about? (Signal.) *Rocks.*
- (Write to show:)

1.	R
2.	S
3.	M
4.	B
5.	R

- Here's what you should have for number 5. Raise your hand if you got it right. ✔
9. Raise your hand if you got everything right. ✔ You really know about these characters. Maybe some time later **you** can tell **me** what they would say.

EXERCISE 8   Classification

1. Everybody, find the next page in your workbook. ✔
- (Hold up workbook. Point to first half.) These boxed pictures show two classes. One class has **one** kind of thing in it, the other class has **more** kinds of things in it.
- Touch the picture that shows only **one** kind of thing. ✔
- What kind of thing is that in the picture? (Signal.) *Rakes.*
2. Touch the picture that shows **more** than one kind of thing. ✔
- Raise your hand if you can figure out the name of the class shown in that picture. ✔
- Everybody, what's the name of that class? (Signal.) *Tools.*
- Everybody, circle the picture that shows **more** kinds of things. ✔
3. Everybody, touch the picture that shows **one** kind of thing. ✔
- The rakes in that picture should be green with black handles. What colors? (Signal.) *Green with black handles.*
- Mark a rake in that picture. ✔
4. Touch the picture that shows **more** kinds of things. The rakes in that picture should be black with red handles. What colors? (Signal.) *Black with red handles.*
- Mark a rake in that picture. ✔

EXERCISE 9   Materials

1. (Hold up workbook. Point to second half.)
2. Here's a coloring rule for the picture. If an object is made of concrete, color it blue or orange. What's the rule? (Signal.) *If an object is made of concrete, color it blue or orange.*
3. (Repeat step 2 until firm.)
4. Mark the objects made of concrete. ✔
5. Here's another coloring rule for this picture. If an object is made of wood, color it red. What's the rule? (Signal.) *If an object is made of wood, color it red.*
6. (Repeat step 5 until firm.)
7. Make a red mark on one of the objects made of wood. ✔
8. Here's one more thing to do. Part of the chair is missing. What part is missing? (Signal.) *The back.*
- Yes, the back. Before you color the chair, follow the dots and make the back.

Objectives

- Identify an object based on its characteristics. (Exercise 1)
- Construct a verbal analogy. (Exercise 2)
- Given a calendar, identify the day and date for "today" and "tomorrow" and one week from today. (Exercise 3)
- Generate statements involving "can do" and "cannot do." (Exercise 4)
- Name four classes containing a common noun and answer questions about members of those classes. (Exercise 5)
- Write three sentences about story characters. (Exercise 6)

EXERCISE 1 Description

1. I'm going to tell you about an object you know. But I'm going to call it a funny name. See if you can figure out what object I'm talking about.
2. (Hold up one finger.)
- People walk on a ferp. Say that. (Signal.) *People walk on a ferp.*
- (Hold up two fingers.)
- A ferp is made of concrete. Say that. (Signal.) *A ferp is made of concrete.*
- (Hold up three fingers.)
- Houses have a ferp in front of them. Say that. (Signal.) *Houses have a ferp in front of them.*
3. Everybody, say all the things you know about a ferp. Get ready.
- (Hold up one finger.) *People walk on a ferp.*
- (Hold up two fingers.) *A ferp is made of concrete.*
- (Hold up three fingers.) *Houses have a ferp in front of them.*
4. (Repeat steps 2 and 3 until firm.)
5. Everybody, tell me what am I calling a ferp. (Pause.) Get ready. (Signal.) *A sidewalk.*
6. I couldn't fool you. It's really a sidewalk. How do you know a ferp is a sidewalk? (Call on a child. Idea: *People walk on it. It's made of concrete. Houses have them in front of them.*)
7. How would you like to have a ferp next to your bed? (Children respond.)

EXERCISE 2 Analogies

1. We're going to make up an analogy that tells what you do with tools.
- What's the analogy going to tell? (Signal.) *What you do with tools.*
2. Here are the tools you're going to use in the analogy: a hammer and a saw.
- Which tools? (Signal.) *A hammer and a saw.*
3. Name the first tool. (Signal.) *A hammer.*
- Tell me what you do with that tool. (Call on a child. Accept reasonable answers but use: *Pound nails.*)
- Everybody, what's the first part of the analogy? (Signal.) *A hammer is to pounding nails.*
- (Repeat step 3 until firm.)
4. Now name the second tool. Get ready. (Signal.) *A saw.*
- Tell me what you do with that tool. Get ready. (Signal.) *Cut wood.*
- So what's the second part of the analogy? (Signal.) *A saw is to cutting wood.*
- (Repeat step 4 until firm.)
5. (Repeat steps 3 and 4 until firm.)
6. Now you're going to say the whole analogy. First you're going to tell what you do with a hammer, and then you're going to tell what you do with a saw.
- Say the analogy. Get ready. (Signal.) *A hammer is to pounding nails as a saw is to cutting wood.*
- Again. Say the analogy. (Signal.) *A hammer is to pounding nails as a saw is to cutting wood.*
7. You made up an analogy that tells what you do with a hammer and what you do with a saw. Good job.

EXERCISE 3 Calendar

1. (Present calendar.)
- We're going to talk about today, tomorrow, and one week from today.
2. Tell me the day of the week it is today. Get ready. (Signal.)
- Tell me the day of the week it will be tomorrow. Get ready. (Signal.)
- Tell me the day of the week it will be one week from today. Get ready. (Signal.)
3. (Repeat step 2 until firm.)
4. Now the dates.
- Tell me today's date. Get ready. (Signal.)
- Look at the calendar. ✔
- Tell me the date it will be one week from today. Get ready. (Signal.)
5. Once more.
- Listen: Tell me today's date. Get ready. (Signal.)
- Tell me tomorrow's date. Get ready. (Signal.)
- Tell me the date it will be one week from today. Get ready. (Signal.)
6. (Repeat step 5 until firm.)

EXERCISE 4 Can Do

1. I'm going to ask questions about a boy and a button.
2. Everybody, can a boy use a button to comb his hair? (Signal.) *No.*
- Say the statement. Get ready. (Signal.) *A boy cannot use a button to comb his hair.*
3. Everybody, can a boy sew a button on a shirt? (Signal.) *Yes.*
- Say the statement. Get ready. (Signal.) *A boy can sew a button on a shirt.*
4. (Call on one child.) Your turn. Make up another statement that tells something a boy can do with a button. (After the child makes the statement, call on the group.)
- Say that statement about what a boy can do with a button. Get ready. (Signal.) (The group repeats the child's statement.)

5. (Call on another child.)
- Your turn. Now make up a statement that tells something a boy cannot do with a button. (After the child makes the statement, call on the group.)
- Say that statement about what a boy cannot do with a button. Get ready. (Signal.) (The group repeats the child's statement.)

EXERCISE 5 Classification

1. Today we're going to talk about a fat baby. We can put a fat baby into four different classes. See how many classes you can name, starting with the smallest class.
2. Everybody, what's the smallest class for a fat baby? (Signal.) *Fat babies.*
- What's the next bigger class? (Signal.) *Babies.*
- What's the next bigger class? (Signal.) *People.*
- What's the biggest class? (Signal.) *Living things.*
- (Accept any other correct responses, but use: *fat babies, babies, people, living things.*)
3. (Repeat step 2 until firm.)
4. What is the one thing you would find in all those four classes? (Signal.) *A fat baby.*
5. Would you find a woman in all those classes? (Signal.) *No.*
- Name two of those classes you would find a woman in. (Pause.) Get ready. (Tap 2 times.) *People. Living things.*
6. We can put a baby into four different classes.
- Would you find a firefighter in all those four classes? (Signal.) *No.*
- Name two of those classes you would find a firefighter in. (Pause.) Get ready. (Tap 2 times.) *People. Living things.*

EXERCISE 6 Sentence Construction

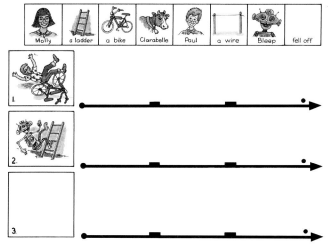

1. Everybody, open your workbook to Lesson 73. Write your name at the top of the page. ✔
- You're going to write sentences. The words that you'll use are in the boxes at the top of the page. All the boxes, except one, have a picture.
2. Everybody, touch the first box. ✔
Who is that? (Signal.) *Molly.*
And her name is written below.
- Touch the next box. ✔
What is that? (Signal.) *A ladder.*
- Touch the next box. ✔
What is that? (Signal.) *A bike.*
- Touch the next box. ✔
Who is that? (Signal.) *Clarabelle.*
- Touch the next box. ✔
Who is that? (Signal.) *Paul.*
- Touch the next box. ✔
What is that? (Signal.) *A wire.*
- Touch the next box. ✔
Who is that? (Signal.) *Bleep.*

- Touch the last box. ✔
- That box just has some words. I'll tell you the words: **fell off.** What words? (Signal.) *Fell off.*
- That's what the characters did in pictures 1 and 2.
- There is no picture 3. I guess you'll just have to make a picture for 3 when we're all done.
3. Everybody, touch picture 1 by the top arrow. ✔
- Who is in that picture? (Signal.) *Paul.*
- What did Paul fall off? (Signal.) *A bike.*
- Here's the sentence for picture 1: Paul fell off a bike. Everybody, say that sentence. (Signal.) *Paul fell off a bike.*
- Write sentence 1. Raise your hand when you're finished. (Observe children.)
4. Now you're going to write a sentence for picture 2.
- Everybody, who is in that picture? (Signal.) *Bleep.*
- What did Bleep fall off? (Signal.) *A ladder.*
- Here's the sentence for picture 2: Bleep fell off a ladder. Everybody, say that sentence. (Signal.) *Bleep fell off a ladder.*
- Write sentence 2. Raise your hand when you're finished. (Observe children.)
5. There is no picture 3. So here's what you'll do: First you'll make up a sentence that tells what the picture will show. You can write a sentence that uses any of the characters in the boxes. But don't write a sentence we've already done. Write your sentence. Raise your hand when you're finished. (Observe children.)
6. Draw a picture for sentence 3.

Objectives

- Construct a verbal analogy. (Exercise 1)
- Discriminate between true and false statements and generate true and false statements. (Exercise 2)
- Given a calendar, identify the day and date for "today" and "tomorrow" and one week from today. (Exercise 3)
- Discriminate between same and different actions. (Exercise 4)
- Given a common noun, answer questions involving "can do." (Exercise 5)
- Listen to a short story and answer questions involving "who," "when," "why," "where" and "what". (Exercise 6)
- Write three sentences about story characters. (Exercise 7)
- Follow coloring rules involving classes and subclasses. (Exercise 8)
- Follow coloring rules involving materials. (Exercise 9)

EXERCISE 1 Analogies

1. We're going to make up an analogy that tells what you put in containers.
- What's the analogy going to tell? (Signal.) *What you put in containers.*
2. Here are the containers you're going to use in the analogy: a suitcase and a glass. Which containers? (Signal.) *A suitcase and a glass.*
3. Name the first container. (Signal.) *A suitcase.*
- Tell me what you put in that container. Get ready. (Signal.) *Clothing.* Yes, clothing.
- So what's the first part of the analogy? (Signal.) *A suitcase is to clothing.*
- (Repeat step 3 until firm.)
4. Now name the second container. Get ready. (Signal.) *A glass.*
- Tell me what you put in that container. Get ready. (Signal.) *Water.* Yes, water.
- So what's the second part of the analogy? (Signal.) *A glass is to water.*
- (Repeat step 4 until firm.)
5. (Repeat steps 3 and 4 until firm.)
6. Now you're going to say the whole analogy. First you're going to tell what you put in a suitcase, and then you're going to tell what you put in a glass.
- Say the analogy. Get ready. (Signal.) *A suitcase is to clothing as a glass is to water.*
- Again. Say the analogy. (Signal.) *A suitcase is to clothing as a glass is to water.*
7. You made up an analogy that tells what you put in a suitcase and what you put in a glass. Good job.

EXERCISE 2 True—False

1. I'm going to make up statements. Some of these statements are true and some are false. You tell me about each statement.
2. An apartment building is not a vehicle. True or false? (Signal.) *True.*
- Scissors can cut cloth. True or false? (Signal.) *True.*
- The moon grows in the ground. True or false? (Signal.) *False.*
- A pitcher is not used to rake leaves. True or false? (Signal.) *True.*
- A hammer is not made of cheese. True or false? (Signal.) *True.*
- (Repeat step 2 until firm.)
3. Your turn. Make up a statement about scissors that is true. (Call on three children. Praise each acceptable statement and have the group repeat it. Then say:) Everybody, that statement is . . . (Signal.) *true.*
4. Your turn. Make up a statement about scissors that is false. (Call on three children. Praise each acceptable statement and have the group repeat it. Then say:) Everybody, that statement is . . . (Signal.) *false.*

EXERCISE 3 Calendar

1. (Present calendar.)
- We're going to talk about today, tomorrow, and one week from today.

2. Tell me the day of the week it is today. Get ready. (Signal.)
- Tell me the day of the week it will be tomorrow. Get ready. (Signal.)
- Tell me the day of the week it will be one week from today. Get ready. (Signal.)
3. (Repeat step 2 until firm.)
4. Now the dates.
- Tell me today's date. Get ready. (Signal.)
- Look at the calendar. ✔
- Tell me the date it will be one week from today. Get ready. (Signal.)
5. Once more.
- Listen: Tell me today's date. Get ready. (Signal.)
- Tell me tomorrow's date. Get ready. (Signal.)
- Tell me the date it will be one week from today. Get ready. (Signal.)
6. (Repeat step 5 until firm.)

EXERCISE 4   Actions

1. Here's the first action game. Get ready.
- Everybody, smile. (Signal.) Good. Stop smiling.
- Now tell me if I do the same thing you did or something different. Watch me. (Smile.) Did I do the same thing or something different? (Signal.) *The same thing.*
- Watch me. (Frown.) Did I do the same thing or something different? (Signal.) *Something different.*
- Watch me. (Clap.) Did I do the same thing or something different? (Signal.) *Something different.*
2. Here's the next action game. Get ready.
- Everybody, touch both your ears. (Signal.) Good.
- Stop touching your ears.
- Now tell me if I do the same thing you did or something different. Watch me. (Touch your nose.) Did I do the same thing or something different? (Signal.) *Something different.*
- Watch me. (Touch one ear.) Did I do the same thing or something different? (Signal.) *Something different.*
- Watch me. (Touch both your ears.) Did I do the same thing or something different? (Signal.) *The same thing.*

EXERCISE 5   Can Do

1. Everybody, I'm going to call on individual children to name things we can do with a pencil.

2. (Call on one child.)
- What's one thing we can do with a pencil? (After the child gives a correct response, call on the group.) Let's all say the whole thing. Get ready. (Signal.) (The group repeats the child's response.)
3. (Call on another child.)
- What's another thing we can do with a pencil? (After the child gives a correct response, call on the group.) Let's all name those things we can do with a pencil.
- What's the first thing?
- (Hold up one finger.) (The group repeats the first response.)
- What's the second thing?
- (Hold up two fingers.) (The group repeats the second response.)
4. (Call on another child.)
- What's another thing we can do with a pencil? (After the child gives a correct response, call on the group.) Let's all name those things we can do with a pencil.
- What's the first thing?
- (Hold up one finger.) (The group repeats the first response.)
- What's the second thing?
- (Hold up two fingers.) (The group repeats the second response.)
- What's the third thing?
- (Hold up three fingers.) (The group repeats the third response.)
5. Now I'm going to call on individual children to name things we can**not** do with a pencil.
6. (Call on another child.)
- What's one thing we cannot do with a pencil? (After the child gives a correct response, call on the group.) Let's all say the whole thing. Get ready. (Signal.) (The group repeats the child's response.)
7. (Call on another child.)
- What's another thing we cannot do with a pencil? (After the child gives a correct response, call on the group.) Let's all name those things we cannot do with a pencil.
- What's the first thing?
- (Hold up one finger.) (The group repeats the first response.)
- What's the second thing?
- (Hold up two fingers.) (The group repeats the second response.)

8. (Call on another child.)
- What's another thing we cannot do with a pencil? (After the child gives a correct response, call on the group.) Let's all name those things we cannot do with a pencil.
- What's the first thing?
- (Hold up one finger.) (The group repeats the first response.)
- What's the second thing?
- (Hold up two fingers.) (The group repeats the second response.)
- What's the third thing?
- (Hold up three fingers.) (The group repeats the third response.)

EXERCISE 6 Who—What—When—Where—Why

1. Listen to this story.
- A girl is playing baseball in the park. Her team won the game because she hit a home run. After the game was over, her team yelled, "Hooray."
- (Repeat the story.)
2. Who hit the home run? (Signal.) *The girl.*
- Where was she playing ball? (Signal.) *In the park.*
- Why did her team win the game? (Signal.) *Because she hit a home run.*
- What did the girl do to win the game? (Signal.) *She hit a home run.*
- When did her team yell, "Hooray"? (Signal.) *After the game was over.*
3. (Repeat step 2 until firm.)

WORKBOOK

| a rat | a bed | Roger | Clarabelle | a chair | a swing | Bleep | sat on |

EXERCISE 7 Sentence Construction

1. Everybody, open your workbook to Lesson 74. Write your name at the top of the page. ✔
- You're going to make up sentences. The words that you'll use are in the boxes at the top of the page. All the boxes except one have a picture.
2. Everybody, touch the first box. ✔
- Who is that? (Call on a child. Idea: *A rat.*) Yes, that's a picture of **a rat.**
- Touch the next box. ✔
  What is that? (Signal.) *A bed.*
- Touch the next box. ✔
  Who is that? (Signal.) *Roger.*
- Touch the next box. ✔
  Who is that? (Signal.) *Clarabelle.*
- Touch the next box. ✔
  What is that? (Signal.) *A chair.*
- Touch the next box. ✔
  What is that? (Signal.) *A swing.*
- Touch the next box. ✔
  Who is that? (Signal.) *Bleep.*
- Touch the last box. ✔
  That box just has two words. I'll tell you those words: **sat on.** What words? (Signal.) *Sat on.*
- That's what the characters did in pictures 1 and 2.
- There is no picture for 3. I guess you'll have to make a picture for 3 when we're all done.
3. Everybody, touch picture 1 by the top arrow. ✔
- Who is in that picture? (Signal.) *Roger.*
4. Everybody, say a sentence that tells what Roger did in picture 1. (Signal.) *Roger sat on a chair.*
- (Repeat step 4 until firm.)
5. Your turn: Write the first sentence. Remember, Roger's name starts with a capital **R.** Write your sentence on arrow 1. Raise your hand when you're finished. (Observe children and give feedback.)
6. Now you're going to make up a sentence for picture 2.
- Everybody, who is in that picture? (Signal.) *Clarabelle.*
7. Everybody, say a sentence that tells what Clarabelle did in picture 2. (Signal.) *Clarabelle sat on a bed.*
- (Repeat step 7 until firm.)

8. Your turn: Write the sentence for picture 2. Raise your hand when you're finished. **(Observe children and give feedback.)**

9. There is no picture 3. So here's what you'll do: First you'll make up a sentence that tells what the picture will show. You can write a sentence that uses any of the characters in the boxes. But don't write a sentence we've already done. Write your sentence. Raise your hand when you're finished. **(Observe children and give feedback.)**

10. I'm going to call on several children to read their sentence for picture 3.
   - (Call on a child to read sentence 3. Repeat with several children.)
   - (Praise original sentences that take the form: *(Name) sat on* _____.)

11. Let's make sure you can read all of your sentences.
   - (Call on several children:) Read all three sentences you wrote.
   - (Praise children who read appropriate sentences in correct order.)

12. Later, you'll have to draw a picture for sentence 3. Remember, your picture will show what your sentence says.
   - (Call on several children:) What will your picture show?
   - (Praise those children whose response tells about their sentence.)

13. I'll show you some of the better pictures later.

EXERCISE 8 Classification

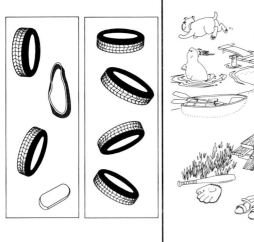

1. Everybody, find the next page in your workbook. ✔
   - (Hold up workbook. Point to first half.)

2. Touch the picture that shows only **one** kind of thing. ✔
   - What kind of thing is that in the picture? (Signal.) *Tires.*

3. Touch the picture that shows **more** than one kind of thing. ✔
   - Raise your hand if you can figure out the name of the class shown in that picture. ✔
   - Everybody, what's the name of that class? (Signal.) *Things made of rubber.*
   - (Repeat step 3 until firm.)

4. Everybody, circle the picture that shows **more** kinds of things. ✔

5. Everybody, touch the picture that shows **one** kind of thing. ✔
   - The tires in that picture should be black. What color? (Signal.) *Black.*
   - Mark a tire in that picture. ✔

6. Touch the picture that shows **more** kinds of things. ✔
   - The tires in that picture should be black and blue. What colors? (Signal.) *Black and blue.*
   - Mark a tire in that picture. ✔

EXERCISE 9 Materials

1. (Hold up workbook. Point to second half.)

2. Here's a coloring rule for the picture. If an object is made of leather, color it purple or blue. What's the rule? (Signal.) *If an object is made of leather, color it purple or blue.*
   - (Repeat step 2 until firm.)

3. Mark the objects made of leather. ✔

4. Here's another coloring rule for this picture. If an object is made of wood, color it yellow or red. What's the rule? (Signal.) *If an object is made of wood, color it yellow or red.*
   - (Repeat step 4 until firm.)

5. Mark the objects made of wood. ✔

6. Here's one more thing to do. Part of the boat is missing. What part is missing? (Signal.) *The hull.*
   - Yes, the hull. Before you color the boat, follow the dots and make the hull.

LESSON 75

Objectives

- Construct verbal analogies. (Exercise 1)
- Name three classes containing a common noun and answer questions about members of those classes. (Exercise 2)
- Discriminate between true and false statements and generate true and false statements. (Exercise 3)
- Given a calendar, identify the day and date for "today" and "tomorrow" and one week from today. (Exercise 4)
- Identify an object based on its characteristics. (Exercise 5)
- Answer questions involving previously learned calendar facts. (Exercise 6)
- Write three sentences about story characters. (Exercise 7)
- Follow coloring rules involving classes and subclasses. (Exercise 8)
- Follow coloring rules involving parts of a whole. (Exercise 9)

EXERCISE 1 Analogies

1. We're going to make up **two** analogies.
- We're going to make up analogies about a deer and a fish. Which animals? (Signal.) *A deer and a fish.*
2. The first analogy tells how the animals move.
- How does a deer move? (Call on a child. Accept all reasonable answers, but use: *Runs.*)
- How does a fish move? (Signal.) *Swims.*
3. So a deer is to running as a fish is to . . . (Signal.) *swimming.*
- Say that analogy about a deer and a fish. Get ready. (Signal.) *A deer is to running as a fish is to swimming.*
4. Listen: A deer is to running as a fish is to swimming. Does that analogy tell **where** you **find** the animals? (Signal.) *No.*
5. Listen: A deer is to running as a fish is to swimming. Does that analogy tell how the animals move? (Signal.) *Yes.*
6. Listen: A deer is to running as a fish is to swimming. Does that analogy tell what parts the animals have? (Signal.) *No.*
7. (Repeat steps 4 through 6 until firm.)
8. We made up an analogy that tells how the animals move. The next analogy tells where you find the animals.
- Where do you find a deer? (Call on a child. Accept all reasonable answers, but use: *in the forest.*)
- Where do you find a fish? (Call on a child. Accept all reasonable answers, but use: *in the water.*)

9. A deer is to the forest as a fish is to the . . . (Signal.) *water.*
- Say that analogy about a deer and a fish. Get ready. (Signal.) *A deer is to the forest as a fish is to the water.*
10. We made up an analogy that tells how the animals move. Then we made up an analogy that tells where you find the animals. Let's see if you can say both those analogies.
11. Think. Say the analogy that tells how the animals move. (Pause.) Get ready. (Signal.) *A deer is to running as a fish is to swimming.*
- Think. Say the analogy that tells where you find the animals. (Pause.) Get ready. (Signal.) *A deer is to the forest as a fish is to the water.*
12. (Repeat step 11 until firm.)

EXERCISE 2 Classification

1. Today we're going to talk about cheddar cheese. We can put cheddar cheese into three different classes. See how many classes you can name, starting with the smallest class.
2. Everybody, what's the smallest class for cheddar cheese? (Signal.) *Cheddar cheese.*
- What's the next bigger class? (Signal.) *Cheese.*
- What's the biggest class? (Signal.) *Food.*
- (Accept any other correct responses, but use: *cheddar cheese, cheese, food.*)
3. (Repeat step 2 until firm.)

4. What is one kind of object you would find in all those classes? (Signal.) *Cheddar cheese.*

5. Would you find a cracker in all those classes? (Signal.) *No.*
- Name the class you would find a cracker in. (Pause.) Get ready. (Signal.) *Food.*

EXERCISE 3   True—False

1. I'm going to make up statements. Some of these statements are true and some are false. You tell me about each statement.

2. Lions live in the jungle. True or false? (Signal.) *True.*
- A paper clip is made of paper. True or false? (Signal.) *False.*
- An airplane does not go in the air. True or false? (Signal.) *False.*
- A barn is not furniture. True or false? (Signal.) *True.*
- You find a slide at a playground. True or false? (Signal.) *True.*
- (Repeat step 2 until firm.)

3. Your turn. Make up a statement about an airplane that is true. (Call on three children. Praise each acceptable statement and have the group repeat it. Then say:) Everybody, that statement is . . . (Signal.) *true.*

4. Your turn. Now make up a statement about an airplane that is false. (Call on three children. Praise each acceptable statement and have the group repeat it. Then say:) Everybody, that statement is . . . (Signal.) *false.*

EXERCISE 4   Calendar

1. (Present calendar.)
- We're going to talk about today, tomorrow, and one week from today.

2. Tell me the day of the week it is today. Get ready. (Signal.)
- Tell me the day of the week it will be tomorrow. Get ready. (Signal.)
- Tell me the day of the week it will be one week from today. Get ready. (Signal.)
3. (Repeat step 2 until firm.)

4. Now the dates.
- Tell me today's date. Get ready. (Signal.)
- Look at the calendar. ✔
- Tell me the date it will be one week from today. Get ready. (Signal.)

5. Once more.
   Listen: Tell me today's date. Get ready. (Signal.)
- Tell me tomorrow's date. Get ready. (Signal.)
- Tell me the date it will be one week from today. Get ready. (Signal.)
6. (Repeat step 5 until firm.)

EXERCISE 5   Description

1. I'm going to tell you about an object you know. But I'm going to call it a funny name. See if you can figure out what object I'm talking about.

2. (Hold up one finger.)
- A wum can be made of leather. Say that. (Signal.) *A wum can be made of leather.*
- (Hold up two fingers.)
- A wum is a container. Say that. (Signal.) *A wum is a container.*
- (Hold up three fingers.)
- You carry money and other small things in a wum. Say that. (Signal.) *You carry money and other small things in a wum.*

3. Everybody, say all the things you know about a wum. Get ready.
- (Hold up one finger.) *A wum can be made of leather.*
- (Hold up two fingers.) *A wum is a container.*
- (Hold up three fingers.) *You carry money and other small things in a wum.*
4. (Repeat steps 2 and 3 until firm.)

5. What kind of container am I calling a wum? (Call on a child. Accept appropriate responses, but use: *purse.*)

6. I couldn't fool you. It's really a purse. How do you know a wum is not a suitcase? (Call on a child. Idea: *Because you don't carry money in it.*)

EXERCISE 6   Calendar Facts

1. We're going to talk about the calendar.
2. Everybody, how many months are in a year? (Signal.) *Twelve.*
- Say the whole thing. (Signal.) *There are twelve months in a year.*

3. Name the months of the year through December. Get ready. (Signal.) *January, February, March, April, May, June, July, August, September, October, November, December.*
- (Repeat step 3 until firm.)

4. How many days are in a week? (Signal.) *Seven.*
- Say the whole thing. (Signal.) *There are seven days in a week.*
5. Everybody, name the seven days of the week. Get ready. (Signal.) *Sunday, Monday, Tuesday, Wednesday, Thursday, Friday, Saturday.*
- (Repeat step 5 until firm.)
6. Everybody, how many seasons are there in a year? (Signal.) *Four.*
- Say the seasons of the year. Get ready. (Signal.) *Winter, spring, summer, fall.*
7. Everybody, tell me what day it is today. Get ready. (Signal.)
- Tell me what day it was yesterday. Get ready. (Signal.)
- Tell me what day it will be tomorrow. Get ready. (Signal.)
8. How many days are there in a year? (Signal.) *365.*
- How many weeks are in a year? (Signal.) *52.*
9. (Repeat step 8 until firm.)

WORKBOOK

EXERCISE 7 Sentence Construction

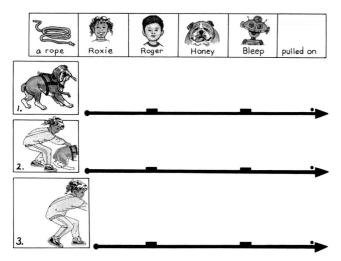

1. Everybody, open your workbook to Lesson 75. Write your name. ✔
- You're going to write sentences that tell what the characters did in the pictures. The words are written at the top of the page.
- Touch the box with the rope in it. ✔
  The words in that box say **a rope.** What words? (Signal.) *A rope.*

- Touch the next box. ✔
  What's the name in that box? (Signal.) *Roxie.*
- Touch the next box. ✔
  What's the name in that box? (Signal.) *Roger.*
- Touch the next box. ✔
  What's the name in that box? (Signal.) *Honey.*
- Touch the next box. ✔
  What's the name in that box? (Signal.) *Bleep.*
- Touch the last box. ✔
  The words in that box are **pulled on.** What words? (Signal.) *Pulled on.*
- That's what the characters did in pictures 1 and 2.
2. Everybody, touch picture 1 by the top arrow. ✔
- Who is in that picture? (Signal.) *Honey.*
- Honey is pulling on something. What's Honey pulling on? (Signal.) *A rope.*
- Everybody, say the sentence that tells what Honey pulled on in picture 1. (Signal.) *Honey pulled on a rope.*
- Right, something is stuck and Honey is trying to pull it out by pulling on a rope.
- Listen to the sentence that tells what Honey did: **Honey pulled on a rope.**
3. Your turn: Write that sentence on arrow 1. Remember, Honey's name begins with a capital **H.** Raise your hand when you're finished.
   (Observe children and give feedback.)
4. Now you're going to write a sentence for picture 2. Who is pulling on Honey in that picture? (Signal.) *Roxie.*
- Write a sentence that tells what Roxie did in picture 2. Raise your hand when you're finished.
  (Observe children and give feedback.)
- (Call on a child:) Read the whole sentence you wrote about Roxie. (Signal.) *Roxie pulled on Honey.*
5. Picture 3 is not finished. Somebody is supposed to be pulling on Roxie, but nobody is pulling on her in the picture.
- Your turn: Write a sentence for picture 3. You can write a sentence that uses any name we haven't used. Write your sentence. Raise your hand when you're finished.
  (Observe children and give feedback.)
6. I'm going to call on several children to read their sentence for picture 3.

- (Call on a child to read sentence 3. Repeat with several children.)
  (Praise original sentences that take the form: *(Name) pulled on Roxie.*)

7. Let's make sure you can read all of your sentences.
- (Call on several children:) Read all three sentences you wrote.
- (Praise appropriate responses.)

8. Later, you'll have to finish the picture for sentence 3. Remember, your picture will show what your sentence says.
- (Call on several children:) What will your picture show?
- (Praise those children whose response tells about their sentence.)

9. I'll show you some of the better pictures later.

EXERCISE 8 Classification

1. Everybody, find the next page. ✔
- (Hold up workbook. Point to first half.)
2. Touch the picture that shows only **one** kind of thing. ✔
- What kind of thing is that in the picture? (Signal.) *Shirts.*
3. Touch the picture that shows **more** than one kind of thing. ✔
- Raise your hand if you can figure out the name of the class shown in that picture. ✔
- Everybody, what's the name of that class? (Signal.) *Things made of cloth.*

4. Listen: The class that is larger is the class that has **more** kinds of things. What does the class that is **larger** have? (Signal.) *More kinds of things.*
5. Everybody, circle the class that is **larger.** ✔
- Everybody, touch the picture of the class that is **smaller.** ✔
- How many kinds of things are in the class that is **smaller?** (Signal.) *One.*
6. The shirts in the picture of the **smaller** class should be red. What color? (Signal.) *Red.*
- Mark a shirt in that picture. ✔
7. Touch the picture that shows the **larger** class. ✔
- The shirts in the picture of the **larger** class should be black and green. What colors? (Signal.) *Black and green.*
- Mark a shirt in that picture. ✔

EXERCISE 9 Part—Whole

1. (Hold up workbook. Point to second half.)
2. Now look at the window. ✔
- Here's a coloring rule for the window. Listen: Color the panes yellow. What's the rule? (Signal.) *Color the panes yellow.*
- Mark the panes. ✔
3. Here's another coloring rule for the window. Listen: Color the lock red. What's the rule? (Signal.) *Color the lock red.*
- Mark the lock. ✔
4. Here's another coloring rule for the window. Listen: Color the frame brown. What's the rule? (Signal.) *Color the frame brown.*
- Mark the frame. ✔
5. Part of the window is missing. What part is missing? (Signal.) *The handle.*
- Yes, the handle. Before you color the window, you're going to follow the dots with your pencil to make the handle.

Objectives

- Discriminate between true and false statements and generate true and false statements. (Exercise 1)
- Listen to a short story and answer questions involving "who," "when," "why," "where" and "what". (Exercise 2)
- Given a calendar, identify the day and date for "today" and "tomorrow" and one week from today. (Exercise 3)
- Identify an object based on its characteristics. (Exercise 4)
- Construct verbal analogies. (Exercise 5)
- **Identify absurdities involving materials.** (Exercise 6)
- **Identify absurdities in a sentence.** (Exercise 7)
- Write three sentences about story characters. (Exercise 8)
- Follow coloring rules involving classes and subclasses. (Exercise 9)
- Complete an analogy involving use. (Exercise 10).

EXERCISE 1   **True—False**

1. I'm going to make up statements. Some of these statements are true and some are false. You tell me about each statement.

2. Chickens give milk.
   True or false? (Signal.) *False.*
   - You cannot eat clothing.
   True or false? (Signal.) *True.*
   - Shoes can be made of leather.
   True or false? (Signal.) *True.*
   - Monkeys do not have wings.
   True or false? (Signal.) *True.*
   - You can keep a car in a garage.
   True or false? (Signal.) *True.*
   - (Repeat step 2 until firm.)

3. Your turn. Make up a statement about shoes that is true. (Call on individual children. Praise each acceptable statement and have the group repeat it. Then say:) Everybody, that statement is . . . (Signal.) *true.*

4. Your turn. Make up a statement about shoes that is false. (Call on individual children. Praise each acceptable statement and have the group repeat it. Then say:) Everybody, that statement is . . . (Signal.) *false.*

EXERCISE 2   **Who—What—When—Where—Why**

1. Listen to this story.
   - The pilot was flying an airplane. She saw a big storm coming, so she landed the airplane at an airport. After the pilot landed, the passengers got out of the airplane.

- (Repeat the story.)
2. Tell what the pilot was flying. Get ready. (Signal.) *An airplane.*
   - Tell where the pilot landed the airplane. Get ready. (Signal.) *At an airport.*
   - Tell who got out of the airplane. Get ready. (Signal.) *The passengers.*
   - Tell why the pilot landed. Get ready. (Signal.) *She saw a big storm coming.*
   - Tell when the passengers got out of the airplane. Get ready. (Signal.) *After the pilot landed.*
3. (Repeat step 2 until firm.)

EXERCISE 3   **Calendar**

1. (Present calendar.)
   - We're going to talk about today, tomorrow, and one week from today.
2. Tell me the day of the week it is today. Get ready. (Signal.)
   - Tell me the day of the week it will be tomorrow. Get ready. (Signal.)
   - Tell me the day of the week it will be one week from today. Get ready. (Signal.)
3. (Repeat step 2 until firm.)
4. Now the dates.
   - Tell me today's date. Get ready. (Signal.)
   - Look at the calendar. ✔
   - Tell me the date it will be one week from today. Get ready. (Signal.)

5. Once more.
- Listen: Tell me today's date. Get ready. (Signal.)
- Tell me tomorrow's date. Get ready. (Signal.)
- Tell me the date it will be one week from today. Get ready. (Signal.)
6. (Repeat step 5 until firm.)

EXERCISE 4   Description

1. I'm going to tell you about an object you know. But I'm going to call it a funny name. See if you can figure out what object I'm talking about.
2. (Hold up one finger.)
   A wup is an animal. Say that. (Signal.) *A wup is an animal.*
- (Hold up two fingers.)
   A wup lives on a farm. Say that. (Signal.) *A wup lives on a farm.*
- (Hold up three fingers.)
   A wup lays eggs. Say that. (Signal.) *A wup lays eggs.*
3. Everybody, say all the things you know about a wup. Get ready.
- (Hold up one finger.) *A wup is an animal.*
- (Hold up two fingers.) *A wup lives on a farm.*
- (Hold up three fingers). *A wup lays eggs.*
4. (Repeat steps 2 and 3 until firm.)
5. Everybody, tell me what kind of animal I am calling a wup. (Pause.) Get ready. (Signal.) *A chicken.*
   (Accept other good answers.)
6. I couldn't fool you. It's really a chicken. How do you know a wup is a chicken? (Call on a child. Idea: *It's an animal. It lives on a farm. It lays eggs.*)

EXERCISE 5   Analogies

1. We're going to make up **two** analogies.
- We're going to make up analogies about a purse and a bottle. Which containers? (Signal.) *A purse and a bottle.*
2. The first analogy tells what the containers are made of.
- What is a purse made of? (Call on a child. Accept all reasonable answers, but use: *leather.*)

- What is a bottle made of? (Call on a child. Accept all reasonable answers, but use: *glass.*)
3. A purse is to leather as a bottle is to . . . (Signal.) *glass.*
- Say that analogy about a purse and a bottle. Get ready. (Signal.) *A purse is to leather as a bottle is to glass.*
4. Listen: A purse is to leather as a bottle is to glass. Does that analogy tell what you **put** in the containers? (Signal.) *No.*
5. Listen: A purse is to leather as a bottle is to glass. Does that analogy tell where you find the containers? (Signal.) *No.*
6. Listen: A purse is to leather as a bottle is to glass. Does that analogy tell what the containers are made of? (Signal.) *Yes.*
7. (Repeat steps 4 through 6 until firm.)
8. We made up an analogy that tells what the containers are made of. The next analogy tells what you put in the containers.
- What do you put in a purse? (Call on a child. Accept all reasonable answers, but use: *money.*)
- What do you put in a bottle? (Call on a child. Accept all reasonable answers, but use: *water.*)
9. A purse is to money as a bottle is to . . . (Signal.) *water.*
10. We made up an analogy that tells what the containers are made of. Then we made up an analogy that tells what you put in the containers. Let's see if you can say both those analogies.
11. Think. Say the analogy that tells what the containers are made of. (Pause.) Get ready. (Signal.) *A purse is to leather as a bottle is to glass.*
- Think. Say the analogy that tells what you put in the containers. (Pause.) Get ready. (Signal.) *A purse is to money as a bottle is to water.*
12. (Repeat step 11 until firm.)

EXERCISE 6   Materials

1. A man wants to make a fence.
- Are some fences made of cloth? (Signal.) *No.*
- What's absurd about a fence that is made of cloth? (Call on individual children. Praise good answers, such as: *It wouldn't be strong. The wind would blow it down.*)

2. Everybody, are some fences made of glass? (Signal.) *No.*
- What's absurd about a fence that is made of glass? (Call on individual children. Praise good answers, such as: *It would break. It cuts.*)
3. Everybody, are some fences made of metal? (Signal.) *Yes.*
- Why can metal be used to make fences? (Call on individual children. Praise good answers, such as: *It's strong. It won't fall down.*)

EXERCISE 7 Absurdity

1. You'll listen to this story and tell me what's absurd about it.
2. A boy put his fish on a leash.
- What did he do with his fish? (Signal.) *Put it on a leash.*
3. Then he went for a walk with his fish.
- Where did he go with his fish? (Signal.) *For a walk.*
4. Now tell me some things that are absurd about that story. (Call on individual children. Praise all appropriate responses.)

WORKBOOK

EXERCISE 8 Sentence Construction

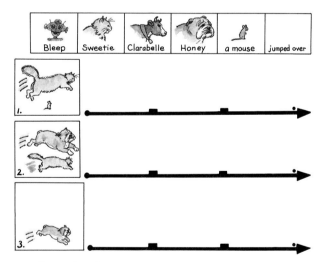

1. Everybody, open your workbook to Lesson 76. Write your name. ✔
- You're going to write sentences that tell what the characters did in the pictures. The words are written at the top of the page.

- Touch the picture of a **mouse.** ✔
  The words in that box say **a mouse.**
  Everybody, what words? (Signal.) *A mouse.*
- Touch the **last** box. ✔
  The words in that box are **jumped over.**
  What words? (Signal.) *Jumped over.*
- That's what the characters did in pictures 1 and 2.
2. Everybody, touch picture 1 by the top arrow. ✔
  Who is jumping in that picture? (Signal.) *Sweetie.*
- Sweetie is jumping over something. What's Sweetie jumping over? (Signal.) *A mouse.*
- Everybody, say a sentence that tells what Sweetie did in picture 1. (Signal.) *Sweetie jumped over a mouse.*
- Yes, **Sweetie jumped over a mouse.**
3. Your turn: Write that sentence on arrow 1. Remember, Sweetie's name begins with a capital **S.** Raise your hand when you're finished.
  (Observe children and give feedback.)
4. Now you're going to write a sentence for picture 2. Who is jumping over Sweetie in that picture? (Signal.) *Honey.*
- Write a sentence that tells what Honey did in picture 2. Raise your hand when you're finished.
  (Observe children and give feedback.)
- Everybody, read the whole sentence you wrote about Honey. (Signal.) *Honey jumped over Sweetie.*
5. Picture 3 is not finished. Somebody is supposed to be jumping over Honey, but nobody is jumping over her in the picture.
- Your turn: Write a sentence for picture 3. You can write a sentence that uses any name we haven't used. Write your sentence. Raise your hand when you're finished.
  (Observe children and give feedback.)
6. I'm going to call on several children to read their sentence.
- (Call on a child to read sentence 3. Repeat with several children.)
- (Praise original sentences that take the form: *[A name other than Sweetie] or [A mouse] jumped over Honey.*)

7. Let's make sure you can read all of your sentences.
• (Call on several children:) Read all three sentences you wrote.
• (Praise appropriate responses.)
8. Later, you'll have to finish the picture for sentence 3. Remember, your picture should show what your sentence says.
• (Call on several children:) What will your picture show? (Praise children whose response tells about their sentence.)
9. I'll show you some of the better pictures later.

EXERCISE 9 **Classification**

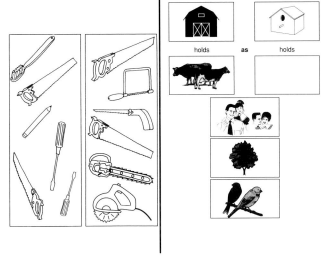

1. Everybody, find the next page. ✔
• (Hold up workbook. Point to first half.)
2. Touch the picture that shows only **one** kind of thing. ✔
• What kind of thing is that in the picture? (Signal.) *Saws.*
3. Touch the picture that shows **more** than one kind of thing. ✔
• Raise your hand if you can figure out the name of the class shown in that picture. ✔
• Everybody, what's the name of that class? (Signal.) *Tools.*
4. Listen: The class that is larger is the class that has **more** kinds of things. What does the class that is **larger** have? (Signal.) *More kinds of things.*

5. Everybody, circle the class that is **larger.** ✔
• Everybody, touch the picture of the class that is **smaller.** ✔
• How many kinds of things are in the class that is **smaller?** (Signal.) *One.*
6. The saws in that picture of the **smaller** class should be blue with red handles. What colors? (Signal.) *Blue with red handles.*
• Mark a saw in that picture. ✔
7. Touch the picture that shows the **larger** class. ✔
• The saws in the picture of the **larger** class should be yellow with brown handles. What colors? (Signal). *Yellow with brown handles.*
• Mark a saw in that picture. ✔

EXERCISE 10 **Analogies**

1. (Hold up workbook. Point to second half.)
2. The pictures show something and what it holds.
3. Touch the barn. ✔
• The picture that's right below shows what it holds. Everybody, what does a barn hold? (Signal.) *Cows.*
• Tell me about a barn. Get ready. (Signal.) *A barn holds cows.*
4. Touch the birdhouse. ✔
• One of the pictures below shows what it holds. Touch the picture that shows what a birdhouse holds. ✔
• Everybody, what does a birdhouse hold? (Signal.) *Birds.*
• Tell me about a birdhouse. Get ready. (Signal.) *A birdhouse holds birds.*
• Listen: A barn holds cows as a birdhouse holds birds.
5. Say the whole analogy about a barn and a birdhouse. Get ready. (Signal.) *A barn holds cows as a birdhouse holds birds.*
6. (Repeat step 5 until firm.)
7. Draw a line from the birdhouse to what it holds. (Observe children and give feedback.)

LESSON 77

Objectives

- Identify absurdities involving materials. (Exercise 1)
- **Recite the definition of "synonym."** (Exercise 2)
- Given a calendar, identify the day and date for "today" and "tomorrow" and one week from today. (Exercise 3)
- Construct verbal analogies. (Exercise 4)
- Identify how common objects are the same and different. (Exercise 5)
- **Replace a word in a sentence with a synonym.** (Exercise 6)
- Identify an object based on its characteristics. (Exercise 7)
- Discriminate between true and false statements and generate true and false statements. (Exercise 8)
- Make up an ending to a new story based on familiar story grammar. (Exercise 9)
- Put on a play to show a familiar story. (Exercise 10)
- Make a picture consistent with the details of a story. (Exercise 11)

EXERCISE 1 Materials

1. A woman wants to make a drinking glass.
- Are some glasses made of ice? (Signal.) *No.*
- What's absurd about a glass that is made of ice? (Call on individual children. Praise good answers, such as: *It would melt.*)
2. Everybody, are some glasses made of glass? (Signal.) *Yes.*
- Why can glass be used to make glasses? (Call on individual children. Praise good answers, such as: *It will hold water. It's easy to hold.*)
3. Everybody, are some glasses made of cloth? (Signal.) *No.*
- What's absurd about a glass that is made of cloth? (Call on individual children. Praise good answers, such as: *Water would go through it. You couldn't hold on to it.*)

EXERCISE 2 Synonyms

1. We're going to learn what **synonym** means.
2. Synonym. Say that. (Signal.) *Synonym.*
- (Repeat until firm.)
3. Listen to the rule. A synonym is a word that means the same thing as another word.
4. Listen again: A synonym is a word that means the same thing as another word. Let's say that. Get ready. (Signal.) (Respond with the children.) *A synonym is a word that means the same thing as another word.*
5. All by yourselves. Say the rule. Get ready. (Signal.) *A synonym is a word that means the same thing as another word.*
6. (Repeat steps 4 and 5 until firm.)

7. What do we call a word that means the same thing as another word? (Signal.) *A synonym.*
- Say the rule. Get ready. (Signal.) *A synonym is a word that means the same thing as another word.*

EXERCISE 3 Calendar

1. (Present calendar.)
- We're going to talk about today, tomorrow, and one week from today.
2. Tell me the day of the week it is today. Get ready. (Signal.)
- Tell me the day of the week it will be tomorrow. Get ready. (Signal.)
- Tell me the day of the week it will be one week from today. Get ready. (Signal.)
3. (Repeat step 2 until firm.)
4. Now the dates.
- Tell me today's date. Get ready. (Signal.)
- Look at the calendar. ✔
- Tell me the date it will be one week from today. Get ready. (Signal.)
5. Once more. Listen: Tell me today's date. Get ready. (Signal.)
- Tell me tomorrow's date. Get ready. (Signal.)
- Tell me the date it will be one week from today. Get ready. (Signal.)
6. (Repeat step 5 until firm.)

EXERCISE 4 Analogies

1. We're going to make up **two** analogies.
- We're going to make up analogies about a frog and a cow. Which animals? (Signal.) *A frog and a cow.*
2. The first analogy tells what the animals say.
- What does a frog say? (Call on a child. Accept all reasonable answers, but use: *ribbit.*)
- What does a cow say? (Signal.) *Moo.*
3. A frog is to ribbiting as a cow is to . . . (Signal.) *mooing.*
- Say that analogy about a frog and a cow. Get ready. (Signal.) *A frog is to ribbiting as a cow is to mooing.*
4. Listen: A frog is to ribbiting as a cow is to mooing. Does that analogy tell how the animals move? (Signal.) *No.*
5. Listen: A frog is to ribbiting as a cow is to mooing. Does that analogy tell what the animals say? (Signal.) *Yes.*
6. Listen: A frog is to ribbiting as a cow is to mooing. Does that analogy tell where you find the animals? (Signal.) *No.*
7. (Repeat steps 4 through 6 until firm.)
8. We made up an analogy that tells what the animals say. The next analogy tells how the animals move.
- How does a frog move? (Call on a child. Accept all reasonable answers, but use: *hops.*)
- How does a cow move? (Call on a child. Accept all reasonable answers, but use: *walks.*)
9. A frog is to hopping as a cow is to . . . (Signal.) *walking.*
- Say that analogy about a frog and a cow. Get ready. (Signal.) *A frog is to hopping as a cow is to walking.*
10. We made up an analogy that tells what the animals say. Then we made up an analogy that tells how the animals move. Let's see if you can say both those analogies.
11. Think. Say the analogy that tells what the animals say. (Pause.) Get ready. (Signal.) *A frog is to ribbiting as a cow is to mooing.*
- Think. Say the analogy that tells how the animals move. (Pause.) Get ready. (Signal.) *A frog is to hopping as a cow is to walking.*
12. (Repeat step 11 until firm.)

EXERCISE 5 Same—Different

1. We're going to talk about how things are the same and how they are different.
2. Listen: A pencil and chalk. Think of them. See if you can name two ways they are the same. (Call on individual children. Have the group repeat each correct answer. Then say:) You told me how a pencil and chalk are . . . (Signal.) *the same.*
3. Listen: A pencil and chalk. Think of them. See if you can name two ways they are different. (Call on individual children. Have the group repeat each correct answer. Then say:) You told me how a pencil and chalk are . . . (Signal.) *different.*

EXERCISE 6 Synonyms

1. Let's make up statements that have synonyms.
2. Listen: I'm going to shut the door. Say that. (Signal.) *I'm going to shut the door.*
3. Here's a statement that has a synonym for shut: I'm going to close the door. Say that. (Signal.) *I'm going to close the door.*
4. I'll say one of the statements. You say the statement that has a synonym. My turn: I'm going to close the door. Your turn. Say the statement that has a synonym. (Signal.) *I'm going to shut the door.*
- (Repeat step 4 until firm.)
5. Here's another one.
6. Listen: The pencil is skinny. Say that. (Signal.) *The pencil is skinny.*
7. Here's a statement that has a synonym: The pencil is thin. Say that. (Signal.) *The pencil is thin.*
8. (Repeat steps 6 and 7 until firm.)
9. I'll say one of the statements. You say the statement that has a synonym. My turn: The pencil is skinny. Your turn. (Signal.) *The pencil is thin.*
- (Repeat step 9 until firm.)

EXERCISE 7 Description

1. I'm going to tell you about an object you know. But I'm going to call it a funny name. See if you can figure out what object I'm talking about.

2. (Hold up one finger.)
- A zatch is made of cloth. Say that. (Signal.) *A zatch is made of cloth.*
- (Hold up two fingers.)
- A zatch is clothing. Say that. (Signal.) *A zatch is clothing.*
- (Hold up three fingers.)
- You wear a zatch in the water. Say that. (Signal.) *You wear a zatch in the water.*

3. Everybody, say all the things you know about a zatch. Get ready.
- (Hold up one finger.) *A zatch is made of cloth.*
- (Hold up two fingers.) *A zatch is clothing.*
- (Hold up three fingers.) *You wear a zatch in the water.*

4. (Repeat steps 2 and 3 until firm.)

5. Everybody, what kind of clothing am I calling a zatch? (Pause.) (Signal.) *A swimsuit.*

6. I couldn't fool you. It's really a swimsuit. How do you know a zatch is a swimsuit? (Call on a child. Idea: *It's cloth. It's clothing. You wear it in the water.*)

7. How would you like to wear a zatch in the snow? (Children respond.)

EXERCISE 8 True—False

1. I'm going to make up statements. Some of these statements are true and some are false. You tell me about each statement.

2. A book is made of paper. True or false? (Signal.) *True.*
- A doll is not a food. True or false? (Signal.) *True.*
- You put clothes in a jar. True or false? (Signal.) *False.*
- You find a motorcycle in a library. True or false? (Signal.) *False.*
- A boy cannot ride on a horse's back. True or false? (Signal.) *False.*
- (Repeat step 2 until firm.)

3. Your turn. Make up a statement about a book that is true. (Call on three children. Praise each acceptable statement and have the group repeat it. Then say:) Everybody, that statement is . . . (Signal.) *true.*

4. Your turn. Make up a statement about a book that is false. (Call on three children. Praise each acceptable statement and have the group repeat it. Then say:) Everybody, that statement is . . . (Signal.) *false.*

EXERCISE 9 Sweetie And The Mirror

Story Completion

1. Here's another story about Sweetie. But the last part is missing.

One day the woman who owned Sweetie took him to somebody's house. When Sweetie started wandering around the house, he saw something that he had never seen before: a mirror. That mirror was on a door, and the mirror went all the way to the floor.

Sweetie had never seen a mirror that close to the floor. And he didn't even know that it was a mirror.

To him, it just looked like part of the room. But there was something in that room that made Sweetie very, very upset. He saw a cat standing there. Sweetie said, "What is that ugly yellow cat doing here?"

- Everybody, who was that ugly yellow cat that Sweetie saw? (Signal.) *Sweetie.*
- Was there **really** another cat in the room? (Signal.) *No.*

Sweetie decided to show that cat that **he** was the boss. So Sweetie arched his back. And that other yellow cat arched its back at the same time.

- Why did that other yellow cat arch its back when Sweetie arched his back? (Call on a child. Idea: *Because that cat **is** Sweetie.*)
- I think poor Sweetie is going to get very confused.

Then Sweetie made the meanest face he could make.

- What did the other cat do when Sweetie made a mean face? (Signal.) *Made a mean face.*

That other yellow cat made a mean face at the same time Sweetie did.

Sweetie said, "I'll show this cat who is boss."

Sweetie crouched down and moved toward the other yellow cat.

- What did the other yellow cat do? (Signal.) *Crouched down and moved toward Sweetie.*
- Right, the other yellow cat crouched down and moved toward Sweetie. Get a picture of those cats coming closer and closer together.

Sweetie held up his left paw and showed how long and sharp his claws were. The yellow cat did the same thing, except with its right paw.

- Wow. Sweetie held up his **left** paw, and the cat in the mirror did that with his **right** paw.

Sweetie said to himself, "That cat is ugly, but it has to be the **fastest** cat I ever saw. When I do something, it seems to do the same thing at the same time I do it."

Then Sweetie said to himself, "It's time to teach this cat a lesson." So he crouched down, leaped at the yellow cat and . . .

2. That's all there is to the story. We're going to have to make up the ending ourselves. Remember, Sweetie gets fooled and then he always says something at the end of these stories.
- Here's where the story stops: Sweetie crouched down, leaped at the yellow cat and . . .
- Now think of what happened to fool Sweetie. Tell what happened when Sweetie jumped. Then tell what Sweetie **thought** happened and what Sweetie said at the end of the story. (Call on several children. Praise ideas such as: *Sweetie bonked himself on the mirror. Then Sweetie said something like, "That yellow cat may be ugly, but he sure can hit hard and fast."*)
3. So here's an ending to the story. See if this is a good one.

Sweetie crouched down and leaped at the yellow cat. Bonk. Sweetie banged his head against the mirror and went flying. He rolled around on the floor and finally sat up and looked at the cat in the mirror. Sweetie said to himself, "That sure is an ugly cat, but let me tell you, that cat is fast and that cat can really hit hard."

EXERCISE 10   Putting On a Play

Sweetie And The Mirror

1. Let's see if we have two children who can act out that story about Sweetie. One child will play Sweetie. The other child will play the cat in the mirror.
- (Call on two children. Tell one:) You're Sweetie.
- (Tell the other:) You're the cat in the mirror.
- (Have children face each other about 10 feet apart.)
2. Okay, I'll tell each part of the story. Then I'll tell our cats to act out that part.

Sweetie saw the cat in the mirror. Sweetie arched his back. And the cat in the mirror did the same thing.

- Go cats. ✔

Next Sweetie made the meanest face he could make. And the cat in the mirror did the same thing.

- Go cats. ✔

Next Sweetie crouched down and moved toward the yellow cat, closer, closer, closer, and the cat in the mirror did the same thing.

- Go cats. ✔

Now Sweetie held up his **left** paw and showed his claws. And the cat in the mirror held up its **right** paw, the same way.

- Remember, Sweetie, your **left** paw. Cats go. ✔

Next Sweetie crouched down and leaped at the yellow cat and went sprawling.

- Cats, be careful and don't **really** bang into each other. Go. ✔

Now Sweetie is completely fooled by the mirror and he says something to himself.

- Say it, Sweetie. (Idea: *"That sure is an ugly-looking cat, but let me tell you, that cat is fast and that cat can really hit hard."*)
3. That was pretty good. Maybe next time, we can do it again with a different Sweetie and a different cat in the mirror.

EXERCISE 11 Story Details

1. Everybody, find lesson 77 in your workbook. Write your name at the top of the page. ✔

2. Touch Sweetie. ✔
- What is Sweetie doing? (Call on a child. Idea: *Holding up his left paw; showing how long and sharp his claws are.*)
- Everybody, which paw is Sweetie holding up? (Signal.) *His left paw.*
3. Now touch the picture in the mirror. ✔
- Everybody, which paw is the cat in the mirror holding up? (Signal.) *His right paw.*
- What's going to happen right after this picture? (Call on a child. Idea: *Sweetie will crouch down and leap at the yellow cat in the mirror.*)
4. Uh-oh, poor Sweetie. Too bad he doesn't know about mirrors. Maybe you can practice this story in a mirror at home. But don't do any real leaping at that mirror.
- Later you can color the picture. Remember, Sweetie and the cat in the mirror look exactly the same.

Objectives

- Generate statements involving "can do" and "cannot do." (Exercise 1)
- Given a calendar, identify the day and date for "today" and "tomorrow" and one week from today. (Exercise 2)
- Construct verbal analogies. (Exercise 3)
- Replace a word in a sentence with a synonym. (Exercise 4)
- Identify how common objects are the same and different. (Exercise 5)
- Discriminate between true and false statements and generate true and false statements. (Exercise 6)
- Identify an object based on its characteristics. (Exercise 7)
- Write three sentences about story characters. (Exercise 8)

EXERCISE 1 Can Do

1. I'm going to ask questions about a man and a jump rope.
2. Everybody, can a man cut a jump rope? (Signal.) *Yes.*
- Say the statement. Get ready. (Signal.) *A man can cut a jump rope.*
3. Everybody, can a man keep the rain off him with a jump rope? (Signal.) *No.*
- Say the statement. Get ready. (Signal.) *A man cannot keep the rain off him with a jump rope.*
4. (Call on a child.)
- Your turn. Make up another statement that tells something a man can do with a jump rope. (After the child makes the statement, call on the group.) Say the statement. Get ready. (Signal.) (The group repeats the child's statement.)
5. (Call on another child.)
 Make up a statement that tells something a man cannot do with a jump rope.
 (After the child makes the statement, call on the group.) Say the statement. Get ready. (Signal.) (The group repeats the child's statement.)

EXERCISE 2 Calendar

1. (Present calendar.)
- We're going to talk about today, tomorrow, and one week from today.
2. Tell me the day of the week it is today. Get ready. (Signal.)
- Tell me the day of the week it will be tomorrow. Get ready. (Signal.)
- Tell me the day of the week it will be one week from today. Get ready. (Signal.)
3. (Repeat step 2 until firm.)

4. Now the dates.
- Tell me today's date. Get ready. (Signal.)
- Look at the calendar. ✔
- Tell me the date it will be one week from today. Get ready. (Signal.)
5. Once more. Listen: Tell me today's date. Get ready. (Signal.)
- Tell me tomorrow's date. Get ready. (Signal.)
- Tell me the date it will be one week from today. Get ready. (Signal.)
6. (Repeat step 5 until firm.)

EXERCISE 3 Analogies

1. We're going to make up **two** analogies.
- We're going to make up analogies about an airplane and a fish. Which objects? (Signal.) *An airplane and a fish.*
2. The first analogy tells where you find the objects.
- Where do you find an airplane? (Call on a child. Accept all reasonable answers, but use: *In the air.*)
- Where do you find a fish? (Call on a child. Accept all reasonable answers, but use: *In the water.*)
3. An airplane is to the air as a fish is to . . . (Signal.) *the water.*
- Say that analogy about an airplane and a fish. Get ready. (Signal.) *An airplane is to the air as a fish is to the water.*

4. Listen: An airplane is to the air as a fish is to the water. Does that analogy tell how the objects move? (Signal.) *No.*

5. Listen: An airplane is to the air as a fish is to the water. Does that analogy tell what you do with the objects? (Signal.) *No.*

6. Listen: An airplane is to the air as a fish is to the water. Does that analogy tell where you find the objects? (Signal.) *Yes.*

7. (Repeat steps 4 through 6 until firm.)

8. We made up an analogy that tells where you find the objects. The next analogy tells what class the objects are in.

• What class is an airplane in? (Signal.) *Vehicles.*

• What class is a fish in? (Call on a child. Accept all reasonable answers, but use: *animals.*)

9. An airplane is to vehicles as a fish is to . . . (Signal.) *animals.*

• Say that analogy about an airplane and a fish. Get ready. (Signal.) *An airplane is to vehicles as a fish is to animals.*

10. We made up an analogy that tells where you find the objects. Then we made up an analogy that tells what class the objects are in. Let's see if you can say both those analogies.

11. Think. Say the analogy that tells where you find the objects. (Pause.) Get ready. (Signal.) *An airplane is to the air as a fish is to the water.*

• Think. Say the analogy that tells what class the objects are in. (Pause.) Get ready. (Signal.) *An airplane is to vehicles as a fish is to animals.*

12. (Repeat step 11 until firm.)

EXERCISE 4   Synonyms

1. We're going to talk about synonyms.

2. Remember the rule: A synonym is a word that means the same thing as another word. Say that. Get ready. (Signal.) *A synonym is a word that means the same thing as another word.*

• (Repeat step 2 until firm.)

3. What's a word that means the same thing as another word? (Signal.) *A synonym.*

• Say the rule. Get ready. (Signal.) *A synonym is a word that means the same thing as another word.*

4. Let's make up statements that mean the same thing as other statements.

5. Listen: The book is thin. Say that. (Signal.) *The book is thin.*

6. Here's the statement that has a synonym: the book is skinny. Say that. (Signal.) *The book is skinny.*

7. I'll say one of the statements. You say the statement that has a synonym. My turn: The book is thin. Your turn. (Signal.) *The book is skinny.*

8. (Repeat steps 5 through 7 until firm.)

9. Here's another one.

10. Listen: Please close the window. Say that. (Signal.) *Please close the window.*

11. Here's a statement that has a synonym: Please shut the window. Say that. (Signal.) *Please shut the window.*

12. I'll say one of the statements. You say the statement that has a synonym. My turn: Please close the window. Your turn. (Signal.) *Please shut the window.*

13. (Repeat steps 11 and 12 until firm.)

EXERCISE 5   Same—Different

1. We're going to talk about how things are the same and how they are different.

• Listen: A flower and a tree. Think of them. See if you can name two ways they are the same. (Call on individual children. Have the group repeat each correct answer. Then say:) You told me how a flower and a tree are . . . (Signal.) *the same.*

• Listen: A flower and a tree. Think of them. See if you can name two ways they are different. (Call on individual children. Have the group repeat each correct answer. Then say:) You told me how a flower and a tree are . . . (Signal.) *different.*

2. Here's another one.

• Listen: A rabbit and a monkey. Think of them. See if you can name two ways they are the same. (Call on individual children. Have the group repeat each correct answer. Then say:) You told me how a rabbit and a monkey are . . . (Signal.) *the same.*

• Listen: A rabbit and a monkey. Think of them. See if you can name two ways they are different. (Call on individual children. Have the group repeat each correct answer. Then say:) You told me how a rabbit and a monkey are . . . (Signal.) *different.*

EXERCISE 6   True—False

1. I'm going to make up statements. Some of these statements are true and some are false. You tell me about each statement.
2. You cannot sit on a chair. True or false? (Signal.) *False.*
- Snakes have legs. True or false? (Signal.) *False.*
- Farm animals can live in barns. True or false? (Signal.) *True.*
- A blanket is made of cloth. True or false? (Signal.) *True.*
- A container does not grow in the ground. True or false? (Signal.) *True.*
- (Repeat step 2 until firm.)
3. Your turn. Make up a statement about snakes that is true. (Call on three children. Praise each acceptable statement and have the group repeat it. Then say:) Everybody, that statement is . . . (Signal.) *true.*
4. Your turn. Make up a statement about snakes that is false. (Call on three children. Praise each acceptable statement and have the group repeat it. Then say:) Everybody, that statement is . . . (Signal.) *false.*

EXERCISE 7   Description

1. I'm going to tell you about an object you know. But I'm going to call it a funny name. See if you can figure out what object I'm talking about.
2. (Hold up one finger.)
- A quimp can be made of plastic. Say that. (Signal.) *A quimp can be made of plastic.*
- (Hold up two fingers.)
- A quimp has bristles. Say that. (Signal.) *A quimp has bristles.*
- (Hold up three fingers.)
- You use a quimp to brush your hair. Say that. (Signal.) *You use a quimp to brush your hair.*
3. Everybody, say all the things you know about a quimp. Get ready.
- (Hold up one finger.) *A quimp can be made of plastic.*
- (Hold up two fingers.) *A quimp has bristles.*
- (Hold up three fingers.) *You use a quimp to brush your hair.*
4. (Repeat steps 2 and 3 until firm.)
5. Everybody, what kind of object am I calling a quimp? (Pause.) (Signal.) *A hairbrush.*

6. Yes, a quimp is a hairbrush. How do you know a quimp is a hairbrush? (Call on a child. Idea: *It can be made of plastic. It has bristles. You use it to brush your hair.*)
7. How would you like to use a quimp to write something? (Children respond.)

WORKBOOK

EXERCISE 8   Sentence Construction

1. Everybody, open your workbook to Lesson 78. Write your name at the top of the page. ✔
- You're going to write sentences that tell what each character carried.
2. Everybody, touch the picture of the rocks. ✔ The word under that picture is **rocks.**
- Touch the next picture. ✔ The word is **Sweetie.**
- Touch the next picture. ✔ The word is **Honey.**
- Touch the next picture. ✔ The word is **skunks.**
- Touch the next picture. ✔ The word is **hats.**
- Touch the next box. ✔ The word in that box is **carried.** That's what the characters will do in your sentences.
- Touch the last picture. ✔ The word is **paint.**
3. Now look at the pictures along the arrows. ✔
- On arrow 1 is a picture of Roxie. She's carrying a basket, but we can't see what she's carrying in that basket.

- Touch arrow 2. ✔
- Who is in the picture? (Signal.) *Paul.* He's carrying a basket, but we can't see what's in his basket.
- Touch arrow 3. ✔
- Who is in the picture? (Signal.) *Clarabelle.* Clarabelle is carrying a basket, but we can't see what's in that basket, either.
4. Listen: You're going to write a sentence for Roxie. The first part of your sentence will say: **Roxie carried.** Then you'll write what she carried. I think I know what that is.
- Your turn: Write **Roxie carried** and then tell what you think she carried. Raise your hand when you've finished the sentence for arrow 1.
  (Observe children and give feedback.)
- (Call on several children:) Read your whole sentence about Roxie.
  (Praise appropriate sentences.)
5. Everybody, touch arrow 2. ✔
- Write a sentence about Paul. Tell what you think he carried. I think I know what that is. Raise your hand when you've finished the sentence for arrow 2.
  (Observe children and give feedback.)

- (Call on several children:) Read your whole sentence about Paul.
- (Praise appropriate sentences.)
6. Everybody, touch arrow 3. ✔
- Write a sentence about Clarabelle. Tell what you think she carried. I don't have any idea what that could be. It might be something very silly. Raise your hand when you've finished the sentence for arrow 3.
  (Observe children and give feedback.)
- (Call on several children:) Read your whole sentence about Clarabelle.
- (Praise appropriate sentences.)
7. Later you can fix up the pictures so they show what the different characters carried. You can draw things sticking out of the top of the baskets. Some of you may have pictures of Clarabelle that are pretty funny.

Objectives

- Construct verbal analogies. (Exercise 1)
- Given a calendar, identify the day and date for "today" and "tomorrow" and one week from today. (Exercise 2)
- Identify an object based on its characteristics. (Exercise 3)
- Replace a word in a sentence with a synonym. (Exercise 4)
- Identify absurdities involving materials. (Exercise 5)
- Identify how common objects are the same and different. (Exercise 6)
- Name members of a class and subclass and identify the bigger class. (Exercise 7)
- Identify absurdities involving use. (Exercise 8)
- Listen to part of a familiar story and recall the story ending. (Exercise 9)
- Put on a play to show a familiar story. (Exercise 10)
- Make a picture consistent with the details of a story. (Exercise 11)

EXERCISE 1 Analogies

1. We're going to make up **two** analogies.
- We're going to make up analogies about a glass and a wagon. Which objects? (Signal.) *A glass and a wagon.*
2. The first analogy tells what class the objects are in.
- What class is a glass in? (Call on a child. Accept all reasonable answers, but use: *containers.*)
- What class is a wagon in? (Call on a child. Accept all reasonable answers, but use: *vehicles.*)
3. A glass is to containers as a wagon is to . . . (Signal.) *vehicles.*
- Say that analogy about a glass and a wagon. Get ready. (Signal.) *A glass is to containers as a wagon is to vehicles.*
4. Listen: A glass is to containers as a wagon is to vehicles. Does that analogy tell what class the objects are in? (Signal.) *Yes.*
5. Listen: A glass is to containers as a wagon is to vehicles. Does that analogy tell what you do with the objects? (Signal.) *No.*
6. Listen: A glass is to containers as a wagon is to vehicles. Does that analogy tell where you find the objects? (Signal.) *No.*
7. (Repeat steps 4 through 6 until firm.)
8. We made up an analogy that tells what class the objects are in. The next analogy tells what the objects are made of.
- What is a glass made of? (Call on a child. Accept all reasonable answers, but use: *glass.*)

- What is a wagon made of? (Call on a child. Accept all reasonable answers, but use: *metal.*)
9. A wagon is to metal as a glass is to . . . (Signal.) *glass.*
- Say that analogy about a wagon and a glass. Get ready. (Signal.) *A wagon is to metal as a glass is to glass.*
10. We made up an analogy that tells what class the objects are in. Then we made up an analogy that tells what the objects are made of. Let's see if you can say both those analogies.
11. Think. Say an analogy that tells what the objects are made of. (Pause.) Get ready. (Signal.) *A wagon is to metal as a glass is to glass.*
- Think. Say an analogy that tells what class the objects are in. (Pause.) Get ready. (Signal.) *A wagon is to vehicles as a glass is to containers.*
12. (Repeat step 11 until firm.)

EXERCISE 2 Calendar

1. (Present calendar.)
- We're going to talk about today, tomorrow, and one week from today.
2. Tell me the day of the week it is today. Get ready. (Signal.)
- Tell me the day of the week it will be tomorrow. Get ready. (Signal.)
- Tell me the day of the week it will be one week from today. Get ready. (Signal.)
3. (Repeat step 2 until firm.)

4. Now the dates.
- Tell me today's date. Get ready. (Signal.)
- Look at the calendar. ✔
- Tell me the date it will be one week from today. Get ready. (Signal.)
5. Once more.
- Listen: Tell me today's date. Get ready. (Signal.)
- Tell me tomorrow's date. Get ready. (Signal.)
- Tell me the date it will be one week from today. Get ready. (Signal.)
6. (Repeat step 5 until firm.)

EXERCISE 3   Description

1. I'm going to tell you about an object you know. But I'm going to call it a funny name. See if you can figure out what object I'm talking about.
2. (Hold up one finger.)
- A sips is a tool. Say that. (Signal.) *A sips is a tool.*
- (Hold up two fingers.)
- A sips has a handle and a blade. Say that. (Signal.) *A sips has a handle and a blade.*
- (Hold up three fingers.)
- You use a sips to cut boards. Say that. (Signal.) *You use a sips to cut boards.*
3. Everybody, say all the things you know about a sips. Get ready.
- (Hold up one finger.) *A sips is a tool.*
- (Hold up two fingers.) *A sips has a handle and a blade.*
- (Hold up three fingers.) *You use a sips to cut boards.*
4. (Repeat steps 2 and 3 until firm.)
5. Everybody, tell me what kind of tool I am calling a sips. (Pause.) Get ready. (Signal.) *A saw.*
6. Yes, a sips is a saw. How do you know a sips is a saw? (Call on a child. Idea: *It's a tool. It has a handle and a blade. You use it to cut boards.*)
7. How would you like to use a sips to cut your hair? (Children respond.)

EXERCISE 4   Synonyms

1. A synonym for under is below.
2. Listen: The dog was lying under the table. Say that. (Signal.) *The dog was lying under the table.*

3. Here's the statement that has a synonym. The dog was lying below the table. Say that. (Signal.) *The dog was lying below the table.*
4. I'll say one of the statements. You say the statement with the synonym. My turn: The dog was lying below the table. Your turn. (Signal.) *The dog was lying under the table.*
- (Repeat step 4 until firm.)

EXERCISE 5   Materials

1. Are some schools made of paper? (Signal.) *No.*
- What's absurd about a school that is made of paper? (Call on individual children. Praise good answers, such as: *The wind would blow it down. The walls wouldn't stay up.*)
2. Everybody, are some schools made of concrete? (Signal.) *Yes.*
- Why can concrete be used to make schools? (Call on individual children. Praise good answers, such as: *It's strong. The wind can't blow it down.*)
3. Everybody, are some schools made of rubber? (Signal.) *No.*
- What's absurd about a school that is made of rubber? (Call on individual children. Praise good answers, such as: *The walls would bend. It wouldn't stand up.*)

EXERCISE 6   Same—Different

1. We're going to talk about how things are the same and how they are different.
2. Listen: Scissors and a knife. Think of them. See if you can name two ways they are the same. (Call on individual children. Have the group repeat each correct answer. Then say:) You told me how scissors and a knife are . . . (Signal.) *the same.*
3. Listen: Scissors and a knife. Think of them. See if you can name two ways they are different. (Call on individual children. Have the group repeat each correct answer. Then say:) You told me how scissors and a knife are . . . (Signal.) *different.*
4. Here's another one. Listen: A pencil and chalk. Think of them. See if you can name two ways they are the same. (Call on individual children. Have the group repeat each correct answer. Then say:) You told me how a pencil and chalk are . . . (Signal.) *the same.*

5. Listen: A pencil and chalk. Think of them. See if you can name two ways they are different. (Call on individual children. Have the group repeat each correct answer. Then say:) You told me how a pencil and chalk are . . . (Signal.) *different.*

EXERCISE 7 Classification

1. We're going to talk about classes.
2. The class of writing tools is made up of many kinds of writing tools. I'll name some kinds of writing tools in the class of writing tools. Listen: crayons, pencils, pens, chalk. You name some kinds of tools in the class of writing tools. (Call on individual children. Praise reasonable answers.)
3. If we took all writing tools from the class of tools, would there be any kinds of tools left? (Signal.) *Yes.*
4. Name some kinds of tools that would be left. (Call on individual children. Praise appropriate responses.)
5. Think about this. If we took all the crayons from the class of writing tools, would there be any writing tools left? (Signal.) *Yes.*
6. Name some kinds of writing tools that would be left. (Call on individual children. Praise all acceptable answers: that is, any kind of writing tool except crayons.)
7. Yes, if we took all the crayons from the class of writing tools, there would still be writing tools left. So which class is bigger, the class of crayons or the class of writing tools? (Signal.) *The class of writing tools.*
8. Tell me how you know. Get ready. (Signal.) *The class of writing tools has more kinds of things in it.*
• (Repeat until firm.)
9. Think big. Tell me which class is bigger, the class of writing tools or the class of tools. (Pause.) Get ready. (Signal.) *The class of tools.*
10. Think big. Tell me which class is bigger, the class of crayons or the class of writing tools. (Pause.) Get ready. (Signal.) *The class of writing tools.*

EXERCISE 8 Absurdity

1. Listen to this story and tell me what's absurd about it.
2. A girl rode a chair to the dentist's office.
• What did the girl ride to the dentist's office? (Signal.) *A chair.*

3. Then the dentist brushed her teeth with a carrot.
• What did the dentist do to the girl? (Signal.) *Brushed her teeth with a carrot.*
4. Now tell me some things that are absurd about that story. (Call on individual children. Praise all appropriate responses.)

EXERCISE 9 Sweetie And The Mirror

Review

1. I'm going to read you the story about **Sweetie and the Mirror** again. Then we're going to act it out.

One day the woman who owned Sweetie took him to somebody's house. When Sweetie started wandering around the house, he saw something that he had never seen before: a mirror. That mirror was on a door, and the mirror went all the way to the floor.

Sweetie had never seen a mirror that close to the floor. And he didn't even know that it was a mirror.

To him, it just looked like part of the room. But there was something in that room that made Sweetie very, very upset. He saw a cat standing there. Sweetie said, "What is that ugly yellow cat doing here?"

Sweetie decided to show that cat that **he** was the boss. So Sweetie arched his back. And that other yellow cat arched its back at the same time.

Then Sweetie made the meanest face he could make. That other yellow cat made a mean face at the same time Sweetie did.

Sweetie said, "I'll show this cat who is boss."

Sweetie crouched down and moved toward the other yellow cat. The other yellow cat did the same thing.

Sweetie held up his left paw and showed how long and sharp his claws were. The yellow cat did the same thing, except with its right paw.

Sweetie said to himself, "That cat is ugly, but it has to be the fastest cat I ever saw. When I do something, it seems to do the same thing at the same time I do it."

Then Sweetie said to himself, "It's time to teach this cat a lesson." So he crouched down, leaped at that yellow cat and . . .

2. That's all there is to the story. Raise your hand if you remember the good ending for this story. Remember, Sweetie gets fooled and then he always says something at the end of these stories.

• Tell what happened when Sweetie jumped. Then tell what Sweetie **thought** happened and what Sweetie said at the end of the story.

• (Call on several children. Praise ideas such as: *Sweetie bonked himself on the mirror. Then Sweetie said something like, "That yellow cat may be ugly, but he sure can hit hard and fast."*)

3. So here's our ending to the story:

Sweetie crouched down and leaped at the yellow cat. Bonk. Sweetie banged his head against the mirror and went flying. He rolled around on the floor and finally sat up and looked at the cat in the mirror. Sweetie said to himself, "That sure is an ugly cat, but let me tell you, that cat is fast and that cat can really hit hard."

EXERCISE 10 Putting On a Play

Sweetie And The Mirror

1. Let's see if we have two children who can act out that story about Sweetie. One child will play Sweetie. The other child will play the cat in the mirror.

• (Call on two children. Tell one:) You're Sweetie.
(Tell the other:) You're the cat in the mirror.
(Have children face each other about 10 feet apart.)

2. Okay, I'll tell each part of the story. Then I'll tell our cats to act out that part.

Sweetie saw the cat in the mirror. Sweetie arched his back. And the cat in the mirror did the same thing.

• Go cats. ✔

Next Sweetie made the meanest face he could make. And the cat in the mirror did the same thing.

• Go cats. ✔

Next Sweetie crouched down and moved toward the yellow cat, closer, closer, closer. And the cat in the mirror did the same thing.

• Go cats. ✔

Now Sweetie held up his **left** paw and showed his claws. And the cat in the mirror held up its **right** paw, the same way.

• Remember, Sweetie, your **left** paw. Go cats. ✔

Next Sweetie crouched down and leaped at the yellow cat and went sprawling.

• Cats, be careful and don't **really** bang into each other. Go. ✔

Now Sweetie is completely fooled by the mirror and he says something to himself.

• Say it, Sweetie.
(Idea: *That sure is an ugly-looking cat, but let me tell you, that cat is fast and that cat can really hit hard.*)

3. That was good acting.

EXERCISE 11 Story Details

1. Everybody, open your workbook to Lesson 79. Write your name at the top of the page. ✔
2. Touch Sweetie. ✔
- What is Sweetie doing? (Call on a child. Ideas: *Lying on his back; lying on the floor.*)
- What took place just **before** this picture? (Call on a child. Idea: *Sweetie bonked his head on the mirror.*) Yes, that's why Sweetie is on the floor. He bonked his head on the mirror.
- Right **after** this picture, Sweetie is going to say something to himself. What will he say to himself? (Call on a child. Idea: *That sure is an ugly-looking cat, but let me tell you, that cat is fast and that cat can really hit hard.*)
3. Later you can color the picture.

LESSON 80

Objectives

- Construct verbal analogies. (Exercise 1)
- Identify an object based on its characteristics. (Exercise 2)
- Given a calendar, identify the day and date for "today" and "tomorrow" and one week from today. (Exercise 3)
- **Name common synonyms.** (Exercise 4)
- Identify absurdities involving materials. (Exercise 5)
- **Identify absurdities involving condition.** (Exercise 6)
- **Write rhyming sentences given picture cues.** (Exercise 7)
- Follow coloring rules involving classes and subclasses. (Exercise 8)
- Construct verbal analogies. (Exercise 9)

EXERCISE 1 Analogies

1. We're going to make up **two** analogies.
- We're going to make up analogies about a monkey and a barn. Which objects? (Signal.) *A monkey and a barn.*
2. The first analogy tells where you find the objects.
- Where do you find a monkey? (Call on a child. Accept all reasonable answers, but use: *in the jungle.*)
- Where do you find a barn? (Call on a child. Accept all reasonable answers, but use: *on the farm.*)
3. A monkey is to the jungle as a barn is to . . . (Signal.) *the farm.*
- Say that analogy about a monkey and a barn. Get ready. (Signal.) *A monkey is to the jungle as a barn is to the farm.*
4. Listen: A monkey is to the jungle as a barn is to the farm. Does that analogy tell what parts the objects have? (Signal.) *No.*
5. Listen: A monkey is to the jungle as a barn is to the farm. Does that analogy tell what class the objects are in? (Signal.) *No.*
6. Listen: A monkey is to the jungle as a barn is to the farm. Does that analogy tell where you find the objects? (Signal.) *Yes.*
7. (Repeat steps 4 through 6 until firm.)
8. We made up an analogy that tells where you find the objects. The next analogy tells what class the objects are in.

- What class is a monkey in? (Call on a child. Accept all reasonable answers, but use: *Animals.*)
- What class is a barn in? (Call on a child. Accept all reasonable answers, but use: *Buildings.*)
9. A monkey is to animals as a barn is to . . . (Signal.) *buildings.*
- Say that analogy about a monkey and a barn. Get ready. (Signal.) *A monkey is to animals as a barn is to buildings.*
10. We made up an analogy that tells where you find the objects. Then we made up an analogy that tells what class the objects are in. Let's see if you can say both those analogies.
11. Think. Say the analogy that tells where you find the objects. (Pause.) Get ready. (Signal.) *A monkey is to the jungle as a barn is to the farm.*
- Think. Say the analogy that tells what class the objects are in. (Pause.) Get ready. (Signal.) *A monkey is to animals as a barn is to buildings.*
12. (Repeat step 11 until firm.)

EXERCISE 2 Description

1. I'm going to tell you about an object you know. But I'm going to call it a funny name. See if you can figure out what object I'm talking about.

2. (Hold up one finger.)
A frip is a person. Say that. (Signal.) *A frip is a person.*
- (Hold up two fingers.) A frip uses building tools. Say that. (Signal.) *A frip uses building tools.*
- (Hold up three fingers.) A frip builds houses. Say that. (Signal.) *A frip builds houses.*
3. Everybody, say all the things you know about a frip. Get ready.
- (Hold up one finger.) *A frip is a person.*
- (Hold up two fingers.) *A frip uses building tools.*
- (Hold up three fingers.) *A frip builds houses.*
4. (Repeat steps 2 and 3 until firm.)
5. Everybody, tell me what kind of person I am calling a frip. (Pause.) Get ready. (Signal.) *A carpenter.*
6. How do you know a frip is a carpenter? (Call on a child. Idea: *It's a person; it uses building tools; it builds houses.*)
7. How would you like to have a frip build your house? (Children respond.)

EXERCISE 3 Calendar

1. (Present calendar.)
- We're going to talk about today, tomorrow, and one week from today.
2. Tell me the day of the week it is today. Get ready. (Signal.)
- Tell me the day of the week it will be tomorrow. Get ready. (Signal.)
- Tell me the day of the week it will be one week from today. Get ready. (Signal.)
3. (Repeat step 2 until firm.)
4. Now the dates.
- Tell me today's date. Get ready. (Signal.)
- Look at the calendar. ✔
- Tell me the date it will be one week from today. Get ready. (Signal.)
5. Once more.
- Listen: Tell me today's date. Get ready. (Signal.)
- Tell me tomorrow's date. Get ready. (Signal.)
- Tell me the date it will be one week from today. Get ready. (Signal.)
6. (Repeat step 5 until firm.)

EXERCISE 4 Synonyms

1. I'll say some synonyms.
2. Listen: big. A synonym of big is large. What's a synonym of big? (Signal.) *Large.*
3. Listen: small. A synonym of small is little. What's a synonym of small? (Signal.) *Little.*
4. Everybody, let's play a synonym game. I'll say a word. You say a word that means the same thing.
5. Listen: Tell me a synonym for thin. Get ready. (Signal.) *Skinny.*
- Listen: Tell me a synonym for shut. Get ready. (Signal.) *Close.*
- Listen: Tell me a synonym for large. Get ready. (Signal.) *Big.*
- Listen: Tell me a synonym for little. Get ready. (Signal.) *Small.*
6. (Repeat step 5 until firm.)

EXERCISE 5 Materials

1. Are some doors made of paper? (Signal.) *No.*
- What's absurd about a door that is made of paper? (Call on individual children. Praise good answers, such as: *It would tear. It wouldn't keep the wind and rain out.*)
2. Are some doors made of wood? (Signal.) *Yes.*
- Why can wood be used to make doors? (Call on individual children. Praise good answers, such as: *It is strong. It will keep out the wind and the rain.*)

EXERCISE 6 Absurdity

1. Listen to this statement and figure out what is absurd about it: A car that was out of gas drove up the hill.
- Say the statement. Get ready. (Signal.) *A car that was out of gas drove up the hill.*
- What's absurd about that statement? (Call on a child. Praise all reasonable responses, then say:) Yes, a car that's out of gas can't drive up a hill.
2. Here's another absurd statement. Figure out what's absurd about this one. Listen: A boy was three years older than his mother.
- Say the statement. Get ready. (Signal.) *A boy was three years older than his mother.*
- What's absurd about that statement? (Call on a child. Praise all reasonable responses; then say:) Yes, a boy can't be older than his mother.

EXERCISE 7 Sentence Writing

| cone | the | fox |

The _____

_____

_____

_____

1. Everybody, open your workbook to Lesson 80. Write your name at the top of the page. ✔
• You're going to write sentences that rhyme.
• Touch the picture of the fox and the ram. ✔
• The fox had a bone. The ram had something that rhymes with **bone.** What did the ram have? (Signal.) *A cone.*
   Yes, **the ram had a cone.**
2. Say the sentence for the ram. Get ready. (Signal.) *The ram had a cone.*
• Say the sentence for the fox. Get ready. (Signal.) *The fox had a bone.*
3. (Repeat step 2 until firm.)
4. The word box above the picture shows how to spell the words **cone, the** and **fox.** You can figure out how to spell the other words.
5. Write the sentence for the fox. Remember to start with a capital and end with a period. The first word is already written for you with a capital **T.** Pencils down when you're finished.
   (Observe children and give feedback.)
• Now go to the next line and write the sentence for the ram. Pencils down when you're finished.
   (Observe children and give feedback.)
6. (Call on individual children to read both their sentences.)

EXERCISE 8 Classification

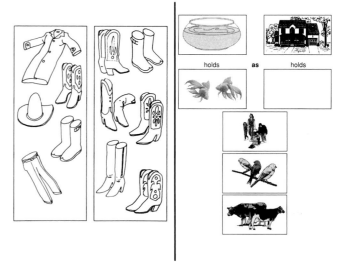

1. Everybody, find the next page in your workbook. ✔
• (Hold up workbook. Point to first half.)
2. Touch the picture that shows only **one** kind of thing. ✔
• What kind of thing is that in the picture? (Signal.) *Boots.*
3. Touch the picture that shows **more** than one kind of thing. ✔
• Raise your hand if you can figure out the name of the class shown in that picture. ✔
• Everybody, what's the name of that class? (Signal.) *Clothing.*
4. Listen: The class that is larger is the class that has **more** kinds of things. What does the class that is **larger** have? (Signal.) *More kinds of things.*
5. Everybody, circle the class that is **larger.** ✔
• Everybody, touch the picture of the class that is **smaller.** ✔
• How many kinds of things are in the class that is **smaller?** (Signal.) *One.*
6. The boots in that picture of the **smaller** class should be brown and yellow. What colors? (Signal.) *Brown and yellow.*
• Mark a boot in that picture. ✔
7. Touch the picture that shows the **larger** class. ✔
• The boots in the picture of the **larger** class should be black and red. What colors? (Signal.) *Black and red.*
• Mark a boot in that picture. ✔

EXERCISE 9 Analogies

1. (Hold up workbook. Point to second half.)
- The pictures show something and what it holds.
2. Touch the fishbowl. ✔
- The picture that's right below shows what it holds. Everybody, what does a fishbowl hold? (Signal.) *Fish.*
3. Touch the house. ✔
- One of the pictures below shows what it holds. Touch the picture that shows what a house holds. ✔
- Everybody, what does a house hold? (Signal.) *People.*

4. Tell me about a fishbowl. Get ready. (Signal.) *A fishbowl holds fish.*
- Tell me about a house. Get ready. (Signal.) *A house holds people.*
5. Say the whole analogy about a fishbowl and a house. Get ready. (Signal.) *A fishbowl holds fish as a house holds people.*
6. (Repeat step 5 until firm.)
7. Draw a line from the house to what it holds.
- (Observe children and give feedback.)

Objectives

- Identify an object based on its characteristics. (Exercises 1 & 7)
- Construct verbal analogies. (Exercise 2)
- Identify absurdities of use. (Exercise 3)
- Given a calendar, identify the day and date for "today" and "tomorrow" and one week from today. (Exercise 4)
- Generate statements involving "can do" and "cannot do." (Exercise 5)
- Replace a word in a sentence with a synonym. (Exercise 6)
- Write rhyming sentences given picture cues. (Exercise 8)
- Name members of a class and subclass and identify the bigger class. (Exercise 9)
- Construct verbal analogies. (Exercise 10)

EXERCISE 1   **Description**

1. I'm going to tell you about an object you know. But I'm going to call it a funny name. See if you can figure out what object I'm talking about.
2. (Hold up one finger.) You find a crench on a farm. Say that. (Signal.) *You find a crench on a farm.*
- (Hold up two fingers.) A crench is a vehicle. Say that. (Signal.) *A crench is a vehicle.*
- (Hold up three fingers.) You use a crench to plow fields. Say that. (Signal.) *You use a crench to plow fields.*
3. Everybody, say all the things you know about a crench. Get ready.
- (Hold up one finger.) *You find a crench on a farm.*
- (Hold up two fingers.) *A crench is a vehicle.*
- (Hold up three fingers.) *You use a crench to plow fields.*
4. (Repeat steps 2 and 3 until firm.)
5. Everybody, what kind of object am I calling a crench? (Pause.) (Signal.) *A tractor.*
6. How do you know a crench is a tractor? (Call on a child. Idea: *You find it on a farm. It's a vehicle. You use it to plow fields.*)
7. How would you like to ride a crench to school? (Children respond.)

EXERCISE 2   **Analogies**

1. We're going to make up **two** analogies.
- We're going to make up analogies about a bed and milk. Which objects? (Signal.) *A bed and milk.*

2. The first analogy tells what you do with the objects.
- What do you do with a bed? (Call on a child. Accept all reasonable answers, but use: *sleep in it.*)
- What do you do with milk? (Call on a child. Accept all reasonable answers, but use: *drink it.*)
3. A bed is to sleeping in as milk is to . . . (Signal.) *drinking.*
- Say that analogy about a bed and milk. Get ready. (Signal.) *A bed is to sleeping in as milk is to drinking.*
4. Listen: A bed is to sleeping in as milk is to drinking. Does that analogy tell what you do with the objects? (Signal.) *Yes.*
5. Listen: A bed is to sleeping in as milk is to drinking. Does that analogy tell what parts the objects have? (Signal.) *No.*
6. Listen: A bed is to sleeping in as milk is to drinking. Does that analogy tell where you find the objects? (Signal.) *No.*
7. (Repeat steps 4 through 6 until firm.)
8. We made up an analogy that tells what you do with the objects. The next analogy tells what class the objects are in.
- What class is a bed in? (Call on a child. Accept all reasonable answers, but use: *furniture.*)
- What class is milk in? (Call on a child. Accept all reasonable answers, but use: *food.*)
9. A bed is to furniture as milk is to . . . (Signal.) *food.*
- Say that analogy about a bed and milk. Get ready. (Signal.) *A bed is to furniture as milk is to food.*

10. We made up an analogy that tells what you do with the objects. Then we made up an analogy that tells what class the objects are in. Let's see if you can say both those analogies.

11. Think. Say the analogy that tells what you do with the objects. (Pause.) Get ready. (Signal.) *A bed is to sleeping in as milk is to drinking.*

• Think. Say the analogy that tells what class the objects are in. (Pause.) Get ready. (Signal.) *A bed is to furniture as milk is to food.*

12. (Repeat step 11 until firm.)

EXERCISE 3 Absurdity

1. Figure out what's wrong with the story. There was a woman. She wanted to wash the dishes, so she got out the broom.

• Tell me what's wrong with that story. (Call on a child. Praise all reasonable responses.)

2. Here's another story. Figure out what's wrong with this one. There was a man. He went for a walk in the rain. He wore a bathing suit so that he wouldn't get wet.

• Tell me what's wrong with that story. (Call on a child. Praise reasonable responses.)

3. Let's figure out what should have happened.

• What should the woman have used to wash the dishes? (Call on several children. Accept all reasonable responses.)

• What should the man have used to keep dry? (Call on several children. Accept all reasonable responses.)

EXERCISE 4 Calendar

1. (Present calendar.)

• We're going to talk about today, tomorrow, and one week from today.

2. Tell me the day of the week it is today. Get ready. (Signal.)

• Tell me the day of the week it will be tomorrow. Get ready. (Signal.)

• Tell me the day of the week it will be one week from today. Get ready. (Signal.)

3. (Repeat step 2 until firm.)

4. Now the dates.

• Tell me today's date. Get ready. (Signal.)

• Look at the calendar. ✔

• Tell me the date it will be one week from today. Get ready. (Signal.)

5. Once more.

• Listen: Tell me today's date. Get ready. (Signal.)

• Tell me tomorrow's date. Get ready. (Signal.)

• Tell me the date it will be one week from today. Get ready. (Signal.)

6. (Repeat step 5 until firm.)

EXERCISE 5 Can Do

1. I'm going to ask questions about a boy and a suitcase.

2. Everybody, can a boy drop a suitcase? (Signal.) *Yes.*

• Say the statement. Get ready. (Signal.) *A boy can drop a suitcase.*

3. Everybody, can a boy swim in a suitcase? (Signal.) *No.*

• Say the statement. Get ready. (Signal.) *A boy cannot swim in a suitcase.*

4. (Call on one child.)

• Your turn. Make up another statement that tells something a boy can do with a suitcase. (After the child makes the statement, call on the group.) Say that statement about what a boy can do with a suitcase. Get ready. (Signal.) (The group repeats the child's statement.)

5. (Call on another child.)

• Your turn. Make up a statement that tells something a boy cannot do with a suitcase. (After the child makes the statement, call on the group.) Say that statement about what a boy cannot do with a suitcase. Get ready. (Signal.) (The group repeats the child's statement.)

EXERCISE 6 Synonyms

1. I'll say some synonyms.

2. Listen: yell. A synonym of yell is shout. What's a synonym of yell? (Signal.) *Shout.*

3. Listen: above. A synonym of above is over. What's a synonym of above? (Signal.) *Over.*

4. Let's use synonyms to make up statements that mean the same thing as other statements.

5. Listen: The wagon is big. Say that. (Signal.) *The wagon is big.*

- Say the statement that has a synonym for big. Get ready. (Signal.) *The wagon is large.*
6. Listen: Tell me a synonym for the word under. Get ready. (Signal.) *Below.*
- Listen: The dog was under the table. Say the statement that has a synonym for under. Get ready. (Signal.) *The dog was below the table.*
7. Listen: Tell me a synonym for the word shout. Get ready. (Signal.) *Yell.*
- Tell me another way of saying she shouted at the dog. Get ready. (Signal.) *She yelled at the dog.*

EXERCISE 7   Description

1. I'm going to tell you about an object you know. But I'm going to call it a funny name. See if you can figure out what object I'm talking about.
2. (Hold up one finger.)
- A mool is a person. Say that. (Signal.) *A mool is a person.*
- (Hold up two fingers.)
- A mool rides in a big truck. Say that. (Signal.) *A mool rides in a big truck.*
- (Hold up three fingers.)
- A mool puts out fires. Say that. (Signal.) *A mool puts out fires.*
3. Everybody, say all the things you know about a mool. Get ready.
- (Hold up one finger.) *A mool is a person.*
- (Hold up two fingers.) *A mool rides in a big truck.*
- (Hold up three fingers.) *A mool puts out fires.*
4. (Repeat steps 2 and 3 until firm.)
5. Everybody, what kind of person am I calling a mool? (Pause.) (Signal.) *A firefighter.*
6. How do you know a mool is a firefighter? (Call on a child. Idea: *It's a person. It rides in a big truck. It puts out fires.*)
7. How would you like to have a mool give you a ride to school? (Children respond.)

EXERCISE 8   Sentence Writing

cake   fox

_____
_____
_____
_____

1. Everybody, open your workbook to Lesson 81. Write your name at the top of the page. ✔
- You're going to write sentences that rhyme.
- Touch the picture of the fox and the ram. ✔
- The picture shows what the fox and the ram had. What did the fox have? (Signal.) *A cake.*
- Yes, **the fox had a cake.**
- What did the ram have? (Signal.) *A rake.* Yes, **the ram had a rake.**
2. Say the sentence for the fox. Get ready. (Signal.) *The fox had a cake.*
- Say the sentence for the ram. Get ready. (Signal.) *The ram had a rake.*
3. (Repeat step 2 until firm.)
4. The word box shows how to spell the words **cake** and **fox.** You can figure out how to spell the other words.
5. Write the sentence for the fox. Remember to start with a capital and end with a period. Pencils down when you're finished. (Observe children and give feedback.)
6. (Call on individual children to read both their sentences.)

EXERCISE 9   Classification

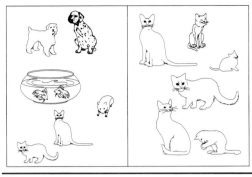

1. Everybody, find the next page in your workbook. ✔
• (Hold up workbook. Point to first half.)
2. Touch the picture that shows only **one** kind of thing. ✔
• What kind of thing is that in the picture? (Signal.) *Cats.*
3. Touch the picture that shows **more** than one kind of thing. ✔
• Raise your hand if you can figure out the name of the class shown in that picture. ✔
• Everybody, what's the name of that class? (Signal.) *Pets.* Yes, pets.
4. (Repeat step 3 until firm.)
5. Listen: The class that is larger is the class that has **more** kinds of things. What does the class that is **larger** have? (Signal.) *More kinds of things.*
6. Everybody, circle the class that is **larger.** ✔
• Everybody, touch the picture of the class that is **smaller.** ✔
• How many kinds of things are in the class that is **smaller?** (Signal.) *One.*

7. The cats in the picture of the **smaller** class should be yellow. What color? (Signal.) *Yellow.*
• Mark a cat in that picture. ✔
8. Touch the picture that shows the **larger** class. The cats in the picture of the **larger** class should be brown and orange. What colors? (Signal.) *Brown and orange.*
• Mark a cat in that picture. ✔

EXERCISE 10   Analogies

1. (Hold up workbook. Point to second half.)
• These pictures show something and what it holds.
2. Touch the purse. ✔
• The picture that's right below shows what it holds. Everybody, what does a purse hold? (Signal.) *Money.*
• Tell me about a purse. Get ready. (Signal.) *A purse holds money.*
3. Touch the lake. ✔
• One of the pictures below shows what it holds. Touch the picture that shows what a lake holds. ✔
• Everybody, what does a lake hold? (Signal.) *Fish.*
• Tell me about a lake. Get ready. (Signal.) *A lake holds fish.*
4. Tell me about a purse. Get ready. (Signal.) *A purse holds money.*
• Tell me about a lake. Get ready. (Signal.) *A lake holds fish.*
5. Say the whole analogy about a purse and a lake. Get ready. (Signal.) *A purse holds money as a lake holds fish.*
6. (Repeat step 5 until firm.)
7. Draw a line from the lake to what it holds. (Observe children and give feedback.)

Objectives

- **Identify the relationship between the components of an analogy. (Exercises 1 & 5)**
- Given a calendar, identify the day and date for "today" and "tomorrow" and one week from today. (Exercise 2)
- Identify cardinal directions. (Exercise 3)
- Identify an object based on its characteristics. (Exercise 4)
- Answer questions about a familiar story. (Exercise 6)
- **Use clues to eliminate members of a familiar class. (Exercise 7)**

EXERCISE 1   Analogies

1. You're going to figure out what an analogy is about.
2. Listen to this: A boat is to water as an airplane is to . . . (Signal.) *air.*
3. What class are a boat and an airplane in? (Signal.) *Vehicles.*
- Yes, vehicles. Our analogy tells something about vehicles.
4. A boat is to water as an airplane is to air.
- Does our analogy tell where you find the vehicles? (Signal.) *Yes.*
- Does our analogy tell what parts they have? (Signal.) *No.*
- Does our analogy tell what they are made of? (Signal.) *No.*
- Does our analogy tell what color they are? (Signal.) *No.*
- Our analogy tells where you find them.
- (Repeat step 4 until firm.)
5. Where do you find a boat? (Signal.) *In water.*
- Say the **first** part of the analogy. Get ready. (Signal.) *A boat is to water.*
6. Where do you find an airplane? (Signal.) *In air.*
- Say the **next** part of the analogy. Get ready. (Signal.) *An airplane is to air.*
7. Tell me what the analogy tells about the vehicles. Get ready. (Signal.) *Where you find them.*
8. Everybody, say the whole analogy. Get ready. (Signal.) *A boat is to water as an airplane is to air.*
9. (Repeat steps 7 and 8 until firm.)

EXERCISE 2   Calendar

1. (Present calendar.)
- We're going to talk about today, tomorrow, and one week from today.
2. Tell me the day of the week it is today. Get ready. (Signal.)
- Tell me the day of the week it will be tomorrow. Get ready. (Signal.)
- Tell me the day of the week it will be one week from today. Get ready. (Signal.)
3. (Repeat step 2 until firm.)
4. Now the dates.
- Tell me today's date. Get ready. (Signal.)
- Look at the calendar. ✔
- Tell me the date it will be one week from today. Get ready. (Signal.)
5. Once more.
- Listen: Tell me today's date. Get ready. (Signal.)
- Tell me tomorrow's date. Get ready. (Signal.)
- Tell me the date it will be one week from today. Get ready. (Signal.)
6. (Repeat step 5 until firm.)

EXERCISE 3   Map Reading

Note: Have the directions cards in place.

1. Everybody, stand up. ✔

2. You're going to face north. (Pause.) Get ready. (Signal.) (The children face north.)
- What are you doing? (Signal.) *Facing north.*
- Say the statement. Get ready. (Signal.) *I am facing north.*
3. Everybody, you're going to face east. (Pause.) Get ready. (Signal.) (The children face east.)
- What are you doing? (Signal.) *Facing east.*
- Say the statement. Get ready. (Signal.) *I am facing east.*
4. Everybody, you're going to face west. (Pause.) Get ready. (Signal.) (The children face west.)
- What are you doing? (Signal.) *Facing west.*
- Say the statement. Get ready. (Signal.) *I am facing west.*
5. (Repeat steps 2 through 4 until firm.)
6. (Point south.) Tell me the direction I'm pointing. (Pause.) Get ready. (Signal.) *South.*
- Say the statement. Get ready. (Signal.) *You are pointing south.*
7. (Point east.) Tell me the direction I'm pointing. (Pause.) Get ready. (Signal.) *East.*
- Say the statement. Get ready. (Signal.) *You are pointing east.*
8. (Repeat steps 6 and 7 until firm.)

EXERCISE 4 Description

1. I'm going to tell you about an object you know. But I'm going to call it a funny name. See if you can figure out what object I'm talking about.
2. (Hold up one finger.)
   A fribble is a person. Say that. (Signal.) *A fribble is a person.*
- (Hold up two fingers.)
- A fribble works in a school. Say that. (Signal.) *A fribble works in a school.*
- (Hold up three fingers.)
- A fribble works in a library. Say that. (Signal.) *A fribble works in a library.*
3. Everybody, say all the things you know about a fribble. Get ready.
- (Hold up one finger.) *A fribble is a person.*
- (Hold up two fingers.) *A fribble works in a school.*
- (Hold up three fingers.) *A fribble works in a library.*
4. (Repeat steps 2 and 3 until firm.)

5. Everybody, what kind of person am I calling a fribble? (Pause.) (Signal.) *A librarian.*
6. I couldn't fool you. It's really a librarian. How do you know a fribble is a librarian? (Call on a child. Idea: *It's a person; it works in a school; it works in a library.*)
7. How would you like to see a fribble throwing a book to a dog? (Children respond.)

EXERCISE 5 Analogies

1. You're going to figure out what an analogy is about.
2. Listen to this: A frog is to ribbiting as a cat is to . . . (Signal.) *meowing.*
3. What class are a frog and a cat in? (Signal.) *Animals.*
- Yes, animals. Our analogy tells something about animals.
4. A frog is to ribbiting as a cat is to meowing.
- Does our analogy tell what parts the animals have? (Signal.) *No.*
- Does our analogy tell where you find them? (Signal.) *No.*
- Does our analogy tell what they say? (Signal.) *Yes.*
- Does our analogy tell how they move? (Signal.) *No.*
- Our analogy tells what they say.
- (Repeat step 4 until firm.)
5. Say the first part of the analogy. Get ready. (Signal.) *A frog is to ribbiting.*
6. Say the next part of the analogy. Get ready. (Signal.) *A cat is to meowing.*
7. Tell me what the analogy tells about the animals. Get ready. (Signal.) *What they say.* Yes, what they say.
8. Everybody, say the whole analogy. Get ready. (Signal.) *A frog is to ribbiting as a cat is to meowing.*
9. (Repeat step 7 and 8 until firm.)

EXERCISE 6   The Bragging Rats Race

Story Review

- Everybody, let's see how well you remember the story about the bragging rats. I'll stop when I'm reading the story. See if you can tell me what happens next in the story.

    A bunch of rats lived near a pond that was on a farm. The rats got along well, except for two of them.

- Everybody, what did the other rats call these two rats? (Signal.) *The bragging rats.*
- Who remembers why the other rats called them the bragging rats? (Call on a child. Idea: *The two rats were always bragging, quarreling and arguing about something.*)
- Let's see if you are right.

    The other rats called these two the bragging rats because they were always bragging, quarreling and arguing about something.

    One day they'd argue about who could eat the most. Another day they'd squabble and quarrel over who was the best looking. Neither one of them was very good looking.

- Why weren't these rats very good looking? (Call on a child. Idea: *One rat had the longest tail you've ever seen on a rat; the other had the biggest, yellowest teeth.*)
- Let's see if you are right.

    One rat was a big gray rat with the longest tail you've ever seen on a rat. The other one wasn't big, but he had the biggest, yellowest teeth you ever saw.

    The other rats in the bunch didn't pay much attention to the bragging and quarreling until the two rats started bragging about . . . something.

- What was that? (Call on a child. Idea: *Who was the fastest rat in the whole bunch.*)
- Everybody, how long did this argument go on? (Signal.) *For days.*
- Let's see if you are right.

    This quarrel went on for days, and the other rats got pretty sick of listening to the rats shout and yell and brag about how fast they were.

    On the third day of their quarrel, they almost got into a fight. The rat with the yellow teeth was saying, "I'm so fast that I could run circles around you while you ran as fast as you could."

- Listen: What did the big gray rat say to that? (Call on a child. Idea: *That he could run circles around the other rat's circles.*)
- Let's see if you are right.

    The big gray rat said, "Oh, yeah? Well, I could run circles around your circles. That's how fast I am."

    The two rats continued yelling at each other until somebody had a plan to stop the arguing.

- Everybody, who was that? (Signal.) *The wise old rat.*
- What was the wise old rat's plan? (Call on a child. Idea: *To have a race.*)
- Let's see if you are right.

    The two rats continued yelling at each other until a wise old rat said, "Stop! We are tired of listening to all this shouting and yelling and bragging. There is a way to find out who is the fastest rat on this farm."

    The wise old rat continued, "We will have a race for any rat that wants to race. Everybody will line up . . ."

- Who remembers where the rats are supposed to run in this race? (Call on a child. Idea: *To the pond and back.*)
- Let's see if you are right.

Here's what the wise old rat said:

"Everybody will line up, run down the path to the pond, then run back. The first rat to get back is the winner. And then we'll have no more arguing about which rat can run the fastest."

The rats agreed, and early the next morning they were lined up, ready for the big race.

- Everybody, how many rats were in this race? (Signal.) *Six.*
- How many rats didn't **finish** the race? (Signal.) *Two.*
- Why didn't those rats **finish** the race? (Call on a child. Idea: *They tumbled into the pond.*)
- Everybody, who ended up winning the race? (Signal.) *A little black rat.*
- Let's see if you are right.

Six rats entered the race. The bragging rats were lined up right next to each other, making mean faces and mumbling about how fast they were going to run.

The rats put their noses close to the ground, ready to take off like a flash.

"Everybody, steady," the wise old rat said. "Everybody, ready. Go!"

The rats took off toward the pond. The big gray rat got ahead of the others, with the yellow-toothed rat right behind him. But just before they got to the pond, the yellow-toothed rat stepped on the long tail of the gray rat, and both rats tumbled over and over in a cloud of dust. They tumbled down the dusty path and right into the pond.

The other rats finished the race. The winner was a little black rat. It was hard for her to finish the race because she was laughing so hard over the bragging rats, who were still splashing and sputtering around in the pond.

After the race, all the other rats went back to the pond. The bragging rats were still splashing and sputtering. The wise old rat said to them, "So now we know who the fastest runner on this farm is. It's neither one of you, so we will have no more arguments from either of you about who can run the fastest!"

- But did the rats stop arguing? (Signal.) *No.*
- What did they argue about next? (Call on a child. Idea: *Who was the fastest swimmer.*)
- Let's see if you are right.

The bragging rats looked at each other. Then the rat with yellow teeth suddenly smiled and said, "I may not be the fastest **runner** in this bunch, but there is no rat in the world that can **swim** as fast as I can."

"Oh, yeah?" said the gray rat. "I can swim so fast that I could go all the way across the pond without even getting my fur wet."

The wise old rat and the other rats just walked away from the pond, slowly shaking their heads.

- What do you think the bragging rats were doing while the others walked away? (Call on a child. Idea: *Bragging and arguing.*)
- Why were the others shaking their heads? (Call on a child. Idea: *Because the bragging rats were still arguing.*)
- The race didn't really settle anything, did it? Those bragging rats just seem to brag about anything.

EXERCISE 7 Classification

A.

1. Everybody, open your workbook to Lesson 82. Write your name at the top of the page. ✔
• All the things are in the **same** class. Everybody, what class is that? (Signal.) *Vehicles.*
2. Touch the top picture. ✔
Everybody, what kind of vehicle is that? (Signal.) *A rowboat.*
• Touch the next picture. ✔
What vehicle? (Signal.) *A car.*
• Touch the next picture. ✔
What vehicle? (Signal.) *A bicycle.*
• Touch the next picture. ✔
What vehicle? (Signal.) *A bus.*
• Touch the next picture. ✔
What vehicle? (Signal.) *A train.*
• Touch the next picture. ✔
What vehicle? (Signal.) *A motorcycle.*
3. Who can start at the top and name all the vehicles? (Call on several children. Praise children who name all the vehicles in order.)
4. You're going to make a flap out of each vehicle. Listen carefully: Cut along the dotted lines. Stop cutting at the end of each dotted line and don't cut anywhere except on a dotted line. Then each of your vehicles will be a flap. Remember, just cut along the dotted lines. Raise your hand when you're finished.
(Observe children and give feedback.)

5. You're going to play a mystery game. It's a very hard game. Here's how it works: I'll tell you clues about the mystery vehicle. After each clue, you'll be able to fold over some pictures that could **not** be the mystery vehicle. After I give you the last clue, you'll know which vehicle is the mystery vehicle because it will be the **only** picture that is **not** folded over. Does that game sound pretty tough?
6. Here's the first clue about the mystery vehicle: This vehicle has wheels. Everybody, say that clue. (Signal.) *This vehicle has wheels.*
• Not all the vehicles have wheels. If it does **not** have wheels, it can **not** be the mystery vehicle. So fold over any vehicle that does **not** have wheels. Just turn it over the way you would turn a page in a book. Raise your hand when you're finished.
(Observe children and give feedback.)
• Everybody, which vehicle did you fold over? (Signal.) *The rowboat.*
• Why did you fold over the rowboat? (Call on a child. Idea: *A rowboat does not have wheels.*)
7. Here's another clue about the mystery vehicle: This vehicle has windows. Everybody, say that clue. (Signal.) *This vehicle has windows.*
• Listen: If it does **not** have windows, it can **not** be the mystery vehicle, so fold over any vehicle that does **not** have windows. Raise your hand when you're finished. (Observe children and give feedback.)
• Which vehicles did you fold over? (Call on a child. Idea: *The bicycle and motorcycle.*)
• Why did you fold over the bicycle and motorcycle? (Call on a child. Idea: *A bicycle and a motorcycle do not have windows.*)
8. Here's another clue about the mystery vehicle: This vehicle can hold **more** than ten people. Everybody, say that clue. (Signal.) *This vehicle can hold more than ten people.*
• Listen: If it can **not** hold more than ten people, it can **not** be the mystery vehicle, so fold over any vehicle that can **not** hold more than ten people. Raise your hand when you're finished. (Observe children and give feedback.)

- Everybody, which vehicle did you fold over? (Signal.) *The car.*
- Why did you fold over the car? (**Call on a child.** Idea: *A car cannot hold more than ten people.*)

9. Here's the last clue about the mystery vehicle: This vehicle runs on tracks. Everybody, say that clue. (Signal.) *This vehicle runs on tracks.*
- Listen: Fold over the picture that could **not** be the mystery vehicle. ✔
- Everybody, which vehicle did you fold over? (Signal.) *The bus.*
- Why did you fold over the bus? (**Call on a child.** Idea: *A bus does not run on tracks.*)

10. You figured out which vehicle is the mystery vehicle. It should be the **only** picture that is **not** folded over. Everybody, which vehicle is the mystery vehicle? (Signal.) *The train.*

- Raise your hand if you figured out the mystery vehicle. ✔

11. I gave you four clues that let you figure out the mystery vehicle. Let's see how many of those clues you remember.
- What was one of the clues? (**Call on a child.** Accept appropriate response.)

12. What was another clue? (**Call on a child.** Accept appropriate response.) (Repeat step 12 until all clues have been identified.)

13. Who can name all four clues about the mystery vehicle? (**Call on several children.** Praise any child who can name at least three clues.)

14. You did such a good job on the mystery game that we'll play it again next time.

Objectives

- Identify the relationship between the components of an analogy. (Exercise 1)
- **Generate questions to find a word's definition.** (Exercise 2)
- Given a calendar, identify the day and date for "today" and "tomorrow" and one week from today. (Exercise 3)
- Identify cardinal directions. (Exercise 4)
- Replace a word in a sentence with a synonym and generate sentences using synonyms for given words. (Exercise 5)
- Generate statements involving "can do" and "cannot do." (Exercise 6)
- **Identify the number of days in a month** and answer questions involving previously learned calendar facts. (Exercise 7)
- Write rhyming sentences given picture cues. (Exercise 8)
- Follow coloring rules for classes and subclasses. (Exercise 9)
- Construct verbal analogies. (Exercise 10)

EXERCISE 1 Analogies

1. You're going to figure out what an analogy is about.
2. Listen to this: A bottle is to glass as a bag is to . . . (Signal.) *paper.*
3. What class are a bottle and a bag in? (Signal.) *Containers.*
- Yes, containers. Our analogy tells something about containers.
4. A bottle is to glass as a bag is to paper.
- Does our analogy tell what you put in the containers? (Signal.) *No.*
- Does our analogy tell what they are made of? (Signal.) *Yes.*
- Does our analogy tell what parts they have? (Signal.) *No.*
- Does our analogy tell what color they are? (Signal.) *No.*
- Our analogy tells what they are made of.
- (Repeat step 4 until firm.)
5. What is a bottle made of? (Signal.) *Glass.*
- Say the **first** part of the analogy. Get ready. (Signal.) *A bottle is to glass.*
6. What is a bag made of? (Signal.) *Paper.*
- Say the **next** part of the analogy. Get ready. (Signal.) *A bag is to paper.*
7. Tell me what the analogy tells about containers. Get ready. (Signal.) *What they are made of.*
8. Everybody, say the whole analogy. Get ready. (Signal.) *A bottle is to glass as a bag is to paper.*
9. (Repeat steps 7 and 8 until firm.)

EXERCISE 2 Questioning Skills

> *Note:* The children are not to memorize the words presented in this task.

1. I'll say a word and ask a question about what that word means.
2. Here's the word: **applaud.** Say that word. (Signal.) *Applaud.*
3. Here's the question: What does the word applaud mean? Now you ask me what the word applaud means. Get ready. (Signal.) *What does the word applaud mean?*
- (Repeat step 3 until everyone can ask the question.)
4. I'll tell you what applaud means. Applaud is a synonym for clap.
- Everybody, show me how you applaud. Get ready. (Signal.) (Praise the children by saying:) Good applauding.
5. Here's another word: **slumber.** Say that word. (Signal.) *Slumber.*
6. Now ask me what the word slumber means. Get ready. (Signal.) *What does the word slumber mean?*
7. I'll tell you what slumber means. Slumber is a synonym for sleep.
- Everybody, show me how you look when you're slumbering. Get ready. (Signal.) (Praise the children by saying:) You look just like you're slumbering.
8. Here's another word: **patella.** Say that word. (Signal.) *Patella.*

9. Now ask me what the word patella means. Get ready. (Signal.) *What does the word patella mean?*
10. I'll tell you what patella means. Patella is a synonym for knee cap.
* Everybody, touch your patella. Get ready. (Signal.)
(Praise the children by saying:) You're touching your patella.

EXERCISE 3 Calendar

1. (Present calendar.)
* We're going to talk about today, tomorrow, and one week from today.
2. Tell me the day of the week it is today. Get ready. (Signal.)
* Tell me the day of the week it will be tomorrow. Get ready. (Signal.)
* Tell me the day of the week it will be one week from today. Get ready. (Signal.)
3. (Repeat step 2 until firm.)
4. Now the dates.
* Tell me today's date. Get ready. (Signal.)
* Look at the calendar. ✔
* Tell me the date it will be one week from today. Get ready. (Signal.)
5. Once more.
* Listen: Tell me today's date. Get ready. (Signal.)
* Tell me tomorrow's date. Get ready. (Signal.)
* Tell me the date it will be one week from today. Get ready. (Signal.)
6. (Repeat step 5 until firm.)

EXERCISE 4 Map Reading

Note: Have the directions cards in place.

1. Everybody, stand up. ✔
2. Everybody, you're going to face east. (Pause.) Get ready. (Signal.) (The children face east.) What are you doing? (Signal.) *Facing east.*
* Say the statement. Get ready. (Signal.) *I am facing east.*
3. Everybody, you're going to face west. (Pause.) Get ready. (Signal.) (The children face west.) What are you doing? (Signal.) *Facing west.*
* Say the statement. Get ready. (Signal.) *I am facing west.*
4. Everybody, you're going to face south. (Pause.) Get ready. (Signal.) (The children face south.) What are you doing? (Signal.) *Facing south.*
* Say the statement. Get ready. (Signal.) *I am facing south.*
5. (Repeat steps 2 through 4 until firm.)
6. Everybody, sit down.
7. (Point north.) Tell me the direction I'm pointing. (Pause.) Get ready. (Signal.) *North.*
* Say the statement. Get ready. (Signal.) *You are pointing north.*
* Yes, if I drove all day in this direction, I would be going north.

EXERCISE 5 Synonyms

1. What do we call two words that mean the same thing? (Signal.) *Synonyms.*
2. Listen: The chicken is skinny. Say that. (Signal.) *The chicken is skinny.*
- Make up a new statement with a synonym for skinny. (Pause.) Get ready. (Signal.) *The chicken is thin.*
- The chicken is skinny. The chicken is thin. The statements mean the same thing because **skinny** and **thin** are synonyms.
- (Repeat step 2 until firm.)
3. Listen: The ball is under the table. Say that. (Signal.) *The ball is under the table.*
- Make up a new statement with a synonym for under. (Pause.) Get ready. (Signal.) *The ball is below the table.*
- The ball is under the table. The ball is below the table.
- (Repeat step 3 until firm.)
4. Listen: Shut the window.
- Make up a new statement with a synonym for shut. (Pause.) Get ready. (Signal.) *Close the window.*
- (Repeat step 4 until firm.)

EXERCISE 6 Can Do

1. I'm going to ask questions about a woman and a pencil.
2. Everybody, can a woman grow a pencil? (Signal.) *No.*
- Say the statement. Get ready. (Signal.) *A woman cannot grow a pencil.*
3. Everybody, can a woman sharpen a pencil? (Signal.) *Yes.*
- Say the statement. Get ready. (Signal.) *A woman can sharpen a pencil.*
4. (Call on one child.)
- Your turn. Make up another statement that tells something a woman can do with a pencil. (After the child makes the statement, call on the group.) Say the statement about what a woman can do with a pencil. Get ready. (Signal.) (The group repeats the child's statement.)

5. (Call on another child.)
- Your turn. Make up a statement that tells something a woman can**not** do with a pencil. (After the child makes the statement, call on the group.) Say the statement about what a woman cannot do with a pencil. Get ready. (Signal.) (The group repeats the child's statement.)

EXERCISE 7 Calendar Facts

1. Here are some more calendar facts.
2. Some months have thirty days; some months have thirty-one days. Most months have thirty-one days. How many days do most months have? (Signal.) *Thirty-one.*
3. But the month of February usually has only twenty-eight days. What month has only twenty-eight days? (Signal.) *February.*
4. (Repeat steps 2 and 3 until firm.)
5. Everybody, how many days are there in a year? (Signal.) *365.*
- Say the whole thing. Get ready. (Signal.) *There are 365 days in a year.*
- (Repeat step 5 until firm.)
6. Everybody, how many days are in a week? (Signal.) *Seven.*
- Say the whole thing. Get ready. (Signal.) *There are seven days in a week.*
7. Everybody, name the seven days of the week. Get ready. (Signal.) *Sunday, Monday, Tuesday, Wednesday, Thursday, Friday, Saturday.*
- (Repeat step 7 until firm.)
8. How many months are in a year? (Signal.) *Twelve.*
- Say the whole thing. Get ready. (Signal.) *There are twelve months in a year.*
9. Name the months of the year through December. Get ready. (Signal.) *January, February, March, April, May, June, July, August, September, October, November, December.*
- (Repeat step 9 until firm.)

10. How many weeks are in a year? (Signal.) *52.*
   • Say the whole thing. Get ready. (Signal.)
     There are 52 weeks in a year.
   • (Repeat step 10 until firm.)
11. How many seasons are in a year?
   (Signal.) *Four.*
   • Say the seasons of the year. Get ready.
     (Signal.) *Winter, spring, summer, fall.*
   • How many weeks are in a year? (Signal.) *52.*
12. Everybody, tell me what day it is today. Get
   ready. (Signal.)
   • Tell me what day it was yesterday. Get
     ready. (Signal.)
   • Tell me what day it will be tomorrow. Get
     ready. (Signal.)

WORKBOOK

EXERCISE 8 Sentence Writing

fish bird under coat

_____

_____

_____

_____

1. Everybody, open your workbook to
   Lesson 83. Write your name at the top of
   the page. ✔
   • You're going to write sentences that rhyme.
   • Touch the picture of the fish and the bird. ✔
   • The picture shows the fish under
     something and the bird under something.
     What is the fish under? (Signal.) *A boat.*
     Yes, **the fish is under a boat.**
   • What is the bird under? (Signal.) *A coat.*
2. Say the sentence for the bird. Get ready.
   (Signal.) *The bird is under a coat.*
   • Say the sentence for the fish. Get ready.
     (Signal.) *The fish is under a boat.*
3. (Repeat step 2 until firm.)

4. The word box shows how to spell the
   words **fish, bird, under** and **coat.** You can
   figure out how to spell the other words.
5. Write the sentence for the fish. Remember
   to start with a capital and end with a
   period. Pencils down when you're finished.
   (Observe children and give feedback.)
   • Now go to the next line and write the
     sentence for the bird. Pencils down when
     you're finished.
     (Observe children and give feedback.)
6. (Call on individual children to read both
   their sentences.)

EXERCISE 9 Classification

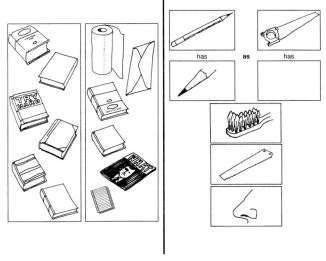

1. Everybody, find the next page in your
   workbook. ✔
   • (Hold up workbook. Point to first half.)
2. The picture that shows only **one** kind of
   thing is the **smaller** class. ✔
   • Touch the picture of the **smaller** class. ✔
   • What kind of thing is that in the picture?
     (Signal.) *Books.*
3. Everybody, circle the picture that shows
   more kinds of things. ✔
   • Everybody, what's the name of the **larger**
     class? (Signal.) *Things made of paper.*
4. Everybody, touch the picture of the class
   that is **smaller.** ✔
   • The books in the picture of the **smaller**
     class should be red or blue. What colors?
     (Signal.) *Red or blue.*

- Mark two books in that picture. ✔
5. Touch the picture that shows the **larger** class. ✔
- The books in that picture should be purple or yellow. What colors? (Signal.) *Purple or yellow.*
- Mark two books in that picture. ✔

EXERCISE 10 Analogies

1. (Hold up workbook. Point to second half.)
2. The pictures show objects and their parts.
3. Touch the pencil. ✔
- The picture that's right below shows what part it has. Everybody, what part does a pencil have? (Signal.) *A point.*
4. Touch the saw. ✔
- One of the pictures below shows what part it has. Touch the picture that shows what part a saw has. ✔
- Everybody, what part does a saw have? (Signal.) *A blade.*
5. Tell me about a pencil. Get ready. (Signal.) *A pencil has a point.*
- Tell me about a saw. Get ready. (Signal.) *A saw has a blade.*
6. Say the whole analogy about a pencil and a saw. Get ready. (Signal.) *A pencil has a point as a saw has a blade.*
7. (Repeat step 6 until firm.)
8. Draw a line from the saw to the part it has. (Observe children and give feedback.)

Objectives

- Answer questions involving previously learned calendar facts. (Exercise 1)
- Given a calendar, identify the day and date for "today" and "tomorrow" and one week from today. (Exercise 2)
- Identify the relationship between the components of an analogy. (Exercise 3)
- Replace a word in a sentence with a synonym. (Exercise 4)
- Write rhyming sentences given picture cues. (Exercise 5)
- **Label cardinal directions on a map.** (Exercise 6)
- Follow coloring rules involving classes and subclasses. (Exercise 7)

EXERCISE 1 Calendar Facts

1. Here are some calendar facts.
2. Some months have thirty days; some months have thirty-one days. Most months have thirty-one days. How many days do most months have? (Signal.) *Thirty-one.*
3. But the month of February usually has only twenty-eight days. What month has only twenty-eight days? (Signal.) *February.*
4. (Repeat steps 2 and 3 until firm.)
5. Everybody, how many days are there in a year? (Signal.) *365.*
- Say the statement. Get ready. (Signal.) *There are 365 days in a year.*
- (Repeat step 5 until firm.)
6. Everybody, how many days are in a week? (Signal.) *Seven.*
- Say the statement. Get ready. (Signal.) *There are seven days in a week.*
7. Everybody, name the seven days of the week. Get ready. (Signal.) *Sunday, Monday, Tuesday, Wednesday, Thursday, Friday, Saturday.*
- (Repeat step 7 until firm.)
8. How many months are in a year? (Signal.) *Twelve.*
- Say the statement. Get ready. (Signal.) *There are twelve months in a year.*
9. Name the months of the year through December. Get ready. (Signal.) *January, February, March, April, May, June, July, August, September, October, November, December.*
- (Repeat step 9 until firm.)

10. How many weeks are in a year? (Signal.) *52.*
- Say the statement. Get ready. (Signal.) *There are 52 weeks in a year.*
- (Repeat step 10 until firm.)
11. How many seasons are in a year? (Signal.) *Four.*
- Say the seasons of the year. Get ready. (Signal.) *Winter, spring, summer, fall.*

EXERCISE 2 Calendar

1. (Present calendar.)
- We're going to talk about today, tomorrow, and one week from today.
2. Tell me the day of the week it is today. Get ready. (Signal.)
- Tell me the day of the week it will be tomorrow. Get ready. (Signal.)
- Tell me the day of the week it will be one week from today. Get ready. (Signal.)
3. (Repeat step 2 until firm.)
4. Now the dates.
- Tell me today's date. Get ready. (Signal.)
- Look at the calendar. ✔
- Tell me the date it will be one week from today. Get ready. (Signal.)
5. Once more.
- Listen: Tell me today's date. Get ready. (Signal.)
- Tell me tomorrow's date. Get ready. (Signal.)
- Tell me the date it will be one week from today. Get ready. (Signal.)
6. (Repeat step 5 until firm.)

EXERCISE 3 Analogies

1. You're going to figure out what an analogy is about.
2. Listen to this: A paintbrush is to painting things **as** a hammer is to . . . (Call on a child. Accept all reasonable answers, but use: *pounding nails.*)
3. Everybody, what class are a paintbrush and a hammer in? (Signal.) *Tools.*
- Yes, tools. Our analogy tells something about tools.
4. A paintbrush is to painting things as a hammer is to pounding nails.
- Does our analogy tell what the tools are made of? (Signal.) *No.*
- Does our analogy tell where you find the tools? (Signal.) *No.*
- Does our analogy tell what parts they have? (Signal.) *No.*
- Does our analogy tell what you do with the tools? (Signal.) *Yes.*
- (Repeat step 4 until firm.)
- Our analogy tells what you do with tools.
5. What do you do with a paintbrush? (Signal.) *Paint things.*
- Say the first part of the analogy. Get ready. (Signal.) *A paintbrush is to painting things.*
6. What do you do with a hammer? (Signal.) *Pound nails.*
- Say the next part of the analogy. Get ready. (Signal.) *A hammer is to pounding nails.*
7. Tell me what the analogy tells about tools. Get ready. (Signal.) *What you do with them.* Yes, what you do with them.
8. Everybody, say the whole analogy. Get ready. (Signal.) *A paintbrush is to painting things as a hammer is to pounding nails.*
9. (Repeat steps 7 and 8 until firm.)

EXERCISE 4 Synonyms

1. What do we call two words that mean the same thing? (Signal.) *Synonyms.*
2. Listen: I'm going to shout. Say that. (Signal.) *I'm going to shout.*
- Make up a new statement with a synonym for **shout.** (Pause.) Get ready. (Signal.) *I'm going to yell.*
- I'm going to shout. I'm going to yell. The statements mean the same thing because **shout** and **yell** are synonyms.
- (Repeat step 2 until firm.)

3. Listen: The box is big. Say that. (Signal.) *The box is big.*
- Make up a new statement with a synonym for **big.** (Pause.) Get ready. (Signal.) *The box is large.*
- The box is big. The box is large.
- (Repeat step 3 until firm.)
4. Listen: The suitcase is under the bed. Say that. (Signal.) *The suitcase is under the bed.*
- Make up a new statement with a synonym for **under.** (Pause.) Get ready. (Signal.) *The suitcase is below the bed.*
- The suitcase is under the bed. The suitcase is below the bed.
- (Repeat step 4 until firm.)

WORKBOOK

EXERCISE 5 Sentence Writing

hat

_____

_____

_____

_____

1. Everybody, open your workbook to Lesson 84. Write your name at the top of the page. ✔
- You're going to write sentences that rhyme.
- Touch the picture of the man and the ram. ✔
- The picture shows what the man and the ram had. What did the man have? (Signal.) *A bat.*
- What did the ram have? (Signal.) *A hat.*
2. Say the sentence for the man. Get ready. (Signal.) *The man had a bat.*
- Say the sentence for the ram. Get ready. (Signal.) *The ram had a hat.*
3. (Repeat step 2 until firm.)
4. The word box shows how to spell the word **hat.** You can figure out how to spell the other words.

5. Write the sentence for the man. Remember to start with a capital and end with a period. Pencils down when you're finished.
   (Observe children and give feedback.)

- Now go to the next line and write the sentence for the ram. Pencils down when you're finished.
  (Observe children and give feedback.)

6. (Call on individual children to read both their sentences.)

EXERCISE 6 Map Reading

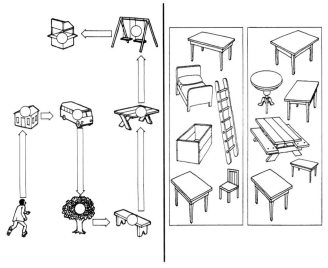

1. Everybody, find the next page in your workbook. ✔
- (Hold up workbook. Point to first half.)
2. Everybody, find the arrows. ✔
3. This picture is a map of where the man skated. You're going to color the arrows orange and write the directions on the objects. Remember to start from the man.
4. Everybody, color the first arrow orange. Do it. ✔
- Now write the letter that shows the direction the man skated. Pencils down when you're finished. ✔
5. You'll do the rest of the arrows later. Remember to write the letter for each arrow.

EXERCISE 7 Classification

1. (Hold up workbook. Point to second half.)
2. Touch the picture of the **smaller** class. ✔
- What kind of thing is that in the picture? (Signal.) *Tables.*
3. Everybody, circle the picture that shows the **larger** class. ✔
- Everybody, what's the name of the larger class? (Signal.) *Things made of wood.*
4. Everybody, touch the picture of the class that is **smaller.** ✔
- The tables in that picture of the **smaller** class should be green or blue. What colors? (Signal.) *Green or blue.*
- Mark two tables in that picture. ✔
5. Touch the picture that shows the **larger** class. ✔
- The tables in that picture should be black or brown. What colors? (Signal.) *Black or brown.*
- Mark two tables in that picture. ✔

Objectives

- Replace a word in a sentence with a synonym. (Exercise 1)
- Identify an object based on its characteristics. (Exercise 2)
- Given a calendar, identify the day and date for "today" and "tomorrow" and one week from today. (Exercise 3)
- Identify cardinal directions. (Exercise 4)
- Listen to a short story and answer questions involving "who," "when," "why," "where" and "what". (Exercise 5)
- Generate questions to find a word's definition. (Exercise 6)
- Listen to a short story and answer questions involving "who," "when," "why," "where" and "what". (Exercise 7)
- Identify absurdities involving use and condition. (Exercise 8)
- Use clues to eliminate members of a familiar class. (Exercise 9)
- Relate a familiar story grammar to a picture that indicates the sequence of events for a new story. (Exercise 10)

EXERCISE 1 Synonyms

1. I'm going to make up a story. You're going to say the story too, but you are going to use synonyms.
2. There was a boy who was very thin.
- What's a synonym for **thin?** (Signal.) *Skinny.*
- So there was a boy who was very . . . (Signal.) *skinny.*
3. This boy really liked to shout.
- What's a synonym for **shout?** (Signal.) *Yell.*
- So this boy really liked to . . . (Signal.) *yell.*
4. One day he got in the closet and closed the door.
- What's the synonym for **closed?** (Signal.) *Shut.*
- So one day he got in the closet and . . . (Signal.) *shut the door.*
5. Let's do that story one more time and go a little faster.
6. There was a boy who was very thin. Say that. (Signal.) *There was a boy who was very thin.*
- Now say that statement with a synonym for **thin.** Get ready. (Signal.) *There was a boy who was very skinny.*
7. This boy really liked to shout. Say that. (Signal.) *This boy really liked to shout.*
- Now say that statement with a synonym for **shout.** Get ready. (Signal.) *This boy really liked to yell.*

8. One day he got in the closet and closed the door. Say that. (Signal.) *One day he got in the closet and closed the door.*
- Now say that statement with a synonym for **closed.** Get ready. (Signal.) *One day he got in the closet and shut the door.*

EXERCISE 2 Description

1. I'm going to say two things about something you know. See if you can figure out what I'm talking about.
2. (Hold up one finger.) Prest is a month of the year.
- (Hold up two fingers.) Prest always comes after September.
3. Everybody, tell me what you know about Prest. Get ready.
- (Hold up one finger.) *Prest is a month of the year.*
- (Hold up two fingers.) *Prest always comes after September.*
4. (Repeat step 3 until firm.)
5. Everybody, tell me what Prest is. Get ready. (Signal.) *October.*
6. (Repeat steps 3 and 5 until firm.)

EXERCISE 3 Calendar

1. (Present calendar.)
- We're going to talk about today, tomorrow, and one week from today.
2. Tell me the day of the week it is today. Get ready. (Signal.)
- Tell me the day of the week it will be tomorrow. Get ready. (Signal.)
- Tell me the day of the week it will be one week from today. Get ready. (Signal.)
3. (Repeat step 2 until firm.)
4. Now the dates.
- Tell me today's date. Get ready. (Signal.)
- Look at the calendar. ✔
- Tell me the date it will be one week from today. Get ready. (Signal.)
5. Once more.
- Listen: Tell me today's date. Get ready. (Signal.)
- Tell me tomorrow's date. Get ready. (Signal.)
- Tell me the date it will be one week from today. Get ready. (Signal.)
6. (Repeat step 5 until firm.)

EXERCISE 4 Map Reading

Note: Have the directions cards in place.

1. Everybody, stand up. ✔
2. Everybody, you're going to face west. (Pause.) Get ready. (Signal.) (The children face west.) What are you doing? (Signal.) *Facing west.*
- Say the statement. Get ready. (Signal.) *I am facing west.*
3. Everybody, you're going to face north. (Pause.) Get ready. (Signal.) (The children face north.) What are you doing? (Signal.) *Facing north.*
- Say the statement. Get ready. (Signal.) *I am facing north.*
4. Everybody, you're going to face south. (Pause.) Get ready. (Signal.) (The children face south.) What are you doing? (Signal.) *Facing south.*
- Say the statement. Get ready. (Signal.) *I am facing south.*
5. (Repeat steps 2 through 4 until firm.)
6. Everybody, sit down.

7. (Point east.) Tell me the direction I'm pointing. (Pause.) Get ready. (Signal.) *East.*
- Say the statement. Get ready. (Signal.) *You are pointing east.*
- Yes, if I pulled a wagon for fifteen minutes in this direction, I would be going east.
8. (Point north.) Tell me the direction I'm pointing. (Pause.) Get ready. (Signal.) *North.*
- Say the statement. Get ready. (Signal.) *You are pointing north.*
- Yes, if I pulled a wagon for one hour in this direction, I would be going north.
9. (Repeat steps 7 and 8 until firm.)

EXERCISE 5 Who—What—When—Where—Why

1. Listen to this story.
- The ball was on the table. A boy hit the ball, and it fell off the table. Then the boy picked it up and put it in his pocket.
- (Repeat the story.)
2. Tell where the ball was first. Get ready. (Signal.) *On the table.*
- Tell who hit the ball. Get ready. (Signal.) *A boy.*
- Tell what the boy picked up. Get ready. (Signal.) *The ball.*
- Tell why the ball fell off the table. Get ready. (Signal.) *A boy hit it.*
- Tell where the boy put the ball. Get ready. (Signal.) *In his pocket.*
3. (Repeat step 2 until firm.)

EXERCISE 6 Questioning Skills

Note: The children are not to memorize the words presented in this task.

1. I'll say a word and ask a question about what that word means.
2. Here's the word: **chortle.** Say that word. (Signal.) *Chortle.*
- Here's the question: What does the word chortle mean? Now you ask me the question about what the word chortle means. Get ready. (Signal.) *What does the word chortle mean?*

3. I'll tell you what chortle means. Chortle is a synonym for laugh.
- Everybody, show me how you chortle. (Praise the children by saying:) You are really chortling.
4. Here's another word: **promenade.** Say that word. (Signal.) *Promenade.*
- Here's the question: What does the word promenade mean? Now you ask me the question about what the word promenade means. Get ready. (Signal.) *What does the word promenade mean?*
5. I'll tell you what promenade means. Promenade is a synonym for walk.
- Show me how you promenade. (Call on a child. Praise child by saying:) Good promenading.

EXERCISE 7   Who—What—When—Where—Why

1. Listen to this story.
2. The cow was in the pasture. It was noon time. The sun was bright, so she closed her eyes. A fly came up to the cow and sat on her back. The cow scared the fly away by swishing her tail.
- (Repeat the story.)
3. Tell what the cow did to scare away the fly. Get ready. (Signal.) *Swished her tail.*
- Tell where the cow was. Get ready. (Signal.) *In the pasture.*
- Tell who sat on the cow's back. Get ready. (Signal.) *The fly.*
- Tell why the cow closed her eyes. Get ready. (Signal.) *The sun was bright.*
- Tell when the cow closed her eyes. Get ready. (Signal.) *Noon time.*
- (Repeat step 3 until firm.)

EXERCISE 8   Absurdity

1. Listen to this statement and figure out what is absurd about it.
2. He dug a hole with his shirt. Say the statement. Get ready. (Signal.) *He dug a hole with his shirt.*
3. What's absurd about that statement? (Call on a child.)
(Praise all reasonable responses, then say:) Yes, he couldn't dig a hole with his shirt.
4. Here's another absurd statement.

5. Listen: Figure out what's absurd about this one. Missy burned her tongue on cold milk. Say the statement. Get ready. (Signal.) *Missy burned her tongue on cold milk.*
6. What's absurd about that statement? (Call on a child.)
(Praise all reasonable responses, then say:) Yes, Missy couldn't burn her tongue on cold milk.

WORKBOOK

EXERCISE 9   Classification

1. Everybody, open your workbook to Lesson 85. Write your name at the top of the page. ✔
- This page has the same pictures as an earlier mystery game. Today, I'll give you different clues for a different mystery vehicle.
- Listen carefully: Cut along the dotted line. Stop cutting at the end of each dotted line. Then each of your vehicles will be a flap. Remember, just cut along the dotted line. Raise your hand when you're finished. (Observe children and give feedback.)
- You're going to play the mystery game again. Remember how it works: I'll tell you clues about the mystery vehicle. After each clue, you'll be able to fold over some pictures that could **not** be the mystery vehicle. After I give you the last clue, you'll know which vehicle is the mystery vehicle because it will be the **only** picture that is **not** folded over.

2. Here's the first clue about the mystery vehicle: This vehicle can go much faster than a bicycle. That's fast. Everybody, say that clue. (Signal.) *This vehicle can go much faster than a bicycle.*

- Listen: If it can **not** go faster than a bicycle, it can **not** be the mystery vehicle, so fold over every vehicle that can **not** go faster than a bicycle. Raise your hand when you're finished.
  (Observe children and give feedback.)
- Which vehicles did you fold over? (Call on a child. Idea: *The rowboat and bicycle.*)
- Why did you fold over the rowboat and bicycle? (Call on a child. Idea: *A rowboat and a bicycle cannot go faster than a bicycle.*)

3. Here's another clue about the mystery vehicle: This vehicle can go on roads and streets. Everybody, say that clue. (Signal.) *This vehicle can go on roads and streets.*

- Listen: If it doesn't go on roads and streets, it can **not** be the mystery vehicle, so fold over every vehicle that does **not** go on roads and streets. Raise your hand when you're finished.
  (Observe children and give feedback.)
- Everybody, which vehicle did you fold over? (Signal.) *The train.*
- Why did you fold over the train? (Call on a child. Idea: *A train does not go on roads and streets.*)

4. Here's another clue about the mystery vehicle: This vehicle can fit inside a regular garage. Everybody, say that clue. (Signal.) *This vehicle can fit inside a regular garage.*

- Listen: If it can **not** fit inside a regular garage, it can **not** be the mystery vehicle, so fold over every vehicle that can **not** fit inside a regular garage. Raise your hand when you're finished.
  (Observe children and give feedback.)
- Everybody, which vehicle did you fold over? (Signal.) *The bus.*
- Why did you fold over the bus? (Call on a child. Idea: *A bus cannot fit inside a regular garage.*)

5. Here's the last clue about the mystery vehicle: This vehicle has only two wheels. Everybody, say that clue. (Signal.) *This vehicle has only two wheels.*

- Listen: Fold over the flap that could **not** be the mystery vehicle. ✔
- Everybody, which vehicle did you fold over? (Signal.) *The car.*
- Why did you fold over the car? (Call on a child. Idea: *A car has more than two wheels.*)

6. You figured out which vehicle is the mystery vehicle. It should be the **only** picture that is **not** folded over. Everybody, which vehicle is the mystery vehicle? (Signal.) *The motorcycle.*

- Raise your hand if you figured out the mystery vehicle. ✔

7. I gave you four clues that let you figure out the mystery vehicle. Let's see how many of those clues you remember.

- What was one of the clues? (Call on a child. Accept appropriate response.)

8. What was another clue? (Call on a child. Accept appropriate response.) (Repeat step 8 until all clues have been identified.)

9. Who can name all four clues about the mystery vehicle? (Call on several children. Praise any child who can name at least three clues.)

EXERCISE 10 Sequence Story

Roger And Sweetie

1. Everybody, find the next page in your workbook. ✔

2. This picture shows another story about Roger, but I don't know what that story is. I don't have anything written in my book. Maybe you can help me out. You can see that Roger's jacket is on top of that fence by number 5. That's where his jacket was at the **end** of the story. I don't think Roger would have put his jacket there, so far away and all tangled up. I think he put it at number 1. I'll bet he took it off because it's a warm day.

- What do you think? (Children respond.)

3. But I can't figure out how that jacket could have moved around. Can you find a clue in the picture that would explain how his jacket moved all the way to that fence? That's a pretty heavy jacket. It would take a pretty strong animal to move it.

- Raise your hand if you can find an animal in the picture strong enough to move Roger's jacket. ✔

- Everybody, what animal did you find? (Signal.) *Sweetie.*

4. But I wonder **how** Sweetie moved that jacket, or **why** Sweetie moved that jacket.

- Who has an idea about where Sweetie was when Roger put his jacket down? (Call on a child. Idea: *Next to Roger.*)

- I'll bet Sweetie wasn't very happy getting all tangled up in that jacket.

5. Look at the numbers in the picture and raise your hand when you think you can tell the whole story. Remember, you have to tell **why** Roger took his jacket off, what the jacket landed on, and then all the places the jacket went. Remember, you also have to tell **why** the jacket is at number 5, but why Sweetie is not in that jacket.

6. (Call on several children to tell the story. Tell the other children to follow along and raise their hand if something is missed. Praise stories that have these details:
It was warm so Roger took off his jacket and put it next to him;
He put it on Sweetie, who got tangled up in it;
Sweetie took off and climbed the tree;
Sweetie fell from the tree into the puddle;
Sweetie ran into the bushes;
Sweetie jumped up on the fence;
The jacket got caught on the fence and Sweetie fell out; and Sweetie was wet and confused.)

7. Later you can color the picture. Sweetie really looks confused again.

Objectives

- Identify the relationship between the components of an analogy. (Exercise 1)
- Given a calendar, identify the day and date for "today" and "tomorrow" and one week from today. (Exercise 2)
- Given a common noun, answer questions involving "can do." (Exercise 3)
- Replace a word in a sentence with a synonym. (Exercise 4)
- **Discriminate between synonyms and opposites.** (Exercise 5)
- Generate questions to find a word's definition. (Exercise 6)
- Identify an object based on its characteristics. (Exercise 7)
- Listen to a short story and answer questions involving "who," "when," "why," "where" and "what". (Exercise 8)
- Write rhyming sentences given picture cues. (Exercise 9)
- Follow coloring rules involving classes and subclasses. (Exercise 10)
- Follow coloring rules involving materials. (Exercise 11)

EXERCISE 1 **Analogies**

1. You're going to figure out what an analogy is about.
2. Listen to this: A restaurant is to eating as a hotel is to . . . (Signal.) *sleeping.*
3. What class are a restaurant and a hotel in? (Signal.) *Buildings.*
- Yes, buildings. Our analogy tells something about buildings.
4. A restaurant is to eating as a hotel is to sleeping.
- Does our analogy tells what the buildings are made of? (Signal.) *No.*
- Does our analogy tell what you do in them? (Signal.) *Yes.*
- Does our analogy tell what parts they have? (Signal.) *No.*
- Does our analogy tell what color they are? (Signal.) *No.*
- Our analogy tell what you do in them.
- (Repeat step 4 until firm.)
5. What do you do in a restaurant?(Signal.) *Eat.*
- Say the first part of the analogy. Get ready. (Signal.) *A restaurant is to eating.*
6. What do you do in a hotel? (Signal.) *Sleep.*
- Say the next part of the analogy. Get ready. (Signal.) *A hotel is to sleeping.*

7. Tell me what the analogy tells about the buildings. Get ready. (Signal.) *What you do in them.* Yes, what you do in them.
8. Everybody, say the whole analogy. Get ready. (Signal.) *A restaurant is to eating as a hotel is to sleeping.*
9. (Repeat steps 7 and 8 until firm.)

EXERCISE 2 **Calendar**

1. (Present calendar.)
- We're going to talk about today, tomorrow, and one week from today.
2. Tell me the day of the week it is today. Get ready. (Signal.)
- Tell me the day of the week it will be tomorrow. Get ready. (Signal.)
- Tell me the day of the week it will be one week from today. Get ready. (Signal.)
3. (Repeat step 2 until firm.)
4. Now the dates.
- Tell me today's date. Get ready. (Signal.)
- Look at the calendar. ✔
- Tell me the date it will be one week from today. Get ready. (Signal.)
5. Once more.
- Listen: Tell me today's date. Get ready. (Signal.)
- Tell me tomorrow's date. Get ready. (Signal.)
- Tell me the date it will be one week from today. Get ready. (Signal.)
6. (Repeat step 5 until firm.)

EXERCISE 3   Can Do

1. Everybody, I'm going to call on individual children to name things we can do with a shirt.
2. (Call on one child.)
- What's one thing we can do with a shirt? (After the child gives a correct response, call on the group.) Let's all say the whole thing. Get ready. (Signal.) (The group repeats the child's response.)
3. (Call on another child.)
   What's another thing we can do with a shirt? (After the child gives a correct response, call on the group.) Let's all name those things we can do with a shirt.
- What's the first thing? (Hold up one finger.) (The group repeats the first response.)
- What's the second thing? (Hold up two fingers.) (The group repeats the second response.)
4. (Call on another child.)
   What's another thing we can do with a shirt? (After the child gives a correct response, call on the group.) Let's all name those things we can do with a shirt.
- What's the first thing? (Hold up one finger.) (The group repeats the first response.)
- What's the second thing? (Hold up two fingers.) (The group repeats the second response.)
- What's the third thing? (Hold up three fingers.) (The group repeats the third response.)
5. Now I'm going to call on individual children to name things we cannot do with a shirt.
6. (Call on one child.)
   What's one thing we cannot do with a shirt? (After the child gives a correct response, call on the group.) Let's all say the whole thing. Get ready. (Signal.) (The group repeats the child's response.)

7. (Call on another child.)
   What's another thing we cannot do with a shirt? (After the child gives a correct response, call on the group.) Let's all name those things we cannot do with a shirt.
- What's the first thing? (Hold up one finger.) (The group repeats the first response.)
- What's the second thing? (Hold up two fingers.) (The group repeats the second response.)
8. (Call on another child.) What's another thing we cannot do with a shirt? (After the child gives a correct response, call on the group.) Let's all name those things we cannot do with a shirt.
- What's the first thing? (Hold up one finger.) (The group repeats the first response.)
- What's the second thing? (Hold up two fingers.) (The group repeats the second response.)
- What's the third thing? (Hold up three fingers.) (The group repeats the third response.)

EXERCISE 4   Synonyms

1. Listen: A dog lived below a house. Say that. (Signal.) *A dog lived below a house.*
- Now say that statement using a synonym for **below.** Get ready. (Signal.) *A dog lived under a house.*
2. This dog was very large. Say that. (Signal.) *This dog was very large.*
- Now say that statement using a synonym for **large.** Get ready. (Signal.) *This dog was very big.*
3. The boy yelled, "Come out." Say that. (Signal.) *The boy yelled, "Come out."*
- Now say that statement using a synonym for **yelled.** Get ready. (Signal.) *The boy shouted, "Come out."*

EXERCISE 5   Synonyms/Opposites

1. Tell me if I name synonyms or opposites. Think big.
2. Listen: Big. Large. Say those words. (Signal.) *Big. Large.*
- Are they synonyms or opposites? (Signal.) *Synonyms.*
- (Repeat step 2 until firm.)
3. Listen: Above. Over. Say those words. (Signal.) *Above. Over.*
- Are they synonyms or opposites? (Signal.) *Synonyms.*
- (Repeat step 3 until firm.)
4. Listen: Fast. Slow. Say those words. (Signal.) *Fast. Slow.*
- Are they synonyms or opposites? (Signal.) *Opposites.*
- (Repeat step 4 until firm.)
5. (Repeat steps 2 through 4 until firm.)

EXERCISE 6   Questioning Skills

1. I'm going to tell a story. When you hear a word you don't know, say **stop.**
2. A boy was looking at an (pause) **illustration.** (Children should say *stop.*)
- Everybody, what word don't you know? (Signal.) *Illustration.*
- Ask the question about what the word illustration means. Get ready. (Signal.) *What does the word illustration mean?*
- I'll tell you what illustration means. Illustration is a synonym for **picture.** What is illustration a synonym for? (Signal.) *Picture.*
- If the boy was looking at an illustration, he was looking at a . . . (Signal.) *picture.*
3. Here's more of the story.
- The picture showed a large (pause) **feline.** (Children should say *stop.*)
- Everybody, what word don't you know? (Signal.) *Feline.*
- Ask the question about what the word feline means. Get ready. (Signal.) *What does the word feline mean?*
- I'll tell you what feline means. Feline is a synonym for cat. What is feline a synonym for? (Signal.) *Cat.*
- So if the boy was looking at an illustration of a feline, he was looking at a picture of a . . . (Signal.) *cat.*

4. Here's more of the story.
- The boy said: "That is a cat I (pause) **cherish.**" (Children should say *stop.*)
- Everybody, what word don't you know? (Signal.) *Cherish.*
- Ask the question about what the word cherish means. Get ready. (Signal.) *What does the word cherish mean?*
- I'll tell you what cherish means. Cherish means **adore.** What does cherish mean? (Signal.) *Adore.*
- So if the boy cherished the cat, he adored the cat.
5. So then the boy took the illustration of the feline he cherished and hung it on his wall. That's the end of the story.

EXERCISE 7   Description

1. I'm going to say two things about something you know. See if you can figure out what I'm talking about.
2. (Hold up one finger.) Strooms is the name of a class.
- (Hold up two fingers.) All strooms take you places.
3. Everybody, tell me what you know about strooms. Get ready.
- (Hold up one finger.) *Strooms is the name of a class.*
- (Hold up two fingers.) *All strooms take you places.*
4. (Repeat step 3 until firm.)
5. Everybody, tell me what strooms are. Get ready. (Signal.) *Vehicles.*
6. (Repeat steps 3 and 5 until firm.)
7. Here's another one.
- (Hold up one finger.) An eem is found in a classroom.
- (Hold up two fingers.) An eem is used to erase chalkboards.
8. Everybody, tell me what you know about an eem.
- (Hold up one finger.) *An eem is found in a classroom.*
- (Hold up two fingers.) *An eem is used to erase chalkboards.*
9. (Repeat step 8 until firm.)
10. Everybody, tell me what an eem is. Get ready. (Signal.) *An eraser.*
11. (Repeat steps 9 and 10 until firm.)

EXERCISE 8 Who—What—When—Where—Why

1. Listen to this story.
2. The teacher was teaching spelling. He got a phone call that told him to go to the office. Before the teacher went to the office, he asked the students to open their books, and they did.
   - (Repeat the story.)
3. Tell what the teacher was doing first. Get ready. (Signal.) *Teaching spelling.*
   - Tell where the teacher went. Get ready. (Signal.) *To the office.*
   - Tell who opened books. Get ready. (Signal.) *The students.*
   - Tell why the teacher went to the office. Get ready. (Signal.) *He got a phone call.*
   - Tell when the teacher asked the students to open their books. Get ready. (Signal.) *Before he went to the office.*
   - (Repeat step 3 until firm.)

WORKBOOK

EXERCISE 9 Sentence Writing

1. Everybody, open your workbook to Lesson 86. Write your name at the top of the page. ✔
   - You're going to write sentences that rhyme.
   - Touch the picture of the car and the bug. ✔
   - The picture shows the car on something and the bug on something. What is the car on? (Signal.) *A road.*
   - Yes, **the car is on a road.**
   - What is the bug on? (Signal.) *A toad.*

2. Say the sentence for the car. Get ready. (Signal.) *The car is on a road.*
   - Say the sentence for the bug. Get ready. (Signal.) *The bug is on a toad.*
3. (Repeat step 2 until firm.)
4. The word box shows how to spell the words **car, toad** and **bug.** You can figure out how to spell the other words.
5. Write the sentence for the car. Remember to start with a capital and end with a period. Pencils down when you're finished. (Observe children and give feedback.)
   - Now go to the next line and write the sentence for the bug. Pencils down when you're finished.
     (Observe children and give feedback.)
6. (Call on individual children to read both their sentences.)

EXERCISE 10 Classification

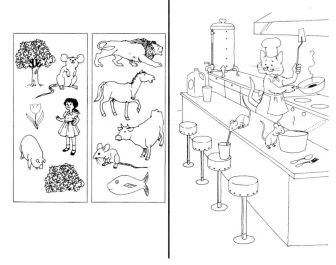

1. Everybody, find the next page in your workbook. ✔
   - (Hold up workbook. Point to first half.)
2. Touch the picture of the **smaller** class. ✔
   - What kind of thing is that in the picture? (Signal.) *Animals.*
3. Everybody, circle the picture that shows the **larger** class. ✔
   - Everybody, what's the name of the **larger** class? (Signal.) *Living things.*
4. Everybody, touch the picture of the class that is **smaller.** ✔
   - The animals in the picture of the **smaller** class should be blue. What color? (Signal.) *Blue.*
   - Mark an animal in that picture. ✔

5. Touch the picture that shows the **larger** class.
- The animals in that picture should be red. What color? (Signal.) *Red.*
- Mark an animal in that picture. ✔

EXERCISE 11 Materials

1. (Hold up workbook. Point to second half.)
2. Here's a coloring rule for this picture. If an object is made of metal, color it blue or red. What's the rule? (Signal.) *If an object is made of metal, color it blue or red.*
- (Repeat step 2 until firm.)
3. Mark two of the objects made of metal. ✔
4. Here's another coloring rule for this picture. If an object could be made of plastic, color it orange. What's the rule? (Signal.) *If an object could be made of plastic, color it orange.*
- (Repeat step 4 until firm.)

5. Make an orange mark on one of the objects that could be made of plastic. ✔
6. Here's one more thing to do.
- Part of the pot is missing. What part is missing? (Signal.) *The handle.*
- Yes, the handle. Before you color the pot, follow the dots with your pencil to make the handle.
7. Remember—the marks show you what color to make the metal objects and the plastic objects.
(Observe children and give feedback.)

LESSON 87

Objectives

- Identify the relationship between the components of an analogy. (Exercise 1)
- Identify an object based on its characteristics. (Exercise 2)
- Given a calendar, identify the day and date for "today" and "tomorrow" and one week from today. (Exercise 3)
- Generate questions to find a word's definition. (Exercise 4)
- Replace a word in a sentence with a synonym. (Exercise 5)
- **Write three sentences.** (Exercise 6)
- Collect data on groups and tell whether statements about groups are true or false. (Exercise 7)

EXERCISE 1 Analogies

1. You're going to figure out what an analogy is about.
2. Listen to this: A purse is to money as a suitcase is to . . . (Signal.) *clothes.*
3. What class are a purse and a suitcase in? (Signal.) *Containers.*
- Yes, containers. Our analogy tells something about containers.
4. A purse is to money as a suitcase is to clothes.
- Does our analogy tell what color the containers are? (Signal.) *No.*
- Does our analogy tell what parts they have? (Signal.) *No.*
- Does our analogy tell what you put in the containers? (Signal.) *Yes.*
- Does our analogy tell where you find the containers? (Signal.) *No.*
- Our analogy tells what you put in them.
- (Repeat step 4 until firm.)
5. What do you put in a purse? (Signal.) *Money.*
- Say the first part of the analogy. Get ready. (Signal.) *A purse is to money.*
6. What do you put in a suitcase? (Signal.) *Clothes.*
- Say the next part of the analogy. Get ready. (Signal.) *A suitcase is to clothes.*
7. Tell me what the analogy tells about the containers. Get ready. (Signal.) *What you put in them.*
- Yes, what you put in them.
8. Everybody, say the whole analogy. Get ready. (Signal.) *A purse is to money as a suitcase is to clothes.*
9. (Repeat steps 7 and 8 until firm.)

EXERCISE 2 Description

1. I'm going to say two things about something you know. See if you can figure out what I'm talking about.
2. (Hold up one finger.) Greem is an action.
- (Hold up two fingers.) When you greem, you use a pencil and paper.
3. Everybody, tell me what you know about greem.
- (Hold up one finger.) *Greem is an action.*
- (Hold up two fingers.) *When you greem, you use a pencil and paper.*
4. (Repeat step 3 until firm.)
5. Tell me what greem is. (Call on a child. Accept correct responses but use: *writing or drawing.*)
6. Everybody, tell me what greem is. Get ready. (Signal.) *Writing or drawing.*
7. (Repeat steps 3 through 6 until firm.)

EXERCISE 3 Calendar

1. (Present calendar.)
- We're going to talk about today, tomorrow, and one week from today.
2. Tell me the day of the week it is today. Get ready. (Signal.)
- Tell me the day of the week it will be tomorrow. Get ready. (Signal.)
- Tell me the day of the week it will be one week from today. Get ready. (Signal.)
3. (Repeat step 2 until firm.)
4. Now the dates.
- Tell me today's date. Get ready. (Signal.)
- Look at the calendar. ✔
- Tell me the date it will be one week from today. Get ready. (Signal.)

5. Once more.
- Listen: Tell me today's date. Get ready. (Signal.)
- Tell me tomorrow's date. Get ready. (Signal.)
- Tell me the date it will be one week from today. Get ready. (Signal.)
6. (Repeat step 5 until firm.)

EXERCISE 4 Questioning Skills

1. I'm going to tell a story. When you hear a word you don't know, say **stop.**
2. A man was (pause) **laboring.** (Children should say *stop.*)
- Everybody, what word don't you know? (Signal.) *Laboring.*
- Ask the question about what the word laboring means. Get ready. (Signal.) *What does the word laboring mean?*
- I'll tell you what laboring means. Laboring is a synonym for **working.**
- What is laboring a synonym for? (Signal.) *Working.*
- If the man was laboring, he was . . . (Signal.) *working.*
3. Here's more of the story.
- He broke one of his (pause) **phalanges.** (Children should say *stop.*)
- Everybody, what word don't you know? (Signal.) *Phalanges.*
- Ask the question about what the word phalanges means. Get ready. (Signal.) *What does the word phalanges mean?*
- I'll tell you what phalanges means. Phalanges is a synonym for **finger bones.**
- What is phalanges a synonym for? (Signal.) *Finger bones.*
4. If the man was laboring and he broke one of his phalanges, he was working and he broke one of his . . . (Signal.) *finger bones.*
- Do you think he felt very well? (Children respond.)
- That's the end of the story.

EXERCISE 5 Synonyms

1. Listen: A woman had a very big plate. Say that. (Signal.) *A woman had a very big plate.*
- Now say that statement using a synonym for **big.** Get ready. (Signal.) *A woman had a very large plate.*

2. She put the plate under a cup in her cabinet. Say that. (Signal.) *She put the plate under a cup in her cabinet.*
- (Repeat until firm.)
3. Now say that statement using a synonym for **under.** Get ready. (Signal.) *She put the plate below a cup in her cabinet.*
4. But the woman couldn't shut the cabinet door. Say that. (Signal.) *But the woman couldn't shut the cabinet door.*
- Now say that statement using a synonym for **shut.** Get ready. (Signal.) *But the woman couldn't close the cabinet door.*
5. And here is the end of the story. She said: "I must find a smaller plate or get a new cabinet."
- What do you think she should do? (Call on individual children. After a child answers, ask:) Why do you think so? (Children respond.)

EXERCISE 6 Sentence Writing

his	her	socks	shoes	feet

1. Everybody, open your workbook to Lesson 87. Write your name. ✔
- You're going to write sentences that do not rhyme.
- Touch the picture of the feet. ✔
- The picture shows what his feet had and what her feet had. What did his feet have? (Signal.) *Socks.*
- What did her feet have? (Signal.) *Shoes.*

2. Say the sentence for what his feet had. Get ready. (Signal.) *His feet had socks.*
- Say the sentence for what her feet had. Get ready. (Signal.) *Her feet had shoes.*
3. (Repeat step 2 until firm.)
4. The word box shows how to spell the words **his, her, socks, shoes,** and **feet.** You can figure out how to spell the other words.
5. Write the sentence for what his feet had. Pencils down when you're finished. ✔
- Now go to the next line and write the sentence for what her feet had. Pencils down when you're finished. ✔
6. (Call on individual children to read both their sentences.)

EXERCISE 7 Data Collection

1. Everybody, find the next page. ✔
- We're going to learn how to settle an argument some people you know were having.

Roxie's neighbors were talking one day. They were talking about Roxie's rock garden.

Paul is one of Roxie's neighbors. He said, "Roxie has more **pink** rocks than any other color."

"No, no," Molly said. (She is another one of Roxie's neighbors.) "Roxie has more **brown** rocks than any other color."

A third neighbor said this: "Bleep. You are both wrong. There are more **gray** rocks than any other color."

- Everybody, which neighbor was that? (Signal.) *Bleep.*
- How could these neighbors figure out who was right about Roxie's rocks? (Call on a child. Idea: *Count the rocks.*)
2. Everybody, look at the picture. That picture shows part of a rock garden. The whole garden is like this part. It has just as many rocks of each color. Some of the rocks have a letter. One letter is **P.** Those are **pink** rocks. Take out your **pink** crayon and make a pink mark on all the pink rocks in the rock garden. Do it fast. Raise your hand when you're finished.
(Observe children and give feedback.)
3. Look at the big box below the picture. Touch the rock that has a **P** on it. ✔
- Right after that rock are the words **pink rocks.** Then there's an empty box. Write the number for the pink rocks in that box. Count all the pink rocks in the rock garden and write that number in the top box. Raise your hand when you're finished.
(Observe children and give feedback.)
- Everybody, what number did you write for pink rocks? (Signal.) *Nine.*
4. Now do the same thing for the **brown** rocks. Make a brown mark on each rock in the rock garden that has a letter **B** on it. The **B** is for brown rocks. After you make your **brown** marks, count the **brown** rocks in the rock garden and write that number in the box for **brown** rocks. Raise your hand when you're finished.
(Observe children and give feedback.)
- Everybody, what number did you write for brown rocks? (Signal.) *Six.*
5. Now do the same thing for the **gray** rocks. Make a gray mark on each rock in the rock garden that has a letter **G** on it. The **G** is for **gray** rocks. After you make your gray marks, count the gray rocks in the rock garden and write that number in the box for **gray** rocks. Raise your hand when you're finished.
(Observe children and give feedback.)
- Everybody, what number did you write for the gray rocks? (Signal.) *Ten.*

6. Get ready to read the numbers one more time. Listen: How many pink rocks are there? (Signal.) *Nine.*

- How many brown rocks are there? (Signal.) *Six.*
- How many gray rocks are there? (Signal.) *Ten.*

7. Let's see who was right about the rocks in Roxie's yard. Paul said that there are more **pink** rocks than any other color. Think about it. Is that statement true or false? (Signal.) *False.*

- Molly said that there are more **brown** rocks than any other color. Is that statement true or false? (Signal.) *False.*
- The third neighbor said, "Bleep . . . There are more **gray** rocks than any other color." Is that statement true or false? (Signal.) *True.*
- Everybody, what's the name of the neighbor who was right about the rocks? (Signal.) *Bleep.*
- That Bleep. Sometimes he says things that are **true** and sometimes he says things that are **false.** You just never know.

8. Before we leave this picture, there's one more box to fill out. The words before that box say **other rocks.** What kind of rocks would go in there? (Call on a child. Idea: *Rocks that are not pink, brown or gray.*)

- In the picture are some rocks that are **white** and some rocks that are **black.** Those are the **other rocks.** To find the number for the **other rocks,** you have to count all the rocks that you haven't counted. If a rock is white or if it is black, you count it. Count all the rocks that are white or black, and write that number in the last box. Raise your hand when you're finished.
(Observe children and give feedback.)
- Everybody, how many other rocks are there? (Signal.) *Nine.*

9. Later you can color the pink, brown and gray rocks.

Objectives

- Identify the relationship between the components of an analogy. (Exercise 1)
- Name members of a class and subclass and identify the bigger class. (Exercise 2)
- Given a calendar, identify the day and date for "today" and "tomorrow" and one week from today. (Exercise 3)
- Identify an object based on its characteristics. (Exercise 4)
- Replace a word in a sentence with a synonym. (Exercise 5)
- Write rhyming sentences given picture cues. (Exercise 6)
- Use clues to eliminate members of a familiar class. (Exercise 7)

EXERCISE 1   Analogies

1. You're going to figure out what an analogy is about.
2. Listen to this: A lion is to the jungle as a fish is to . . . (Signal.) *the water.*
3. What class are a lion and a fish in? (Signal.) *Animals.*
- Yes, animals. Our analogy tells us something about animals.
4. A lion is to the jungle as a fish is to the water.
- Does our analogy tell how the animals move? (Signal.) *No.*
- Does our analogy tell what color they are? (Signal.) *No.*
- Does our analogy tell where you find them? (Signal.) *Yes.*
- Does our analogy tell what parts they have? (Signal.) *No.*
- Our analogy tells where you find them.
- (Repeat step 4 until firm.)
5. Where do you find a lion? (Signal.) *In the jungle.*
- Say the first part of the analogy. Get ready. (Signal.) *A lion is to the jungle.*
6. Where do you find a fish? (Signal.) *In the water.*
- Say the next part of the analogy. Get ready. (Signal.) *A fish is to the water.*
7. Tell me what the analogy tells about the animals. Get ready. (Signal.) *Where you find them.* Yes, where you find them.
8. Everybody, say the whole analogy. Get ready. (Signal.) *A lion is to the jungle as a fish is to the water.*
9. (Repeat steps 7 and 8 until firm.)

EXERCISE 2   Classification

1. We're going to talk about classes.
2. If we took all cups from the class of containers, would there be any kinds of containers left? (Signal.) *Yes.*
3. Name some kinds of containers that would be left. (Call on individual children. Praise appropriate responses: any kind of container except cups.)
4. The class of cups is made up of many kinds of cups. I'll name some kinds of cups in the class of cups. Listen: Plastic cups, metal cups. You name some kinds of cups in the class of cups. (Call on individual children. Praise reasonable answers such as: *china cups* and *paper cups.*)
5. Think about this. If we took all the paper cups from the class of cups, would there be any cups left? (Signal.) *Yes.*
6. Name some kinds of cups that would be left. (Call on individual children. Praise all acceptable answers: any kind of cup except paper cups.)
7. Yes, if we took all the paper cups from the class of cups, there would still be cups left. So which class is bigger, the class of paper cups or the class of cups? (Signal.) *The class of cups.*
8. Tell me how you know. Get ready. (Signal.) *The class of cups has more kinds of things in it.*
- (Repeat until firm.)
9. Everybody, think big. Tell me which class is bigger, the class of containers or the class of cups. (Pause.) Get ready. (Signal.) *The class of containers.*
10. Everybody, think big. Tell me which class is bigger, the class of paper cups or the class of cups. (Pause.) Get ready. (Signal.) *The class of cups.*

EXERCISE 3 Calendar

1. (Present calendar.)
- We're going to talk about today, tomorrow, and one week from today.
2. Tell me the day of the week it is today. Get ready. (Signal.)
- Tell me the day of the week it will be tomorrow. Get ready. (Signal.)
- Tell me the day of the week it will be one week from today. Get ready. (Signal.)
3. (Repeat step 2 until firm.)
4. Now the dates.
- Tell me today's date. Get ready. (Signal.)
- Look at the calendar. ✔
- Tell me the date it will be one week from today. Get ready. (Signal.)
5. Once more.
- Listen: Tell me today's date. Get ready. (Signal.)
- Tell me tomorrow's date. Get ready. (Signal.)
- Tell me the date it will be one week from today. Get ready. (Signal.)
6. (Repeat step 5 until firm.)

EXERCISE 4 Description

1. I'm going to say two things about something you know. See if you can figure out what I'm talking about.
2. (Hold up one finger.)
- Trast is an action.
- (Hold up two fingers.)
- When you trast, both legs leave the ground at once.
3. Everybody, tell me what you know about trast.
- (Hold up one finger.) *Trast is an action.*
- (Hold up two fingers.) *When you trast, both legs leave the ground at once.*
4. (Repeat step 3 until firm.)
5. Everybody, tell me what trast is. Get ready. (Signal.) *Jump.*
6. (Repeat steps 3 and 5 until firm.)

EXERCISE 5 Synonyms

1. Listen: a synonym for over is above.
2. I'll say one statement. You say the statement that means **the same thing.** My turn. The kite is above the tree. Your turn. Get ready. (Signal.) *The kite is over the tree.*
- (Repeat step 2 until firm.)

3. I'll say a statement. You say the statement that means **the same thing.** My turn. The dog was under the house. Your turn. Get ready. (Signal.) *The dog was below the house.*
- (Repeat step 3 until firm.)

EXERCISE 6 Sentence Writing

| bird | man |

1. Everybody, open your workbook to Lesson 88. Write your name at the top of the page. ✔
- You're going to write sentences.
- Touch the picture of the bird and the bug. ✔
- The picture shows the bird on something and the bug on something. What is the bird on? (Signal.) *A van.*
- Yes, **the bird is on a van.**
- What is the bug on? (Signal.) *A man.*
2. Say the sentence for the bird. Get ready. (Signal.) *The bird is on a van.*
- Say the sentence for the bug. Get ready. (Signal.) *The bug is on a man.*
3. (Repeat step 2 until firm.)
4. The word box shows how to spell the words **bird** and **man.** You can figure out how to spell the other words.
5. Write the sentence for the bird. Remember to start with a capital and end with a period. Pencils down when you're finished. (Observe children and give feedback.)

- Now go to the next line and write the sentence for the bug. Pencils down when you're finished.
  (Observe children and give feedback.)
6. (Call on individual children to read both their sentences.)

EXERCISE 7 Classification

1. Everybody, find the next page. ✔
- All the things under the letter A are in the **same** class. Everybody, what class is that? (Signal.) *Animals.*
2. Touch the top picture. ✔
   Everybody, what kind of animal is that? (Signal.) *A bird.*
- Touch the next picture. ✔
  What animal? (Signal.) *A goldfish.*
  Yes, a goldfish.
- Touch the next picture. ✔
  What animal? (Signal.) *A snake.*
- Touch the next picture. ✔
  What animal? (Signal.) *A dog.*
- Touch the next picture. ✔
  What animal? (Signal.) *A rabbit.*
- Touch the next picture. ✔
  What animal? (Signal.) *An elephant.*
3. Who can start at the top and name all the animals? (Call on several children. Praise children who name all the animals in order.)
4. Everybody, make a flap out of each animal. Cut carefully. Don't cut anywhere except on a dotted line. Raise your hand when you're finished. You have 1 minute. (Observe children and give feedback.)

5. (After 1 minute, say:) You're going to play a mystery game. It's a very hard game. Here's how it works: I'll tell you clues about the mystery animal. After each clue, you'll be able to fold over some pictures that could **not** be the mystery animal. After I give you the last clue, you'll know which animal is the mystery animal because it will be the **only** picture that is **not** folded over.
6. Here's the first clue about the mystery animal: This animal has legs. Everybody, say that clue. (Signal.) *This animal has legs.*
- Not all the animals have legs. If it does **not** have legs, it can **not** be the mystery animal. So fold over any animal that does **not** have legs. Raise your hand when you're finished. (Observe children and give feedback.)
- Everybody, which animals did you fold over? (Signal.) *The goldfish and snake.*
- Why did you fold over the goldfish and the snake? (Signal.) *Because they don't have legs.*
7. Here's another clue about the mystery animal: This animal is smaller than a car. Everybody, say that clue. (Signal.) *This animal is smaller than a car.*
- Listen: If it is **not** smaller than a car, it can **not** be the mystery animal, so fold over any animal that is **not** smaller than a car. Raise your hand when you're finished. (Observe children and give feedback.)
- Everybody, which animal did you fold over? (Signal.) *The elephant.*
- Why did you fold over the elephant? (Signal.) *Because it's **not** smaller than a car.*
8. Here's the last clue about the mystery animal: This animal can fly. Everybody, say that clue. (Signal.) *This animal can fly.*
- Listen: Fold over the pictures that could **not** be the mystery animal. ✔
- Everybody, which animals did you fold over? (Signal.) *The dog and rabbit.*
- Why did you fold over the dog and the rabbit? (Signal.) *Because they don't fly.*
9. You figured out which animal is the mystery animal. It should be the only picture that is **not** folded over. Everybody, which animal is the mystery animal? (Signal.) *The bird.*
- Raise your hand if you figured out the mystery animal. ✔

10. I gave you three clues that let you figure out the mystery animal. Let's see how many of those clues you remember.
   - What was one of the clues? (Call on a child. Accept appropriate response.)
11. What was another clue? (Call on a child. Accept appropriate response.)
   (Repeat step 11 until all clues have been identified.)
12. Who can name all three clues about the mystery animal? (Call on several children. Praise any child who can name at least two clues.)
13. Unfold each flap so you can see all the animals again and I'll tell you about another mystery animal. ✔
14. Here's the first clue about the mystery animal: This animal can move along the ground. Everybody, say that clue. (Signal.) *This animal can move along the ground.*
   - Listen: Fold over every picture that could **not** be the mystery animal. That's any animal that can **not** move along the ground. Raise your hand when you're finished. (Observe children and give feedback.)
   - Everybody, which animal did you fold over? (Signal.) *The goldfish.*
   - Why did you fold over the goldfish? (Signal.) *Because the goldfish cannot move along the ground.*
15. Here's another clue about the mystery animal: This animal has four legs. Everybody, say that clue. (Signal.) *This animal has four legs.*
   - Listen: Fold over every picture that could **not** be the mystery animal. That's every animal that does **not** have four legs. Raise your hand when you're finished. (Observe children and give feedback.)

   - Everybody, which animals did you fold over? (Signal.) *The snake and bird.*
   - Why did you fold over the snake and the bird? (Signal.) *Because they do not have four legs.*
16. Here's the last clue about the mystery animal: This animal has a trunk. Everybody, say that clue. (Signal.) *This animal has a trunk.*
   - Listen: Fold over every picture that could **not** be the mystery animal.
   - Everybody, which animals did you fold over? (Signal.) *The rabbit and dog.*
   - Why did you fold over the rabbit and the dog? (Signal.) *Because they do not have a trunk.*
17. You figured out which animal is the mystery animal. Everybody, which animal is the mystery animal? (Signal.) *The elephant.*
   - Raise your hand if you figured out the mystery animal. ✔
18. I gave you three clues that let you figure out the mystery animal. Let's see how many of those clues you remember.
   - What was one of the clues? (Call on a child. Accept reasonable response.)
19. What was another clue? (Call on a child. Accept reasonable response.)
   (Repeat step 19 until all clues have been identified.)
20. Who can name all three clues about the mystery animal? (Call on several children. Praise any child who can name at least two clues.)

Objectives

- Name four classes containing a common noun and answer questions about members of those classes. (Exercise 1)
- Identify an object based on its characteristics. (Exercise 2)
- Replace a word in a sentence with a synonym. (Exercise 3)
- Answer questions involving previously learned calendar facts. (Exercise 4)
- Listen to a short story and answer questions involving "who," "when," "why," "where" and "what." (Exercise 5)
- Name objects that could be made of a given material. (Exercise 6)
- Identify absurdities of ability and use. (Exercise 7)
- Write rhyming sentences given picture cues. (Exercise 8)
- Construct verbal analogies. (Exercise 9)
- **Write class names next to members of the class.** (Exercise 10)

EXERCISE 1   Classification

1. Today we're going to talk about a rocking chair. We can put a rocking chair into four different classes.
2. See how many classes you can name, starting with the smallest class.
- Everybody, what's the smallest class? Get ready. (Signal.) *Rocking chairs.*
- What's the next bigger class? (Signal.) *Chairs.*
- What's the next bigger class? (Signal.) *Furniture.*
- What's the biggest class? (Signal.) *Things made of wood.*
- (Accept any other correct responses, but use: *rocking chairs, chairs, furniture, things made of wood.*)
3. (Repeat step 2 until firm.)
4. What is one kind of object you would find in all those classes? (Signal.) *A rocking chair.*
5. Think of these classes: rocking chairs, chairs, furniture, things made of wood.
- Would you find a wooden folding chair in all those classes? (Signal.) *No.*
- Name three of those classes you would find a wooden folding chair in. (Pause.) Get ready. (Tap 3 times.) *Chairs. Furniture. Things made of wood.*
6. Would you find a wooden table in all those classes? (Signal.) *No.*
- Name two of those classes you would find a wooden table in. (Pause.) Get ready. (Tap 2 times.) *Furniture. Things made of wood.*

EXERCISE 2   Description

1. I'm going to say two things about something you know. See if you can figure out what I'm talking about.
2. (Hold up one finger.)
- Meel is a day.
- (Hold up two fingers.)
- Meel always comes after Sunday.
3. Everybody, tell me what you know about Meel.
- (Hold up one finger.) *Meel is a day.*
- (Hold up two fingers.) *Meel always comes after Sunday.*
4. (Repeat step 3 until firm.)
5. Everybody, tell me what Meel is. Get ready. (Signal.) *Monday.*
6. (Repeat steps 3 and 5 until firm.)
7. Here's another one.
- (Hold up one finger.) Kroost is an action.
- (Hold up two fingers.) When you kroost, you look at words in a book.
8. Everybody, tell me what you know about kroost.
- (Hold up one finger.) *Kroost is an action.*
- (Hold up two fingers.) *When you kroost, you look at words in a book.*
9. (Repeat step 8 until firm.)
10. Everybody, tell me what kroost is. (Pause.) Get ready. (Signal.) *Read.*
11. (Repeat steps 8 and 10 until firm.)

EXERCISE 3 Synonyms

1. Let's make up statements that mean the same thing as other statements.
2. Listen: The horse is well. Say that. (Signal.) *The horse is well.*
- Here's a statement that means **the same thing:** The horse is healthy. Say that. (Signal.) *The horse is healthy.*
3. I'll say one of the statements. You say the statement that means the same thing. My turn: The horse is well. Your turn. Get ready. (Signal.) *The horse is healthy.*
- (Repeat step 3 until firm.)

EXERCISE 4 Calendar Facts

1. You learned calendar facts.
- Everybody, how many days are in a week? (Signal.) *Seven.*
- Everybody, say the days of the week. Get ready. (Signal.) *Sunday, Monday, Tuesday, Wednesday, Thursday, Friday, Saturday.*
2. How many weeks are in a year? (Signal.) *52.*
- Say the fact. Get ready. (Signal.) *There are 52 weeks in a year.*
3. How many days are in a year? (Signal.) *365.*
- Say the fact. Get ready. (Signal.) *There are 365 days in a year.*
4. How many seasons are in a year? (Signal.) *Four.*
- Name the four seasons. Get ready. (Signal.) *Winter, spring, summer, fall.*
5. How many months are in a year? (Signal.) *12.*
- Everybody, say the months. Get ready. (Signal.) *January, February, March, April, May, June, July, August, September, October, November, December.*
6. (Repeat step 5 until firm.)
7. What day of the week is it today? (Signal.)
- What day of the week will it be tomorrow? (Signal.)
- What's today's date? (Signal.)

EXERCISE 5 Who—What—When—Where—Why

1. Listen to this story.
- The woman was digging in her garden. She dug up a lot of carrots. Her hands got very dirty. Before the woman washed her hands, she gave her rabbit a carrot.
- (Repeat the story.)
2. Tell why the woman's hands got dirty. (Call on a child. Idea: *She was digging.*)
- Everybody, tell who the woman gave a carrot to. Get ready. (Signal.) *Her rabbit.*
- Did the woman give the rabbit a carrot before she washed her hands or after she washed her hands? (Signal.) *Before she washed her hands.*
- Tell where the woman was. Get ready. (Signal.) *In her garden.*
- Tell what the woman gave her rabbit. Get ready. (Signal.) *A carrot.*
3. (Repeat step 2 until firm.)

EXERCISE 6 Materials

1. Think of things that are made of glass.
- Let's see who can name at least three things made of glass. (Call on individual children to name objects made of glass. Each child should name at least three things.)
2. Everybody, think of things that are made of rubber.
- Let's see who can name at least three things made of rubber. (Call on individual children to name objects made of rubber. Each child should name at least three things.)
3. Everybody, think of things that are made of cloth.
- Let's see who can name at least three things made of cloth. (Call on individual children to name objects made of cloth. Each child should name at least three things.)

EXERCISE 7 Absurdity

1. Listen to this statement and figure out what is absurd about it.
- Her horse cooked dinner for her. Say the statement. (Signal.) *Her horse cooked dinner for her.*
- What's absurd about that statement? (Call on one child. Praise all reasonable responses; then say:) Yes, her horse couldn't cook dinner for her.
2. Here's another absurd statement. Figure out what's absurd about this one.
- Listen: He carried his lemonade home in his glove. Say the statement. (Signal.) *He carried his lemonade home in his glove.*
- What's absurd about that statement? (Call on one child. Praise all reasonable responses; then say:) Yes, you can't carry lemonade in a glove.

WORKBOOK

EXERCISE 8 Sentence Writing

| mole | under | coat |

1. Everybody, open your workbook to Lesson 89. Write your name at the top of the page. ✔
- You're going to write sentences that rhyme.
- Touch the picture of the mole and the rat. ✔
- The picture shows the mole under something and the rat under something. What is the mole under? (Signal.) *A goat.*
- What is the rat under? (Signal.) *A coat.*

2. Say the sentence for the mole. Get ready. (Signal.) *The mole is under a goat.*
- Say the sentence for the rat. Get ready. (Signal.) *The rat is under a coat.*
3. (Repeat step 2 until firm.)
4. The word box shows how to spell the words **mole, under** and **coat.** You can figure out how to spell the other words.
5. Write the sentence for the mole. Remember to start with a capital and end with a period. Pencils down when you're finished. (Observe children and give feedback.)
- Now go to the next line and write the sentence for the rat. Pencils down when you're finished. (Observe children and give feedback.)
6. (Call on individual children to read both their sentences.)

EXERCISE 9 Analogies

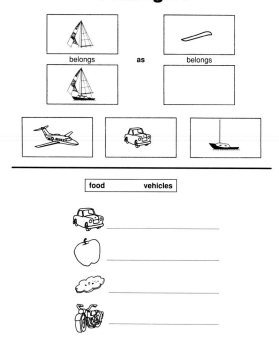

1. Everybody, find the next page. ✔
- (Hold up workbook. Point to first half.)
2. The pictures show parts and the objects those parts belong to.
3. Touch the sail. ✔
- The picture that's right below shows what it belongs to. Everybody, what does a sail belong to? (Signal.) *A sailboat.*
4. Touch the wing. ✔
- One of the pictures below shows what it belongs to. Touch the picture that shows what a wing belongs to. ✔
- Everybody, what does it belong to? (Signal.) *An airplane.*

5. Tell me about a sail. Get ready. (Signal.) *A sail belongs to a sailboat.*
- Tell me about a wing. Get ready. (Signal.) *A wing belongs to an airplane.*
6. Say the whole analogy about a sail and a wing. Get ready. (Signal.) *A sail belongs to a sailboat as a wing belongs to an airplane.*
7. (Repeat step 6 until firm.)
8. Draw a line from the wing to what it belongs to.
   (Observe children and give feedback.)

EXERCISE 10 Classification

1. (Hold up workbook. Point to second half.)
2. Everybody, I'll read the words in the box. You touch the words.
- First word: Food. ✔
- Next word: Vehicles. ✔
- Yes, food and vehicles.
3. Everybody, touch the car. Is a car in the class of food or in the class of vehicles? (Signal.) *Vehicles.*

- Yes, a car is in the class of vehicles. Copy the word **vehicles** next to the car.
   (Observe children and give feedback.)
4. Everybody, touch the apple. Is an apple in the class of food or in the class of vehicles? (Signal.) *Food.*
- Yes, an apple is in the class of food. Copy the word **food** next to the apple.
   (Observe children and give feedback.)
5. Everybody, touch the cookie. Is a cookie in the class of food or in the class of vehicles? (Signal.) *Food.*
- Yes, a cookie is in the class of food. Copy the word **food** next to the cookie.
   (Observe children and give feedback.)
6. Everybody, touch the motorcycle. Is a motorcycle in the class of food or in the class of vehicles? (Signal.) *Vehicles.*
- Yes, a motorcycle is in the class of vehicles. Copy the word **vehicles** next to the motorcycle.
   (Observe children and give feedback.)

LESSON 90

Objectives

- Replace a word in a sentence with a synonym (Exercise 1)
- Identify an object based on its characteristics. (Exercise 2)
- Generate questions to find a word's definition. (Exercise 3)
- Construct verbal analogies. (Exercise 4)
- Answer questions involving previously learned calendar facts. (Exercise 5)
- Write rhyming sentences given picture cues. (Exercise 6)
- Label cardinal directions on a map. (Exercise 7)
- Follow coloring rules involving classes and subclasses. (Exercise 8)

EXERCISE 1 Synonyms

1. I'll say a statement. You say the statement that means **the same thing.** My turn: The child is well. Your turn. Get ready. (Signal.) *The child is healthy.*
- (Repeat step 1 until firm.)
2. Here's another one.
3. Listen: The baby is weeping. Say that. (Signal.) *The baby is weeping.*
- Here's a statement that means the same thing: The baby is crying. Say that. (Signal.) *The baby is crying.*
- (Repeat step 3 until firm.)
4. I'll say one of the statements. You say the statement that means **the same thing.** My turn: The baby is weeping. Your turn. Get ready. (Signal.) *The baby is crying.*
- (Repeat step 4 until firm.)

EXERCISE 2 Description

1. I'm going to say two things about something you know. See if you can figure out what I'm talking about.
2. (Hold up one finger.) Zool is a season.
- (Hold up two fingers.)
In some places it snows in zool.
3. Everybody, tell me what you know about zool.
- (Hold up one finger.) *Zool is a season.*
- (Hold up two fingers.) *In some places it snows in zool.*
4. (Repeat step 3 until firm.)
5. Everybody, tell me what zool is. Get ready. (Signal.) *Winter.*
6. (Repeat steps 3 and 5 until firm.)

7. Here's another one.
- (Hold up one finger.) A tatting is a place.
- (Hold up two fingers.) You see a diving board at a tatting.
8. Everybody, tell me what you know about a tatting.
- (Hold up one finger.) *A tatting is a place.*
- (Hold up two fingers.) *You see a diving board at a tatting.*
9. (Repeat step 8 until firm.)
10. Everybody, tell me what a tatting is. Get ready. (Signal.) *A swimming pool.*
11. (Repeat steps 8 and 10 until firm.)

EXERCISE 3 Questioning Skills

1. I'm going to tell a story. When you hear a word you don't know, say **stop.**
2. A girl was (pause) **wailing.** (Children are to say *stop.*)
- Everybody, what word don't you know? (Signal.) *Wailing.*
- Ask the question about what the word wailing means. Get ready. (Signal.) *What does the word wailing mean?*
- I'll tell you what wailing means. Wailing is a synonym for **crying.** What is wailing a synonym for? (Signal.) *Crying.*
- So if the girl was wailing, she was . . . (Signal.) *crying.*
3. Here's more of the story.
- Her finger was (pause) **lacerated.** (Children are to say *stop.*)

- Everybody, what word don't you know? (Signal.) *Lacerated.*
- Ask the question about what the word lacerated means. Get ready. (Signal.) *What does the word lacerated mean?*
- I'll tell you what lacerated means. Lacerated is a synonym for **cut.** What is lacerated a synonym for? (Signal.) *Cut.*
4. So the girl was wailing because her finger was lacerated. How do you think her finger felt? (Children respond.)
   That's the end of the story.

EXERCISE 4   Analogies

1. We're going to make up an analogy.
2. Everybody, tell me what class a tree and a flower are in. Get ready. (Signal.) *Plants.*
   Yes, plants.
3. We're going to make up an analogy that tells a part each plant has.
- What's the analogy going to tell? (Signal.) *A part each plant has.*
4. Name some parts that a tree has. (Call on individual children. Repeat all reasonable answers.)
- Let's say a tree has a trunk.
5. Name some parts that a flower has. (Call on individual children. Repeat all reasonable answers.)
- Let's say a flower has a stem.
6. A tree is to a trunk as a flower is to a stem. Everybody, say the analogy about the parts a tree and a flower have. Get ready. (Signal.) *A tree is to a trunk as a flower is to a stem.*
- (Repeat step 6 until firm.)

7. What does our analogy tell about each plant? (Call on a child. Idea: *A part each plant has.*)
8. Everybody, say our analogy one more time. Get ready. (Signal.) *A tree is to a trunk as a flower is to a stem.*
9. (Repeat steps 7 and 8 until firm.)

EXERCISE 5   Calendar Facts

1. You learned calendar facts.
- Everybody, how many days are in a week? (Signal.) *Seven.*
- Everybody, say the days of the week. Get ready. (Signal.) *Sunday, Monday, Tuesday, Wednesday, Thursday, Friday, Saturday.*
2. How many weeks are in a year? (Signal.) *52.*
- Say the fact. Get ready. (Signal.) *There are 52 weeks in a year.*
3. How many days are in a year? (Signal.) *365.*
- Say the fact. Get ready. (Signal.) *There are 365 days in a year.*
4. How many seasons are in a year? (Signal.) *Four.*
- Name the four seasons. Get ready. (Signal.) *Winter, spring, summer, fall.*
5. (Repeat steps 1 through 4 until firm.)
6. How many months are in a year? (Signal.) *12.*
- Everybody, say the months. Get ready. (Signal.) *January, February, March, April, May, June, July, August, September, October, November, December.*
- (Repeat step 6 until firm.)
7. What day of the week is it today? (Signal.)
- What day of the week will it be tomorrow? (Signal.)
- What's today's date? (Signal.)

EXERCISE 6   Sentence Writing

ant   cake

_____

_____

_____

_____

1. Everybody, open your workbook to Lesson 90. Write your name at the top of the page. ✔
• You're going to write sentences that rhyme.
• Touch the picture of the ant and the goat. ✔
• The picture shows the ant in something and the goat in something. What is the ant in? (Signal.) *A cake.*
• What is the goat in? (Signal.) *A lake.*
2. Say the sentence for the ant. Get ready. (Signal.) *The ant is in a cake.*
• Say the sentence for the goat. Get ready. (Signal.) *The goat is in a lake.*
3. (Repeat step 2 until firm.)
4. The word box shows how to spell the words **ant** and **cake.** You can figure out how to spell the other words.
5. Write the sentence for the ant. Remember to start with a capital and end with a period. Pencils down when you're finished. (Observe children and give feedback.)
• Now go to the next line and write the sentence for the goat. Pencils down when you're finished. (Observe children and give feedback.)
6. (Call on individual children to read both their sentences.)

EXERCISE 7   Map Reading

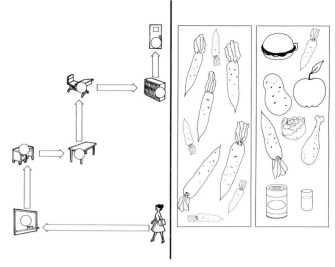

1. Everybody, find the next page. ✔
• (Hold up workbook. Point to first half.)
2. Find the arrows. ✔
• The arrows show where the woman went.
3. Start at the picture of the woman and figure out which direction each arrow is pointing. Write the letter for each direction in the circle. Pencils down when you're finished. (Observe children and give feedback.)

EXERCISE 8   Classification

1. (Hold up workbook. Point to second half.)
2. Touch the picture of the **smaller** class. ✔
• What kind of thing is that in the picture? (Signal.) *Carrots.*
3. Everybody, circle the picture that shows the **larger** class. ✔
• Everybody, what's the name of the **larger** class? (Signal.) *Food.*
• (Repeat step 3 until firm.)
4. Everybody, touch the picture of the class that is **smaller.** ✔
• The carrots in that picture of the **smaller** class should be orange. What color? (Signal.) *Orange.*
• Mark a carrot in that picture. ✔
5. Touch the picture that shows the **larger** class. ✔
• The carrots in that picture should be red or yellow. What colors? (Signal.) *Red or yellow.*
• Mark two carrots in that picture. ✔

Objectives

- **Name common synonyms and opposites.** (Exercise 1)
- Identify an object based on its characteristics. (Exercise 2)
- Replace a word in a sentence with a synonym. (Exercise 3)
- Construct verbal analogies. (Exercise 4)
- Listen to a short story and answer questions involving "who," "when," "why," "where" and "what". (Exercise 5)
- Answer questions involving previously learned calendar facts. (Exercise 6)
- Write rhyming sentences given picture cues. (Exercise 7)
- **Ask questions to figure out the "mystery" picture.** (Exercise 8)

EXERCISE 1 Synonyms/Opposites

1. Everybody, let's play a game. I'll say a word. You say a word that means the same thing.
- Listen: Tell me a synonym for **under.** Get ready. (Signal.) *Below.*
- Listen: Tell me a synonym for **over.** Get ready. (Signal.) *Above.*
- Listen: Tell me a synonym for **below.** Get ready. (Signal.) *Under.*
- Listen: Tell me a synonym for **above.** Get ready. (Signal.) *Over.*
2. I'll say a word. You tell me the opposite.
- Listen: Tell me the opposite of **happy.** Get ready. (Signal.) *Sad.*
- Listen: Tell me the opposite of **starting.** Get ready. (Signal.) *Finishing.*

EXERCISE 2 Description

1. I'm going to say two things about something you know. See if you can figure out what I'm talking about.
2. (Hold up one finger.) A krast is a person.
- (Hold up two fingers.) A krast puts out fires.
3. Everybody, tell me what you know about a krast.
- (Hold up one finger.) *A krast is a person.*
- (Hold up two fingers.) *A krast puts out fires.*
4. (Repeat step 3 until firm.)
5. Everybody, tell me what a krast is. Get ready. (Signal.) *A firefighter.*
6. (Repeat steps 3 and 5 until firm.)

EXERCISE 3 Synonyms

1. We're going to make up statements that mean the same thing.
2. What do we call two words that mean the same thing? (Signal.) *Synonyms.*
3. Listen: Children like to shout. Say that. (Signal.) *Children like to shout.*
- Say that statement using a synonym for **shout.** Get ready. (Signal.) *Children like to yell.*
- Children like to shout. Children like to yell. Those statements mean the same thing because shout and yell are synonyms.
4. Listen: The nurse is weeping. Say that. (Signal.) *The nurse is weeping.*
- Say that statement using a synonym for **weeping.** Get ready. (Signal.) *The nurse is crying.*
- (Repeat step 4 until firm.)
5. Listen: The bird flew over the house. Say that. (Signal.) *The bird flew over the house.*
- Say that statement using a synonym for **over.** Get ready. (Signal.) *The bird flew above the house.*

EXERCISE 4 Analogies

1. We're going to make up an analogy.
2. Everybody, tell me what class a carrot and milk are in. Get ready. (Signal.) *Food.* Yes, food.
3. We're going to make up an analogy that tells what color each food is. What's the analogy going to tell? (Signal.) *What color each food is.*
4. Tell me the color a carrot is. (Signal.) *Orange.* Yes, a carrot is to orange.
5. Tell me the color milk is. (Signal.) *White.* Yes, milk is to white.
6. Everybody, say the whole analogy about what colors a carrot and milk are. Get ready. (Signal.) *A carrot is to orange as milk is to white.*
   • (Repeat step 6 until firm.)
7. What does our analogy tell about each food? Get ready. (Signal.) *What color it is.*
8. Everybody, say our analogy one more time. Get ready. (Signal.) *A carrot is to orange as milk is to white.*
9. (Repeat steps 7 and 8 until firm.)

EXERCISE 5 Who—What—When—Where—Why

1. Listen to this story.
   • A cat and dog were playing in the yard. The dog chased the cat, so the cat hissed at the dog. Then the dog crawled under the fence. After the dog left, the cat ate dinner.
   • (Repeat the story.)
2. Did the dog leave first or did the cat eat dinner first? (Signal.) *The dog left first.*
   • Tell where the cat and dog were playing. Get ready. (Signal.) *In the yard.*
   • Tell who chased the cat. Get ready. (Signal.) *The dog.*
   • Tell why the cat hissed at the dog. Get ready. (Signal.) *Because the dog chased it.*
   • Tell what the dog crawled under. Get ready. (Signal.) *The fence.*
   • Tell when the cat ate dinner. Get ready. (Signal.) *After the dog left.*
3. (Repeat step 2 until firm.)

EXERCISE 6 Calendar Facts

1. You learned calendar facts.
   • Everybody, how many days are in a week? (Signal.) *Seven.*
   • Everybody, say the days of the week. Get ready. (Signal.) *Sunday, Monday, Tuesday, Wednesday, Thursday, Friday, Saturday.*
2. How many weeks are in a year? (Signal.) *52.*
   • Say the fact. Get ready. (Signal.) *There are 52 weeks in a year.*
3. How many days are in a year? (Signal.) *365.*
   • Say the fact. Get ready. (Signal.) *There are 365 days in a year.*
4. How many seasons are in a year? (Signal.) *Four.*
   • Name the four seasons. Get ready. (Signal.) *Winter, spring, summer, fall.*
5. (Repeat steps 1 through 4 until firm.)
6. How many months are in a year? (Signal.) *12.*
   • Everybody, say the months. Get ready. (Signal.) *January, February, March, April, May, June, July, August, September, October, November, December.*
   • (Repeat step 6 until firm.)
7. What day of the week is it today? (Signal.)
   • What day of the week will it be tomorrow? (Signal.)
   • What's today's date? (Signal.)

WORKBOOK

EXERCISE 7 Sentence Writing

clock   will   sing

_____

_____

_____

1. Everybody, open your workbook to Lesson 91. Write your name. ✔

• You're going to write sentences that rhyme. Touch the picture of the man and the clock. ✔

• The picture shows what the man will do and what the clock will do. What will the man do? (Signal.) *Sing.*

• What will the clock do? (Signal.) *Ring.*

2. Say the sentence for the man. Get ready. (Signal.) *The man will sing.*

• Say the sentence for the clock. Get ready. (Signal.) *The clock will ring.*

3. (Repeat step 2 until firm.)

4. The word box shows how to spell the words **clock, will** and **sing.** You can figure out how to spell the other words.

5. Write the sentence for the man. Remember to start with a capital and end with a period. Pencils down when you're finished. (Observe children and give feedback.)

• Now go to the next line and write the sentence for the clock. Pencils down when you're finished.
(Observe children and give feedback.)

6. (Call on individual children to read both their sentences.)

EXERCISE 8 Questioning

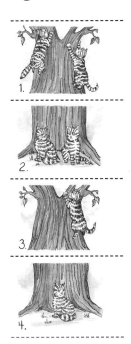

1. Everybody, find the next page. ✔

• Make a flap out of each picture. Cut carefully. Don't cut anywhere except on a dotted line. Do it fast. Raise your hand when you're finished. ✔

2. We're going to play the question game that is **really** tough. If you're very smart, you can find out the right picture in only two questions. You have to really think. Let's see if you can do it in only **two** questions.

3. (**Key:** The target picture is number 2—two cats sitting next to a tree.)

• Here we go. I'm thinking about one of the pictures. Raise your hand if you want to ask a question.

• (Call on a child with hand raised. Accept good questions. That is, a question that asks either about the number of cats or the location—not **both.**)

• (After a good question, say:) That's a good question. Here's the answer. (Tell the children the answer.)

• Fold over **all** the pictures that could **not** be the mystery picture. Raise your hand when you're finished.
(Observe children and give feedback.)

• Tell me the numbers for the pictures that you can still see. (Call on a child. Confirm correct response.)

4. Raise your hand if you have another good question. (Call on a child with hand raised. After a good question, say:) That's a good question. Here's the answer. (Tell the children the answer.)

• Fold over **all** the pictures that could **not** be the mystery picture. Raise your hand when you're finished.
(Observe children and give feedback.)

• Tell me the numbers for the pictures that you can still see. (Call on a child. Confirm correct response.)

5. (After you answer **two** questions, tell the group either:)

You found the mystery picture in **only** two questions. Good for you.	(or)	You asked **two** questions, but you **didn't** find the mystery picture. Let's start over and try again. Unfold each flap. See if you can ask **really** good questions this time. (Repeat steps 3 and 4.)

6. (When children have found the mystery picture in only two questions, say:) Everybody, what's the number of the picture I was thinking of? (Signal.) *Two.*
- How many cats are in that picture? (Signal.) *Two.*
- What are the cats doing? (Signal.) *Sitting.*
- You found the picture I was thinking of and it took you only two questions.

7. (**Key:** The target picture is number 4—one cat sitting next to a tree.)
- New game. Unfold each flap so you can see all four pictures again. ✔
- I'm thinking of a different picture. Ask me questions, and I'll tell you the answers. Raise your hand if you want to ask a question. (Call on a child with hand raised. After a good question, say:) That's a good question. Here's the answer. (Tell the children the answer.)
- Fold over **all** the pictures that could not be the mystery picture. Raise your hand when you're finished. (Observe children and give feedback.)
- Tell me the numbers for the pictures that you can still see. (Call on a child. Confirm correct response.)

8. Raise your hand if you have another good question. (Call on a child with hand raised. After a good question, say:) That's a good question. Here's the answer. (Tell the children the answer.)

- Fold over **all** the pictures that could **not** be the mystery picture. Raise your hand when you're finished. (Observe children and give feedback.)
- Tell me the numbers for the pictures that you can still see. (Call on a child. Confirm correct response.)

9. (After you answer **two** questions, tell the group either:)

You found the mystery picture in **only** two questions. Good for you.	(or)	You asked **two** questions, but you **didn't** find the mystery picture. Let's start over and try again. Unfold each flap. See if you can ask **really** good questions this time. (Repeat steps 7 and 8.)

10. (When children have found the mystery picture in only two questions, say:) Everybody, what's the number of the picture I was thinking of? (Signal.) *Four.*
- How many cats are in that picture? (Signal.) *One.*
- What is the cat in that picture doing? (Signal.) *Sitting.*
- You found the picture I was thinking of and it took you only two questions.

Objectives

- Listen to a short story and answer questions involving "who," "when," "why," "where" and "what". (Exercise 1)
- Generate questions to find a word's definition. (Exercise 2)
- Given a calendar, identify the day and date for "today" and "tomorrow" and one week from today. (Exercise 3)
- Identify an object based on its characteristics. (Exercise 4)
- Name common synonyms. (Exercise 5)
- Write rhyming sentences given picture cues. (Exercise 6)
- Ask questions to figure out the "mystery" picture. (Exercise 7)

EXERCISE 1 Who—What—When—Where—Why

1. Listen to this story.
- The alligator was in the river. He was hungry, so he ate a fish. After the alligator ate the fish, he went for a swim.
- (Repeat the story.)
- What did the alligator do first—eat the fish or go for a swim? (Signal.) *Eat the fish.*
2. Tell where the alligator was. Get ready. (Signal.) *In the river.*
- Tell what the alligator did first. Get ready. (Signal.) *He ate a fish.*
- Tell who ate a fish. Get ready. (Signal.) *The alligator.*
- Tell why the alligator ate a fish. Get ready. (Signal.) *He was hungry.*
- Tell when the alligator went for a swim. Get ready. (Signal.) *After he ate a fish.*
3. (Repeat step 2 until firm.)

EXERCISE 2 Questioning Skills

1. I'm going to tell a story. When you hear a word you don't know, say **stop.**
2. This morning a boy (pause) **arose.** (Children should say *stop.*)
- Ask the question about what the word arose means. Get ready. (Signal.) *What does the word arose mean?*
- Arose is a synonym for **got up.** What is arose a synonym for? (Signal.) *Got up.*
- So if a boy arose, he . . . (Signal.) *got up.*

3. Here's more of the story. He put on his (pause) **garments.** (Children should say *stop.*)
- Ask the question about what the word garments means. Get ready. (Signal.) *What does the word garments mean?*
- Garments is a synonym for **clothes.** What is garments a synonym for? (Signal.) *Clothes.*
- So if a boy arose and put on his garments, he got up and put on his . . . (Signal.) *clothes.*
4. Here's more of the story.
- Then he said to his mother (pause) **farewell.** (Children should say *stop.*)
- Ask the question about what the word farewell means. Get ready. (Signal.) *What does the word farewell mean?*
- Farewell is a synonym for **goodbye.** What is farewell a synonym for? (Signal.) *Goodbye.*
5. So the boy arose and put on his garments. Then he said farewell to his mother. What do you think she said to him? (Children respond.)
- That's the end of the story.

EXERCISE 3   Calendar

1. (Present calendar.) We're going to talk about today, tomorrow, and one week from today.
2. Tell me the day of the week it is today. Get ready. (Signal.)
• Tell me the day of the week it will be tomorrow. Get ready. (Signal.)
• Tell me the day of the week it will be one week from today. Get ready. (Signal.)
3. (Repeat step 2 until firm.)
4. Now the dates. Tell me today's date. Get ready. (Signal.)
• Look at the calendar. ✔
• Tell me the date it will be one week from today. Get ready. (Signal.)
5. Once more. Listen: Tell me today's date. Get ready. (Signal.)
• Tell me tomorrow's date. Get ready. (Signal.)
• Tell me the date it will be one week from today. Get ready. (Signal.)
6. (Repeat step 5 until firm.)

EXERCISE 4   Description

1. I'm going to say two things about something you know. See if you can figure out what I'm talking about.
2. (Hold up one finger.) Stram is a day of the week.
• (Hold up two fingers.) Stram always comes before Wednesday.
3. Everybody, tell me what you know about stram. (Hold up one finger.) *Stram is a day of the week.*
• (Hold up two fingers.) *Stram always comes before Wednesday.*
4. (Repeat step 3 until firm.)
5. Everybody, tell me what stram is. Get ready. (Signal.) *Tuesday.*
6. (Repeat steps 3 and 4 until firm.)
7. Here's another one.
8. (Hold up one finger.) Merl is an action.
• (Hold up two fingers.) When you merl, you move your legs very fast.

9. Everybody, tell me what you know about merl. (Hold up one finger.) *Merl is an action.*
• (Hold up two fingers.) *When you merl, you move your legs very fast.*
10. (Repeat step 9 until firm.)
11. Everybody, tell me what merling is. (Pause.) Get ready. (Signal.) *Running.*
12. (Repeat steps 9 and 11 until firm.)

EXERCISE 5   Synonyms

1. Everybody, let's play a game. I'll say a word. You say a synonym. Listen: What's a synonym for **weeping?** (Signal.) *Crying.*
• Listen: What's a synonym for **small?** (Signal.) *Little.*
• Listen: What's a synonym for **crying?** (Signal.) *Weeping.*
• Listen: What's a synonym for **large?** (Signal.) *Big.*
2. (Repeat step 1 until firm.)

WORKBOOK

EXERCISE 6   Sentence Writing

baby	plane	cry

_____
_____
_____
_____

1. Everybody, open your workbook to Lesson 92. Write your name. ✔
• You're going to write sentences that rhyme.

- Touch the picture of the plane and the baby. ✔
- The picture shows what the plane will do and what the baby will do. What will the plane do? (Signal.) *Fly.*
- What will the baby do? (Signal.) *Cry.*
2. Say the sentence for the plane. Get ready. (Signal.) *The plane will fly.*
- Say the sentence for the baby. Get ready. (Signal.) *The baby will cry.*
3. (Repeat step 2 until firm.)
4. The word box shows how to spell the words **baby, plane** and **cry.** You can figure out how to spell the other words.
5. Write the sentence for the plane. Remember to start with a capital and end with a period. Pencils down when you're finished. (Observe children and give feedback.)
- Now go to the next line and write the sentence for the baby. Pencils down when you're finished. (Observe children and give feedback.)
6. (Call on individual children to read both their sentences.)

EXERCISE 7   Questioning

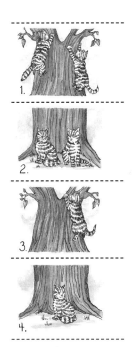

1. Everybody, find the next page. ✔
- You've seen this picture before, but this time I'll be thinking about a different mystery picture.
- Make a flap out of each picture. Cut carefully. Don't cut anywhere except on a dotted line. Raise your hand when you're finished. ✔

2. Remember, if you're really smart, you can find out the right picture in only **two** questions. You have to really think. Let's see if you can do it in only two questions.
3. (**Key:** The target picture is number 3—one cat climbing a tree.)
- Here we go. I'm thinking about one of the pictures. Raise your hand if you want to ask a question. (**Call on a child with hand raised. Accept good questions. That is, a question that asks either about the number of cats or the location—not both.**)
- (After a good question, say:) That's a good question. Here's the answer. (Tell children the answer.)
- Fold over **all** the pictures that could **not** be the mystery picture. Raise your hand when you're finished. (Observe children and give feedback.)
- Tell me the numbers for the pictures that you can still see. (Call on a child. Confirm correct response.)
4. Raise your hand if you have another good question. (Call on a child with hand raised. After a good question, say:) That's a good question. Here's the answer. (Tell children the answer.)
- Fold over **all** the pictures that could **not** be the mystery picture. Raise your hand when you're finished. (Observe children and give feedback.)
- Tell me the numbers for the pictures that you can still see. (Call on a child. Confirm correct response.)
5. (After you answer **two** questions, tell the group either:)

You found the mystery picture in **only** two questions. Good for you.	(or)	You asked **two** questions, but you **didn't** find the mystery picture. Let's start over and try again. Unfold each flap. See if you can ask **really** good questions this time. (Repeat steps 3 and 4.)

6. (When children have found the mystery picture in only two questions, say:) Everybody, what's the number of the picture I was thinking of? (Signal.) *Three.*

- How many cats are in that picture? (Signal.) *One.*
- What is that cat doing? (Signal.) *Climbing a tree.*
- You found the picture I was thinking of and it took you only two questions.

7. (**Key:** The target picture is number 1—two cats climbing a tree.)

- New game. Unfold each flap so you can see all four pictures again. ✔
- I'm thinking of a different picture. Ask me questions, and I'll tell you the answers. Raise your hand if you want to ask a question. (Call on a child with hand raised. After a good question, say:) That's a good question. Here's the answer. (Tell children the answer.)
- Fold over **all** the pictures that could **not** be the mystery picture. Raise your hand when you're finished. (Observe children and give feedback.)
- Tell me the numbers for the pictures that you can still see. (Call on a child. Confirm correct response.)

8. Raise your hand if you have another good question. (Call on a child with hand raised. After a good question, say:) That's a good question. Here's the answer. (Tell children the answer.)

- Fold over **all** the pictures that could **not** be the mystery picture. Raise your hand when you're finished. (Observe children and give feedback.)
- Tell me the numbers for the pictures that you can still see. (Call on a child. Confirm correct response.)

9. (After you answer **two** questions, tell the group either:)

| You found the mystery picture in **only** two questions. Good for you. | (or) | You asked **two** questions, but you **didn't** find the mystery picture. Let's start over and try again. Unfold each flap. See if you can ask **really** good questions this time. (Repeat steps 7 and 8.) |

10. (When children have found the mystery picture in only two questions, say:) Everybody, what's the number of the picture I was thinking of? (Signal.) *One.*

- How many cats are in that picture? (Signal.) *Two.*
- What are the cats in that picture doing? (Signal.) *Climbing a tree.*
- You found the picture I was thinking of and it took you only two questions.

Objectives

- Construct verbal analogies. (Exercise 1)
- Given a calendar, identify the day and date for "today" and "tomorrow" and one week from today. (Exercise 2)
- Identify an object based on its characteristics. (Exercise 3)
- Construct verbal analogies. (Exercise 4)
- Identify an object based on its characteristics. (Exercise 5)
- Write rhyming sentences given picture cues. (Exercise 6)
- Label cardinal directions on a map. (Exercise 7)
- Write class names next to members of the class. (Exercise 8)

EXERCISE 1 Analogies

1. We're going to make up an analogy.
2. Everybody, tell me what class pencils and scissors are in. Get ready. (Signal.) *Tools.* Yes, tools.
3. We're going to make up an analogy that tells what you do with the tools. What's the analogy going to tell? (Signal.) *What you do with the tools.*
4. Tell me what you do with pencils. (Call on a child. Accept draw but use: *write.*) Yes, you write with pencils.
5. Tell me what you do with scissors. (Signal.) *Cut.* Yes, you cut with scissors.
6. Everybody, say the analogy about what you do with pencils and scissors. Get ready. (Signal.) *Pencils are to writing as scissors are to cutting.*
   - (Repeat step 6 until firm.)
7. Tell me what our analogy tells about each tool. Get ready. (Signal.) *What you do with it.*
8. Everybody, say our analogy one more time. Get ready. (Signal.) *Pencils are to writing as scissors are to cutting.*
9. (Repeat steps 7 and 8 until firm.)

EXERCISE 2 Calendar

1. (Present calendar.) We're going to talk about today, tomorrow, and one week from today.

2. Tell me the day of the week it is today. Get ready. (Signal.)
   - Tell me the day of the week it will be tomorrow. Get ready. (Signal.)
   - Tell me the day of the week it will be one week from today. Get ready. (Signal.)
3. (Repeat step 2 until firm.)
4. Now the dates. Tell me today's date. Get ready. (Signal.)
   - Look at the calendar. ✔
   - Tell me the date it will be one week from today. Get ready. (Signal.)
5. Once more. Listen: Tell me today's date. Get ready. (Signal.)
   - Tell me tomorrow's date. Get ready. (Signal.)
   - Tell me the date it will be one week from today. Get ready. (Signal.)
6. (Repeat step 5 until firm.)

EXERCISE 3 Description

1. I'm going to say two things about something you know. See if you can figure out what I'm talking about.
2. (Hold up one finger.) Kreest is a holiday.
   - (Hold up two fingers.) People decorate trees at Kreest.
3. Everybody, tell me what you know about Kreest.
   - (Hold up one finger.) *Kreest is a holiday.*
   - (Hold up two fingers.) *People decorate trees at Kreest.*
4. (Repeat step 3 until firm.)
5. Everybody, tell me what Kreest is. Get ready. (Signal.) *Christmas.*
6. (Repeat steps 3 and 5 until firm.)

EXERCISE 4 Analogies

1. We're going to make up an analogy.
2. Everybody, tell me what class a frog and a butterfly are in. Get ready. (Signal.) *Animals.* Yes, animals.
3. We're going to make up an analogy that tells how each animal moves.
- What's the analogy going to tell? (Signal.) *How each animal moves.*
4. Tell me how a frog moves. Get ready. (Signal.) *Hops.* Yes, a frog hops.
5. Tell me how a butterfly moves. Get ready. (Signal.) *Flies.* Yes, a butterfly flies.
6. Everybody, say the analogy about how a frog and a butterfly move. Get ready. (Signal.) *A frog is to hopping as a butterfly is to flying.*
- (Repeat step 6 until firm.)
7. Tell me what our analogy tells about each animal. Get ready. (Signal.) *How each animal moves.*
8. Everybody, say our analogy one more time. Get ready. (Signal.) *A frog is to hopping as a butterfly is to flying.*
- (Repeat step 8 until firm.)

EXERCISE 5 Description

1. I'm going to say two things about something you know. See if you can figure out what I'm talking about.
2. (Hold up one finger.) A morl is a person.
- (Hold up two fingers.) A morl helps a doctor.
3. Everybody, tell me what you know about a morl. (Hold up one finger.) *A morl is a person.*
- (Hold up two fingers.) *A morl helps a doctor.*
4. (Repeat step 3 until firm.)
5. Everybody, tell me what a morl is. Get ready. (Signal.) *A nurse.*
6. (Repeat steps 3 and 5 until firm.)
7. Here's another one.
8. (Hold up one finger.) Met is a holiday.
- (Hold up two fingers.) Children wear costumes on Met.

9. Everybody, tell me what you know about Met. (Hold up one finger.) *Met is a holiday.*
- (Hold up two fingers.) *Children wear costumes on Met.*
10. (Repeat step 9 until firm.)
11. Everybody, tell me what Met is. Get ready. (Signal.) *Halloween.*
12. (Repeat steps 9 and 11 until firm.)

WORKBOOK

EXERCISE 6 Sentence Writing

> *Note:* Remind children to start their sentences with a capital and end them with a period.

mail

_____
_____
_____
_____

1. Everybody, open your workbook to Lesson 93. Write your name. ✔
- You're going to write sentences.
- Touch the picture of the man and the cat. ✔
- The picture shows what the man had and what the cat had. What did the man have? (Signal.) *Mail.*
- What did the cat have? (Signal.) *A pail.*
2. Say the sentence for the man. Get ready. (Signal.) *The man had mail.*
- Say the sentence for the cat. Get ready. (Signal.) *The cat had a pail.*
3. (Repeat step 2 until firm.)
4. The word box shows how to spell the word **mail.** You can figure out how to spell the other words.

5. Write the sentence for the man. Pencils down when you're finished. ✔

• Now go to the next line and write the sentence for the cat. Pencils down when you're finished. ✔

6. (Call on individual children to read both their sentences.)

EXERCISE 7 **Map Reading**

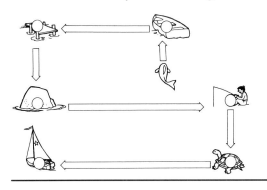

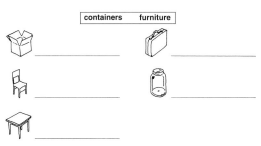

1. Everybody, find the next page. ✔

• (Hold up workbook. Point to first half.) Everybody, touch the fish. ✔

2. This picture is a map of where the fish swam. You're going to color the arrows brown and write the directions on the objects. Remember to start from the fish.

3. Everybody, color the first arrow brown. Do it. ✔

• Now write the letter that shows the direction the fish swam. Pencils down when you're finished. ✔

4. You'll do the rest of the arrows later. Remember to write the letter for each arrow.

EXERCISE 8 **Classification**

1. (Hold up workbook. Point to second half.) Everybody, I'll read the words in the box. You touch the words.
First word: Containers. ✔

• Next word: Furniture. ✔
Yes, containers and furniture.

2. Everybody, put your finger under the picture of a box. ✔
Is a box in the class of containers or in the class of furniture? (Signal.) *Containers.* Yes, a box is in the class of containers.

• Copy the word **containers** next to the box. ✔

• Read what you wrote. (Signal.) *Containers.*

3. Everybody, put your finger under the chair. ✔
Is a chair in the class of containers or in the class of furniture? (Signal.) *Furniture.* Yes, a chair is in the class of furniture.

• Copy the word **furniture** next to the chair. ✔

• Read what you wrote. (Signal.) *Furniture.*

4. Everybody, read the words you wrote. (Signal.) *Containers. Furniture.*

• Later you can write the class words that go with the other pictures.

LESSON 94

Objectives

- Identify an object based on its characteristics. (Exercise 1)
- Replace a word in a sentence with a synonym. (Exercise 2)
- Generate questions to find a word's definition. (Exercise 3)
- Construct verbal analogies. (Exercise 4)
- Listen to a short story and answer questions involving "who," "when," "why," "where" and "what". (Exercise 5)
- **Apply an if-then rule based on the occurrence of events.** (Exercise 6)
- Write sentences given picture cues. (Exercise 7)

EXERCISE 1 Description

1. I'm going to say two things about something you know. See if you can figure out what I'm talking about.
2. (Hold up one finger.) A strem is a person.
- (Hold up two fingers.) A strem fixes teeth.
3. Everybody, tell me what you know about a strem. (Hold up one finger.) *A strem is a person.*
- (Hold up two fingers.) *A strem fixes teeth.*
4. (Repeat step 3 until firm.)
5. Everybody, tell me what a strem is. Get ready. (Signal.) *A dentist.*
6. (Repeat steps 3 and 5 until firm.)
7. Here's another one.
8. (Hold up one finger.) Drons is the name of a big class.
- (Hold up two fingers.) Drons are all the things that grow in the ground.
9. Everybody, tell me what you know about drons. (Hold up one finger.) *Drons is the name of a big class.*
- (Hold up two fingers.) *Drons are all the things that grow in the ground.*
10. (Repeat step 9 until firm.)
11. Everybody, tell me what drons are. Get ready. (Signal.) *Plants.*
12. (Repeat steps 9 and 11 until firm.)

EXERCISE 2 Synonyms

1. We're going to make up statements that mean the same thing.
2. What do we call two words that mean the same thing? (Signal.) *Synonyms.*

3. Listen: The animal is well. Say that. (Signal.) *The animal is well.*
- Say that statement using a synonym for **well.** Get ready. (Signal.) *The animal is healthy.*
- (Repeat step 3 until firm.)
4. The animal is well. The animal is healthy. Those statements mean the same thing because **well** and **healthy** are synonyms.
5. Listen: The container is small. Say that. (Signal.) *The container is small.*
- Say that statement using a synonym for **small.** Get ready. (Signal.) *The container is little.*
- (Repeat step 5 until firm.)
6. Listen: The umbrella is over my head. Say that. (Signal.) *The umbrella is over my head.*
- Say that statement using a synonym for over. Get ready. (Signal.) *The umbrella is above my head.*
- (Repeat step 6 until firm.)

EXERCISE 3 Questioning Skills

1. I'm going to tell a story. When you hear a word you don't know, say **stop.**
- A boy went to the **emporium.** (The children are to say *stop.*)
- Everybody, what word don't you know? (Signal.) *Emporium.*
- Ask the question about what the word emporium means. Get ready. (Signal.) *What does the word emporium mean?*
- I'll tell you what emporium means. Emporium is a synonym for **store.** What is emporium a synonym for? (Signal.) *Store.*
- So if a boy went to the emporium, he went to the . . . (Signal.) *store.*

2. Here's more of the story. He purchased a **velocipede.** (The children are to say *stop.*)
- Everybody, what word don't you know? (Signal.) *Velocipede.*
- Ask the question about what the word velocipede means. Get ready. (Signal.) *What does the word velocipede mean?*
- I'll tell you what velocipede means. Velocipede is a synonym for **bicycle.** What is velocipede a synonym for? (Signal.) *Bicycle.*
3. So a boy went to the emporium and purchased a velocipede. Would you like to do the same thing? (Children respond.)
- That's the end of the story.

EXERCISE 4   Analogies

1. We're going to make up an analogy.
2. Everybody, tell me what class a bowl and a pitcher are in. Get ready. (Signal.) *Containers.* Yes, containers.
3. We're going to make up an analogy that tells what you put in each container. What's the analogy going to tell? (Signal.) *What you put in each container.*
4. Name some things that you put in a bowl. (Call on individual children. Repeat all reasonable answers.)
- Let's say you put soup in a bowl.
5. Name some things that you put in a pitcher. (Call on individual children. Repeat all reasonable answers.)
- Let's say you put milk in a pitcher.
6. Everybody, say the analogy about what you put in a bowl and a pitcher. Get ready. (Signal.) *A bowl is to soup as a pitcher is to milk.*
- (Repeat step 6 until firm.)
7. What does our analogy tell about each container? (Signal.) *What you put in it.*
8. Everybody, say our analogy one more time. Get ready. (Signal.) *A bowl is to soup as a pitcher is to milk.*
9. (Repeat steps 7 and 8 until firm.)

EXERCISE 5   Who—What—When—Where—Why

1. Listen to this story.
- The ball was on the table. A boy hit the ball, and it fell off the table. Then the boy picked it up and put it in his pocket.
- (Repeat the story.)
2. Tell where the ball was first. Get ready. (Signal.) *On the table.*
- Tell who hit the ball. Get ready. (Signal.) *A boy.*
- Tell what the boy picked up. Get ready. (Signal.) *The ball.*
- Tell why the ball fell off the table. Get ready. (Signal.) *A boy hit it.*
- Tell where the boy put the ball. Get ready. (Signal.) *In his pocket.*
3. (Repeat step 2 until firm.)

WORKBOOK

EXERCISE 6   If-Then Application

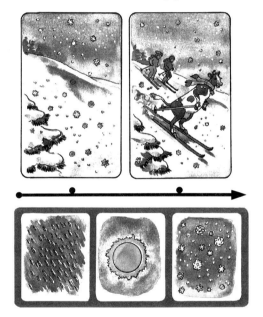

1. Everybody, open your workbook to Lesson 94. Write your name. ✔
- This is a new kind of game. It shows what Clarabelle will do and when she'll do it.
2. Everybody, touch the arrow. ✔
- The first picture shows what the weather is going to do. Everybody, what's coming out of the sky in that picture? (Signal.) *Snow.*
- Touch the second picture. ✔
- That picture shows what Clarabelle will do. Everybody, what will Clarabelle do? (Signal.) *Go skiing.*

3. We have to make up a rule for these pictures. The rule starts with **if.** The **if** part tells about the **first** picture. Listen to the **if** part: If it snows . . .
   - Your turn: If it snows, what will happen? (Signal.) *Clarabelle will go skiing.* Yes, if it snows, Clarabelle will go skiing.
4. Everybody, say the **if** rule. (Signal.) *If it snows, Clarabelle will go skiing.*
   - (Repeat step 4 until firm.)
5. That's the rule for these pictures. Look at the pictures below the arrow. ✔
   - They show things that **might** happen. You have to figure out what Clarabelle will do.
   - Touch the first picture **below** the arrow. ✔
   - Everybody, what's happening in that picture? (Signal.) *It's raining.*
   - My turn: What will Clarabelle do if it rains? We don't know. We only know what she'll do if it **snows.**
   - Your turn: What will Clarabelle do if it rains? (Signal.) *We don't know.* Right, we don't know.
6. Touch the second picture below the arrow. ✔
   - What's happening in that picture? (Call on a child. Idea: *The sun's shining.*)
   - Think big. Everybody, what will Clarabelle do if the sun shines? (Signal.) *We don't know.* Right, we don't know.
7. Touch the last picture below the arrow. ✔
   - Everybody, what's happening in that picture? (Signal.) *It's snowing.*
   - Everybody, what will Clarabelle do if it snows? (Signal.) *Go skiing.*
   - Right, that's the rule: If it snows, Clarabelle will go skiing.
8. Two of the pictures below the arrow show things that our rule does **not** tell us about. So we don't know what Clarabelle will do if these things happen. Listen: Cross out the two pictures that show things our rule does **not** tell us about. Raise your hand when you're finished.
   (Observe children and give feedback.)
9. (Call on a child:) Which two pictures did you cross out? (Idea: *The picture that shows it's raining and the picture that shows the sun's shining.*)
   - Why did you cross them out? (Call on a child. Idea: *Our rule does not tell us about them.*)

10. Raise your hand if you crossed out the pictures of it raining and the sun shining. ✔
    - I couldn't fool you with this new kind of **if** rule, could I?

EXERCISE 7   Sentence Writing

Note: Remind children to start their sentences with a capital and end them with a period.

| woman | rock |

_____

_____

_____

_____

1. Everybody, find the next page. ✔
   - You're going to write sentences that do not rhyme.
   - Touch the picture of the woman and the man. ✔
   - The picture shows what the woman had and what the man had. What did the woman have? (Signal.) *A ring.*
   - What did the man have? (Signal.) *A rock.* Yes, a **rock.**
2. Say the sentence for what the woman had. Get ready. (Signal.) *The woman had a ring.*
   - Say the sentence for what the man had. Get ready. (Signal.) *The man had a rock.*
3. (Repeat step 2 until firm.)
4. The word box shows how to spell the words **woman** and **rock.** You can figure out how to spell the other words.
5. Write the sentence for what the woman had. Pencils down when you're finished. ✔
   - Now go to the next line and write the sentence for what the man had. Pencils down when you're finished. ✔
6. (Call on individual children to read both their sentences.)

Objectives

- Construct verbal analogies. (Exercise 1)
- Identify an object based on its characteristics. (Exercise 2)
- Name things that a statement does NOT tell. (Exercise 3)
- Listen to a short story and answer questions involving "who," "when," "why," "where" and "what". (Exercise 4)
- Discriminate between synonyms and opposites. (Exercise 5)
- Apply an if-then rule based on the occurrence of events. (Exercise 6)
- Write class names next to members of the class. (Exercise 7)
- Follow coloring rules involving materials. (Exercise 8)

EXERCISE 1 Analogies

1. We're going to make up an analogy.
2. Everybody, tell me what class a barn and a house are in. Get ready. (Signal.) *Buildings.* Yes, buildings.
3. We're going to make up an analogy that tells what lives in each building. What's the analogy going to tell? (Signal.) *What lives in each building.*
4. Name some things that live in a barn. (Call on individual children. Repeat all reasonable answers.)
- Let's say horses live in a barn.
5. Name some things that live in a house. (Call on individual children. Repeat all reasonable answers.)
- Let's say people live in a house.
6. Everybody, say the analogy about horses and people. Get ready. (Signal.) *Horses are to a barn as people are to a house.*
- (Repeat step 6 until firm.)
7. What does our analogy tell about each building? (Signal.) *What lives in it.*
8. Everybody, say our analogy one more time. Get ready. (Signal.) *Horses are to a barn as people are to a house.*
9. (Repeat steps 7 and 8 until firm.)

EXERCISE 2 Description

1. I'm going to say two things about something you know. See if you can figure out what I'm talking about.
2. (Hold up one finger.) An eem is a big place.
- (Hold up two fingers.) There is lots of salt water in an eem.
3. Everybody, tell me what you know about an eem. (Hold up one finger.) *An eem is a big place.*
- (Hold up two fingers.) *There is lots of salt water in an eem.*
4. (Repeat step 3 until firm.)
5. Everybody, tell me what an eem is. Get ready. (Signal.) *An ocean.*
6. (Repeat steps 3 and 5 until firm.)

EXERCISE 3 Statements

1. Listen to this statement.
2. Melissa gave him a piece of pie. Everybody, say that statement. (Signal.) *Melissa gave him a piece of pie.*
3. Does that statement tell if he likes pie? (Signal.) *No.*
- Does that statement tell what Melissa gave him? (Signal.) *Yes.*

- Does that statement tell what Melissa is doing now? (Signal.) *No.*
- Does that statement tell what Melissa did? (Signal.) *Yes.*
- Does that statement tell if he ate the piece of pie? (Signal.) *No.*

4. Melissa gave him a piece of pie. Everybody, say that statement again. (Signal.) *Melissa gave him a piece of pie.*

5. Name three things that statement does not tell you. (Call on individual children. Repeat all three correct responses.)

6. You have named three things the statement does not tell us.
- Name the first thing. (Hold up one finger.) (The children give the first response.)
- Name the second thing. (Hold up two fingers.) (The children give the second response.)
- Name the third thing. (Hold up three fingers.) (The children give the third response.)
- (Repeat step 6 until all children can name the three things in order.)

EXERCISE 4 Who—What—When—Where—Why

1. Listen to this story.
- The girl was in school. She told a funny joke. The children laughed because they liked the joke. After the children stopped laughing, they all went back to work.
- (Repeat the story.)

2. Tell what the girl did. Get ready. (Signal.) *Told a funny joke.*
- Tell why the class laughed. (Call on a child. Idea: *They liked the joke.*)
- Tell who went back to work. Get ready. (Signal.) *The children.*
- Tell when the children went back to work. Get ready. (Signal.) *After they stopped laughing.*
- Tell where the girl was. Get ready. (Signal.) *In school.*

3. (Repeat step 2 until firm.)

EXERCISE 5 Synonyms/Opposites

1. Tell me if I name synonyms or opposites. Think big.

2. Listen: Big. Large. Say those words. (Signal.) *Big. Large.*
- Are they synonyms or opposites? (Signal.) *Synonyms.*
- (Repeat step 2 until firm.)

3. Listen: Above. Over. Say those words. (Signal.) *Above. Over.*
- Are they synonyms or opposites? (Signal.) *Synonyms.*
- (Repeat step 3 until firm.)

4. Listen: Fast. Slow. Say those words. (Signal.) *Fast. Slow.*
- Are they synonyms or opposites? (Signal.) *Opposites.*
- (Repeat step 4 until firm.)

5. (Repeat steps 2 through 4 until firm.)

WORKBOOK

EXERCISE 6 If-Then Application

1. Everybody, open your workbook to Lesson 95. Write your name. ✔
- This arrow shows another **if** game. The first picture shows what **Sweetie** might do. The second picture shows what **Honey** will do.

2. Look at the pictures carefully and see if you can figure out the **if** rule. Remember, you have to start with **if.** Then you tell what happens in the **first** picture. Then you tell what **Honey** will do. Raise your hand when you're ready to tell the **if** rule. ✔
   - (Call on a child:) Say the **if** rule for these pictures.
     (Idea: *If Sweetie chases Andrea, Honey will bite Sweetie's tail.*) Yes, if Sweetie chases Andrea, Honey will bite Sweetie's tail.
3. Everybody, say the **if** rule. (Signal.) *If Sweetie chases Andrea, Honey will bite Sweetie's tail.*
     (Repeat step 3 until firm.)
4. That's the rule for these pictures. Look at the pictures below the arrow. ✔
   - They show things that **might** happen. You have to figure out what Honey will do.
   - Touch the first picture **below** the arrow. ✔
   - What's happening in that picture? (Call on a child. Idea: *Sweetie is chasing the bragging rats.*)
   - My turn: What will Honey do if Sweetie chases the bragging rats? We don't know. We only know what she'll do if Sweetie chases **Andrea.**
   - Your turn: What will Honey do if Sweetie chases the bragging rats? (Signal.) *We don't know.* Right, we don't know.
5. Touch the second picture below the arrow. ✔ What's happening in that picture? (Call on a child. Idea: *Sweetie is chasing Andrea.*)
   - Think big. Everybody, what will Honey do if Sweetie chases Andrea? (Signal.) *Bite Sweetie's tail.*
   - Right, that's the rule: If Sweetie chases Andrea, Honey will bite Sweetie's tail.
6. Touch the last picture below the arrow. ✔
   - What's happening in that picture? (Call on a child. Idea: *Sweetie is chasing a butterfly.*)
   - Everybody, what will Honey do if Sweetie chases a butterfly? (Signal.) *We don't know.* Right, we don't know.

7. Two of the pictures below the arrow show things that our rule doesn't tell us about. So we don't know what Honey will do if these things happen.
   Listen: Cross out the two pictures that show things our rule does **not** tell us about. Raise your hand when you're finished. (Observe children and give feedback.)
8. (Call on a child:) Which two pictures did you cross out?
   (Idea: *The picture that shows Sweetie chasing the bragging rats and the picture that shows Sweetie chasing a butterfly.*)
   - Why did you cross them out? (Call on a child. Idea: *Our rule doesn't tell us about them.*)
9. Raise your hand if you crossed out the pictures of Sweetie chasing the bragging rats and Sweetie chasing the butterfly. ✔
   - Good for you.

EXERCISE 7   Classification

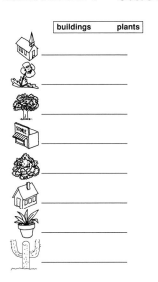

1. Everybody, find the next page. ✔
   - (Hold up workbook. Point to first half.)
     Everybody, I'll read the words in the box. You touch the words.
     First word: Buildings. ✔
   - Next word: Plants. ✔
     Yes, buildings and plants.

2. Everybody, put your finger under the church. ✔
- Is a church in the class of buildings or in the class of plants? (Signal.) *Buildings.* Yes, a church is in the class of buildings.
- Copy the word **buildings** next to the church. ✔
- Read what you wrote. (Signal.) *Buildings.*
3. Everybody, put your finger under the flower. ✔ Is a flower in the class of buildings or in the class of plants? (Signal.) *Plants.*
- Yes, a flower is in the class of plants. Copy the word **plants** next to the flower. ✔ Read what you wrote. (Signal.) *Plants.*
4. Everybody, read the words you wrote. (Signal.) *Buildings. Plants.*
5. Later you can write the class words that go with the other pictures.

EXERCISE 8 Materials

1. (Hold up workbook. Point to second half.)
2. Here's a coloring rule for this picture. If an object is made of wood, color it black or brown. What's the rule? (Signal.) *If an object is made of wood, color it black or brown.*
- (Repeat step 2 until firm.)
3. Mark two of the objects made of wood. ✔
4. Here's another coloring rule for this picture. If an object is made of cloth, color it orange. What's the rule? (Signal.) *If an object is made of cloth, color it orange.*
- (Repeat step 4 until firm.)
5. Make an orange mark on one of the objects made of cloth. ✔
6. Here's one more thing to do. Part of the shirt is missing. What part is missing? (Signal.) *The sleeve.* Yes, the sleeve.
- Before you color the shirt, follow the dots and make the sleeve.
7. Remember—the marks show you what color to make the wood objects and the cloth objects.

Objectives

- Construct verbal analogies. (Exercise 1)
- Identify an object based on its characteristics. (Exercise 2)
- Name common synonyms and opposites. (Exercise 3)
- Name things that a statement does NOT tell. (Exercise 4)
- Generate questions to find a word's definition. (Exercise 5)
- Identify an object based on its characteristics. (Exercise 6)
- Write rhyming sentences given picture cues. (Exercise 7)
- **Cooperatively develop utterances for familiar story characters.** (Exercise 8)

EXERCISE 1   Analogies

1. We're going to make up an analogy.
2. Everybody, tell me what class a table and a chair are in. Get ready. (Signal.) *Furniture.* Yes, furniture.
3. We're going to make up an analogy that tells what you do on each piece of furniture. What's the analogy going to tell? (Signal.) *What you do on each piece of furniture.*
4. Tell me what you do on a table. (Call on individual children. Repeat all reasonable answers.)
- Let's say you eat on a table.
5. Tell me what you do on a chair. Get ready. (Signal.) *Sit on it.* Yes, you sit on a chair.
6. Everybody, say the analogy about what you do on a table and on a chair. Get ready. (Signal.) *A table is to eating as a chair is to sitting.*
- (Repeat step 6 until firm.)
7. What does our analogy tell about each piece of furniture? (Signal.) *What you do on it.*
8. Everybody, say our analogy one more time. Get ready. (Signal.) *A table is to eating as a chair is to sitting.*
9. (Repeat steps 7 and 8 until firm.)

EXERCISE 2   Description

1. I'm going to say two things about something you know. See if you can figure out what I'm talking about.
2. (Hold up one finger.)
   A nerpor is a place.
- (Hold up two fingers.)
   You find swings and slides at a nerpor.

3. Everybody, tell me what you know about a nerpor.
- (Hold up one finger.) *A nerpor is a place.*
- (Hold up two fingers.) *You find swings and slides at a nerpor.*
4. (Repeat step 3 until firm.)
5. Everybody, tell me what a nerpor is. Get ready. (Signal.) *A playground.*
6. (Repeat steps 3 and 5 until firm.)

EXERCISE 3   Synonyms/Opposites

1. Everybody, let's play a game. I'll say a word. You say a word that means the same thing.
- Listen: Tell me a synonym for **healthy.** Get ready. (Signal.) *Well.*
- Listen: Tell me a synonym for **big.** Get ready. (Signal.) *Large.*
- Listen: Tell me a synonym for **well.** Get ready. (Signal.) *Healthy.*
- Listen: Tell me a synonym for **large.** Get ready. (Signal.) *Big.*
2. It's time for some opposites.
- Listen: Tell me the opposite of **large.** Get ready. (Signal.) *Small.*
- Listen: Tell me the opposite of **feeling well.** Get ready. (Signal.) *Feeling sick.*
- Listen: Tell me the opposite of **over.** Get ready. (Signal.) *Under.*

EXERCISE 4   Statements

1. Listen to this statement.
2. Darwin will play football tomorrow. Everybody, say that statement. (Signal.) *Darwin will play football tomorrow.*
3. Does that statement tell what Darwin is doing now? (Signal.) *No.*

- Does that statement tell what Darwin did yesterday? (Signal.) *No.*
- Does that statement tell what Darwin will do tomorrow? (Signal.) *Yes.*
- Does that statement tell if Darwin is big? (Signal.) *No.*

4. Darwin will play football tomorrow. Everybody, say that statement again. (Signal.) *Darwin will play football tomorrow.*

5. Name three things the statement does not tell you. (Call on individual children. Repeat three correct responses.)

6. You have named three things the statement does not tell us.
- Name the first thing. (Hold up one finger.) (The children give the first response.)
- Name the second thing. (Hold up two fingers.) (The children give the second response.)
- Name the third thing. (Hold up three fingers.) (The children give the third response.)
- (Repeat step 6 until all children can name the three things in order.)

EXERCISE 5 Questioning Skills

1. I'm going to tell a story. When you hear a word you don't know, say **stop.**

2. A girl was **forlorn.** (The children are to say *stop.*) Everybody, what word don't you know? (Signal.) *Forlorn.*
- Ask the question about what the word forlorn means. Get ready. (Signal.) *What does the word forlorn mean?*
- I'll tell you what forlorn means. Forlorn is a synonym for **sad.** What is forlorn a synonym for? (Signal.) *Sad.*
- If a girl was forlorn, she was . . . (Signal.) *sad.*

3. Here's more of the story. Her family was **relocating.** (The children are to say *stop.*) Everybody, what word don't you know? (Signal.) *Relocating.*
- Ask the question about what the word relocating means. Get ready. (Signal.) *What does the word relocating mean?*
- I'll tell you what relocating means. Relocating is a synonym for **moving.** What is relocating a synonym for? (Signal.) *Moving.*

- If a girl was forlorn because her family was relocating, she was sad because her family was . . . (Signal.) *moving.*

4. Here's more of the story. They were going to another **municipality.** (The children are to say *stop.*) Everybody, what word don't you know? (Signal.) *Municipality.*
- Ask the question about what the word municipality means. Get ready. (Signal.) *What does the word municipality mean?*
- I'll tell you what municipality means. Municipality is a synonym for **city.** What is municipality a synonym for? (Signal.) *City.*

5. If a girl was forlorn because her family was relocating to another municipality, she was sad because her family was moving to another . . . (Signal.) *city.*
How would you like to move to another city? (Children respond.)
- That's the end of the story.

EXERCISE 6 Description

1. I'm going to say two things about something you know. See if you can figure out what I'm talking about.

2. (Hold up one finger.) Dorns is the name of a big class.
- (Hold up two fingers.) Dorns have roofs and walls.

3. Everybody, tell me what you know about dorns.
- (Hold up one finger.) *Dorns is the name of a big class.*
- (Hold up two fingers.) *Dorns have roofs and walls.*

4. (Repeat step 3 until firm.)

5. Everybody, tell me what dorns are. Get ready. (Signal.) *Buildings.*

6. (Repeat steps 3 and 5 until firm.)

7. Here's another one.

8. (Hold up one finger.) Nerp is an action.
- (Hold up two fingers.) When you nerp, you chew food and swallow it.

9. Everybody, tell me what you know about nerp. (Hold up one finger.) *Nerp is an action.*
• (Hold up two fingers.) *When you nerp, you chew food and swallow it.*
10. (Repeat step 9 until firm.)
11. Everybody, tell me what nerping is. Get ready. (Signal.) *Eating.*
12. (Repeat steps 9 and 11 until firm.)

WORKBOOK

EXERCISE 7 Sentence Writing

1. Everybody, open your workbook to Lesson 96. Write your name. ✔
• You're going to write sentences.
• Touch the picture of the cat and the boat. ✔
• The picture shows what kind of tail the cat had and what kind of sail the boat had. What kind of tail did the cat have? (Signal.) *A short tail.*
• What kind of sail did the boat have? (Signal.) *A big sail.*
2. Say the sentence for the cat. Get ready. (Signal.) *The cat had a short tail.*
• Say the sentence for the boat. Get ready. (Signal.) *The boat had a big sail.*
3. (Repeat step 2 until firm.)
4. The word box shows how to spell the words **short, boat** and **sail.** You can figure out how to spell the other words.
5. Write the sentence for the cat. Pencils down when you're finished. ✔

• Now go to the next line and write the sentence for the boat. Pencils down when you're finished. ✔
6. (Call on individual children to read both their sentences.)

EXERCISE 8 Extrapolation

Note: A complete listing of character descriptions appears in the Teacher's Guide.

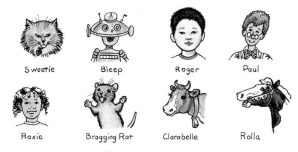

1. Everybody, find the next page. ✔
• (Hold up workbook. Point to top half.) Find the characters. ✔
• We're going to work in teams. (Divide the class into four teams.)
2. These are pictures of characters you know and their names are under the pictures. What I'm going to do is circle a couple of names for each team. Then that team will have to give us a clue about each character by saying something that the character would say.
• (Circle the following names on one child's worksheet in each team:
   Team 1.   Circle **Paul** and **Bragging Rat.**
   Team 2.   Circle **Bleep** and **Roxie.**
   Team 3.   Circle **Sweetie** and **Roger.**
   Team 4.   Circle **Clarabelle** and **Rolla.**)
• Don't show any of the other teams the names that I've circled.

3. Here's what you're going to do: Each team will give a clue. They'll say something that one of their circled characters would say. If I circled Bleep's name, you'd say something that Bleep would say. If I circled Clarabelle's name, you'd say something that Clarabelle would say.

- So here's what I want each team to do: Make up clues for the names I've circled. Whisper the clues so that nobody outside your team can hear them. When you have clues for both the names I've circled, raise your hand. Remember, the clue has to be something the character would say. ✔

4. (After hands are raised, point to team 1.) Team 1 will give us the first clue. Everybody else will make a line under the name for that character. If the clue is something Sweetie would say, you'll draw a line under the name **Sweetie.** If the clue is something that Bleep would say, you'll draw a line under the name **Bleep.**

5. (Call on a child in team 1.) Tell us the clue for one of your characters. (Child gives either a clue for Paul, for example, *"Painting pink and purple plums is perfect,"* or gives a boastful Bragging Rat clue.)

- (If the clue is **not** good, say:) Say something else that character would say.
- (If the clue **is** good, say:) Everybody who is **not** in team 1, underline the name of the character. ✔
- Everybody who is **not** in team 1, raise your hand if you know who that character is. ✔
- Everybody, whose name did you underline? (Children respond.)

6. (Call on another child in team 1.) Tell us the clue for your **other** character. (Child responds.)

- Everybody who is **not** in team 1, raise your hand if you know who that character is. ✔
- (If the clue is good, say:) Everybody who is **not** on team 1, underline the name of the character. ✔
- Everybody, whose name did you underline? (Children respond.)

7. Let's give team 2 a turn. (Call on a child in team 2.) Tell us the clue for one of your characters. (Child gives either a clue for Bleep, which is likely to include the word "Bleep" or a clue for rock-collecting Roxie.)

- Everybody who is **not** in team 2, raise your hand if you know who that character is. ✔
- (If the clue is **not** good, say:) Say something else that character would say.
- (If the clue **is** good, say:) Everybody who is **not** in team 2, underline the name of the character. ✔
- Everybody, whose name did you underline? (Children respond.)

8. (Call on another child in team 2.) Tell us the clue for your **other** character. (Child responds.)

- Everybody who is **not** in team 2, raise your hand if you know who that character is. ✔
- (If the clue is good, say:) Everybody who is **not** in team 2, underline the name of the character. ✔
- Everybody, whose name did you underline? (Children respond.)

9. Let's give team 3 a turn. (Call on a child in team 3.) Tell us the clue for one of your characters. (Child gives either a clue for mean Sweetie or hat-losing Roger.)

- Everybody who is **not** in team 3, raise your hand if you know who that character is. ✔
- (If the clue is good, say:) Everybody who is **not** in team 3, underline the name of the character. ✔
- Everybody, whose name did you underline? (Children respond.)

10. (Call on another child in team 3.) Tell us the clue for your **other** character. (Child responds.)

- Everybody who is **not** in team 3, raise your hand when you know who the character is. ✔
- (If the clue is good, say:) Everybody who is **not** in team 3, underline the name of the character. ✔
- Everybody, whose name did you underline? (Children respond.)

11. Let's give the last team a turn. (Call on a child in team 4.) Tell us a clue for one of your characters. (Child gives either a clue for silly Clarabelle cow who wants to do what others do, or a clue for Rolla who wants to be number 1 on the merry-go-round.)

- Everybody who is **not** in team 4, raise your hand when you know who that character is. ✔

- (If the clue is good, say:) Everybody who is **not** in team 4, underline the name of the character. ✔
- Everybody, whose name did you underline? (Children respond.)

12. (Call on another child in team 4.) Tell us the clue for your **other** character. (Child responds.)
   - Everybody who is **not** in team 4, raise your hand if you know who that character is. ✔

- (If the clue is good, say:) Everybody who is **not** in team 4, underline the name of the character. ✔
- Everybody, whose name did you underline? (Children respond.)

13. Wow, you really said some things that sounded just like those characters.

Objectives

- Replace a word in a sentence with a synonym. (Exercise 1)
- Identify absurdities of conditions. (Exercise 2)
- Identify an object based on its characteristics. (Exercise 3)
- Discriminate between synonyms and opposites. (Exercise 4)
- Construct verbal analogies. (Exercise 5)
- Ask questions to figure out the "mystery" picture. (Exercise 6)
- Write class names next to members of the class. (Exercise 7)

EXERCISE 1 Synonyms

1. Listen: a synonym for fast is quick. What's a synonym for fast? (Signal.) *Quick.*
2. I'm going to make up a story.
3. A bird flew above a fish pond. Say that. (Signal.) *A bird flew above a fish pond.*
- Now say that statement using a synonym for **above.** Get ready. (Signal.) *A bird flew over a fish pond.*
4. The bird tried to catch the fish under the water. Say that. (Signal.) *The bird tried to catch the fish under the water.*
- Now say that statement using a synonym for **under.** Get ready. (Signal.) *The bird tried to catch the fish below the water.*
5. But the fish were too fast for the bird. Say that. (Signal.) *But the fish were too fast for the bird.*
- Now say that statement using a synonym for **fast.** Get ready. (Signal.) *But the fish were too quick for the bird.*
6. And here is the end of the story.
7. The bird said: "If I want to eat, I will have to move faster or go to a fish store." What do you think it should do? (Call on individual children. After a child answers, ask:) Why do you think so? (Children respond.)

EXERCISE 2 Absurdity

1. Listen to this statement and figure out what is absurd about it.
2. The dog is smaller than an ant. Say the statement. (Signal.) *The dog is smaller than an ant.*
3. What's absurd about that statement? (Call on one child.) (Praise all reasonable responses; then say:) Yes, a dog can't be smaller than an ant.
4. Here's another absurd statement. Figure out what's absurd about this one.
5. Listen: Kim was eight years old before she had her third birthday. Say the statement. (Signal.) *Kim was eight years old before she had her third birthday.*
6. What's absurd about that statement? (Call on one child.) (Praise all reasonable responses; then say:) Yes, before your third birthday you're only two, not eight.

EXERCISE 3 Description

1. I'm going to say two things about something you know. See if you can figure out what I'm talking about.
2. (Hold up one finger.) A mool is a tool.
- (Hold up two fingers.) You use a mool to clean your teeth.
3. Everybody, tell me what you know about a mool.
- (Hold up one finger.) *A mool is a tool.*
- (Hold up two fingers.) *You use a mool to clean your teeth.*
4. (Repeat step 3 until firm.)
5. Everybody, tell me what a mool is. Get ready. (Signal.) *A toothbrush.*
6. (Repeat steps 3 and 5 until firm.)
7. Here's another one.

8. (Hold up one finger.) Greem is a holiday.

- (Hold up two fingers.) Kids hunt for eggs on Greem.

9. Everybody, tell me what you know about Greem.

- (Hold up one finger.) *Greem is a holiday.*
- (Hold up two fingers.) *Kids hunt for eggs on Greem.*

10. (Repeat step 9 until firm.)

11. Everybody, tell me what Greem is. Get ready. (Signal.) *Easter.*

12. (Repeat steps 9 and 11 until firm.)

EXERCISE 4   Synonyms/Opposites

1. Tell me if I name synonyms or opposites. Think big.

2. Listen: Below. Under. Say those words. (Signal.) *Below. Under.*

- Are they synonyms or opposites? (Signal.) *Synonyms.*
- (Repeat step 2 until firm.)

3. Listen: Wide. Narrow. Say those words. (Signal.) *Wide. Narrow.*

- Are they synonyms or opposites? (Signal.) *Opposites.*
- (Repeat step 3 until firm.)

4. Listen: Shut. Close. Say those words. (Signal.) *Shut. Close.*

- Are they synonyms or opposites? (Signal.) *Synonyms.*
- (Repeat step 4 until firm.)

5. (Repeat steps 2 through 4 until firm.)

EXERCISE 5   Analogies

1. We're going to make up an analogy.

2. Everybody, tell me what class a coat and a belt are in. Get ready. (Signal.) *Clothing.* Yes, clothing.

3. We're going to make up an analogy that tells a part each piece of clothing has. What's the analogy going to tell? (Signal.) *A part each piece of clothing has.*

4. Name some parts that a coat has. (Call on individual children. Repeat all reasonable answers.)

- Let's say that a coat has a collar.

5. Name some parts that a belt has. (Call on individual children. Repeat all reasonable answers.)

- Let's say that a belt has a buckle.

6. Everybody, say the analogy that tells a part a coat has and a part a belt has. Get ready. (Signal.) *A coat has a collar as a belt has a buckle.*

- (Repeat step 6 until firm.)

7. What does our analogy tell about each piece of clothing? (Signal.) *A part it has.*

8. Everybody, say our analogy one more time. Get ready. (Signal.) *A coat has a collar as a belt has a buckle.*

9. (Repeat steps 7 and 8 until firm.)

WORKBOOK

EXERCISE 6   Questioning

1. Everybody, open your workbook to Lesson 97. Write your name. ✔

- Everybody, we're going to play a question game with teams.
  (Divide the class into four teams.)

2. Make a flap out of each picture. Cut carefully. Raise your hand when you're finished.
  (Observe children and give feedback.)

3. Now, let's play the toughest game of all. We'll see which teams can do it. Remember, if you're **really** smart, your team can find the mystery picture by asking only **three** questions. But they have to be **super** questions. You're working in teams. So your team has to agree on each question before the team asks it. Everybody on a team figures out which questions your team will ask. When your team has your first question, raise your hands and I'll come over. You'll whisper the question to me so that none of the other teams can hear the question. I'll whisper the answer, and you'll fold over the pictures that could **not** be the mystery picture.

4. (**Key:** The target picture is 7—one dog sitting next to a doghouse.)

• You know your **first** question is good if you can fold over **four** pictures after I answer your first question. Remember, you're trying to find the mystery picture in only **three** questions. Raise your hands when your team has a good question.

   Answers:
   (How many dogs?) One.
   (Where is the dog?) Next to a doghouse.
   (What is the dog doing?) Sitting.
   (Do **not** combine answers, such as: **Sitting next to** a doghouse.)

5. (After you answer each team's question, tell the team to fold over the pictures that could **not** be the mystery picture. Then ask them if that was a good question. Remind them by saying:) For a good first question, you can fold over four pictures.

• (Then direct each team to agree on the next question. Tell them:) If it's a good question, you can fold over two pictures.

• (Repeat the procedure for the third question.) If it's a good question, you'll know which picture is the mystery picture.

6. (After any team has found the mystery picture by asking only three questions, tell the class:) We have a winner. We have a team that found the mystery picture by asking only **three** questions.

• (Call on a team member to say the three questions. Do not accept "combined" questions.)

7. Everybody, what's the number of the mystery picture? (Signal.) *Seven.*

• How many dogs are in that picture? (Signal.) *One.*

• What is the dog doing? (Signal.) *Sitting.*

• Where is the dog? (Signal.) *Next to a doghouse.*

8. (**Key:** The target picture is 2—two dogs standing next to a tree.)

• We'll play the game again. Unfold each flap. This time I'm thinking of a different picture. Remember, here's how you know if your **first** question is good. If you can fold over **four** pictures after I answer your first question, it's a good question. If you can fold over only **one** picture, it's **not** a super good question. Remember, you're trying to find the mystery picture in only **three** questions. Raise your hands when your team has a good question.

9. (After any team has found the mystery picture by asking only three questions, tell the class:) We have a winner. We have a team that found the mystery picture by asking only **three** questions.

• (Call on a team member to say the three questions. Do not accept "combined" questions.)

10. Everybody, what's the number of the mystery picture? (Signal.) *Two.*

• How many dogs are in the picture? (Signal.) *Two.*

• What are the dogs doing? (Signal.) *Standing.*

• Where are the dogs? (Signal.) *Next to a tree.*

11. You really knew how to work together and figure out the mystery picture.

EXERCISE 7 Classification

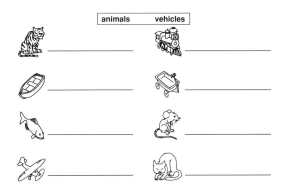

animals   vehicles

1. Everybody, find the next page. ✔
• (Hold up workbook. Point to second half.)
   Everybody, I'll read the words in the box.
   You touch the words.
• First word: Animals. ✔
• Next word: Vehicles. ✔

2. Everybody, put your finger under the tiger. ✔
• Is a tiger in the class of animals or in the
   class of vehicles? (Signal.) *Animals.*
   Yes, a tiger is in the class of animals.
• Copy the word **animals** next to the tiger. ✔
• Read what you wrote. Get ready. (Signal.)
   Animals.
3. Everybody, put your finger under the
   rowboat. ✔
• Is a rowboat in the class of animals or in
   the class of vehicles? (Signal.) *Vehicles.*
   Yes, a rowboat is in the class of vehicles.
• Copy the word **vehicles** next to the
   rowboat. ✔
• Read what you wrote. (Signal.) *Vehicles.*
4. Everybody, read the words you wrote.
   (Signal.) *Animals. Vehicles.*
5. Later you can write the class words that go
   with the other pictures.

Lesson 98

Objectives

- Discriminate between synonyms and opposites. (Exercise 1)
- Name things that a statement does NOT tell. (Exercise 2)
- Name common opposites. (Exercise 3)
- Construct verbal analogies. (Exercise 4)
- **Identify past and future tense.** (Exercise 5)
- Identify an object based on its characteristics. (Exercise 6)
- Write sentences given picture cues. (Exercise 7)
- Label cardinal directions on a map. (Exercise 8)
- Construct analogies given picture cues. (Exercise 9)

EXERCISE 1 Synonyms/Opposites

1. Tell me if I name synonyms or opposites. Think big.
2. Listen: Easy. Difficult. Say those words. (Signal.) *Easy. Difficult.*
  - Are they synonyms or opposites? (Signal.) *Opposites.*
  - (Repeat step 2 until firm.)
3. Listen: Shout. Yell. Say those words. (Signal.) *Shout. Yell.*
  - Are they synonyms or opposites? (Signal.) *Synonyms.*
  - (Repeat step 3 until firm.)
4. Listen: Thin. Skinny. Say those words. (Signal.) *Thin. Skinny.*
  - Are they synonyms or opposites? (Signal.) *Synonyms.*
  - (Repeat step 4 until firm.)
5. (Repeat steps 2 through 4 until firm.)

EXERCISE 2 Statements

1. Listen to this statement.
2. Yesterday Cheryl played baseball. Everybody, say that statement. (Signal.) *Yesterday Cheryl played baseball.*
3. Does that statement tell what Cheryl is doing now? (Signal.) *No.*
  - Does that statement tell who Cheryl played with? (Signal.) *No.*
  - Does that statement tell if Cheryl is a good baseball player? (Signal.) *No.*
  - Does that statement tell what Cheryl did yesterday? (Signal.) *Yes.*
  - Does that statement tell if Cheryl wore a coat? (Signal.) *No.*
4. Yesterday Cheryl played baseball. Everybody, say that statement again. (Signal.) *Yesterday Cheryl played baseball.*
5. Name three things the statement does not tell you. (Call on individual children. Repeat three correct responses.)
6. You have named three things the statement does not tell us.
  - Name the first thing. (Hold up one finger.) (The children give the first response.)
  - Name the second thing. (Hold up two fingers.) (The children give the second response.)
  - Name the third thing. (Hold up three fingers.) (The children give the third response.)
  - (Repeat step 6 until all children can name the three things in order.)

EXERCISE 3 Opposites

1. We're going to play a word game.
2. Everybody, think of a cabinet that is not open. It is the opposite of open. What's the opposite of open? (Signal.) *Shut.*
  - So a cabinet that is the opposite of open is . . . (Signal.) *shut.*
3. Everybody, think of a pot that is not shiny. It is the opposite of shiny. What's the opposite of shiny? (Signal.) *Dull.*
  - A pot that is the opposite of shiny is . . . (Signal.) *dull.*
4. Everybody, think of a dress that is not clean. It is the opposite of clean.

What's the opposite of clean? (Signal.) *Dirty.*

- So a dress that is the opposite of clean is . . . (Signal.) *dirty.*

5. Everybody, think of a woman who is not laughing. She is doing the opposite of laughing. What's the opposite of laughing? (Signal.) *Crying.*

- So a woman who is doing the opposite of laughing is . . . (Signal.) *crying.*

6. Everybody, think of food that is not raw. It is the opposite of raw. What's the opposite of raw? (Signal.) *Cooked.*

- So food that is the opposite of raw is . . . (Signal.) *cooked.*

EXERCISE 4 Analogies

1. We're going to make up an analogy.
2. Everybody, tell me what class a polar bear and an elephant are in. Get ready. (Signal.) *Animals.* Yes, animals.
3. We're going to make up an analogy that tells what color each animal is. What's the analogy going to tell? (Signal.) *What color each animal is.*
4. What color is a polar bear? (Signal.) *White.* Yes, a polar bear is white.
5. What color is an elephant? (Signal.) *Gray.* Yes, an elephant is gray.
6. Everybody, say the analogy about what colors a polar bear and an elephant are. Get ready. (Signal.) *A polar bear is to white as an elephant is to gray.*
- (Repeat step 6 until firm.)
7. What does our analogy tell about each animal? (Signal.) *What color it is.*
8. Everybody, say our analogy one more time. Get ready. (Signal.) *A polar bear is to white as an elephant is to gray.*
9. (Repeat steps 7 and 8 until firm.)

EXERCISE 5 Verb Tense

1. It's time for some statements.
2. Listen: The baby will cry. Say that statement. Get ready. (Signal.) *The baby will cry.*
- Does that statement tell what the baby did or what the baby will do? (Signal.) *What the baby will do.*
3. Listen: The baby cried. Say that statement. Get ready. (Signal.) *The baby cried.*
- Does that statement tell what the baby did or what the baby will do? (Signal.) *What the baby did.*

EXERCISE 6 Description

1. I'm going to say two things about something you know. See if you can figure out what I'm talking about.
2. (Hold up one finger.) *Zorn is a month.*
- (Hold up two fingers.) *Zorn comes between April and June.*
3. Everybody, tell me what you know about Zorn.
- (Hold up one finger.) *Zorn is a month.*
- (Hold up two fingers.) *Zorn comes between April and June.*
4. (Repeat step 3 until firm.)
5. Everybody, tell me what Zorn is. Get ready. (Signal.) *May.*
6. (Repeat steps 3 and 5 until firm.)
7. Here's another one.
8. (Hold up one finger.) *A tast is a tool that cuts wood.*
- (Hold up two fingers.) *A tast has a blade with teeth.*
9. Everybody, tell me what you know about a tast.
- (Hold up one finger.) *A tast is a tool that cuts wood.*
- (Hold up two fingers.) *A tast has a blade with teeth.*
10. (Repeat step 9 until firm.)
11. Everybody, tell me what a tast is. Get ready. (Signal.) *A saw.*
12. (Repeat steps 9 and 11 until firm.)

EXERCISE 7 Sentence Writing

Note: Remind children to start their sentences with a capital and end them with a period.

| girl | boy | sock |

_____

_____

_____

_____

1. Everybody, open your workbook to Lesson 98. Write your name. ✔
- You're going to write sentences that do not rhyme.
- Touch the picture of the boy and the girl. ✔
- The picture shows what the boy had and what the girl had. What did the boy have? (Signal.) *A sock.* Yes, a **sock.**
- What did the girl have? (Signal.) *A hat.* Yes, a **hat.**
2. Say the sentence for what the boy had. Get ready. (Signal.) *The boy had a sock.*
- Say the sentence for what the girl had. Get ready. (Signal.) *The girl had a hat.*
3. (Repeat step 2 until firm.)
4. The word box shows how to spell the words **girl, boy,** and **sock.** You can figure out how to spell the other words.

5. Write the sentence for what the boy had. Pencils down when you're finished. ✔
- Now go to the next line and write the sentence for what the girl had. Pencils down when you're finished. ✔
6. (Call on individual children to read both their sentences.)

EXERCISE 8 Map Reading

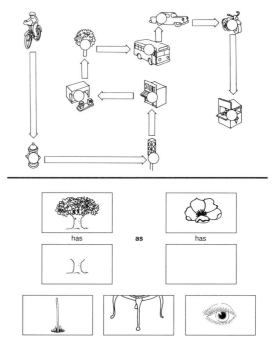

1. Everybody, find the next page. ✔
- (Hold up workbook. Point to top half.) Everybody, touch the boy. ✔
2. This picture is a map of where the boy rode a bike. You're going to color the arrows green and write the directions on the objects. Remember to start from the boy on the bike.
3. Everybody, color the first arrow green. Do it. ✔
- Now write the letter that shows the direction the boy rode. Pencils down when you're finished.
4. You'll do the rest of the arrows later.

EXERCISE 9　Analogies

1. (Hold up workbook. Point to bottom half.)
- The pictures show objects and their parts.
2. Touch the tree. ✔
3. The picture that's right below shows what part it has. Everybody, what part does a tree have? (Signal.) *A trunk.*
- Tell me about a tree. Get ready. (Signal.) *A tree has a trunk.*
4. Touch the flower. ✔
- One of the pictures below shows what part it has. Touch the picture that shows what part a flower has. ✔
- Everybody, what part? (Signal.) *A stem.*
- Tell me about a flower. Get ready. (Signal.) *A flower has a stem.*
5. Tell me about a tree. Get ready. (Signal.) *A tree has a trunk.*
- Tell me about a flower. Get ready. (Signal.) *A flower has a stem.*
6. Say the whole analogy about a tree and a flower. Get ready. (Signal.) *A tree has a trunk as a flower has a stem.*
7. (Repeat step 6 until firm.)
8. Draw a line from the flower to what part it has. (Observe children and give feedback.)

Objectives

- Identify objects based on characteristics. (Exercise 1)
- Replace a word in a sentence with a synonym. (Exercise 2)
- Answer questions involving previously learned calendar facts **and identify how many days in each month.** (Exercise 3)
- Construct verbal analogies. (Exercise 4)
- Generate questions to find a word's definition. (Exercise 5)
- Listen to a short story and answer questions involving "who," "when," "why," "where" and "what". (Exercise 6)
- Apply an if-then rule based on the occurrence of events. (Exercise 7)
- Write sentences given picture cues. (Exercise 8)

EXERCISE 1 Description

1. I'm going to say two things about something you know. See if you can figure out what I'm talking about.
2. (Hold up one finger.) A ketting is a place.
- (Hold up two fingers.) You can play in the sand and swim in the water at a ketting.
3. Everybody, tell me what you know about a ketting.
- (Hold up one finger.) *A ketting is a place.*
- (Hold up two fingers.) *You can play in the sand and swim in the water at a ketting.*
4. (Repeat step 3 until firm.)
5. Everybody, tell me what a ketting is. Get ready. (Signal.) *A beach.*
6. (Repeat steps 3 and 5 until firm.)
7. Here's another one.
8. (Hold up one finger.) A prast is a person.
- (Hold up two fingers.) A prast makes things out of wood.
9. Everybody, tell me what you know about a prast.
- (Hold up one finger.) *A prast is a person.*
- (Hold up two fingers.) *A prast makes things out of wood.*
10. (Repeat step 9 until firm.)
11. Everybody, tell me what a prast is. Get ready. (Signal.) *A carpenter.*
12. (Repeat steps 9 and 11 until firm.)

EXERCISE 2 Synonyms

1. There was a boy who felt very healthy. Say that. (Signal.) *There was a boy who felt very healthy.*
- Now say that statement using a synonym for **healthy.** Get ready. (Signal.) *There was a boy who felt very well.*
2. He liked to run very quickly. Say that. (Signal.) *He liked to run very quickly.*
- Now say that statement using a synonym for **quickly.** Get ready. (Signal.) *He liked to run very fast.*
3. But his yard was too little for him to run in. Say that. (Signal.) *But his yard was too little for him to run in.*
- Now say that statement using a synonym for **little.** Get ready. (Signal.) *But his yard was too small for him to run in.*

EXERCISE 3 Calendar Facts

1. Here are some more calendar facts.
2. Some months have thirty days; some months have thirty-one days. Most months have thirty-one days. How many days do most months have? (Signal.) *Thirty-one.*
3. But the month of February usually has only twenty-eight days. What month has only twenty-eight days? (Signal.) *February.*
4. (Repeat steps 2 and 3 until firm.)
5. Everybody, how many days are there in a year? (Signal.) *365.*
- Say the whole thing. Get ready. (Signal.) *There are 365 days in a year.*
- (Repeat step 5 until firm.)

6. Everybody, how many days are in a week? (Signal.) *Seven.*
- Say the whole thing. Get ready. (Signal.) *There are seven days in a week.*
7. Everybody, name the seven days of the week. Get ready. (Signal.) *Sunday, Monday, Tuesday, Wednesday, Thursday, Friday, Saturday.*
- (Repeat step 7 until firm.)
8. How many months are in a year? (Signal.) *Twelve.*
- Say the whole thing. Get ready. (Signal.) *There are twelve months in a year.*
9. Name the months of the year. Get ready. (Signal.) *January, February, March, April, May, June, July, August, September, October, November, December.*
- (Repeat step 9 until firm.)
10. How many weeks are in a year? (Signal.) *52.*
- Say the whole thing. Get ready. (Signal.) *There are 52 weeks in a year.*
- (Repeat step 10 until firm.)
11. How many seasons are in a year? (Signal.) *Four.*
- Say the seasons of the year. Get ready. (Signal.) *Winter, spring, summer, fall.*
12. How many days does February have? (Signal.) *28.*

EXERCISE 4 Analogies

1. We're going to make up an analogy.
2. Everybody, tell me what class a skyscraper and a barn are in. Get ready. (Signal.) *Buildings.* Yes, buildings.
3. We're going to make up an analogy that tells where you find each building. What's the analogy going to tell? (Signal.) *Where you find each building.*
4. Tell me where you find skyscraper. Get ready. (Signal.) *In a city.* Yes, you find a skyscraper in a city.
5. Tell me where you find a barn. Get ready. (Signal.) *On a farm.* Yes, you find a barn on a farm.
6. Everybody, say the analogy about where you find a skyscraper and a barn. Get ready. (Signal.) *A skyscraper is to a city as a barn is to a farm.*
- (Repeat step 6 until firm.)

7. What does our analogy tell about each building? (Signal.) *Where you find it.*
8. Everybody, say our analogy one more time. Get ready. (Signal.) *A skyscraper is to a city as a barn is to a farm.*
9. (Repeat steps 7 and 8 until firm.)

EXERCISE 5 Questioning Skills

1. I'm going to tell a story. When you hear a word you don't know, say **stop.**
2. The teacher was **agitated.** (The children are to say *stop.*)
- Everybody, what word don't you know? (Signal.) *Agitated.*
- Ask the question about what the word agitated means. Get ready. (Signal.) *What does the word agitated mean?*
- I'll tell you what agitated means. Agitated is a synonym for **upset.** What is agitated a synonym for? (Signal.) *Upset.*
- If a teacher was agitated, she was . . . (Signal.) *upset.*
3. Here's more of the story.
- The class was **clamorous.** (The children are to say *stop.*)
- Everybody, what word don't you know? (Signal.) *Clamorous.*
- Ask the question about what the word clamorous means. Get ready. (Signal.) *What does the word clamorous mean?*
- I'll tell you what clamorous means. Clamorous is a synonym for **noisy.** What is clamorous a synonym for? (Signal.) *Noisy.*
- If the teacher was agitated because the class was clamorous, she was upset because the class was . . . (Signal.) *noisy.*
4. Here's more of the story.
- She told them to stay **mute.** (The children are to say *Stop.*)
- Everybody, what word don't you know? (Signal.) *Mute.*
- Ask the question about what the word mute means. Get ready. (Signal.) *What does the word mute mean?*
- I'll tell you what mute means. Mute is a synonym for **silent.** What is mute a synonym for? (Signal.) *Silent.*
5. The teacher was agitated because the class was clamorous. She told them to stay mute. Do you think they did? (Children respond.)
- That's the end of the story.

EXERCISE 6 Who—What—When—Where—Why

1. Listen to this story.
- Last week a leaf was lying on the grass. The wind blew the leaf onto the sidewalk. Yesterday a girl stepped on the leaf.
- (Repeat the story.)
2. Tell when the leaf was lying on the grass. Get ready. (Signal.) *Last week.*
- Tell why the leaf blew away. Get ready. (Signal.) *The wind blew it.*
- Tell where the leaf landed. Get ready. (Signal.) *On the sidewalk.*
- Tell who stepped on the leaf. Get ready. (Signal.) *A girl.*
- Tell when the girl stepped on the leaf. Get ready. (Signal.) *Yesterday.*
3. (Repeat step 2 until firm.)

WORKBOOK

EXERCISE 7 If-Then Application

1. Everybody, open your workbook to Lesson 99. Write your name. ✔
- This arrow shows another **if** game. The first picture shows what **Roger** is going to do. The second picture shows what Roger's **hat** will do.

2. Look at the pictures carefully and see if you can figure out the **if** rule. Remember, you have to start with **if.** Then you tell what happens in the **first** picture. Then you tell what Roger's **hat** will do. Remember, you have to tell about the **hat.**
Raise your hand when you're ready to tell the **if** rule. ✔
- (Call on a child.) Say the **if** rule for these pictures.
(Idea: *If Roger puts his hat on top of a bird, Roger's hat will end up in the tree.*) Yes, if Roger puts his hat on top of a bird, his hat will end up in the tree.
3. Everybody, say the rule. (Signal.) *If Roger puts his hat on top of a bird, his hat will end up in the tree.*
(Repeat step 3 until firm.)
4. That's the rule for these pictures. Look at the pictures below the arrow. ✔
- They show things that **might** happen.
- Touch the first picture below the arrow. ✔
- What's happening in that picture? (Call on a child. Idea: *Roger is putting his hat on top of a turtle.*)
- Everybody, what will happen if Roger puts his hat on top of a turtle? (Signal.) *We don't know.* Right, we don't know.
5. Touch the second picture below the arrow. ✔
- What's happening in that picture? (Call on a child. Idea: *Roger is putting his hat on top of a bird.*)
- Everybody, what will happen if Roger puts his hat on top of a bird? (Signal.) *The hat will end up in the tree.* Right, if Roger puts his hat on top of a bird, his hat will end up in the tree.

6. Touch the last picture below the arrow. ✔
- What's happening in that picture? (Call on a child. Idea: *Roger is putting his hat on top of a frog.*) Everybody, what will happen if Roger puts his hat on top of a frog? (Signal.) *We don't know.* Right, we don't know.
7. Two of the pictures below the arrow show things that our rule does **not** tell us about. So we don't know what will happen if Roger does these things.
- Listen: Cross out the two pictures that show things our rule does **not** tell us about. Raise your hand when you're finished. (Observe children and give feedback.)
8. (Call on a child.) Which two pictures did you cross out?
(Idea: *The picture that shows Roger putting his hat on top of a turtle and the picture that shows Roger putting his hat on top of a frog.*)
- Why did you cross them out? (Call on a child. Idea: *Our rule doesn't tell us about them.*)
9. Raise your hand if you crossed out the pictures of Roger putting his hat on top of a turtle and Roger putting his hat on top of a frog. ✔
Boy, you are getting so smart about **if** rules.

EXERCISE 8 Sentence Writing

> *Note:* Remind children to start their sentences with a capital and end them with a period.

swim

1. Everybody, find the next page. ✔
- You're going to write sentences that do not rhyme.
- Touch the picture of the girl and the boy. ✔
- The picture shows what the girl will do and what the boy will do. What will the girl do? (Signal.) *Run.*
- What will the boy do? (Signal.) *Swim.*
2. Say the sentence for what the girl will do. Get ready. (Signal.) *The girl will run.*
- Say the sentence for what the boy will do. Get ready. (Signal.) *The boy will swim.*
3. (Repeat step 2 until firm.)
4. The word box shows how to spell the word **swim.** You can figure out how to spell the other words.
5. Write the sentence for what the girl will do. Pencils down when you're finished. ✔
- Now go to the next line and write the sentence for what the boy will do. Pencils down when you're finished. ✔
6. (Call on individual children to read both their sentences.)

LESSON **100**

Objectives

- Name common opposites. (Exercise 1)
- Construct verbal analogies. (Exercise 2)
- **Identify a word based on its characteristics.** (Exercise 3)
- Replace a word in a sentence with a synonym. (Exercise 4)
- Identify absurdities in sentences. (Exercise 5)
- Apply an if-then rule based on the occurrence of events. (Exercise 6)
- Write sentences given picture cues. (Exercise 7)

EXERCISE 1 Opposites

1. Listen: The opposite of far is near. What's the opposite of far? (Signal.) *Near.*
- We're going to play a word game.
2. Everybody, think of a city that is far. What's the opposite of far? (Signal.) *Near.*
- So a city that is the opposite of far is . . . (Signal.) *near.*
3. Everybody, think of meat that is cooked. What's the opposite of cooked? (Signal.) *Raw.*
- So meat that is the opposite of cooked is . . . (Signal.) *raw.*
4. Everybody, think of a bicycle that is safe. What's the opposite of safe? (Signal.) *Dangerous.*
- So a bicycle that is the opposite of safe is . . . (Signal.) *dangerous.*
5. Everybody, think of a house that is dirty. What's the opposite of dirty? (Signal.) *Clean.*
- So a house that is the opposite of dirty is . . . (Signal.) *clean.*
6. Everybody, think of a swimmer who is fast. What's the opposite of fast? (Signal.) *Slow.*
- So a swimmer who is the opposite of fast is . . . (Signal.) *slow.*

EXERCISE 2 Analogies

1. We're going to make up an analogy.
2. Everybody, tell me what class a couch and a table are in. Get ready. (Signal.) *Furniture.* Yes, furniture.
3. We're going to make up an analogy that tells where you find each piece of furniture. What's the analogy going to tell? (Signal.) *Where you find each piece of furniture.*
4. Name some places that you find a couch. (Call on individual children. Repeat all reasonable answers.)
- Let's say that you find a couch in the living room.
5. Name some places that you find a table. (Call on individual children. Repeat all reasonable answers.)
- Let's say that you find a table in the kitchen.
6. Everybody, say the analogy about where you find a couch and a table. Get ready. (Signal.) *A couch is to the living room as a table is to the kitchen.*
- (Repeat step 6 until firm.)
7. What does our analogy tell about each piece of furniture? Get ready. (Signal.) *Where you find it.*
8. Everybody, say our analogy one more time. Get ready. (Signal.) *A couch is to the living room as a table is to the kitchen.*

EXERCISE 3 Description

1. I'm going to say two things about something you know. See if you can figure out what I'm talking about.
2. (Hold up one finger.) Froom is an action.
• (Hold up two fingers.) When you move through water, you froom.
3. Everybody, tell me what you know about froom.
• (Hold up one finger.) *Froom is an action.*
• (Hold up two fingers.) *When you move through water, you froom.*
4. (Repeat step 3 until firm.)
5. Everybody, tell me what frooming is. Get ready. (Signal.) *Swimming.*
6. (Repeat steps 3 and 5 until firm.)
7. Here's another one.
8. (Hold up one finger.) A narp is a person.
• (Hold up two fingers.) A narp plants seed and harvests food.
9. Everybody, tell me what you know about a narp.
• (Hold up one finger.) *A narp is a person.*
• (Hold up two fingers.) *A narp plants seed and harvests food.*
10. (Repeat step 9 until firm.)
11. Everybody, tell me what a narp is. Get ready. (Signal.) *A farmer.*
• (Repeat step 9 and 11 until firm.)

EXERCISE 4 Synonyms

1. We're going to make up statements that mean the same thing.
2. What do we call two words that mean the same thing? (Signal.) *Synonyms.*
3. Listen: The chicken is skinny. Say that. (Signal.) *The chicken is skinny.*
• Make up a new statement using a synonym for **skinny.** Get ready. (Signal.) *The chicken is thin.*
4. Listen: The ball is under the table. Say that. (Signal.) *The ball is under the table.*
• Make up a new statement using a synonym for **under.** Get ready. (Signal.) *The ball is below the table.*
5. Listen: Shut the window. Say that. (Signal.) *Shut the window.*
• Make up a new statement using a synonym for **shut.** Get ready. (Signal.) *Close the window.*

EXERCISE 5 Absurdity

1. Listen to this story and tell me what's absurd about it.
2. A boy rode his tricycle across the lake. Where did the boy ride his tricycle? (Signal.) *Across the lake.*
3. Then he planted the tricycle in the garden. What did he do with the tricycle? (Signal.) *Planted it in the garden.*
4. Now tell me some things that are absurd about that story. (Call on two or three individual children. Ask the first child:) What's one thing that's absurd? (After the child responds, ask other children:) What's another thing that's absurd? (Praise all appropriate responses.)

WORKBOOK

EXERCISE 6 If-Then Application

1. Everybody, open your workbook to Lesson 100. Write your name. ✔
• This arrow shows another **if** game. The first picture shows what **Clarabelle** is going to do. The second picture shows what the **diving board** will do.
2. Look at the pictures carefully and see if you can figure out the **if** rule. Remember, you have to start with **if.** Then you tell what happens in the **first** picture. Then you tell what the **diving board** will do. Remember, for the second picture tell about the **diving board.** Raise your hand when you're ready to tell the **if** rule. ✔

- (Call on a child.) Say the **if** rule for these pictures. (Idea: *If Clarabelle walks out on the diving board, the diving board will break.*) Yes, if Clarabelle walks out on the diving board, the diving board will break.

3. Everybody, say the rule. (Signal.) *If Clarabelle walks out on the diving board, the diving board will break.*
(Repeat step 3 until firm.)

4. That's the rule for these pictures. Look at the pictures below the arrow. ✔

- They show things that **might** happen.
- Touch the first picture below the arrow. ✔
- What's happening in that picture? (Call on a child. Idea: *Clarabelle is walking out on a wire.*)
- Everybody, what will happen if Clarabelle walks out on a wire? (Signal.) *We don't know.* Right, we don't know.

5. Touch the second picture below the arrow. ✔

- What's happening in that picture? (Call on a child. Idea: *Clarabelle is walking across a log.*)
- Everybody, what will happen if Clarabelle walks across a log? (Signal.) *We don't know.* Right, we don't know.

6. Touch the last picture below the arrow. ✔

- What's happening in that picture?
(Call on a child. Idea: *Clarabelle is walking out on the diving board.*)
- Everybody, what will happen if Clarabelle walks out on the diving board? (Signal.) *The diving board will break.*
- Right, that's the rule: If Clarabelle walks out on the diving board, the diving board will break.

7. Two of the pictures below the arrow show things that our rule does **not** tell us about. So we don't know what will happen if Clarabelle does these things. Listen: Cross out the two pictures that show things our rule does **not** tell us about. Raise your hand when you're finished.
(Observe children and give feedback.)

8. (Call on a child.) Which two pictures did you cross out? (Idea: *The picture that shows Clarabelle walking out on a wire and the picture that shows Clarabelle walking across a log.*)

- Why did you cross them out? (Call on a child. Idea: *Our rule doesn't tell us about them.*)

9. Raise your hand if you crossed out the pictures of Clarabelle walking out on a wire and Clarabelle walking across a log. ✔ That's great.

EXERCISE 7 Sentence Writing

> *Note:* Remind children to start their sentences with a capital and end them with a period.

| girl | drink | eat | boy |

1. Everybody, find the next page. ✔

- You're going to write sentences that do not rhyme. Touch the picture of the boy and the girl. ✔
- The picture shows what the boy will do and what the girl will do. What will the boy do? (Signal.) *Eat.*
- What will the girl do? (Signal.) *Drink.*

2. Say the sentence for what the boy will do. Get ready. (Signal.) *The boy will eat.*

- Say the sentence for what the girl will do. Get ready. (Signal.) *The girl will drink.*

3. (Repeat step 2 until firm.)

4. The word box shows how to spell the words **girl, drink, eat,** and **boy.** You can figure out how to spell the other words.

5. Write the sentence for what the boy will do. Pencils down when you're finished. ✔

- Now go to the next line and write the sentence for what the girl will do. Pencils down when you're finished. ✔

6. (Call on individual children to read both their sentences.)

Objectives

- Construct verbal analogies. (Exercise 1)
- **Replace a word in a sentence with an opposite.** (Exercise 2)
- Identify past and present tense. (Exercise 3)
- Identify a word based on its characteristics. (Exercise 4)
- Replace a word in a sentence with a synonym. (Exercise 5)
- Identify absurdities. (Exercise 6)
- Write sentences given picture cues. (Exercise 7)
- Label cardinal directions on a map. (Exercise 8)
- Name members of a class and subclass and identify the bigger class. (Exercise 9)

EXERCISE 1 Analogies

1. We're going to make up an analogy.
2. Everybody, tell me what class a lion and a cat are in. Get ready. (Signal.) *Animals.* Yes, animals.
3. We're going to make up an analogy that tells what each animal says. What's the analogy going to tell? (Signal.) *What each animal says.*
4. Tell me what a lion says. Get ready. (Signal.) *Roar.* Yes, a lion says roar.
5. Tell me what a cat says. Get ready. (Signal.) *Meow.* Yes, meow.
- Here's the first part of the analogy: A lion is to roaring.
6. Everybody, say the whole analogy about what a lion and a cat say. Get ready. (Signal.) *A lion is to roaring as a cat is to meowing.*
- (Repeat step 6 until firm.)
7. What does our analogy tell about each animal? (Signal.) *What each animal says.*
8. Everybody, say our analogy one more time. Get ready. (Signal.) *A lion is to roaring as a cat is to meowing.*

EXERCISE 2 Opposites

1. We're going to play a word game.
2. Listen: The tractor was pushing. Say that statement. (Signal.) *The tractor was pushing.*
- Now say a statement that tells the opposite about what the tractor was doing. Get ready. (Signal.) *The tractor was pulling.*
3. Listen: The building was near. Say that statement. (Signal.) *The building was near.*
- Now say a statement that tells the opposite about where the building was. Get ready. (Signal.) *The building was far.*
4. Listen: The floor was clean. Say that statement. (Signal.) *The floor was clean.*
- Now say a statement that tells the opposite about the floor. Get ready. (Signal.) *The floor was dirty.*
5. Listen: The carrot is raw. Say that statement. (Signal.) *The carrot is raw.*
- Now say a statement that tells the opposite about the carrot. Get ready. (Signal.) *The carrot is cooked.*

EXERCISE 3 Verb Tense

1. It's time for some statements.
- Listen: The boy washed. Say that statement. (Signal.) *The boy washed.*
- Does that statement tell what the boy did or what the boy is doing? (Signal.) *What the boy did.*
2. Listen: The boy is washing. Say that statement. (Signal.) *The boy is washing.*
- Does that statement tell what the boy did or what the boy is doing? (Signal.) *What the boy is doing.*
3. (Repeat step 2 until firm.)
4. One more time. Listen: The boy washed. Say that statement. (Signal.) *The boy washed.*
- What does that statement tell? (Signal.) *What the boy did.*
5. Listen: The boy is washing. Say that statement. (Signal.) *The boy is washing.*
- What does that statement tell? (Signal.) *What the boy is doing.*

6. Say the statement that tells what the boy did. Get ready. (Signal.) *The boy washed.*

7. Say the statement that tells what the boy is doing. Get ready. (Signal.) *The boy is washing.*

8. (Repeat steps 6 and 7 until firm.)

EXERCISE 4   Description

1. I'm going to say two things about something you know. See if you can figure out what I'm talking about.

2. (Hold up one finger.) Sleem is a season.
- (Hold up two fingers.) Leaves turn yellow and red in sleem.

3. Everybody tell me what you know about sleem.
- (Hold up one finger.) *Sleem is a season.*
- (Hold up two fingers.) *Leaves turn yellow and red in sleem.*

4. (Repeat step 3 until firm.)

5. Everybody, tell me what sleem is. Get ready. (Signal.) *Fall.*

6. (Repeat steps 3 and 5 until firm.)

7. Here's another one.

8. (Hold up one finger.) Marl is a time of day.
- (Hold up two fingers.) Most people wake up early in the marl.

9. Everybody, tell me what you know about marl.
- (Hold up one finger.) *Marl is a time of day.*
- (Hold up two fingers.) *Most people wake up early in the marl.*

10. (Repeat step 9 until firm.)

11. Everybody, tell me what marl is. Get ready. (Signal.) *Morning.*

12. (Repeat steps 9 and 11 until firm.)

EXERCISE 5   Synonyms

1. What do we call two words that mean the same thing? (Signal.) *Synonyms.*

2. Listen: I'm going to shout. Say that. (Signal.) *I'm going to shout.*
- Say the statement with a synonym for **shout.** Get ready. (Signal.) *I'm going to yell.*
- (Repeat step 2 until firm.)

3. Listen: The box is big. Say that. (Signal.) *The box is big.*
- Say the statement with a synonym for **big.** Get ready. (Signal.) *The box is large.*
- (Repeat step 3 until firm.)

4. Listen: The suitcase is under the bed. Say that. (Signal.) *The suitcase is under the bed.*
- Say the statement with a synonym for **under.** Get ready. (Signal.) *The suitcase is below the bed.*
- (Repeat step 4 until firm.)

EXERCISE 6   Absurdity

1. Listen to this statement and figure out what is absurd about it.

2. The girl poured some milk from the empty bottle. Say the statement. Get ready. (Signal.) *The girl poured some milk from the empty bottle.*

3. What's absurd about that statement? (Call on one child. Praise all reasonable responses; then say:) Yes, she couldn't pour milk from an empty bottle.

WORKBOOK

EXERCISE 7   Sentence Writing

stick

_____

_____

_____

_____

1. Everybody, open your workbook to Lesson 101. Write your name. ✔
- You're going to write sentences that do not rhyme.
- Touch the picture of the pig and the cat. ✔
- The picture shows what the pig had and what the cat had. What did the pig have? (Signal.) *A stick.*
- What did the cat have? (Signal.) *A cup.*

2. Say the sentence for what the pig had. Get ready. (Signal.) *The pig had a stick.*
• Say the sentence for what the cat had. Get ready. (Signal.) *The cat had a cup.*
3. (Repeat step 2 until firm.)
4. The word box shows how to spell the word **stick.** You can figure out how to spell the other words.
5. Write the sentence for what the pig had. Pencils down when you're finished. ✔
• Now go to the next line and write the sentence for what the cat had. Pencils down when you're finished. ✔
6. (Call on individual children to read both their sentences.)

EXERCISE 8 **Map Reading**

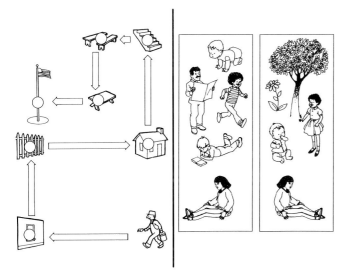

1. Everybody, find the next page. ✔
• (Hold up workbook. Point to first half.) Everybody, touch the painter. ✔

2. This picture is a map of what the painter painted. You're going to color the arrows green and write the directions on the objects. Remember to start from the painter.
3. Everybody, color the first arrow green. Do it. ✔
• Now write the letter that shows the direction the painter went. Use your pencil. ✔
4. You'll do the rest of the arrows later.

EXERCISE 9 **Classification**

1. (Hold up workbook. Point to second half.) Touch the picture of the **smaller** class. ✔
• What kind of thing is that in the picture? (Signal.) *People.*
2. Everybody, circle the picture that shows the **larger** class. ✔
• Everybody, what's the name of the larger class? (Signal.) *Living things.*
3. Everybody, touch the picture of the class that is **smaller.** ✔
• The people in that picture of the **smaller** class should be wearing green or blue clothes. What colors? (Signal.) *Green or blue.*
• Mark two people in that picture. ✔
4. Touch the picture that shows the **larger** class. ✔
• The people in that picture should be wearing purple or yellow clothes. What colors? (Signal.) *Purple or yellow.*
• Mark two people in that picture. ✔

LESSON 102

Objectives

- Identify the relationship between the components of an analogy. (Exercise 1)
- Replace a word in a sentence with an opposite. (Exercise 2)
- Replace a word in a sentence with a synonym. (Exercise 3)
- Name objects that could be made of a given material. (Exercise 4)
- Identify past and present tense. (Exercise 5)
- Write sentences given picture clues. (Exercise 6)
- Write class names next to members of the class. (Exercise 7)
- Label cardinal directions on a map. (Exercise 8)

EXERCISE 1 Analogies

1. I'm going to say some analogies about a table and a bed. Everybody, tell me what class a table and a bed are in. Get ready. (Signal.) *Furniture.*
- See if you can figure out what each analogy **tells** about the furniture.
2. Listen to this analogy. A table is to eating **as** a bed is to . . . (Signal.) *sleeping.*
- Everybody, say that analogy. Get ready. (Signal.) *A table is to eating as a bed is to sleeping.*
3. What does that analogy tell about the table and the bed? (Call on individual children. Praise reasonable responses, but use: *what you do with them.*) Yes, it tells what you do with each piece of furniture.
- (Repeat step 3 until firm.)
4. (Repeat steps 2 and 3 until firm.)
5. Listen to the next analogy. A bed is to a blanket **as** a table is to a . . . (Signal.) *tablecloth.*
- Everybody, say that analogy. Get ready. (Signal.) *A bed is to a blanket as a table is to a tablecloth.*
6. What does that analogy tell about the bed and the table? (Call on individual children. Praise reasonable responses, but use: *what you put on top of them.*) Yes, it tells what you put on top of each piece of furniture.
- (Repeat step 6 until firm.)
7. (Repeat steps 5 and 6 until firm.)

EXERCISE 2 Opposites

1. We're going to play a word game.
2. Listen: A curtain is dirty. Say that statement. (Signal.) *A curtain is dirty.*
- Now say a statement that tells the opposite about the curtain. Get ready. (Signal.) *A curtain is clean.*
3. Listen: The problem was easy. Say that statement. (Signal.) *The problem was easy.*
- Now say a statement that tells the opposite about the problem. Get ready. (Signal.) *The problem was difficult.*
4. Listen: An egg was cooked. Say that statement. (Signal.) *An egg was cooked.*
- Now say a statement that tells the opposite about an egg. Get ready. (Signal.) *An egg was raw.*
5. Listen: The rock is rough. Say that statement. (Signal.) *The rock is rough.*
- Now say a statement that tells the opposite about the rock. Get ready. (Signal.) *The rock is smooth.*

EXERCISE 3 Synonyms

1. I'm going to make up a story.
2. There was a pig that was healthy. Say that. (Signal.) *There was a pig that was healthy.*
- Now say that statement using a synonym for **healthy.** Get ready. (Signal.) *There was a pig that was well.*
3. But the pig was too fat to be quick. Say that. (Signal.) *But the pig was too fat to be quick.*
- Now say that statement using a synonym for **quick.** Get ready. (Signal.) *But the pig was too fat to be fast.*
4. He wished he was thin. Say that. (Signal.) *He wished he was thin.*

- Now say that statement using a synonym for **thin.** Get ready. (Signal.) *He wished he was skinny.*

5. And here is the end of the story.

6. His brother said, "To get thin, you have to stop eating or else do a lot more running." What do you think he should do? (Call on individual children. After a child answers, ask:) What do you think so? (Child responds.)

EXERCISE 4   Materials

1. Think of things that are made of concrete. Let's see who can name at least three things made of concrete. (Call on individual children to name objects made of concrete. Each child should name at least three things.)

2. Everybody, think of things that are made of glass. Let's see who can name at least three things made of glass. (Call on individual children to name objects made of glass. Each child should name at least three things.)

3. Everybody, think of things that are made of metal. Let's see who can name at least three things made of metal. (Call on individual children to name objects made of metal. Each child should name at least three things.)

EXERCISE 5   Verb Tense

1. It's time for some statements. Listen: The girl smiled. Say that statement. (Signal.) *The girl smiled.*

- Does that statement tell what the girl did or what the girl is doing? (Signal.) *What the girl did.*

2. Listen: The girl is smiling. Say that statement. (Signal.) *The girl is smiling.*

- Does that statement tell what the girl did or what the girl is doing? (Signal.) *What the girl is doing.*

3. (Repeat step 2 until firm.)

4. One more time. Listen: The girl smiled. Say that statement. (Signal.) *The girl smiled.*

- What does that statement tell? (Signal.) *What the girl did.*

5. Listen: The girl is smiling. Say that statement. (Signal.) *The girl is smiling.*

- What does that statement tell? (Signal.) *What the girl is doing.*

6. Say the statement that tells what the girl did. Get ready. (Signal.) *The girl smiled.*

7. Say the statement that tells what the girl is doing. Get ready. (Signal.) *The girl is smiling.*

8. (Repeat steps 6 and 7 until firm.)

EXERCISE 6   Sentence Writing

fish cow car

_____
_____
_____
_____

1. Everybody, open your workbook to Lesson 102. Write your name. ✔

- You're going to write sentences that do not rhyme.

- Touch the picture of the cow and the fish. ✔

- The picture shows what the cow had and what the fish had. What did the cow have? (Signal.) *A car.*

- What did the fish have? (Signal.) *A hat.*

2. Say the sentence for what the cow had. Get ready. (Signal.) *The cow had a car.*

- Say the sentence for what the fish had. Get ready. (Signal.) *The fish had a hat.*

3. (Repeat step 2 until firm.)

4. The word box shows how to spell the words **fish, cow,** and **car.** You can figure out how to spell the other words.

5. Write the sentence for what the cow had. Pencils down when you're finished. ✔

- Now go to the next line and write the sentence for what the fish had. Pencils down when you're finished. ✔

6. (Call on individual children to read both their sentences.)

EXERCISE 7   Classification

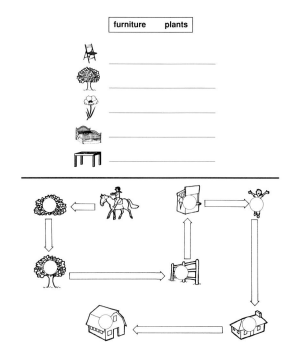

1. Everybody, find the next page. ✔
• (Hold up workbook. Point to top half.) Everybody, I'll read the words in the box. You touch the words.
• First word: Furniture. ✔
• Next word: Plants. ✔
   Yes, furniture and plants.
2. Everybody, put your finger under the chair. ✔

3. Is a chair in the class of furniture or in the class of plants? (Signal.) *Furniture.*
• Copy the word **furniture** next to the chair. ✔
• Read what you wrote. (Signal.) *Furniture.*
4. Everybody, put your finger under the tree. ✔
5. Is a tree in the class of furniture or in the class of plants? (Signal.) *Plants.*
• Copy the word **plants** next to the tree. ✔
• Read what you wrote. (Signal.) *Plants.*
6. Everybody, read the words you wrote. (Signal.) *Furniture. Plants.*
7. Later you can write the class words that go with the pictures.

EXERCISE 8   Map Reading

1. (Hold up workbook. Point to bottom half.) Everybody, touch the horse. ✔
2. This picture is a map of where the girl rode her horse. You're going to color the arrows purple and write the directions on the objects. Remember to start from the girl on the horse.
3. Everybody, color the first arrow purple. Do it. ✔
• Now write the letter that shows the direction the girl rode. Use your pencil. ✔
4. You'll do the rest of the arrows later.

Objectives

- Identify the relationship between the components of an analogy. (Exercise 1)
- Replace a word in a sentence with an opposite. (Exercise 2)
- Name members of a class and subclass and identify the bigger class. (Exercise 3)
- Identify a word based on its characteristics. (Exercise 4)
- Replace a word in a sentence with a synonym. (Exercise 5)
- Write sentences given picture cues. (Exercise 6)
- Construct verbal analogies. (Exercise 7)
- Write class names next to members of the class. (Exercise 8)

EXERCISE 1 Analogies

1. I'm going to say some analogies about a paper bag and a glass.
- Everybody, tell me what class a paper bag and a glass are in. Get ready. (Signal.) *Containers.*
- See if you can figure out what each analogy **tells** about the containers.
2. Listen to this analogy.
- A paper bag is to dry things **as** a glass is to . . . (Signal.) *wet things.*
- Everybody, say that analogy. Get ready. (Signal.) *A paper bag is to dry things as a glass is to wet things.*
3. What does that analogy tell about the paper bag and the glass? (Call on individual children. Praise reasonable responses, but use: *what kind of things they hold.*) Yes, it tells what kind of things each container holds.
- (Repeat step 3 until firm.)
4. (Repeat steps 2 and 3 until firm.)
5. Listen to the next analogy.
- A paper bag is to paper **as** a glass is to . . . (Signal.) *glass.*
- Everybody, say that analogy. Get ready. (Signal.) *A paper bag is to paper as a glass is to glass.*
6. What does that analogy tell about the paper bag and the glass? (Call on individual children. Praise reasonable responses, but use: *what they are made of.*) Yes, it tells what each container is made of.
- (Repeat step 6 until firm.)
7. (Repeat steps 5 and 6 until firm.)

EXERCISE 2 Opposites

1. We're going to play a word game.
2. Listen: The ham is cooked. Say the statement. (Signal.) *The ham is cooked.*
- Now say a statement that tells the opposite about the ham. Get ready. (Signal.) *The ham is raw.*
3. Listen: The bed was narrow. Say the statement. (Signal.) *The bed was narrow.*
- Now say a statement that tells the opposite about the bed. Get ready. (Signal.) *The bed was wide.*
4. Listen: The park was near. Say the statement. (Signal.) *The park was near.*
- Now say a statement that tells the opposite about the park. Get ready. (Signal.) *The park was far.*
5. Listen: The glass is dull. Say the statement. (Signal.) *The glass is dull.*
- Now say a statement that tells the opposite about the glass. Get ready. (Signal.) *The glass is shiny.*
6. Listen: The room is dirty. Say the statement. (Signal.) *The room is dirty.*
- Now say a statement that tells the opposite about the room. Get ready. (Signal.) *The room is clean.*

EXERCISE 3 Classification

1. We're going to talk about classes.
2. If we took all fruit from the class of food, would there be any kinds of food left? (Signal.) *Yes.*
3. Name some kinds of food that would be left. (Call on individual children. Praise appropriate responses.)

4. The class of fruit is made up of many kinds of fruit. I'll name some kinds of fruit in the class of fruit. Listen: Apples, pears. Your turn. Name some kinds of fruit. (Call on individual children. Praise reasonable answers such as *apples, oranges, lemons,* and *plums.*)

5. Think about this. If we took all the apples from the class of fruit, would there be any fruit left? (Signal.) *Yes.*

6. Name some kinds of fruit that would be left. (Call on individual children. Praise all acceptable answers: that is, any kind of fruit except apples.)

7. Yes, if we took all the apples from the class of fruit, there would still be fruit left. So which class is bigger, the class of fruit or the class of apples? (Signal.) *The class of fruit.*
   • Tell me how you know. Get ready. (Signal.) *The class of fruit has more kinds of things in it.*

8. Think big. Tell me which class is bigger, the class of food or the class of fruit? (Signal.) *The class of food.*

9. Think big. Tell me which class is bigger, the class of fruit or the class of apples? (Signal.) *The class of fruit.*

EXERCISE 4 Description

1. I'm going to say two things about something you know. See if you can figure out what I'm talking about.

2. (Hold up one finger.) Frums is the name of a class.
   • (Hold up two fingers.) We use frums to help us do work.

3. Everybody, tell me what you know about frums.
   • (Hold up one finger.) *Frums is the name of a class.*
   • (Hold up two fingers.) *We use frums to help us do work.*

4. (Repeat step 3 until firm.)

5. Everybody, tell me what frums are. Get ready. (Signal.) *Tools.*

6. (Repeat steps 3 and 5 until firm.)

7. Here's another one.

8. (Hold up one finger.) Zeel is a day of the week.

• (Hold up two fingers.) Zeel is the day before Saturday.

9. Everybody, tell me what you know about Zeel.
   • (Hold up one finger.) *Zeel is a day of the week.*
   • (Hold up two fingers.) *Zeel is the day before Saturday.*

10. (Repeat step 9 until firm.)

11. Everybody, tell me what Zeel is. Get ready. (Signal.) *Friday.*

12. (Repeat steps 9 and 11 until firm.)

EXERCISE 5 Synonyms

1. I'm going to make up a story.

2. There was an airplane that was very big.
   • What's a synonym for **big?** (Signal.) *Large.*
   • So there was an airplane that was very . . . (Signal.) *large.*

3. This airplane was very fast.
   • What's a synonym for **fast?** (Signal.) *Quick.*
   • So this airplane was very . . . (Signal.) *quick.*

4. The airplane flew over the clouds.
   • What's a synonym for **over?** (Signal.) *Above.*
   • So the airplane flew . . . (Signal.) *above the clouds.*

5. Let's do that story one more time and go a little faster.

6. There was an airplane that was very big. Say that. (Signal.) *There was an airplane that was very big.*
   • Now say that statement using a synonym for **big.** Get ready. (Signal.) *There was an airplane that was very large.*

7. This airplane was very fast. Say that. (Signal.) *This airplane was very fast.*
   • Now say that statement using a synonym for **fast.** Get ready. (Signal.) *This airplane was very quick.*

8. The airplane flew over the clouds. Say that. (Signal.) *The airplane flew over the clouds.*
   • Now say that statement using a synonym for **over.** Get ready. (Signal.) *The airplane flew above the clouds.*

9. And here is the end of the story.

10. The pilot said, "Here comes a big storm. I'll have to fly higher or else land this airplane." What do you think she should do? (Call on individual children. After a child answers, ask:) Why do you think so?

EXERCISE 6 Sentence Writing

| bird | fly | girl |

_____

_____

_____

1. Everybody, open your workbook to Lesson 103. Write your name. ✔
- You're going to write sentences that do not rhyme.
- Touch the picture of the girl and the bird. ✔
- The picture shows what the girl will do and what the bird will do. What will the girl do? (Signal.) *Sing.*
- What will the bird do? (Signal.) *Fly.*
2. Say the sentence for what the girl will do. Get ready. (Signal.) *The girl will sing.*
- Say the sentence for what the bird will do. Get ready. (Signal.) *The bird will fly.*
3. (Repeat step 2 until firm.)
4. The word box shows how to spell the words **bird, fly,** and **girl.** You can figure out how to spell the other words.
5. Write the sentence for what the girl will do. Pencils down when you're finished. ✔
- Now go to the next line and write the sentence for what the bird will do. Pencils down when you're finished. ✔
6. (Call on individual children to read both their sentences.)

EXERCISE 7 Analogies

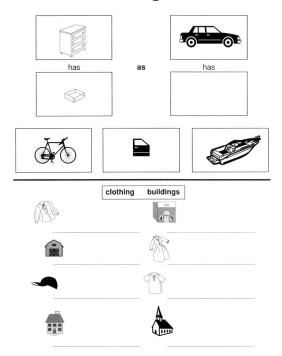

1. Everybody, find the next page. ✔
- (Hold up workbook. Point to top half.)
- The pictures show objects and their parts.
2. Touch the dresser. ✔
3. The picture that's right below shows what part it has. Everybody, what part does a dresser have? (Signal.) *A drawer.*
- Tell me about a dresser. Get ready. (Signal.) *A dresser has a drawer.*
4. Touch the car. ✔
- One of the pictures below shows what parts it has. Touch the picture that shows what part a car has. ✔
- Everybody, what part does a car have? (Signal.) *A door.*
- Tell me about a car. Get ready. (Signal.) *A car has a door.*
5. Tell me about a dresser. Get ready. (Signal.) *A dresser has a drawer.*
- Tell me about a car. Get ready. (Signal.) *A car has a door.*
6. Say the whole analogy about a dresser and a car. Get ready. (Signal.) *A dresser has a drawer as a car has a door.*
7. (Repeat step 6 until firm.)
8. Draw a line from the car to the part it has. (Observe children and give feedback.)

EXERCISE 8 Classification

1. (Hold up workbook. Point to bottom half.) Everybody, I'll read the words in the box. You touch the words.
- First word: Clothing. ✔
- Next word: Buildings. ✔
- Yes, clothing and buildings.
2. Everybody, touch the woman's shirt. ✔
3. Is a shirt in the class of clothing or in the class of buildings? (Signal.) *Clothing.*
- Copy the word **clothing** next to the woman's shirt. ✔

- Read what you wrote. (Signal.) *Clothing.*
4. Everybody, put your finger under the barn. ✔
5. Is a barn in the class of clothing or in the class of buildings? (Signal.) *Buildings.*
- Copy the word **buildings** next to the barn. ✔
- Read what you wrote. (Signal.) *Buildings.*
6. Everybody, read the words you wrote. (Signal.) *Clothing. Buildings.*
7. Later you can write the class words that go with the other pictures.

Objectives

- Identify the cardinal directions. (Exercise 1)
- Identify the relationship between the components of an analogy. (Exercise 2)
- Replace a word in a sentence with an opposite. (Exercise 3)
- Listen to a short story and answer questions involving "who," "when," "why," "where" and "what". (Exercise 4)
- Name three classes containing a common noun and answer questions about members of those classes. (Exercise 5)
- Write sentences given picture cues. (Exercise 6)
- Label cardinal directions on a map. (Exercise 7)
- Follow coloring directions involving smaller and larger classes. (Exercise 8)

EXERCISE 1 Map Reading

1. Let's all stand up. ✔
2. Everybody, you're going to face north. (Pause.) Get ready. (Signal.) (The children face north.)
- What are you doing? (Signal.) *Facing north.*
- Say the statement. Get ready. (Signal.) *I am facing north.*
3. Everybody, you're going to face south. (Pause.) Get ready. (Signal.) (The children face south.)
- What are you doing? (Signal.) *Facing south.*
- Say the statement. Get ready. (Signal.) *I am facing south.*
4. Everybody, you're going to face west. (Pause.) Get ready. (Signal.) (The children face west.)
- What are you doing? (Signal.) *Facing west.*
- Say the statement. Get ready. (Signal.) *I am facing west.*
5. (Repeat steps 2 through 4 until firm.)
6. (Point east.) Tell me the direction I'm pointing. (Pause.) Get ready. (Signal.) *East.*
- Say the statement. Get ready. (Signal.) *You are pointing east.*
  Yes, if I skated for ten minutes in this direction, I would be going east.
7. (Point south.) Tell me the direction I'm pointing. (Pause.) Get ready. (Signal.) *South.*
- Say the statement. Get ready. (Signal.) *You are pointing south.*
  Yes, if I skated for two hours in this direction, I would be going south.
8. (Repeat steps 6 and 7 until firm.)

EXERCISE 2 Analogies

1. I'm going to say some analogies about a frog and a dog.
2. Everybody, tell me what class a frog and a dog are in. Get ready. (Signal.) *Animals.*
3. See if you can figure out what each analogy **tells** about the animals. Listen to this analogy.
4. A frog is to ribbiting **as** a dog is to . . . (Signal.) *barking.*
- Everybody, say that analogy. Get ready. (Signal.) *A frog is to ribbiting as a dog is to barking.*
5. What does that analogy tell about the frog and the dog? (Call on a child. Praise reasonable responses, but use: *what they say.*)
  Yes, it tells what each animal says.
- (Repeat step 5 until firm.)
6. (Repeat steps 4 and 5 until firm.)
7. Listen to the next analogy.
8. A frog is to hopping **as** a dog is to . . . (Signal.) *running.*
- Everybody, say that analogy. Get ready. (Signal.) *A frog is to hopping as a dog is to running.*
9. What does that analogy tell about the frog and the dog? (Call on a child. Praise reasonable responses, but use: *how they move.*)
  Yes, it tells how each animal moves.
- (Repeat step 9 until firm.)
10. (Repeat steps 8 and 9 until firm.)

EXERCISE 3 Opposites

1. I'm going to tell you a story. You have to know your opposites to follow this story.
2. Listen: There was a girl. She was the opposite of noisy. Everybody, what do you know about that girl? Get ready. (Signal.) *She was quiet.*
   Yes, the girl was quiet.
3. This quiet girl went to look at a house. The house was the opposite of big. Everybody, what do you know about that house? Get ready. (Signal.) *It was small.*
   Yes, the house was small.
4. The small house did not have a good floor. The floor was the opposite of safe. Everybody, what do you know about that floor? Get ready. (Signal.) *It was dangerous.*
   Yes, the floor was dangerous.
5. The quiet girl heard a crash inside the house. She was scared and she ran away. She ran the opposite of slowly. What do you know about how that girl ran? (Call on a child. Accept *quickly,* but use *fast.*)
   Yes, the girl ran fast.
6. (Repeat steps 2 through 5 until firm.)
7. Let's see what you remember about that story.
8. Everybody, tell me about the girl. Get ready. (Signal.) *She was quiet.*
   • Tell me about the house. Get ready. (Signal.) *It was small.*
   • Tell me about the floor. Get ready. (Signal.) *It was dangerous.*
   • Tell me how the girl ran. Get ready. (Signal.) *She ran fast.*
   • (Repeat step 8 until firm.)

EXERCISE 4 Who—What—When—Where—Why

1. Listen to this story.
   • The house had a leak, so the woman climbed a ladder to look at the roof. After she got to the top of the house, a dog barked at her.
   • (Repeat the story.)
2. Tell what the woman did. Get ready. (Signal.) *Climbed a ladder.*
   • Tell what barked at the woman. Get ready. (Signal.) *A dog.*
   • Tell when the dog barked at the woman. Get ready. (Signal.) *After she got to the top of the house.*
   • Tell what the woman climbed. Get ready. (Signal.) *A ladder.*
   • Tell why the woman climbed the ladder. Get ready. (Signal.) *To look at the roof.*
3. (Repeat step 2 until firm.)

EXERCISE 5 Classification

1. Today we're going to talk about a kitchen table. We can put a kitchen table into three different classes. See how many classes you can name, starting with the smallest class.
2. Everybody, what's the smallest class for a kitchen table? (Signal.) *Kitchen tables.*
   • What's the next bigger class? (Signal.) *Tables.*
   • What's the biggest class? (Signal.) *Furniture.*
   • (Accept any other correct responses, but use: *kitchen tables, tables, furniture.*)
3. (Repeat step 2 until firm.)
4. What is one kind of object you would find in all those classes? (Signal.) *A kitchen table.*
5. Would you find a chair in all those classes? (Signal.) *No.*
   • Name the class you would find a chair in. Get ready. (Signal.) *Furniture.*

EXERCISE 6 Sentence Writing

stop horse fly

_____

_____

_____

_____

1. Everybody, open your workbook to Lesson 104. Write your name. ✔
• You're going to write sentences that do not rhyme.
• Touch the picture of the man and the horse. ✔
• The picture shows what the man will do and what the horse will do. What will the man do? (Signal.) *Fly.* Yes, **fly.**
• What will the horse do? (Signal.) *Stop.* Yes, **stop.**
2. Say the sentence for what the man will do. Get ready. (Signal.) *The man will fly.*
• Say the sentence for what the horse will do. Get ready. (Signal.) *The horse will stop.*
3. (Repeat step 2 until firm.)
4. The word box shows how to spell the words **stop, horse,** and **fly.** You can figure out how to spell the other words.
5. Write the sentence for what the man will do. Pencils down when you're finished. ✔
• Now go to the next line and write the sentence for what the horse will do. Pencils down when you're finished. ✔
6. (Call on individual children to read both their sentences.)

EXERCISE 7 Map Reading

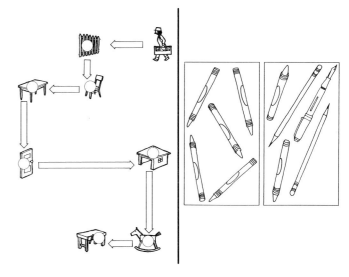

1. Everybody, find the next page. ✔
• (Hold up workbook. Point to first half.) Everybody, touch the carpenter. ✔
2. This picture is a map of what the carpenter fixed. You're going to color the arrows orange and write the directions on the objects. Remember to start from the carpenter.
3. Everybody, color the first arrow orange. Do it. ✔
• Now write the letter that shows the direction the carpenter went. ✔
4. You'll do the rest of the arrows later.

EXERCISE 8 Classification

1. (Hold up workbook. Point to second half.) Touch the picture of the **smaller** class. ✔
• What kind of thing is that in the picture? (Signal.) *Crayons.*
2. Everybody, circle the picture that shows the **larger** class. ✔
• What's the name of the larger class? (Call on a child. Praise reasonable responses, but use: *things you write with.*)
3. Everybody, touch the picture of the class that is **smaller.** ✔
• The crayons in that picture of the **smaller** class should be orange or yellow. What colors? (Signal.) *Orange or yellow.*
• Mark two crayons in that picture. ✔
4. Touch the picture that shows the **larger** class. ✔
• The crayons in that picture should be red or blue. What colors? (Signal.) *Red or blue.*
• Mark two crayons in that picture. ✔

Objectives

- Identify the relationship between the components of an analogy. (Exercise 1)
- Name things that a statement does NOT tell. (Exercise 2)
- Name three classes containing a common noun and answer questions about members of those classes. (Exercise 3)
- Identify words based on characteristics. (Exercise 4)
- Replace a word in a sentence with a synonym. (Exercise 5)
- Write sentences given picture cues. (Exercise 6)
- Ask questions to figure out the "mystery" picture. (Exercise 7)

EXERCISE 1 Analogies

1. I'm going to say some analogies about a tree and a flower.
2. Everybody, tell me what class a tree and a flower are in. Get ready. (Signal.) *Plants.*
3. See if you can figure out what each analogy **tells** about the plants. Listen to this analogy.
4. A tree is to a trunk **as** a flower is to a . . . (Signal.) *stem.*
   - Everybody, say that analogy. Get ready. (Signal.) *A tree is to a trunk as a flower is to a stem.*
5. What does that analogy tell about the tree and the flower? (Call on a child. Praise reasonable responses, but use: *a part they have.*) Yes, it tells a part each plant has.
   - (Repeat step 5 until firm.)
6. (Repeat steps 4 and 5 until firm.)
7. Listen to the next analogy.
8. A tree is to big **as** a flower is to . . . (Signal.) *small.*
   - Everybody, say that analogy. Get ready. (Signal.) *A tree is to big as a flower is to small.*
9. What does that analogy tell about the tree and the flower? (Call on a child. Praise reasonable responses, but use: *what size they are.*) Yes, it tells what size each plant is.
   - (Repeat step 9 until firm.)
10. (Repeat steps 8 and 9 until firm.)

EXERCISE 2 Statements

1. The teacher was reading a newspaper. Everybody, say that statement. Get ready. (Signal.) *The teacher was reading a newspaper.*
2. Does that statement tell what the teacher is doing now? (Signal.) *No.*
   - Does that statement tell what the class was doing? (Signal.) *No.*
   - Does that statement tell what the teacher was doing? (Signal.) *Yes.*
   - Does that statement tell if the teacher was wearing glasses? (Signal.) *No.*
   - Does that statement tell if the teacher was sitting down? (Signal.) *No.*
3. The teacher was reading a newspaper. Everybody, say that statement again. (Signal.) *The teacher was reading a newspaper.*
4. Name three things the statement does not tell you. (Call on individual children. Repeat correct responses.)
5. You have named three things the statement does not tell us.
   - Name the first thing. (Hold up one finger. The children give the first response.)
   - Name the second thing. (Hold up two fingers. The children give the second response.)
   - Name the third thing. (Hold up three fingers. The children give the third response.)
   - (Repeat step 5 until all children can name the three things in order.)

EXERCISE 3　Classification

1. Today we're going to talk about a jet airplane. We can put a jet airplane into three different classes.
2. Everybody, what's the smallest class for a jet airplane? (Signal.) *Jet airplanes.*
   - What's the next bigger class? (Signal.) *Airplanes.*
   - What's the biggest class? (Signal.) *Vehicles.*
   - (Accept any other correct responses, but use: *jet airplanes, airplanes, vehicles.*)
3. (Repeat step 2 until firm.)
4. What is one kind of object you would find in all those classes? (Signal.) *Jet airplane.*
5. Would you find a truck in all those classes? (Signal.) *No.*
   - Name the class you would find a truck in. Get ready. (Signal.) *Vehicles.*
6. Would you find a train in all those classes? (Signal.) *No.*
   - Name the class you would find a train in. Get ready. (Signal.) *Vehicles.*

EXERCISE 4　Description

1. I'm going to say two things about something you know. See if you can figure out what I'm talking about.
2. (Hold up one finger.) A tetting is usually made of leather.
   - (Hold up two fingers.) You use a tetting to hold up your pants.
3. Everybody, tell me what you know about a tetting.
   - (Hold up one finger.) *A tetting is usually made of leather.*
   - (Hold up two fingers.) *You use a tetting to hold up your pants.*
4. (Repeat step 3 until firm.)
5. Everybody, tell me what a tetting is. Get ready. (Signal.) *A belt.*
6. (Repeat steps 3 and 5 until firm.)

7. Here's another one.
8. (Hold up one finger.) A prost is a place.
   - (Hold up two fingers.) You see wild animals in cages at a prost.
9. Everybody, tell me what you know about a prost.
   - (Hold up one finger.) *A prost is a place.*
   - (Hold up two fingers.) *You see wild animals in cages at a prost.*
10. (Repeat step 9 until firm.)
11. Everybody, tell me what a prost is. Get ready. (Signal.) *A zoo.*
12. (Repeat steps 9 and 11 until firm.)

EXERCISE 5　Synonyms

1. We're going to make up statements that mean the same thing.
2. What do we call two words that mean the same thing? (Signal.) *Synonyms.*
3. Listen: The animal is skinny. Say that. (Signal.) *The animal is skinny.*
   - Say the statement with a synonym for **skinny.** Get ready. (Signal.) *The animal is thin.*
   - (Repeat step 3 until firm.)
4. Listen: The container is closed. Say that. (Signal.) *The container is closed.*
   - Say the statement with a synonym for **closed.** Get ready. (Signal.) *The container is shut.*
   - (Repeat step 4 until firm.)
5. Listen: The book is under my desk. Say that. (Signal.) *The book is under my desk.*
   - Say the statement with a synonym for **under.** Get ready. (Signal.) *The book is below my desk.*
   - (Repeat step 5 until firm.)

EXERCISE 6   Sentence Writing

mole   dig

_____
_____
_____
_____

1. Everybody, open your workbook to Lesson 105. Write your name. ✔
   - You're going to write sentences that do not rhyme.
   - Touch the picture of the mole and the fox. ✔
   - The picture shows what the the mole will do and what the fox will do. What will the mole do? (Signal.) *Dig.*
   - What will the fox do? (Signal.) *Sit.*
2. Say the sentence for what the mole will do. Get ready. (Signal.) *The mole will dig.*
   - Say the sentence for what the fox will do. Get ready. (Signal.) *The fox will sit.*
3. (Repeat step 2 until firm.)
4. The word box shows how to spell the words **mole** and **dig.** You can figure out how to spell the other words.
5. Write the sentence for what the mole will do. Pencils down when you're finished. ✔
   - Now go to the next line and write the sentence for what the fox will do. Pencils down when you're finished. ✔
6. (Call on individual children to read both their sentences.)

EXERCISE 7   Questioning

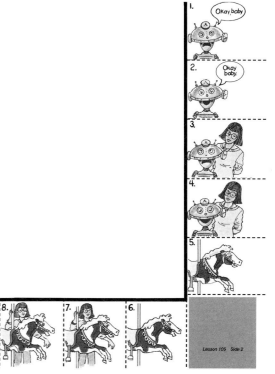

1. Everybody, find the next page. ✔
   - We're going to play a question game with teams again. (Divide class into four teams.)
2. Make a flap out of each picture. Cut carefully. Raise your hand when you're finished.
   (Observe children and give feedback.)
3. Now let's play the tough question game again. We'll see which teams can do it. Remember, if you're **really** smart, your team can find the mystery picture by asking only **three** questions. But they have to be **super** questions. A good first question would let you fold over four pictures. A good second question would let you fold over two more pictures. Remember, in some of the pictures, Bleep is happy and in some of the pictures, Rolla is happy.
   - When your team has your first question, raise your hands and I'll come over. You'll whisper the question to me and I'll whisper the answer. You'll fold over the pictures that could **not** be the mystery picture.
4. (**Key:** The target picture is 2—Bleep alone, smiling and saying, "Okay, baby.")
   - Remember, you're trying to find the mystery picture in only **three** questions. Raise your hands when your team has a good question.

Answers to Possible Questions:

(How many characters are in the picture?) One.
(Is a character talking?) Yes.
(Is a character smiling?) Yes.
(Is a character sad?) No.
(Who is in the picture?) Bleep is in the picture. But you don't know if he's alone.
(Is Molly in the picture?) No.
*(Do **not** combine answers, such as: Bleep is the only character in the picture.)*

5. (After any team has found the mystery picture by asking only three questions, tell the class:) We have a team that found the mystery picture by asking only **three** questions. Tell everybody the questions you asked. (Call on a team member to say the three questions. Do not accept "combined" questions.)

6. Everybody, what's the number of the mystery picture? (Signal.) *Two.*

• How many characters are in the picture? (Signal.) *One.*

• Who is in the picture? (Signal.) *Bleep.* Yes, only Bleep is in the picture.

• How is Bleep feeling? (Signal.) *Happy.*

• Is Bleep saying anything? (Signal.) *Yes.*

• What is he saying? (Signal.) *Okay, baby.*

7. (**Key:** The target picture is 7—Rolla looking sad, Molly next to Rolla.)

• We'll play the game again. Unfold each flap. ✔

• This time I'm thinking of a different picture. Remember to ask good questions because you're trying to find the mystery picture in only **three** questions. Raise your hands when your team has a good question.

8. (After any team has found the mystery picture by asking only three questions, tell the class:) We have a team that found the mystery picture by asking only **three** questions. Tell everybody the questions you asked. (Call on a team member to say the three questions. Do not accept "combined" questions.)

9. Everybody, what's the number of the mystery picture? (Signal.) *Seven.*

• Who is in the picture? (Signal.) *Rolla and Molly.*

• How does Rolla feel? (Signal.) *Sad.*

10. You figured out the mystery picture by asking really good questions.

Objectives

- Identify the relationship between the components of an analogy. (Exercise 1)
- Replace a word in a sentence with an opposite. (Exercise 2)
- Identify an object based on its characteristics. (Exercise 3)
- Discriminate between synonyms and opposites. (Exercise 4)
- Answer questions involving previously learned calendar facts. (Exercise 5)
- Write sentences given picture cues. (Exercise 6)
- Construct verbal analogies. (Exercise 7)
- Follow coloring rules involving materials. (Exercise 8)

EXERCISE 1 Analogies

1. I'm going to say some analogies about a cat and a lion.
2. Everybody, tell me what big class a cat and a lion are in. Get ready. (Signal.) *Animals.*
3. See if you can figure out what each analogy **tells** about the animals. Listen to this analogy.
4. A cat is to small as a lion is to . . . (Signal.) *big.*
   - Everybody, say that analogy. Get ready. (Signal.) *A cat is to small as a lion is to big.*
5. What does that analogy tell about the cat and the lion? (Call on a child. Praise reasonable responses, but use: *what size they are.*) Yes, it tells what size each animal is.
   - (Repeat step 5 until firm.)
6. (Repeat steps 4 and 5 until firm.)
7. Listen to the next analogy.
8. A cat is to meowing **as** a lion is to . . . (Signal.) *roaring.*
   - Everybody, say that analogy. Get ready. (Signal.) *A cat is to meowing as a lion is to roaring.*
9. What does that analogy tell about the cat and the lion? (Call on a child. Praise reasonable responses, but use: *what they say.*) Yes, it tells what each animal says.
   - (Repeat step 9 until firm.)
10. (Repeat steps 8 and 9 until firm.)

EXERCISE 2 Opposites

1. I'm going to tell you a story. You have to know your opposites to follow this story.
2. There was a boy. He was the opposite of dirty. Everybody, what do you know about that boy? (Signal.) *He was clean.* Yes, the boy was clean.
3. This clean boy went out to play in the rain. Soon he was the opposite of dry. Everybody, what do you know about that boy? (Signal.) *He was wet.* Yes, the boy was wet.
4. The wet boy ran to get a towel to dry himself. He ran the opposite of quickly. Everybody, how did the wet boy run? (Signal.) *Slowly.* Yes, the wet boy ran slowly.
5. (Repeat steps 2 through 4 until firm.)
6. Let's see what you remember about that story.
7. Everybody, tell me how the boy looked. Get ready. (Signal.) *Clean.*
   - Tell me how the boy felt when he played in the rain. Get ready. (Signal.) *Wet.*
   - Tell me how the boy ran. Get ready. (Signal.) *Slowly.*
   - (Repeat step 7 until firm.)

EXERCISE 3 Description

1. I'm going to talk about something you know. See if you can figure out what I'm talking about.
2. (Hold up one finger.) A dren is usually made of metal.
   - (Hold up two fingers.) You use a dren to eat soup.

3. Everybody, tell me what you know about a dren.
- (Hold up one finger.) *A dren is usually made of metal.*
- (Hold up two fingers.) *You use a dren to eat soup.*
4. (Repeat step 3 until firm.)
5. Everybody, tell me what a dren is. Get ready. (Signal.) *A spoon.*
6. (Repeat steps 3 and 5 until firm.)

EXERCISE 4   Synonyms/Opposites

1. Tell me if I name synonyms or opposites.
2. Listen: Healthy. Well. Say those words. (Signal.) *Healthy. Well.*
- Are those words synonyms or opposites? (Signal.) *Synonyms.*
- (Repeat step 2 until firm.)
3. Listen: Open. Shut. Say those words. (Signal.) *Open. Shut.*
- Are those words synonyms or opposites? (Signal.) *Opposites.*
- (Repeat step 3 until firm.)
4. Listen: Safe. Dangerous. Say those words. (Signal.) *Safe. Dangerous.*
- Are those words synonyms or opposites? (Signal.) *Opposites.*
- (Repeat step 4 until firm.)
5. (Repeat steps 2 through 4 until firm.)

EXERCISE 5   Calendar Facts

1. You learned calendar facts.
- Everybody, how many days are in a week? (Signal.) *Seven.*
- Everybody, say the days of the week. Get ready. (Signal.) *Sunday, Monday, Tuesday, Wednesday, Thursday, Friday, Saturday.*
2. How many weeks are in a year? (Signal.) *52.*
- Say the fact. Get ready. (Signal.) *There are 52 weeks in a year.*
3. How many days are in a year? (Signal.) *365.*
- Say the fact. Get ready. (Signal.) *There are 365 days in a year.*
4. How many seasons are in a year? (Signal.) *Four.*
- Name the four seasons. Get ready. (Signal.) *Winter, spring, summer, fall.*
5. (Repeat steps 1 through 4 until firm.)

6. How many months are in a year? (Signal.) *12.*
- Everybody, say the months. Get ready. (Signal.) *January, February, March, April, May, June, July, August, September, October, November, December.*
7. (Repeat step 6 until firm.)
8. What day of the week is it today? (Signal.)
- What day of the week will it be tomorrow? (Signal.)
- What's today's date? (Signal.)
9. (Repeat step 8 until firm.)

WORKBOOK

EXERCISE 6   Sentence Writing

| cow   walk |

_____

_____

_____

1. Everybody, open your workbook to Lesson 106. Write your name. ✔
- You're going to write sentences that do not rhyme.
- Touch the picture of the cow and the cat. ✔
- The picture shows what the cow will do and what the cat will do. What will the cow do? (Signal.) *Walk.* Yes, **walk.**
- What will the cat do? (Signal.) *Sit.*
2. Say the sentence for what the cow will do. Get ready. (Signal.) *The cow will walk.*
- Say the sentence for what the cat will do. Get ready. (Signal.) *The cat will sit.*
3. (Repeat step 2 until firm.)

4. The word box shows how to spell the words **cow** and **walk.** You can figure out how to spell the other words.
5. Write the sentence for what the cow will do. Pencils down when you're finished. ✔
• Now go to the next line and write the sentence for what the cat will do. Pencils down when you're finished. ✔
6. (Call on individual children to read both their sentences.)

EXERCISE 7   Analogies

1. Everybody, find the next page. ✔
• (Hold up workbook. Point to first half.)
• The pictures show objects and their parts.
2. Touch the bookcase. ✔
3. The picture that's right below shows what part it **has.** Everybody, what parts? (Signal.) *Shelves.*
• Tell me about a bookcase. Get ready. (Signal.) *A bookcase has shelves.*
4. Touch the flower. ✔
• One of the pictures below shows what parts it **has.** Touch the picture that shows what parts a flower has. ✔
• Everybody, what parts? (Signal.) *Leaves.*
• Tell me about a flower. Get ready. (Signal.) *A flower has leaves.*

5. Tell me about a bookcase. Get ready. (Signal.) *A bookcase has shelves.*
• Tell me about a flower. Get ready. (Signal.) *A flower has leaves.*
6. Say the whole analogy about a bookcase and a flower. Get ready. (Signal.) *A bookcase has shelves as a flower has leaves.*
7. (Repeat step 6 until firm.)
8. Draw a line from the flower to what part it has. (Observe children and give feedback.)

EXERCISE 8   Materials

1. (Hold up workbook. Point to second half.) Everybody, look at the picture. ✔
2. Here's a coloring rule for this picture. If an object could be made of leather, color it purple or black. What's the rule? (Signal.) *If an object could be made of leather, color it purple or black.*
• (Repeat step 2 until firm.)
3. Mark objects made of leather. ✔
4. Here's another coloring rule for this picture. If an object is made of metal, color it yellow. What's the rule? (Signal.) *If an object is made of metal, color it yellow.*
• (Repeat step 4 until firm.)
5. Make a yellow mark on one of the objects made of metal. ✔
6. Here's one more thing to do. Part of the scissors is missing. What part is missing? (Signal.) *The blade.*
• Yes, the blade. Before you color the scissors, follow the dots and make the blade.
7. Remember—the marks show you what color to make the leather objects and the metal objects.

Objectives

- Name four classes containing a common noun and answer questions about members of those classes. (Exercise 1)
- Identify words based on characteristics. (Exercise 2)
- Replace a word in a sentence with an opposite. (Exercise 3)
- Generate questions to find a word's definition. (Exercise 4)
- Discriminate between synonyms and opposites. (Exercise 5)
- Write sentences given picture cues. (Exercise 6)
- Construct verbal analogies. (Exercise 7)
- Write class names next to members of the class. (Exercise 8)

EXERCISE 1   Classification

1. Today we're going to talk about an oak tree. We can put an oak tree into four different classes. See how many classes you can name, starting with the smallest class.
2. Everybody, what's the smallest class for an oak tree? (Signal.) *Oak trees.*
- What's the next bigger class? (Signal.) *Trees.*
- What's the next bigger class? (Signal.) *Plants.*
- What's the biggest class? (Signal.) *Living things.*
- (Accept any other correct responses, but use: *oak trees, trees, plants, living things.*)
3. (Repeat step 2 until firm.)
4. What is one kind of object you would find in all those classes? (Signal.) *An oak tree.*
5. Would you find a palm tree in all those classes? (Signal.) *No.*
- Name three of those classes you would find a palm tree in. Get ready. (Tap 3 times.) *Trees. Plants. Living things.*
6. Would you find a flower in all those classes? (Signal.) *No.*
- Name two of those classes you would find a flower in. Get ready. (Tap 2 times.) *Plants. Living things.*

EXERCISE 2   Description

1. I'm going to say two things about something you know. See if you can figure out what I'm talking about.
2. (Hold up one finger.) Malz is a word.
- (Hold up two fingers.) Malz is a synonym for shout.

3. Everybody, tell me what you know about malz.
- (Hold up one finger.) *Malz is a word.*
- (Hold up two fingers.) *Malz is a synonym for shout.*
4. (Repeat step 3 until firm.)
5. Everybody, tell me what malz is. Get ready. (Signal.) *Yell.*
6. (Repeat steps 3 and 5 until firm.)
7. Here's another one.
8. (Hold up one finger.) Freem is a word.
- (Hold up two fingers.) Freem is the opposite of hot.
9. Everybody, tell me what you know about freem.
- (Hold up one finger.) *Freem is a word.*
- (Hold up two fingers.) *Freem is the opposite of hot.*
10. (Repeat step 9 until firm.)
11. Everybody, tell me what freem is. Get ready. (Signal.) *Cold.*
12. (Repeat steps 9 and 11 until firm.)

EXERCISE 3   Opposites

1. We're going to play a word game.
2. Listen: The team is winning. Say that statement. (Signal.) *The team is winning.*
- Now say a statement that tells the opposite about the team. Get ready. (Signal.) *The team is losing.*
3. Listen: The carrot is raw. Say that statement. (Signal.) *The carrot is raw.*
- Now say a statement that tells the opposite about the carrot. Get ready. (Signal.) *The carrot is cooked.*

EXERCISE 4 Questioning Skills

1. I'm going to tell a story. When you hear a word you don't know, say **stop.**
2. A girl was walking to her (pause) **abode.** (The children are to say *stop.*)
   - Everybody, what word don't you know? (Signal.) *Abode.*
3. Ask the question about what the word abode means. Get ready. (Signal.) *What does the word abode mean?*
4. I'll tell you what abode means. Abode is a synonym for **house.**
   - What is abode a synonym for? (Signal.) *House.*
   - So if the girl was walking to her abode, she was walking to her . . . (Signal.) *house.*
5. Here's more of the story.
6. On the sidewalk she saw a (pause) **serpent.** (The children are to say *stop.*) Everybody, what word don't you know? (Signal.) *Serpent.*
7. Ask the question about what the word serpent means. Get ready. (Signal.) *What does the word serpent mean?*
8. I'll tell you what serpent means. Serpent is a synonym for **snake.**
   - What is serpent a synonym for? (Signal.) *Snake.*
   - So if the girl was walking to her abode and saw a serpent, she was walking to her house and saw . . . (Signal.) *a snake.*
9. Here's more of the story.
10. The girl was (pause) **terrified.** (The children are to say *stop.*) Everybody, what word don't you know? (Signal.) *Terrified.*
11. Ask the question about what the word terrified means. Get ready. (Signal.) *What does the word terrified mean?*
12. I'll tell you what terrified means. Terrified is a synonym for **scared.**
   - What is terrified a synonym for? (Signal.) *Scared.*
13. So if the girl saw a serpent when she was walking to her abode and she was terrified, she saw a snake when she was walking to her house and she was . . . (Signal.) *scared.*
   - Why do you think she was scared? (Children respond.)
   - That's the end of the story.

EXERCISE 5 Synonyms/Opposites

1. Tell me if I name synonyms or opposites. Think big.
2. Listen: Crying. Weeping. Say those words. (Signal.) *Crying. Weeping.*
   - Are those words synonyms or opposites? (Signal.) *Synonyms.*
   - (Repeat step 2 until firm.)
3. Listen: Deep. Shallow. Say those words. (Signal.) *Deep. Shallow.*
   - Are those words synonyms or opposites? (Signal.) *Opposites.*
   - (Repeat step 3 until firm.)
4. Listen: Small. Little. Say those words. (Signal.) *Small. Little.*
   - Are those words synonyms or opposites? (Signal.) *Synonyms.*
   - (Repeat step 4 until firm.)
5. (Repeat steps 2 through 4 until firm.)

WORKBOOK

EXERCISE 6 Sentence Writing

| eat white leaf other |

_____

_____

_____

_____

1. Everybody, open your workbook to Lesson 107. Write your name. ✔
   - You're going to write sentences that do not rhyme.
   - Touch the picture of the fish. ✔
   - The picture shows what the fish will eat. What will the white fish eat? (Signal.) *A leaf.*
   - What will the other fish eat? (Signal.) *A bug.*

2. Say the sentence for what the white fish will eat. Get ready. (Signal.) *The white fish will eat a leaf.*
- Say the sentence for what the other fish will eat. Get ready. (Signal.) *The other fish will eat a bug.*
3. (Repeat step 2 until firm.)
4. The word box shows how to spell the words **eat, white, leaf** and **other.** You can figure out how to spell the rest of the words.
5. Write the sentence for what the white fish will eat. Pencils down when you're finished. ✔
- Now go to the next line and write the sentence for what the other fish will eat. Pencils down when you're finished. ✔
6. (Call on individual children to read both their sentences.)

EXERCISE 7 Analogies

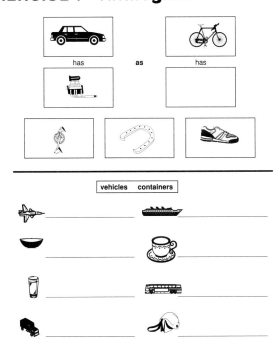

1. Everybody, find the next page. ✔
- (Hold up workbook. Point to top half.)
- The pictures show objects and their parts.
2. Touch the car. ✔
3. The picture that's right below shows what part it has. Everybody, what part does a car have? (Signal.) *An engine.*
- Tell me about a car. Get ready. (Signal.) *A car has an engine.*

4. Touch the bike. ✔
- One of the pictures below shows what part it has. Touch the picture that shows what part a bike has. ✔
- Everybody, what part does a bike have? (Signal.) *Pedals.*
- Tell me about a bike. Get ready. (Signal.) *A bike has pedals.*
5. Tell me about a car. Get ready. (Signal.) *A car has an engine.*
- Tell me about a bike. Get ready. (Signal.) *A bike has pedals.*
6. Say the analogy about a car and a bike. Get ready. (Signal.) *A car has an engine as a bike has pedals.*
7. (Repeat step 6 until firm.)
8. Draw a line from the bike to what part it has. (Observe children and give feedback.)

EXERCISE 8 Classification

1. (Hold up workbook. Point to bottom half.) Everybody, I'll read the words in the box. You touch the words. First word: Vehicles. ✔
- Next word: Containers. ✔
- Yes, vehicles and containers.
2. Everybody, put your finger under the jet. ✔
3. Is a jet in the class of vehicles or in the class of containers? (Signal.) *Vehicles.*
- Copy the word **vehicles** next to the jet. ✔
- Read what you wrote. (Signal.) *Vehicles.*
4. Everybody, put your finger under the bowl. ✔
- Is a bowl in the class of vehicles or in the class of containers? (Signal.) *Containers.*
- Copy the word **containers** next to the bowl. ✔
5. Everybody, read the words you wrote. (Signal.) *Vehicles. Containers.*
6. Later you can write the class words that go with the rest of the pictures.

Objectives

- Identify the relationship between the components of an analogy. (Exercise 1)
- Name objects that could be made of a given material. (Exercise 2)
- Identify objects based on characteristics. (Exercise 3)
- Identify absurdities. (Exercise 4)
- Replace a word in a sentence with an opposite. (Exercise 5)
- Write sentences given picture cues. (Exercise 6)
- Label cardinal directions on a map. (Exercise 7)
- Follow coloring rules involving classes and subclasses. (Exercise 8)

EXERCISE 1 Analogies

1. I'm going to say some analogies about a pencil and a saw.
2. Everybody, tell me what class a pencil and a saw are in. Get ready. (Signal.) *Tools.*
3. See if you can figure out what each analogy **tells** about the tools. Listen to this analogy.
4. A pencil is to a point **as** a saw is to . . . (Call on a child. Accept any reasonable responses; then say:) Let's use blade for this analogy.
   - Everybody, say that analogy. Get ready. (Signal.) *A pencil is to a point as a saw is to a blade.*
5. What does that analogy tell about the pencil and the saw? (Call on a child. Praise reasonable responses, but use: *a part they have.*) Yes, it tells a part each tool has.
   - (Repeat step 5 until firm.)
6. (Repeat steps 4 and 5 until firm.)
7. Listen to the next analogy.
8. A pencil is to writing **as** a saw is to . . . (Call on a child. Accept any reasonable responses; then say:) Let's use sawing for this analogy.
   - Everybody, say that analogy. Get ready. (Signal.) *A pencil is to writing as a saw is to sawing.*
9. What does that analogy tell about the pencil and the saw? (Call on a child. Praise reasonable responses, but use: *what you do with them.*) Yes, it tells what you do with each tool.
   - (Repeat step 9 until firm.)
10. (Repeat steps 8 and 9 until firm.)

EXERCISE 2 Materials

1. Think of things that are made of glass.
   - Let's see who can name at least three things made of glass. (Call on individual children to name objects made of glass. Each child should name at least three things.)
2. Everybody, think of things that are made of metal.
   - Let's see who can name at least three things made of metal. (Call on individual children to name objects made of metal. Each child should name at least three things.)
3. Everybody, think of things that are made of leather.
   - Let's see who can name at least three things made of leather. (Call on individual children to name objects made of leather. Each child should name at least three things.)

EXERCISE 3 Description

1. I'm going to say two things about something you know. See if you can figure out what I'm talking about.
2. (Hold up one finger.) A strim is made of glass.
   - (Hold up two fingers.) You can drink milk from a strim.

3. Everybody, tell me what you know about a strim.
   - (Hold up one finger.) *A strim is made of glass.*
   - (Hold up two fingers.) *You can drink milk from a strim.*
4. (Repeat step 3 until firm.)
5. Everybody, tell me what a strim is. Get ready. (Signal.) *A glass.*
6. (Repeat steps 3 and 5 until firm.)
7. Here's another one.
8. (Hold up one finger.) A torl is a piece of furniture.
   - (Hold up two fingers.) You keep books in a torl.
9. Everybody, tell me what you know about a torl.
   - (Hold up one finger.) *A torl is a piece of furniture.*
   - (Hold up two fingers.) *You keep books in a torl.*
10. (Repeat step 9 until firm.)
11. Everybody, tell me what a torl is. Get ready. (Signal.) *A bookcase.*
12. (Repeat steps 9 and 11 until firm.)

EXERCISE 4 Absurdity

1. Listen to this story and tell me what's absurd about it.
2. A woman turned on the toaster and put some ice cream in the hot toaster. Where did the woman put the ice cream? (Signal.) *In the hot toaster.*
3. Then she put that cold ice cream in a dish. What did the woman do? (Signal.) *Put the cold ice cream in a dish.*
4. Now tell me some things that are absurd about that story. (Call on two or three individual children. Ask the first child:) What's one thing that's absurd? (After the child responds, ask other children:) What's another thing that's absurd? (Praise all appropriate responses.)

EXERCISE 5 Opposites

1. I'm going to tell you a story. You have to know your opposites to follow this story.
2. Listen: There was a pig. The pig was the opposite of clean. Everybody, what do you know about that pig? (Signal.) *It was dirty.* Yes, the pig was dirty.
3. This dirty pig was thirsty. Its mouth was the opposite of wet. Everybody, what do you know about that dirty pig's mouth? (Signal.) *It was dry.* Yes, the dirty pig's mouth was dry.
4. The dirty pig went looking for some water and found a pond. The pond was the opposite of shallow. Everybody, what do you know about that pond? (Signal.) *It was deep.* Yes, the pond was deep.
5. The dirty pig drank some water from the pond. The pig drank the opposite of quickly. Everybody, what do you know about how that pig drank? (Signal.) *It drank slowly.* Yes, the dirty pig drank slowly.
6. (Repeat steps 2 through 5 until firm.)
7. Let's see what you remember about that story.
8. Everybody, tell me about the pig. Get ready. (Signal.) *It was dirty.*
   - Tell me about the dirty pig's mouth. Get ready. (Signal.) *It was dry.*
   - Tell me about the pond. Get ready. (Signal.) *It was deep.*
   - Tell me about how the dirty pig drank. Get ready. (Signal.) *It drank slowly.*
   - (Repeat step 8 until firm.)

EXERCISE 6   Sentence Writing

leaf   other   black

_____

_____

_____

_____

1. Everybody, open your workbook to Lesson 108. Write your name. ✔
• You're going to write sentences that do not rhyme.
• Touch the picture of the ants. ✔
• The picture shows what the black ant will eat and what the other ant will eat. Who will eat a seed? (Signal.) *The black ant.*
• What will the other ant eat? (Signal.) *A leaf.*
2. Say the sentence for what the black ant will eat. Get ready. (Signal.) *The black ant will eat a seed.*
• Say the sentence for what the other ant will eat. Get ready. (Signal.) *The other ant will eat a leaf.*
3. (Repeat step 2 until firm.)
4. The word box shows how to spell the words **leaf, other** and **black.** You can figure out how to spell the other words.
5. Write the sentence for what the black ant will eat. Pencils down when you're finished. ✔
• Now go to the next line and write the sentence for what the other ant will eat. Pencils down when you're finished. ✔
6. (Call on individual children to read both their sentences.)

EXERCISE 7   Map Reading

1. Everybody, find the next page. ✔
• (Hold up workbook. Point to first half.) Everybody, touch the snake. ✔
2. This picture is a map of where the snake crawled. You're going to color the arrows black and write the directions on the objects. Remember to start from the snake.
3. Everybody, color the first arrow black. Do it. ✔
• Now write the letter that shows the direction the snake crawled. ✔
4. You'll do the rest of the arrows later.

EXERCISE 8   Classification

1. (Hold up workbook. Point to second half.) Touch the picture of the **smaller** class. ✔
• What kind of thing is that in the picture? (Signal.) *Pillows.*
2. Everybody, circle the picture that shows the **larger** class. ✔
• Everybody, what's the name of the larger class? (Signal.) *Things made of cloth.*
3. Everybody, touch the picture of the class that is **smaller.** ✔
• The pillows in that picture of the **smaller** class should be blue. What color? (Signal.) *Blue.*
• Mark a pillow in that picture. ✔
4. Touch the picture that shows the **larger** class. ✔
• Each pillow in that picture should have red and yellow stripes. What colors? (Signal.) *Red and yellow.*
• Mark a pillow in that picture. ✔

Objectives

- Identify the relationship between the components of an analogy. (Exercise 1)
- Replace a word in a sentence with an opposite. (Exercise 2)
- **Identify past, present and future tense.** (Exercise 3)
- Generate questions to find a word's definition. (Exercise 4)
- Identify objects based on characteristics. (Exercise 5)
- Apply an if-then rule based on the occurrence of events. (Exercise 6)
- Write sentences given picture cues. (Exercise 7)

EXERCISE 1 Analogies

1. I'm going to say some analogies about a house and a school.
2. Everybody, tell me what class a house and a school are in. Get ready. (Signal.) *Buildings.*
3. See if you can figure out what each analogy **tells** about the buildings. Listen to this analogy.
4. A house is to little **as** a school is to . . . (Signal.) *big.*
- Everybody, say that analogy. Get ready. (Signal.) *A house is to little as a school is to big.*
5. What does that analogy tell about the house and the school? (Call on a child. Praise reasonable responses, but use: *what size they are.*) Yes, it tells what size each building is.
- (Repeat step 5 until firm.)
6. (Repeat steps 4 and 5 until firm.)

EXERCISE 2 Opposites

1. We're going to play a word game.
2. Listen: The ground is rough. Say that statement. (Signal.) *The ground is rough.*
- Now say a statement that tells the opposite of rough. Get ready. (Signal.) *The ground is smooth.*
3. Listen: The clothes are clean. Say that statement. (Signal.) *The clothes are clean.*
- Now say a statement that tells the opposite of clean. Get ready. (Signal.) *The clothes are dirty.*

EXERCISE 3 Verb Tense

1. It's time for some statements.
2. Listen: The rabbit will hop. What does that statement tell? (Signal.) *What the rabbit will do.* Yes, it tells what the rabbit will do.
- What will he do? (Signal.) *Hop.*
3. Listen: The boy jumped. What does that statement tell? (Signal.) *What the boy did.* Yes, it tells what the boy did.
- What did he do? (Signal.) *Jumped.*
4. Listen: The cat is sitting. What does that statement tell? (Signal.) *What the cat is doing.* Yes, it tells what the cat is doing.
- What is he doing? (Signal.) *Sitting.*
5. Listen: The goat ran home. What does that statement tell? (Signal.) *What the goat did.* Yes, it tells what the goat did.
- What did it do? (Signal.) *Ran home.*
6. Listen: The dog is sleeping. What does that statement tell? (Signal.) *What the dog is doing.* Yes, it tells what the dog is doing.
- What is it doing? (Signal.) *Sleeping.*
7. Let's play a statement game.

8. Everybody, say the statement that tells what the dog is doing. Get ready. (Signal.) *The dog is sleeping.*

9. Say the statement that tells what the dog will do. Get ready. (Signal.) *The dog will sleep.*

10. Say the statement that tells what the dog did. Get ready. (Signal.) *The dog slept.*

11. Now say the statement that tells what the dog will do. Get ready. (Signal.) *The dog will sleep.*

12. Now say the statement that tells what the dog did. Get ready. (Signal.) *The dog slept.*

13. (Repeat steps 8 through 12 until firm.)

14. Let's play another statement game.

15. Listen: The boy will jump. What does that statement tell? Get ready. (Signal.) *What the boy will do.*

16. Say the statement. Get ready. (Signal.) *The boy will jump.*

17. Now make up a statement that tells what the boy is doing. Get ready. (Signal.) *The boy is jumping.*

18. Now make up a statement that tells what the boy did. Get ready. (Signal.) *The boy jumped.*

19. (Repeat steps 15 through 18 until firm.)

EXERCISE 4   Questioning Skills

1. I'm going to tell a story. When you hear a word you don't know, say **stop.**

2. A boy went to the **menagerie.** (The children are to say *stop.*) Everybody, what word don't you know? (Signal.) *Menagerie.*

3. Ask the question about what the word menagerie means. Get ready. (Signal.) *What does the word menagerie mean?*

4. I'll tell you what menagerie means. Menagerie is a synonym for **zoo.** What is menagerie a synonym for? (Signal.) *Zoo.*

• If a boy went to the menagerie, he went to the . . . (Signal.) *zoo.*

5. Here's more of the story.

6. He wanted to go into a cage of **simians.** (The children are to say *stop.*)

• Everybody, what word don't you know? (Signal.) *Simians.*

7. Ask the question about what the word simians means. Get ready. (Signal.) *What does the word simians mean?*

8. I'll tell you what simians means. Simians is a synonym for **monkeys.** What is simians a synonym for? (Signal.) *Monkeys.*

9. If a boy went to the menagerie and wanted to go into a cage of simians, he went to the zoo and wanted to go into a cage of . . . (Signal.) *monkeys.*

10. Here's more of the story.

11. But the zoo keeper did not give him **admission.** (The children are to say *stop.*) Everybody, what word don't you know? (Signal.) *Admission.*

12. Ask the question about what the word admission means. Get ready. (Signal.) *What does the word admission mean?*

13. I'll tell you what admission means. Admission is a synonym for **let in.** What is admission a synonym for? (Signal.) *Let in.*

14. So if a boy went to the menagerie and wanted to go into a cage of simians but he was not given admission, he wanted to go into a cage of monkeys but he was not . . . (Signal.) *let in.*

• Would you like to go into a cage full of monkeys?
(Children respond.)

• That's the end of the story.

EXERCISE 5   Description

1. I'm going to say two things about something you know. See if you can figure out what I'm talking about.

2. (Hold up one finger.) An emm is a vehicle.

• (Hold up two fingers.) An emm flies very fast.

3. Everybody, tell me what you know about an emm.

• (Hold up one finger.) *An emm is a vehicle.*

• (Hold up two fingers.) *An emm flies very fast.*

4. (Repeat step 3 until firm.)

5. Everybody, tell me what an emm is. Get ready. (Signal.) *An airplane.*

6. (Repeat steps 3 and 5 until firm.)

7. Here's another one.

8. (Hold up one finger.) A pren is an animal.
- (Hold up two fingers.) A pren flies in the air.
9. Everybody, tell me what you know about a pren.
   - (Hold up one finger.) *A pren is an animal.*
   - (Hold up two fingers.) *A pren flies in the air.*
10. (Repeat step 9 until firm.)
11. Everybody, tell me what a pren is. Get ready. (Signal.) *A bird.*
12. (Repeat steps 9 and 11 until firm.)

WORKBOOK

EXERCISE 6 *If-Then Application*

1. Everybody, open your workbook to Lesson 109. Write your name. ✔
- There are **two** arrows under the pictures.
2. One arrow has the number 1 on it. Touch that arrow. ✔
- Arrow 1 tells what happens in the **first** picture and the **second** picture. The **first** picture shows what Clarabelle is going to do.
- Touch the **first** picture. ✔
- What is Clarabelle going to do? (Call on a child. Idea: *Sit on a chair.*)

- Touch the **second** picture. ✔
- That picture shows what will happen to the chair. Everybody, what will happen to the chair? (Signal.) *It will break.*
3. Raise your hand when you can tell the rule for arrow 1. (Call on several children. Praise responses such as: *If Clarabelle sits on a chair, the chair will break.*) Yes, here's the rule for arrow 1: If Clarabelle sits on a chair, the chair will break.
4. Everybody, say the rule for arrow 1. (Signal.) *If Clarabelle sits on a chair, the chair will break.*
   (Repeat step 4 until firm.)
5. Now touch arrow 2. ✔
- That arrow tells what will happen **if the chair breaks.** Everybody, touch the last picture. ✔
- Two things will happen in the last picture. What will happen to Clarabelle? (Signal.) *She'll fall down.*
- What will the children do in the last picture? (Signal.) *Laugh.*
- Those are the two things that will happen **if the chair breaks.** Clarabelle will fall on the floor. **And** the children will laugh, laugh, laugh.
- Raise your hand when you can say the rule for arrow 2. Remember to start with **if the chair breaks** and to tell the **two** things that will happen **if the chair breaks.** (Call on several children. Praise responses such as: *If the chair breaks, Clarabelle will fall on the floor and the children will laugh, laugh, laugh.*)
- Yes here's the rule for arrow 2: If the chair breaks, Clarabelle will fall on the floor and the children will laugh, laugh, laugh.
6. Everybody, start with **If the chair breaks,** and say the rule for arrow 2. (Signal.) *If the chair breaks, Clarabelle will fall on the floor and the children will laugh, laugh, laugh.*
- (Repeat step 6 until firm.)

7. Everybody, get ready to say both rules.
8. Say the rule for arrow 1. (Signal.) *If Clarabelle sits on a chair, the chair will break.*
• Say the rule for arrow 2. (Signal.) *If the chair breaks, Clarabelle will fall on the floor and the children will laugh, laugh, laugh.* (Repeat step 8 until firm.)
9. That silly Clarabelle. What would you think if she walked into our classroom one day and tried to sit on a chair? (Children respond.)

EXERCISE 7 Sentence Writing

was   rope   rug

_____
_____
_____
_____

1. Everybody, find the next page. ✔
• You're going to write sentences that do not rhyme.
• Touch the picture of the bird and the bug. ✔
• The picture shows what the bird was on and what the bug was on. What was the bird on? (Signal.) *A rope.*
• What was the bug on? (Signal.) *A rug.*
2. Say the sentence for what the bird was on. Get ready. (Signal.) *The bird was on a rope.*
• Say the sentence for what the bug was on. Get ready. (Signal.) *The bug was on a rug.*
3. (Repeat step 2 until firm.)
4. The word box shows how to spell the words **was, rope** and **rug.** You can figure out how to spell the other words.
5. Write the sentence for what the bird was on. Pencils down when you're finished. ✔
• Now go to the next line and write the sentence for what the bug was on. Pencils down when you're finished. ✔
6. (Call on individual children to read both their sentences.)

Objectives

- Replace a word in a sentence with a synonym. (Exercise 1)
- Identify absurdities. (Exercise 2)
- Identify past, present and future tense. (Exercise 3)
- Identify an object based on its characteristics. (Exercise 4)
- Identify the relationship between the components of an analogy. (Exercise 5)
- Write sentences given picture cues. (Exercise 6)
- Write class names next to members of the class. (Exercise 7)
- Label cardinal directions on a map. (Exercise 8)

EXERCISE 1 Synonyms

1. Let's make up statements that mean the same thing as other statements.
2. Listen: The garage is near the house. Say that. (Signal.) *The garage is near the house.*
3. Here's a statement that means the same thing: The garage is close to the house. Say that. (Signal.) *The garage is close to the house.*
4. (Repeat steps 2 and 3 until firm.)
5. I'll say one of the statements. You say the statement that means the same thing. My turn. The garage is close to the house. Your turn. Get ready. (Signal.) *The garage is near the house.*
- (Repeat step 5 until firm.)
6. Listen: A synonym for difficult is hard. What's a synonym for difficult? (Signal.) *Hard.*
7. Listen: The test is hard. Say that. (Signal.) *The test is hard.*
8. Say the statement that means the same thing. My turn. The test is hard. Your turn. Get ready. (Signal.) *The test is difficult.*
- (Repeat step 8 until firm.)

EXERCISE 2 Absurdity

1. Listen to this story and figure out what's wrong with it.
2. There was a lion. The lion wanted something to eat, so he got a saw.
3. Now tell me what's wrong with that story. (Call on a child.)
- (Praise all reasonable responses.)

4. Here's another story. Figure out what's wrong with this one.
5. There was a girl. She wanted to sit down, so she got a typewriter.
6. Now tell me what's wrong with that story. (Call on a child.)
- (Praise all reasonable responses.)
7. Let's figure out what should have happened.
8. What could the lion have gotten to eat? (Call on several children.)
- (Praise all reasonable responses.)
9. What should the girl have gotten to sit on? (Call on several children.)
- (Praise all reasonable responses.)

EXERCISE 3 Verb Tense

1. It's time for some statements. Some tell what somebody did.
2. Listen: The cow is chewing.
   What does that statement tell? (Signal.) *What the cow is doing.*
   Yes, it tells what the cow is doing. What is it doing? (Signal.) *Chewing.*
3. Listen: The girl clapped.
   What does that statement tell? (Signal.) *What the girl did.*
   Yes, it tells what the girl did. What did she do? (Signal.) *Clapped.*
4. Listen: The bear will dance.
   What does that statement tell? (Signal.) *What the bear will do.*
   Yes, it tells what the bear will do. What will he do? (Signal.) *Dance.*

5. Listen: The man fished.
   What does that statement tell? (Signal.)
   What the man did.
   Yes, it tells what the man did.
   What did he do? (Signal.) *Fished.*
6. Listen: The woman is painting.
   What does that statement tell? (Signal.)
   What the woman is doing.
   Yes, it tells what the woman is doing.
   What is she doing? (Signal.) *Painting.*
7. Let's play a statement game.
8. Everybody, say the statement that tells
   what the woman is doing. Get ready.
   (Signal.) *The woman is painting.*
9. Now say the statement that tells what the
   woman did. Get ready. (Signal.) *The woman
   painted.*
10. Now say the statement that tells what the
    woman will do. Get ready. (Signal.) *The
    woman will paint.*
11. (Repeat steps 8 through 10 until firm.)
12. Let's play another statement game.
13. Listen: The boat sailed.
    What does that statement tell? (Signal.)
    What the boat did.
14. Say the statement. Get ready. (Signal.)
    The boat sailed.
15. Now make up a statement that tells what
    the boat is doing. Get ready. (Signal.)
    The boat is sailing.
16. Now make up a statement that tells what
    the boat will do. Get ready. (Signal.)
    The boat will sail.
17. (Repeat steps 13 through 16 until firm.)

EXERCISE 4   Description

1. I'm going to say two things about
   something you know. See if you can figure
   out what I'm talking about.
2. (Hold up one finger.) A speem is a vehicle.
• (Hold up two fingers.) A speem is very big
   and goes in the water.

3. Everybody, tell me what you know about a
   speem.
• (Hold up one finger.) *A speem is a vehicle.*
• (Hold up two fingers.) *A speem is very big
   and goes in the water.*
4. (Repeat step 3 until firm.)
5. Everybody, tell me what a speem is. Get
   ready. (Signal.) *A ship.*
6. (Repeat steps 3 and 5 until firm.)

EXERCISE 5   Analogies

1. I'm going to say some analogies about a
   paintbrush and a hammer.
2. Everybody, tell me what class a paintbrush
   and a hammer are in. Get ready. (Signal.)
   Tools.
3. See if you can figure out what each
   analogy **tells** about the tools. Listen to this
   analogy.
4. A paintbrush is to painting as a hammer is
   to. . . (Signal.) *hammering.*
• Everybody, say that analogy. Get ready.
   (Signal.) *A paintbrush is to painting as a
   hammer is to hammering.*
5. What does that analogy tell about the
   paintbrush and the hammer? (Call on a
   child. Praise reasonable responses, but
   use: *what you do with them.*) Yes, it tells
   what you do with each tool.
• (Repeat step 5 until firm.)
6. (Repeat steps 4 and 5 until firm.)
7. Listen to the next analogy.
8. A paintbrush is to bristles as a hammer is
   to a . . . (Signal.) *head.*
• Everybody, say that analogy. Get ready.
   (Signal.) *A paintbrush is to bristles as a
   hammer is to a head.*
9. What does that analogy tell about the
   paintbrush and the hammer? (Call on a
   child. Praise reasonable responses, but
   use: *a part they have.*) Yes, it tells what part
   each tool has.
• (Repeat step 9 until firm.)
10. (Repeat steps 8 and 9 until firm.)

WORKBOOK

EXERCISE 6 Sentence Construction

Clarabelle	sat on	a hat	Sweetie
Paul	kissed	Molly	a rock
Bleep	painted	a pie	a rat

1. _____

2. _____

3. _____

[ ]

1. Everybody, open your workbook to Lesson 110. Write your name. ✔
- Here's your chance to write silly sentences.
2. Touch the pictures in the first column. ✔
- Your sentences will have to start by telling about one of these characters. You can write sentences about what Clarabelle did, what Paul did or what Bleep did.
- You can write all your sentences about the **same** character or you can write about **different** characters. But remember, your sentences must start out by naming **Clarabelle, Paul** or **Bleep.**
3. Touch the words in the second column. ✔
- These are the words that tell what your character did.
- The words in the top box are **sat on.** Everybody, what words? (Signal.) *Sat on.*
- The word in the next box is **kissed.** What word? (Signal.) *Kissed.*
- The word in the bottom box is **painted.** What word? (Signal.) *Painted.*

- Touch the **top** box again. ✔ Everybody, what words? (Signal.) *Sat on.*
- Touch the next box. ✔ What word? (Signal.) *Kissed.*
- Touch the bottom box. ✔ What word? (Signal.) *Painted.*
- Remember, those are the words you can use to tell what your character did. You can tell that Clarabelle **sat on** something. You can tell that Clarabelle **kissed** something. You can tell that Clarabelle **painted** something. Or you can use a different name. You can tell what **Paul** did or what **Bleep** did.
4. The last two columns of pictures are **what** the character **sat on** or **kissed** or **painted.** I'll read the words. You touch the right pictures.
- **A hat.** ✔
- **Molly.** ✔
- **A pie.** ✔
- **Sweetie.** ✔
- **A rock.** ✔
- **A rat.** ✔
- Remember, those are the **things** that your character **sat on** or **kissed** or **painted.**
5. Your turn: Make up your three sentences. You can make them as silly as you want. Write your first sentence on line 1. Write your next sentence on line 2. Write your last sentence on line 3. Raise your hand when you're finished. (Observe children and give feedback.)
6. (Call on a child to read all three sentences. Praise appropriate sentences. Repeat with several children.)
7. Look at the box at the bottom of the page. ✔
- The box is supposed to have a picture in it. Later you can draw the picture in that box. Draw the picture for the best sentence you made up.

EXERCISE 7 Classification

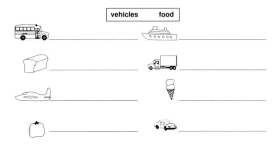

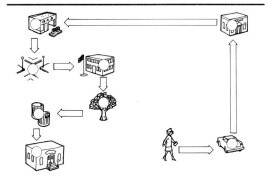

1. Everybody, find the next page. ✔
• (Hold up workbook. Point to top half.)
  Everybody, I'll read the words in the box.
  You touch the words.
• First word: vehicles. ✔
• Next word: food. ✔
  Yes, vehicles and food.

2. Everybody, put your finger under the bus. ✔
• Is a bus in the class of vehicles or in the
  class of food? (Signal.) *Vehicles.*
• Copy the word **vehicles** next to the bus.
• Read what you wrote. (Signal.) *Vehicles.*
3. Everybody, put your finger under the bread. ✔
• Is bread in the class of vehicles or in the
  class of food? (Signal.) *Food.*
• Copy the word **food** next to the bread. ✔
• Read what you wrote. (Signal.) *Food.*
4. Later you can write the class words that go
  with the other pictures.

EXERCISE 8 Map Reading

1. (Hold up workbook. Point to bottom half.)
  Everybody, touch the mail carrier. ✔
2. This picture is a map of where the mail
  carrier walked. You're going to color the
  arrows blue and write the directions on the
  objects. Remember to start from the mail
  carrier.
3. Everybody, color the first arrow blue. Do it. ✔
• Now write the letter that shows the
  direction the mail carrier walked. ✔
4. You'll do the rest of the arrows later.

Objectives

- Follow directions involving synonyms. (Exercise 1)
- Replace a word in a sentence with a synonym. (Exercise 2)
- Answer questions involving previously learned calendar facts. (Exercise 3)
- Replace a word in a sentence with an opposite. (Exercise 4)
- Identify absurdities. (Exercise 5)
- Write sentences given picture cues. (Exercise 6)
- Follow coloring directions involving classes and subclasses. (Exercise 7)
- Construct verbal analogies. (Exercise 8)

EXERCISE 1 **Synonyms**

1. Let's use words that mean the same thing as other words.
2. I'm going to put my hand **near** my mouth. What am I going to do? (Signal.) *Put your hand near your mouth.*
- Watch. (Place your hand near your mouth.) I put my hand **near** my mouth. (Put your hand down.)
3. Now I'm going to put my hand **close to** my mouth. What am I going to do this time? (Signal.) *Put your hand close to your mouth.* (Place your hand close to your mouth.)
   I put my hand **close to** my mouth. (Put your hand down.)
4. I did the same thing because **near** and **close to** mean the same thing. Listen: Because **near** and **close to** mean the same thing. Everybody, say that. (Signal.) *Because **near** and **close to** mean the same thing.*
5. Your turn. Put your hand **near** your mouth. (Signal.) (Wait.) ✔
- Where is your hand? (Signal.) *Near my mouth.*
- Put your hand down. ✔
6. Your turn. Put your hand **close to** your mouth. (Signal.) (Wait.) ✔
- Where is your hand? (Signal.) *Close to my mouth.*
- Put your hand down.
7. Why did you do the same thing both times? (Signal.) *Because **near** and **close to** mean the same thing.*
- (Repeat step 7 until firm.)
8. What do we call any word that means the same thing as another word? (Signal.) *A synonym.*
- So **near** and **close to** are synonyms.

EXERCISE 2 **Synonyms**

1. Listen: A synonym for shiny is bright. What's a synonym for shiny? (Signal.) *Bright.*
2. Let's make up statements that mean the same thing as other statements.
3. I'll say a statement. You say the statement that means the same thing. My turn. The book is hard. Your turn. Get ready. (Signal.) *The book is difficult.*
- (Repeat step 3 until firm.)
4. I'll say a different statement. You say the statement that means the same thing. My turn. The window is shiny. Your turn. Get ready. (Signal.) *The window is bright.*
- (Repeat step 4 until firm.)

EXERCISE 3 **Calendar Facts**

1. We're going to talk about days and months.
2. Everybody, how many months are in a year? (Signal.) *12.*
- Say the whole thing. Get ready. (Signal.) *There are 12 months in a year.*
3. Name the months of the year through December. Get ready. (Signal.) *January, February, March, April, May, June, July, August, September, October, November, December.*
- (Repeat step 3 until firm.)
4. How many days are in a week? (Signal.) *Seven.*
- Say the whole thing. Get ready. (Signal.) *There are seven days in a week.*
5. Everybody, name the seven days of the week. Get ready. (Signal.) *Sunday, Monday, Tuesday, Wednesday, Thursday, Friday, Saturday.*
- (Repeat step 5 until firm.)

6. Everybody, how many seasons are there in a year? (Signal.) *Four.*
- Say the seasons of the year. Get ready. (Signal.) *Winter, spring, summer, fall.*
7. Everybody, tell me what day it was yesterday. Get ready. (Signal.)
- Tell me what day it is today. Get ready. (Signal.)
- Tell me what day it will be tomorrow. Get ready. (Signal.)

EXERCISE 4 Opposites

1. We're going to play a word game.
2. Listen: The window is shut. Say that statement. (Signal.) *The window is shut.*
- Now say a statement that tells the opposite of shut. Get ready. (Signal.) *The window is open.*
3. Listen: The game is easy. Say that statement. (Signal.) *The game is easy.*
- Now say a statement that tells the opposite of easy. Get ready. (Signal.) *The game is difficult.*

EXERCISE 5 Absurdity

1. Listen to this story and figure out what's wrong with it.
2. There was a man. He was going on a trip, so he bought a closet to carry his clothes in.
3. Tell me what's wrong with that story.
   (Call on a child.) (Praise all reasonable responses.)
4. Here's another story. Figure out what's wrong with this one.
5. There was a woman. She wanted to take a bath, so she filled a bottle with water.
6. Tell me what's wrong with that story.
   (Call on a child.) (Praise all reasonable responses.)
7. Let's figure out what should have happened.
8. What could the man have used to carry his clothes in?
   (Call on a child.) (Praise all reasonable responses.)
9. What should the woman have used to take a bath?
   (Call on a child.) (Praise all reasonable responses.)

EXERCISE 6 Sentence Writing

| was | cow | hill |

1. Everybody, open your workbook to Lesson 111. Write your name. ✔
- You're going to write sentences that do not rhyme.
- Touch the picture of the man and the cat. ✔
- The picture shows what the man was on and what the cat was on. What was the man on? (Signal.) *A cow.*
- What was the cat on? (Signal.) *A hill.*
2. Say the sentence for what the man was on. Get ready. (Signal.) *The man was on a cow.*
- Say the sentence for what the cat was on. Get ready. (Signal.) *The cat was on a hill.*
3. (Repeat step 2 until firm.)
4. The word box shows how to spell the words **was, cow,** and **hill.** You can figure out how to spell the other words.
5. Write the sentence for what the man was on. Pencils down when you're finished. ✔
- Now go to the next line and write the sentence for what the cat was on. Pencils down when you're finished. ✔
6. (Call on individual children to read both their sentences.)

EXERCISE 7 Classification

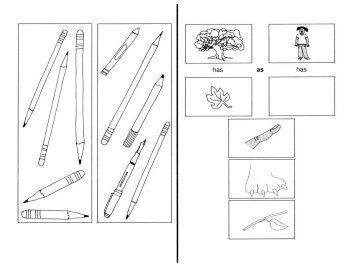

1. Everybody, find the next page. ✔
- (Hold up workbook. Point to first half.) Touch the picture of the **smaller** class. ✔
- What kind of thing is that in the picture? (Signal.) *Pencils.*
2. Everybody, circle the picture that shows the **larger** class. ✔
- What's the name of the larger class? (Call on a child. Praise reasonable responses, but use: *things to write with.*)
3. Everybody, touch the picture of the class that is **smaller.** ✔
- The pencils in that picture of the **smaller** class should be orange. What color? (Signal.) *Orange.*
- Mark a pencil in that picture. ✔
4. Touch the picture that shows the **larger** class. ✔
- The pencils in that picture should have blue and green dots. What colors? (Signal.) *Blue and green.*
- Mark a pencil in that picture. ✔

EXERCISE 8 Analogies

1. (Hold up workbook. Point to second half.)
- The pictures show objects and their parts.
2. Touch the tree. ✔
- The picture that's right below shows what part it has. Everybody, what part does a tree have? (Signal.) *A leaf.*
- Tell me about a tree. Get ready. (Signal.) *A tree has a leaf.*
3. Touch the girl. ✔
- One of the pictures below shows what parts she has. Touch the picture that shows what part a girl has. ✔
- Everybody, what part does a girl have? (Signal.) *A finger.*
- Tell me about a girl. Get ready. (Signal.) *A girl has a finger.*
4. Tell me about a tree. Get ready. (Signal.) *A tree has a leaf.*
- Tell me about a girl. Get ready. (Signal.) *A girl has a finger.*
5. Say the whole analogy about a tree and a girl. Get ready. (Signal.) *A tree has a leaf as a girl has a finger.*
6. (Repeat step 5 until firm.)
7. Draw a line from the girl to the part she has. (Observe children and give feedback.)

Objectives

- Replace a word in a sentence with a synonym. (Exercise 1)
- Listen to a short story and answer questions involving "who," "when," "why," "where" and "what". (Exercise 2)
- Apply narrowing criteria to guess a mystery object. (Exercise 3)
- Identify past, present and future tense. (Exercise 4)
- Identify an object based on its characteristics. (Exercise 5)
- Write sentences given picture cues. (Exercise 6)
- **Read a word and write the opposite of that word.** (Exercise 7)
- Write class names next to members of the class. (Exercise 8)

EXERCISE 1   Synonyms

1. Let's make up statements that mean the same thing as other statements.
2. I'll say one statement. You say the statement that means the same thing. My turn. The question is difficult. Your turn. (Signal.) *The question is hard.*
- (Repeat step 2 until firm.)
3. Here's another one.
4. I'll say one statement. You say the statement that means the same thing. My turn. The rug is near the bed. Your turn. (Signal.) *The rug is close to the bed.*
- (Repeat step 4 until firm.)

EXERCISE 2   Who—What—When—Where—Why

1. Listen to this story.
- It was five o'clock. John felt like running, so he put on his tennis shoes. He ran to the train station where he saw his friend Hector.
- (Repeat the story.)
2. Tell why John put on his tennis shoes. Get ready. (Signal.) *Because he felt like running.*
- Tell what John put on. Get ready. (Signal.) *His tennis shoes.*
- Tell when John put on his tennis shoes. Get ready. (Signal.) *At five o'clock.*
- Tell where John ran to. Get ready. (Signal.) *The train station.*
- Tell who John saw at the train station. Get ready. (Signal.) *His friend Hector.*
3. (Repeat step 2 until firm.)

EXERCISE 3   Description

1. Get ready to play detective and find out what object I'm thinking of. I'll give you two clues.
2. (Hold up one finger.) It's a container.
- (Hold up two fingers.) It's made of glass.
3. Say the two things we know about the object.
- (Hold up one finger.) *It's a container.*
- (Hold up two fingers.) *It's made of glass.*
- (Repeat step 3 until firm.)
4. Those clues don't tell you enough to find the right container. They could tell you about a lot of containers. See how many containers you can name that are made of glass. (Call on individual children. The group is to name at least three containers that are made of glass, such as a *bottle, a glass,* and *a bowl.*)
5. Here's another clue for finding the right object.
6. Listen: This object could hold ketchup or jam in it. Everybody, say that. Get ready. (Signal.) *This object could hold ketchup or jam in it.*
7. Now here are the three things we know about the object.
- (Hold up one finger.) It's a container.
- (Hold up two fingers.) It's made of glass.
- (Hold up three fingers.) This object could hold ketchup or jam in it.

8. Everybody, say all the things we know. Get ready.
   - (Hold up one finger.) *It's a container.*
   - (Hold up two fingers.) *It's made of glass.*
   - (Hold up three fingers.) *This object could hold ketchup or jam in it.*
9. Everybody, tell me what container I am thinking of. Get ready. (Signal.) *A bottle.*

EXERCISE 4   Verb Tense

1. It's time for some statements.
2. Listen: The police officer waved.
   - What does that statement tell? (Signal.) *What the police officer did.*
     Yes, it tells what the police officer did.
   - What did he do? (Signal.) *Waved.*
3. Listen: The turtle is swimming.
   What does that statement tell? Get ready. (Signal.) *What the turtle is doing.*
   Yes, it tells what the turtle is doing.
   - What is it doing? (Signal.) *Swimming.*
4. Listen: The monkey will swing. What does that statement tell? Get ready. (Signal.) *What the monkey will do.* Yes, it tells what the monkey will do.
   - What will he do? (Signal.) *Swing.*
5. Listen: The patient is resting. What does that statement tell? Get ready. (Signal.) *What the patient is doing.* Yes, it tells what the patient is doing.
   - What is she doing? (Signal.) *Resting.*
6. Listen: The nurse will cook.
   What does that statement tell? Get ready. (Signal.) *What the nurse will do.* Yes, it tells what the nurse will do.
   - What will she do? (Signal.) *Cook.*
7. Let's play a statement game.
8. Everybody, say the statement that tells what the nurse will do. Get ready. (Signal.) *The nurse will cook.*
9. I'll say a statement that tells what the nurse is doing. Listen: The nurse is cooking.
   - Now I'll say a statement that tells what the nurse did. Listen: The nurse cooked. Your turn.

10. Say the statement that tells what the nurse will do. Get ready. (Signal.) *The nurse will cook.*
11. Now say the statement that tells what the nurse is doing. Get ready. (Signal.) *The nurse is cooking.*
12. Now say the statement that tells what the nurse did. Get ready. (Signal.) *The nurse cooked.*
13. (Repeat steps 10 through 12 until firm.)
14. Let's play another statement game.
15. Listen: The ice is melting. What does that statement tell? Get ready. (Signal.) *What the ice is doing.*
16. Say the statement. (Signal.) *The ice is melting.*
17. Now make up a statement that tells what the ice did. Get ready. (Signal.) *The ice melted.*
18. Now make up a statement that tells what the ice will do. Get ready. (Signal.) *The ice will melt.*
19. (Repeat steps 15 through 18 until firm.)

EXERCISE 5   Description

1. I'm going to say two things about something you know. See if you can figure out what I'm talking about.
2. (Hold up one finger.) Narz is a season.
   - (Hold up two fingers.) It is usually very hot during narz.
3. Everybody, tell me what you know about narz.
   - (Hold up one finger.) *Narz is a season.*
   - (Hold up two fingers.) *It is usually very hot during narz.*
4. (Repeat step 3 until firm.)
5. Everybody, tell me what narz is. Get ready. (Signal.) *Summer.*
6. (Repeat steps 3 and 5 until firm.)

EXERCISE 6 Sentence Writing

lake   sky   kite

1. Everybody, open your workbook to Lesson 112. Write your name. ✔
• You're going to write sentences that do not rhyme.
• Touch the picture of the box and the kite. ✔
• The picture shows what the box was in and what the kite was in. What was the box in? (Signal.) *A lake.*
• What was the kite in? (Signal.) *The sky.*
2. Say the sentence for what the box was in. Get ready. (Signal.) *The box was in a lake.*
• Say the sentence for what the kite was in. Get ready. (Signal.) *The kite was in the sky.*
3. (Repeat step 2 until firm.)
4. The word box shows how to spell the words **lake, sky** and **kite.** You can figure out how to spell the other words.
5. Write the sentence for what the box was in. Pencils down when you're finished. ✔
• Now go to the next line and write the sentence for what the kite was in. Pencils down when you're finished. ✔
6. (Call on individual children to read both their sentences.)

EXERCISE 7 Opposites

rough	tall	old	pull

1. push _____
2. young _____
3. smooth _____
4. short _____

tools	furniture	plants

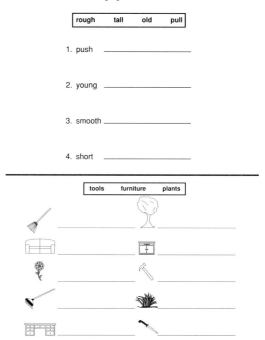

1. Everybody, find the next page. ✔
• (Hold up workbook. Point to top half.) Find the words in the box at the top of your workbook. ✔
• I'll read those words. Touch and follow along: **rough, tall, old, pull.** ✔
2. Your turn. Touch the first word. ✔
• What word? (Signal.) *Rough.*
• Next word. ✔
• What word? (Signal.) *Tall.*
• Next word. ✔
• What word? (Signal.) *Old.*
• Last word. ✔
• What word? (Signal.) *Pull.*
• (Repeat step 2 until firm.)
3. You're going to write words that tell the opposite.
• Touch number 1. ✔
• That word is **push.** What word? (Signal.) *Push.*
• Everybody, what's the opposite of **push?** (Signal.) *Pull.*

4. The word **pull** is in the word box. Copy that word right after the word **push.**
   (Observe children and give feedback.)

5. Touch number 2. ✔
   • That word is **young.** What word? (Signal.) *Young.*
   • Everybody, what's the opposite of **young?** (Signal.) *Old.*

6. The word **old** is in the word box. Copy that word right after the word **young.**
   (Observe children and give feedback.)

7. Touch number 3. ✔
   • That word is **smooth.** What word? (Signal.) *Smooth.*
   • Everybody, what's the opposite of **smooth?** (Signal.) *Rough.*

8. The word **rough** is in the word box. Copy that word right after the word **smooth.**
   (Observe children and give feedback.)

9. Touch number 4. ✔
   • That word is **short.** What word? (Signal.) *Short.*
   • Everybody, which word in the box is the opposite of **short?** (Signal.) *Tall.*

10. Copy the word **tall** right after the word **short.**

EXERCISE 8 Classification

1. (Hold up workbook. Point to bottom half.)
   Everybody, I'll read the words in the box for the bottom part. You touch the words.
   • First word: tools. ✔
   • Next word: furniture. ✔
   • Last word: plants. ✔
   • Yes, tools, furniture, and plants.

2. Everybody, put your finger under the broom. ✔
   • Is a broom in the class of tools, in the class of furniture, or in the class of plants? (Signal.) *Tools.*
   • Copy the word **tools** next to the broom. (Observe children and give feedback.)
   • Read what you wrote. (Signal.) *Tools.*

3. Everybody, put your finger under the couch. ✔
   • Is a couch in the class of tools, in the class of furniture, or in the class of plants? (Signal.) *Furniture.*
   • Copy the word **furniture** next to the couch. (Observe children and give feedback.)
   • Read what you wrote. (Signal.) *Furniture.*

4. Everybody, put your finger under the flower. ✔
   • Is a flower in the class of tools, in the class of furniture, or in the class of plants? (Signal.) *Plants.*
   • Copy the word **plants** next to the flower. (Observe children and give feedback.)
   • Read what you wrote. (Signal.) *Plants.*

5. Later you can write the class words that go with the other pictures.

LESSON 113

Objectives

- Replace a word in a sentence with an opposite. (Exercise 1)
- Given an action, answer questions involving "same" and "different." (Exercise 2)
- Replace a word in a sentence with an opposite. (Exercise 3)
- Generate questions to find a word's definition. (Exercise 4)
- Replace a word in a sentence with a synonym. (Exercise 5)
- Write sentences given picture cues. (Exercise 6)
- Construct verbal analogies. (Exercise 7)
- Read a word and write the opposite of that word. (Exercise 8)

EXERCISE 1 Opposites

1. I'm going to tell you a story. You have to know your opposites to follow this story.
2. Listen: There was a horse. The horse was the opposite of dull. Everybody, what do you know about that horse? (Signal.) *It was shiny.*
   Yes, the horse was shiny.
3. This shiny horse saw some other horses. The other horses were the opposite of clean. Everybody, what do you know about those other horses? (Signal.) *They were dirty.*
   Yes, the other horses were dirty.
4. The dirty horses were not happy. They did the opposite of laugh. Everybody, what do you know about what the dirty horses did? (Signal.) *They cried.*
   Yes, the dirty horses cried.
5. The shiny horse asked the dirty horses to stop crying. The dirty horses said the opposite of no. Everybody, what did they say? (Signal.) *Yes.*
   Yes, the dirty horses said yes.
6. (Repeat steps 2 through 5 until firm.)
7. Let's see what you remember about that story.
8. Everybody, tell me how the first horse looked. (Signal.) *Shiny.*
   - Tell me how the other horses looked. (Signal.) *Dirty.*
   - Tell me what the dirty horses did. (Signal.) *Cried.*
   - Tell me what the dirty horses said. (Signal.) *Yes.*
9. (Repeat step 8 until firm.)

EXERCISE 2 Actions

1. It's time for an action game.
2. Everybody, smile. (Signal.) ✔
   - Good. Now tell me if I do the same thing or something different. Watch me. (Smile.) Did I do the same thing or something different? (Signal.) *The same thing.*
3. Watch me. (Frown.) Did I do the same thing or something different? (Signal.) *Something different.*
4. Watch me. (Smile.) Did I do the same thing or something different? (Signal.) *The same thing.*
5. Everybody, touch both your knees. (Signal.) ✔
   - Good. Stop touching your knees. ✔
   - Now tell me if I do the same thing or something different.
6. Watch me. (Touch your nose.) Did I do the same thing or something different? (Signal.) *Something different.*
7. Watch me. (Touch **one** knee.) Did I do the same thing or something different? (Signal.) *Something different.*
8. Watch me. (Touch both your knees.) Did I do the same thing or something different? (Signal.) *The same thing.*

EXERCISE 3 Opposites

1. We're going to play a word game.
2. Listen: The board is wide. Say that statement. (Signal.) *The board is wide.*
   - Now say a statement that tells the opposite about the board. Get ready. (Signal.) *The board is narrow.*
3. Listen: The tractor is pushing. Say that statement. (Signal.) *The tractor is pushing.*
   - Now say a statement that tells the opposite about the tractor. Get ready. (Signal.) *The tractor is pulling.*
4. (Repeat steps 2 and 3 until firm.)

EXERCISE 4 Questioning Skills

1. I'm going to tell a story. When you hear a word you don't know, say **stop.**
2. A girl had some **currency.** (The children are to say *stop.*) Everybody, what word don't you know? (Signal.) *Currency.*
3. Ask the question about what the word currency means. Get ready. (Signal.) *What does the word currency mean?*
4. I'll tell you what currency means. Currency is a synonym for **money.** What is currency a synonym for? (Signal.) *Money.*
- If a girl had some currency, she had some . . . (Signal.) *money.*
5. Here's more of the story.
6. She went to the **cinema.** (The children are to say *Stop.*) Everybody, what word don't you know? (Signal.) *Cinema.*
7. Ask the question about what the word cinema means. Get ready. (Signal.) *What does the word cinema mean?*
8. I'll tell you what cinema means. Cinema is a synonym for **movies.** What is cinema a synonym for? (Signal.) *Movies.*
- If a girl had some currency and went to the cinema, she had some money and went to . . . (Signal.) *the movies.*
9. Here's more of the story.
10. The movie was **hilarious.** (The children are to say *Stop.*) Everybody, what word don't you know? (Signal.) *Hilarious.*
11. Ask the question about what the word hilarious means. Get ready. (Signal.) *What does the word hilarious mean?*
12. I'll tell you what hilarious means. Hilarious is a synonym for **funny.** What is hilarious a synonym for? (Signal.) *Funny.*
- If a girl had some currency and went to the cinema and the movie was hilarious, she had some money and went to the movies and the movie was funny. Would you like to go to a funny movie?
(Children respond.)
- That's the end of the story.

EXERCISE 5 Synonyms

1. I'll say a statement. You say the statement that means the same thing. My turn. The car is bright. Your turn. Get ready. (Signal.) *The car is shiny.*
2. (Repeat step 1 until firm.)

EXERCISE 6 Sentence Writing

| was | goat | dog |

1. Everybody, open your workbook to Lesson 113. Write your name. ✔
- You're going to write sentences that do not rhyme.
- Touch the picture of the dog and the goat. ✔
- The picture shows what the dog was **on** and what the goat was **in.** What was the dog **on?** (Signal.) *A log.*
- What was the goat **in?** (Signal.) *A log.*
2. Say the sentence for what the dog was on. Get ready. (Signal.) *The dog was on a log.*
- Say the sentence for what the goat was in. Get ready. (Signal.) *The goat was in a log.*
3. (Repeat step 2 until firm.)
4. The word box shows how to spell the words **was, goat,** and **dog.** You can figure out how to spell the other words.
5. Write the sentence for what the dog was on. Pencils down when you're finished. ✔
- Now go to the next line and write the sentence for what the goat was in. Pencils down when you're finished. ✔
6. (Call on individual children to read both their sentences.)

EXERCISE 7 **Analogies**

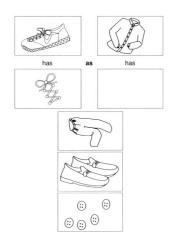

1. Everybody, find the next page. ✔
• (Hold up workbook. Point to first half.)
• The pictures show objects and their parts.
2. Touch the shoe. ✔
• The picture that's right below shows what part it has. Everybody, what part does a shoe have? (Signal.) *Laces.*
• Tell me about a shoe. Get ready. (Signal.) *A shoe has laces.*
3. Touch the shirt. ✔
• One of the pictures below shows what part it has. Touch the picture that shows what part a shirt has. ✔
• Everybody, what part does a shirt have? (Signal.) *Buttons.*
• Tell me about a shirt. Get ready. (Signal.) *A shirt has buttons.*
4. Tell me about a shoe. Get ready. (Signal.) *A shoe has laces.*
• Tell me about a shirt. Get ready. (Signal.) *A shirt has buttons.*
5. Say the whole analogy about a shoe and a shirt. Get ready. (Signal.) *A shoe has laces as a shirt has buttons.*
6. (Repeat step 5 until firm.)
7. Draw a line from the shirt to what part it has. (Observe children and give feedback.)

EXERCISE 8 **Opposites**

win	dry	short	fast

1. slow _____

2. lose _____

3. wet _____

4. tall _____

1. (Hold up workbook. Point to second half.) Find the words in the box. ✔
• I'll read those words. Touch and follow along: **win, dry, short, fast.** ✔
2. Your turn. Touch the first word. ✔
• What word? (Signal.) *Win.*
• Next word. ✔
• What word? (Signal.) *Dry.*
• Next word. ✔
• What word? (Signal.) *Short.*
• Last word. ✔
• What word? (Signal.) *Fast.*
• (Repeat step 2 until firm.)
3. You're going to write words that tell the opposite.
• Touch word 1. ✔
• That word is **slow.** What word? (Signal.) *Slow.*
• Everybody, what's the opposite of **slow?** (Signal.) *Fast.*
4. The word **fast** is in the word box. Copy that word right after the word **slow.** (Observe children and give feedback.)
5. (Repeat step 3 for word 2: **lose.**) (Repeat step 4 for **win.**)
6. (Repeat step 3 for word 3: **wet.**) (Repeat step 4 for **dry.**)
7. (Repeat step 3 for word 4: **tall.**) (Repeat step 4 for **short.**)

Objectives

- Replace a word in a sentence with a synonym. (Exercise 1)
- Name objects that could be made of a given material. (Exercise 2)
- **Identify a place based on its characteristics.** (Exercise 3)
- Name things that a statement does NOT tell. (Exercise 4)
- Given a calendar, identify the day and date for "today" and "tomorrow" and one week from today. (Exercise 5)
- Apply an if-then rule based on the occurrence of events. (Exercise 6)
- Write rhyming sentences given picture cues. (Exercise 7)

EXERCISE 1 Synonyms

1. Let's make up statements that mean the same thing as other statements.
2. Listen: The book is hard. Say that. (Signal.) *The book is hard.*
3. Say the statement that means the same thing. My turn. The book is hard. Your turn. Get ready. (Signal.) *The book is difficult.*
- (Repeat step 3 until firm.)
4. Here's another one.
5. Listen: The window is shiny. Say that. (Signal.) *The window is shiny.*
6. Say the statement that means the same thing. My turn. The window is shiny. Your turn. Get ready. (Signal.) *The window is bright.*
- (Repeat step 6 until firm.)
7. Everybody, let's play a game. I'll say a word. You say a word that means the same thing.
8. Listen: What's a synonym for **well?** (Signal.) *Healthy.*
9. Listen: What's a synonym for **hard?** (Signal.) *Difficult.*
10. Listen: What's a synonym for **large?** (Signal.) *Big.*
11. Listen: What's a synonym for **under?** (Signal.) *Below.*

EXERCISE 2 Materials

1. Think of things that are made of metal.
- Let's see who can name at least three things made of metal. (Call on individual children to name objects made of metal. Each child should name at least three things.)
2. Everybody, think of things that are made of glass.
- Let's see who can name at least three things made of glass. (Call on individual children to name objects made of glass. Each child should name at least three things.)
3. Everybody, think of things that are made of leather.
- Let's see who can name at least three things made of leather. (Call on individual children to name objects made of leather. Each child should name at least three things.)

EXERCISE 3 Description

1. I'm going to say some things about a place. See if you can figure out what I'm talking about.
2. (Hold up one finger.) A krist is a place.
- (Hold up two fingers.) Many people, many streets, and many buildings are in a krist.
3. Everybody, tell me what you know about a krist.
- (Hold up one finger.) *A krist is a place.*
- (Hold up two fingers.) *Many people, many streets, and many buildings are in a krist.*
4. (Repeat step 3 until firm.)
5. Everybody, tell me what a krist is. Get ready. (Signal.) *A city.*
6. (Repeat steps 3 and 5 until firm.)

EXERCISE 4 Statements

1. Listen to this statement.
2. The girls are playing on the slide. Everybody, say that statement. (Signal.) *The girls are playing on the slide.* (Ask individual children the questions in step 3.)
3. Does that statement tell what the girls are doing now? (Signal.) *Yes.*
- Does that statement tell what the boys are doing? (Signal.) *No.*
- Does that statement tell what the boys are playing? (Signal.) *No.*
- Does that statement tell if the girls are tired? (Signal.) *No.*
- Does that statement tell if it is raining? (Signal.) *No.*
4. The girls are playing on the slide. Everybody, say that statement again. (Signal.) *The girls are playing on the slide.*
5. Name three things the statement does not tell you. (Call on individual children. Repeat correct responses.)
6. You have named three things the statement does not tell us.
- Name the first thing. (Hold up one finger.) (The children give the first response.)
- Name the second thing. (Hold up two fingers.) (The children give the second response.)
- Name the third thing. (Hold up three fingers.) (The children give the third response.)
7. (Repeat step 6 until all children can name the three things in order.)

EXERCISE 5 Calendar

1. (Present calendar.)
- We're going to talk about today, tomorrow, and one week from today.
2. Tell me the day of the week it is today. Get ready. (Signal.)
- Tell me the day of the week it will be tomorrow. Get ready. (Signal.)
- Tell me the day of the week it will be one week from today. Get ready. (Signal.)
3. (Repeat step 2 until firm.)
4. Now the dates.
- Tell me today's date. Get ready. (Signal.)
- Look at the calendar. ✔
- Tell me the date it will be one week from today. Get ready. (Signal.)

5. Once more.
- Listen: Tell me today's date. Get ready. (Signal.)
- Tell me tomorrow's date. Get ready. (Signal.)
- Tell me the date it will be one week from today. Get ready. (Signal.)
6. (Repeat step 5 until firm.)

WORKBOOK

EXERCISE 6 If-Then Application

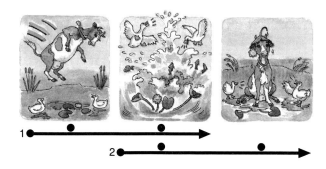

1. Everybody, open your workbook to Lesson 114. Write your name. ✔
- There are **two** arrows under the pictures. The arrow with number **1** next to it tells about two of the pictures.
- Touch the two pictures for arrow **1**. ✔
- Raise your hand if you touched the first picture and the second picture. ✔
- Arrow **2** tells about two pictures. Touch the two pictures for arrow **2**. ✔
- Raise your hand if you touched the second picture and the third picture. ✔
- Remember, each arrow tells about an **if** rule for two pictures.
2. Everybody, touch arrow **1** again. ✔
- Arrow 1 tells what happens in the **first** picture and the **second** picture. The **first** picture shows what Clarabelle is going to do. Touch that picture. ✔
- What is Clarabelle going to do? (Call on a child. Idea: *Jump into the duck pond.*)

- Touch the **second** picture. ✔
  That picture shows what will happen to the water in the duck pond.
- What will happen to the water in the duck pond? (Call on a child. Idea: *It will jump out of the duck pond.*)
- Raise your hand when you can tell the **if** rule for arrow 1. (Call on several children. Idea: *If Clarabelle jumps into the duck pond, the water will jump out of the duck pond.*)
- Yes, here's the rule for arrow 1: If Clarabelle jumps **into** the duck pond, the water will jump **out** of the duck pond.
3. Everybody, say the rule for arrow 1. (Signal.) *If Clarabelle jumps into the duck pond, the water will jump out of the duck pond.*
- (Repeat step 3 until firm.)
4. Now touch arrow **2.** ✔
- That arrow tells what will happen **if the water jumps out of the duck pond.**
- What are the ducks doing in the last picture? (Call on a child. Idea: *The ducks are yelling at Clarabelle.*)
- Raise your hand when you can say the rule for arrow 2. Remember to start with **if** and tell about the second picture, then tell about the last picture. (Call on several children. Idea: *If the water jumps out of the duck pond, the ducks will yell at Clarabelle.*)
- Yes, here's the rule for arrow 2: If the water jumps out of the duck pond, the ducks will yell at Clarabelle.
5. Everybody, say the rule for arrow 2. (Signal.) *If the water jumps out of the duck pond, the ducks will yell at Clarabelle.*
- (Repeat step 5 until firm.)
6. Everybody, get ready to say both rules.
- Say the rule for arrow 1. (Signal.) *If Clarabelle jumps into the duck pond, the water will jump out of the duck pond.*
- Say the rule for arrow 2. (Signal.) *If the water jumps out of the duck pond, the ducks will yell at Clarabelle.*
7. That silly Clarabelle is always causing trouble when she pretends to be something other than a cow.

EXERCISE 7　Sentence Writing

snake

_____
_____
_____

1. Everybody, open your workbook to Lesson 114. Write your name. ✔
- You're going to write sentences that rhyme.
- Touch the picture of the fish and the bug. ✔
- The picture shows where the fish was and where the bug was. Where was the bug? (Signal.) *On a snake.*
- Where was the fish? (Signal.) *In a lake.*
2. Say the sentence for where the fish was. Get ready. (Signal.) *The fish was in a lake.*
- Say the sentence for where the bug was. Get ready. (Signal.) *The bug was on a snake.*
3. (Repeat step 2 until firm.)
4. The word box shows how to spell the word **snake.** You can figure out how to spell the other words.
5. Write the sentence for where the fish was. Pencils down when you're finished. ✔
- Now go to the next line and write the sentence for where the bug was. Pencils down when you're finished. ✔
6. (Call on individual children to read both their sentences.)

LESSON 115

Objectives

- Replace a word in a sentence with an opposite. (Exercise 1)
- Identify absurdities. (Exercise 2)
- Replace a word in a sentence with a synonym. (Exercise 3)
- Identify a word based on its characteristics. (Exercise 4)
- Cooperatively generate an ending for a story. (Exercise 5)
- **Draw pictures to retell a story.** (Exercise 6)

EXERCISE 1 Opposites

1. I'm going to tell you a story. You have to know your opposites to follow this story.
2. Listen: There was a boy. He was the opposite of tall. Everybody, what do you know about that boy? (Signal.) *He was short.* Yes, the boy was short.
3. This short boy had a dog. The dog was the opposite of skinny. Everybody, what do you know about the dog? (Signal.) *It was fat.* Yes, the dog was fat.
4. The short boy and his fat dog went walking down the sidewalk. The sidewalk was the opposite of smooth. Everybody, what do you know about the sidewalk? (Signal.) *It was rough.* Yes, the sidewalk was rough.
5. The boy and his dog found a penny. The penny was the opposite of shiny. Everybody, what do you know about the penny? (Signal.) *It was dull.* Yes, the penny was dull.
6. (Repeat steps 2 through 5 until firm.)
7. Let's see what you remember about that story.
8. Everybody, tell me how the boy looked. (Signal.) *Short.*
- Tell me how the dog looked. (Signal.) *Fat.*
- Tell me how the sidewalk looked. (Signal.) *Rough.*
- Tell me how the penny looked. (Signal.) *Dull.*
- (Repeat step 8 until firm.)

EXERCISE 2 Absurdity

1. Listen to this story and figure out what's wrong with it.
2. There was a girl. She wanted to comb her hair. So she got some scissors.

3. Now tell me what's wrong with that story. (Call on a child.) (Praise all reasonable responses.)
4. Here's another story. Figure out what's wrong with this one.
5. There was a man. He wanted to dig a hole. So he got a belt to dig with.
6. Now tell me what's wrong with that story. (Call on a child.) (Praise all reasonable responses.)
7. Let's figure out what should have happened.
8. What should the girl have used to comb her hair? (Call on several children.) (Praise all reasonable responses.)
9. What could the man have used to dig a hole? (Call on several children.) (Praise all reasonable responses.)

EXERCISE 3 Synonyms

1. Let's make up statements that mean the same thing.
2. Listen: The chairs are the same. Say that. (Signal.) *The chairs are the same.*
3. Here's a statement that means the same thing: The chairs are alike. Say that. (Signal.) *The chairs are alike.*
4. (Repeat steps 2 and 3 until firm.)
5. I'll say one of the statements. You say the statement that means the same thing. My turn. The chairs are alike. Your turn. Get ready. (Signal.) *The chairs are the same.*
- (Repeat step 5 until firm.)

6. Everybody, let's play a game.
   I'll say a word. You say a word that means the same thing.
7. Listen: What's a synonym for **near?** (Signal.) *Close (to).*
8. Listen: What's a synonym for **over?** (Signal.) *Above.*
9. Listen: What's a synonym for **close to?** (Signal.) *Near.*
10. Listen: What's a synonym for **above?** (Signal.) *Over.*
11. (Repeat steps 7 through 10 until firm.)

EXERCISE 4 Description

1. I'm going to say two things about something you know. See if you can figure out what I'm talking about.
2. (Hold up one finger.) A metting is a tool.
• (Hold up two fingers.) You can use a metting to cut meat.
3. Everybody, tell me what you know about a metting.
• (Hold up one finger.) *A metting is a tool.*
• (Hold up two fingers.) *You can use a metting to cut meat.*
4. (Repeat step 3 until firm.)
5. Everybody, tell me what a metting is. Get ready. (Signal.) *A knife.*
6. (Repeat steps 3 and 5 until firm.)
7. Here's another one.
8. (Hold up one finger.) Nerk is a word.
• (Hold up two fingers.) Nerk is the opposite of fast.
9. Everybody, tell me what you know about nerk.
• (Hold up one finger.) *Nerk is a word.*
• (Hold up two fingers.) *Nerk is the opposite of fast.*
10. (Repeat step 9 until firm.)
11. Everybody, tell me what nerk is. Get ready. (Signal.) *Slow.*
12. (Repeat steps 9 and 11 until firm.)

EXERCISE 5 Clarabelle And The Frog Log

Story Completion

1. You're going to work in teams again and figure out the ending to a story. I'll tell the first part. Then your team will figure out a good ending. (Assign children to four teams.)
• Here's the story:

> One day, sixteen green frogs were sitting on a log that was floating in a lake. The log was near the shore of the lake, and the frogs were having a very peaceful time, just sitting and sunning and making frog sounds—"Croak, croak."
>
> Clarabelle was in a field right next to the lake. She saw those happy green frogs all lined up on that floating log and she said to herself, "My, that looks like fun. I would love to sit on that log."
>
> So she tiptoed into the water and approached one end of the floating log. The frogs saw her coming and said, "Hey, what do you think you're doing? Get out of here. Can't you see that this is a frog log, not a cow log?"
>
> But when Clarabelle . . .

• And that's as far as the story goes.
2. Listen: Make up a good ending. Think about what Clarabelle will do, what the log will do and what those sixteen green frogs will do.
• Talk about your ending with your teammates, but remember to whisper. Don't let the members of the other teams hear what you're saying. Raise your hands when your team has a really good ending. (Observe children and give feedback.)
3. (Call on a team member from each team to tell their ending. Praise appropriate endings.)

EXERCISE 6

1. One day, 16 green frogs were sitting on a log that was floating in a lake. The log was near the shore of the lake, and the frogs were having a very peaceful time, just sitting and sunning and making frog sounds – "Croak, croak."

2. Clarabelle was in a field right next to the lake. She saw those happy green frogs all lined up on that floating log and she said to herself, "My, that looks like fun. I would love to sit on that log."

3. So she tiptoed into the water and approached one end of the floating log. The frogs saw her coming and said, "Hey, what do you think you're doing? Get out of here. Can't you see that this is a frog log, not a cow log?"

4. But when Clarabelle _____

```
[ Box 1 ]
[ Box 2 ]
[ Box 3 ]   [ Box 4 ]
```

1. Everybody, open your workbook to Lesson 115. Write your name. ✔
- Here's the whole story I just read.
2. The first part of the story tells what you'll draw in box 1. Listen to that part and remember what you're going to draw in box 1.
- Touch the first word of the story and follow along. ✔
- (Read paragraph 1 at a reasonably slow pace:)

> One day, sixteen green frogs were sitting on a log that was floating in a lake. The log was near the shore of the lake, and the frogs were having a very peaceful time, just sitting and sunning and making frog sounds—"Croak, croak."

- So for picture 1, you'll show that part of the story: those frogs all lined up, sitting and sunning and making frog sounds.
3. The next part of the story tells what you'll draw in box 2.
- Touch the first word after the number 2. ✔ (Read paragraph 2 at a reasonably slow pace:)

> Clarabelle was in a field right next to the lake. She saw those happy green frogs all lined up on that floating log and she said to herself, "My, that looks like fun. I would love to sit on that log."

- So for picture 2, you'll show that part of the story: Clarabelle looking at those green frogs.

4. The next part of the story tells what you'll draw in box 3.
- Touch the first word after the number 3. ✔
- (Read paragraph 3 at a reasonably slow pace:)

> So she tiptoed into the water and approached one end of the floating log. The frogs saw her coming and said, "Hey, what do you think you're doing? Get out of here. Can't you see that this is a frog log, not a cow log?"

- So for picture 3, you'll show that part of the story: Clarabelle tiptoeing out to the log and the frogs are not very happy.
5. Remember, you'll show happy frogs in picture 1. You'll show Clarabelle looking at the frogs in picture 2. You'll show Clarabelle tiptoeing out to that log in picture 3—and the frogs are not very happy.
6. Everybody, touch the first word after the number 4. ✔
- All it says for number 4 is: **But when Clarabelle . . .** You're going to tell me what to write. I'll write it on the board. Then you'll copy it and draw a picture to show the ending.
- (Write on the board:)

> But when Clarabelle

- That's the part that's already written. Tell me the first thing to write: **But when Clarabelle . . .** what? (Call on several children. Write the story ending that the children dictate on the board. Prompt endings that express these ideas: *But when Clarabelle climbed onto the log, the log sunk* or *the log rolled* or *one end of the log went down and the other end of the log went up and the frogs shot up into the air. Clarabelle and the frogs ended up in the water. The frogs were mad at Clarabelle.*)
7. (After the story is completed, say:) Your turn. Copy the whole story. Don't copy the words that are already written, but copy everything else. Write carefully. Raise your hand when you're finished.
(Observe children and give feedback.)
8. Later you can draw the pictures to tell about each part of the story.

Objectives

- **Construct an if-then rule involving missing parts of a whole.** (Exercise 1)
- Replace a word in a sentence with an opposite. (Exercise 2)
- Identify a word based on its characteristics. (Exercise 3)
- Replace a word in a sentence with a synonym. (Exercise 4)
- Name common synonyms. (Exercise 5)
- Write rhyming sentences given picture cues. (Exercise 6)
- Follow coloring rules involving classes and subclasses. (Exercise 7)
- Read a word and write the opposite of that word. (Exercise 8)

EXERCISE 1 If—Then

1. You're going to make up if-then statements.
2. Listen: Does a flashlight work without a battery? (Signal.) *No.*
3. So, if a flashlight doesn't have a battery, what do you know about it? (Signal.) *It won't work.*
4. I'll start with the words "If a flashlight doesn't have a battery," and say the whole statement: **If** a flashlight doesn't have a battery, it won't work.
5. Once more. I'll say the whole if-then statement: **If** a flashlight doesn't have a battery, it won't work.
6. Your turn. Start with the words "If a flashlight doesn't have a battery," and say the whole statement. Get ready. (Signal.) *If a flashlight doesn't have a battery, it won't work.*
- (Repeat step 6 until firm.)
7. Here's another question: Would a bike run well without a back tire? (Signal.) *No.*
8. So, if a bike doesn't have a back tire, what do you know about it? (Signal.) *It won't run.*
9. I'll start with the words "If a bike doesn't have a back tire," and say the whole statement: If a bike doesn't have a back tire, it won't run.
10. Your turn. Start with the words "If a bike doesn't have a back tire," and say the whole statement. Get ready. (Signal.) *If a bike doesn't have a back tire, it won't run.*
- (Repeat step 10 until firm.)

EXERCISE 2 Opposites

1. Let's make up statements with the opposite word.
2. Listen: Cars are safe. Say the statement. (Signal.) *Cars are safe.*
3. Now say a statement with the opposite of safe. Get ready. (Signal.) *Cars are dangerous.*
4. (Repeat steps 2 and 3 until firm.)
5. Now let's make up some more statements.
6. Listen: The egg is raw. Say the statement. (Signal.) *The egg is raw.*
7. Now say a statement with the opposite of raw. Get ready. (Signal.) *The egg is cooked.*
8. (Repeat steps 6 and 7 until firm.)

EXERCISE 3 Description

1. I'm going to say two things about something you know. See if you can figure out what I'm talking about.
2. (Hold up one finger.) Froop is a day.
- (Hold up two fingers.) Froop always comes after Saturday.
3. Everybody, tell me what you know about Froop.
- (Hold up one finger.) *Froop is a day.*
- (Hold up two fingers.) *Froop always comes after Saturday.*
4. (Repeat step 3 until firm.)
5. Everybody, tell me what Froop is. Get ready. (Signal.) *Sunday.*
6. (Repeat steps 3 and 5 until firm.)

7. Here's another one.

8. (Hold up one finger.) A gare can be made of wood.

• (Hold up two fingers.) You use a gare to light a fire.

9. Everybody, tell me what you know about a gare.

• (Hold up one finger.) *A gare can be made of wood.*

• (Hold up two fingers.) *You use a gare to light a fire.*

10. (Repeat step 9 until firm.)

11. Everybody, tell me what a gare is. Get ready. (Signal.) *A match.*

12. (Repeat steps 9 and 11 until firm.)

EXERCISE 4   Synonyms

1. Let's make up statements that mean the same thing as other statements.

2. Listen: We will end our work. Say that. (Signal.) *We will end our work.*

3. Here's a statement that means the same thing: We will finish our work. Say that. (Signal.) *We will finish our work.*

4. (Repeat steps 2 and 3 until firm.)

5. I'll say one of the statements. You say the statement that means the same thing. My turn. We will end our work. Your turn. Get ready. (Signal.) *We will finish our work.*

• (Repeat step 5 until firm.)

EXERCISE 5   Synonyms

1. Everybody, let's play a game.
I'll say a word. You say the synonym.

2. Listen: What's a synonym for **weeping?** (Signal.) *Crying.*

3. Listen: What's a synonym for **shiny?** (Signal.) *Bright.*

4. Listen: What's a synonym for **crying?** (Signal.) *Weeping.*

5. Listen: What's a synonym for **bright?** (Signal.) *Shiny.*

EXERCISE 6   Sentence Writing

| boy | cat | girl |

1. Everybody, open your workbook to Lesson 116. Write your name. ✔

• You're going to write sentences that rhyme.

• Touch the picture of the girl and the boy. ✔

• The picture shows what the girl had and what the boy had. What was the thing the boy had? (Signal.) *A cat.*

• The thing the girl had rhymes with **cat.** What was the thing the girl had? (Signal.) *A hat.*

2. Say the sentence for what the girl had. Get ready. (Signal.) *The girl had a hat.*
Say the sentence for what the boy had. Get ready. (Signal.) *The boy had a cat.*

3. (Repeat step 2 until firm.)

4. The word box shows how to spell the word **cat.** You can figure out how to spell the other words.

5. Write the sentence for what the girl had. Pencils down when you're finished. ✔

• Now go to the next line and write the sentence for what the boy had. Pencils down when you're finished. ✔

6. (Call on individual children to read both their sentences.)

EXERCISE 7 Classification

big	win	push	smooth	open

1. rough _____
2. lose _____
3. shut _____
4. pull _____
5. small _____

1. Everybody, find the next page. ✔
- (Hold up workbook. Point to first half.) Touch the picture of the **smaller** class. ✔
- What kind of thing is that in the picture? (Signal.) *Sailboats.*
2. Everybody, circle the picture that shows the **larger** class. ✔
- Everybody, what's the name of the larger class? (Signal.) *Boats.*
3. Everybody, touch the picture of the class that is **smaller.** ✔
- The sailboats in that picture of the **smaller** class should have orange sails. What color? (Signal.) *Orange.*
- Mark a sail in that picture. ✔
4. Touch the picture that shows the **larger** class. ✔
- The sailboats in that picture should have sails with yellow and green stripes. What colors? (Signal.) *Yellow and green.*
- Mark a sail in that picture. ✔

EXERCISE 8 Opposites

1. (Hold up workbook. Point to second half.) Find the words in the box. ✔
- I'll read those words. Touch and follow along: **big, win, push, smooth, open.** ✔
2. Your turn. Touch the first word. ✔ What word? (Signal.) *Big.*
- Next word. ✔ What word? (Signal.) *Win.*
- Next word. ✔ What word? (Signal.) *Push.*
- Next word. ✔ What word? (Signal.) *Smooth.*
- Last word. ✔ What word? (Signal.) *Open.*
- (Repeat step 2 until firm.)
3. You're going to write words that tell the opposite.
- Touch word 1. ✔
- That word is **rough.** What word? (Signal.) *Rough.*
- Everybody, what's the opposite of **rough?** (Signal.) *Smooth.*
4. The word **smooth** is in the word box. Copy that word right after the word **rough.** (Observe children and give feedback.)
5. (Repeat step 3 for word 2: **lose.**) (Repeat step 4 for **win.**)
6. (Repeat step 3 for word 3: **shut.**) (Repeat step 4 for **open.**)
7. (Repeat step 3 for word 4: **pull.**) (Repeat step 4 for **push.**)
8. (Repeat step 3 for word 5: **small.**) (Repeat step 4 for **big.**)

LESSON 117

Objectives

- Construct an if-then rule involving condition. (Exercise 1)
- Name common synonyms. (Exercise 2)
- Identify words based on characteristics. (Exercise 3)
- Replace a word in a sentence with an opposite. (Exercise 4)
- Answer questions involving previously learned calendar facts. (Exercise 5)
- Write sentences given picture cues. (Exercise 6)
- Write class names next to members of the class. (Exercise 7)
- Label cardinal directions on a map. (Exercise 8)

EXERCISE 1 If—Then

1. You're going to make up if-then statements.
2. Listen: Do you feel better when you are sleepy or when you are rested? (Signal.) *Rested.*
3. I'll start with the words "If you are rested," and say the whole statement: **If** you are rested, you feel better.
4. Your turn. Start with the words "If you are rested," and say the whole statement. Get ready. (Signal.) *If you are rested, you feel better.*
- (Repeat step 4 until firm.)
5. Is a person in better shape when the person exercises regularly or when the person just sits around? (Signal.) *Exercises regularly.*
6. I'll start with the words "If a person exercises regularly," and say the whole statement: **If** a person exercises regularly, the person is in better shape.
7. Your turn. Start with the words "If a person exercises regularly," and say the whole statement. Get ready. (Signal.) *If a person exercises regularly, the person is in better shape.*
- (Repeat step 8 until firm.)
8. Let's do those statements again.
9. Say the statement that tells about you being rested. Get ready. (Signal.) *If you are rested, you feel better.*
10. Say the statement that tells about a person who exercises regularly. Get ready. (Signal.) *If a person exercises regularly, the person is in better shape.*
11. (Repeat steps 9 and 10 until firm.)

EXERCISE 2 Synonyms

1. Everybody, let's play a game. I'll say a word. You say a synonym.
2. What's a synonym for **the same?** (Signal.) *Alike.*
3. What's a synonym for **end?** (Signal.) *Finish.*
4. (Repeat steps 2 and 3 until firm.)

EXERCISE 3 Description

1. I'm going to say two things about something you know. See if you can figure out what I'm talking about.
2. (Hold up one finger.) Sasts are made of metal.
- (Hold up two fingers.) You use sasts to cut paper.
3. Everybody, tell me what you know about sasts.
- (Hold up one finger.) *Sasts are made of metal.*
- (Hold up two fingers.) *You use sasts to cut paper.*
4. (Repeat step 3 until firm.)
5. Everybody, tell me what sasts are. Get ready. (Signal.) *Scissors.*
6. (Repeat steps 3 and 5 until firm.)
7. Here's another one.
8. (Hold up one finger.) Bame is a word.
- (Hold up two fingers.) Bame is the opposite of deep.
9. Everybody, tell me what you know about bame.
- (Hold up one finger.) *Bame is a word.*
- (Hold up two fingers.) *Bame is the opposite of deep.*
10. (Repeat step 9 until firm.)
11. Everybody, tell me what bame is. Get ready. (Signal.) *Shallow.*
12. (Repeat steps 9 and 11 until firm.)

EXERCISE 4   Opposites

1. I'm going to tell you a story. You have to know your opposites to follow this story.
2. Listen: There was a worm. The worm was the opposite of short. Everybody, what do you know about that worm? (Signal.) *It was long.*
   Yes, the worm was long.
3. The worm crawled to the edge of the table. What the worm did was the opposite of safe. So what the worm did was . . . (Signal.) *dangerous.*
   Yes, it was dangerous.
4. The worm slipped off the table and fell on a board. That board was the opposite of rough. Everybody, what do you know about that board? (Signal.) *It was smooth.*
   Yes, the board was smooth.
5. The worm slid down the board and fell into a coffee pot. The pot was the opposite of shut. Everybody, what do you know about that pot? (Signal.) *It was open.*
   Yes, the coffee pot was open.
6. (Repeat steps 2 through 5 until firm.)
7. Let's see what you remember about that story.
8. Everybody, was the worm long or short? (Signal.) *Long.*
   • Did the worm do something safe or dangerous? (Signal.) *Dangerous.*
   • Tell me how the board felt. (Signal.) *Smooth.*
   • Tell me about the coffee pot. (Signal.) *It was open.*
   • (Repeat step 8 until firm.)

EXERCISE 5   Calendar Facts

1. We're going to talk about days and months.
2. Everybody, how many days are in a week? (Signal.) *Seven.*
   • Say the whole thing. Get ready. (Signal.) *There are seven days in a week.*
3. Everybody, name the seven days of the week. Get ready. (Signal.) *Sunday, Monday, Tuesday, Wednesday, Thursday, Friday, Saturday.*
   • (Repeat step 3 until firm.)
4. How many months are in a year? (Signal.) *12.*
   • Say the whole thing. Get ready. (Signal.) *There are 12 months in a year.*

5. Name the months of the year through December. Get ready. (Signal.) *January, February, March, April, May, June, July, August, September, October, November, December.*
   • (Repeat step 5 until firm.)
6. Everybody, how many seasons are there in a year? (Signal.) *Four.*
   • Say the seasons of the year. Get ready. (Signal.) *Winter, spring, summer, fall.*
7. Everybody, tell me what day it was yesterday. Get ready. (Signal.)
   • Tell me what day it is today. Get ready. (Signal.)
   • Tell me what day it will be tomorrow. Get ready. (Signal.)

WORKBOOK

EXERCISE 6   Sentence Writing

duck	barn

1. Everybody, open your workbook to Lesson 117. Write your name. ✔
   • You're going to write sentences that do not rhyme.
   • Touch the picture of the rat and the duck. ✔
   • The picture shows what the rat was on and what the duck was on. What was the rat on? (Signal.) *A barn.*
   • What was the duck on? (Signal.) *A rug.*
2. Say the sentence for what the rat was on. Get ready. (Signal.) *The rat was on a barn.*
   • Say the sentence for what the duck was on. Get ready. (Signal.) *The duck was on a rug.*
3. (Repeat step 2 until firm.)

4. The word box shows how to spell the words **duck** and **barn.** You can figure out how to spell the other words.
5. Write the sentence for what the rat was on. Pencils down when you're finished. ✔
- Now go to the next line and write the sentence for what the duck was on. Pencils down when you're finished. ✔
6. (Call on individual children to read both their sentences.)

EXERCISE 7 Classification

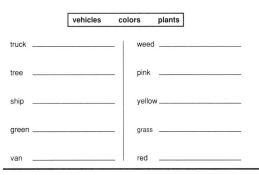

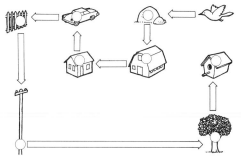

1. Everybody, find the next page. ✔ (Hold up workbook. Point to top half.) Everybody, I'll read the words in the box. You touch the words.
- First word: vehicles. ✔
- Next word: colors. ✔
- Last word: plants. ✔
2. Your turn to read the words in the box.
- First word. What word? (Signal.) *Vehicles.*
- Next word. What word? (Signal.) *Colors.*
- Last word: What word? (Signal.) *Plants.* Yes, vehicles, colors, and plants.
3. Everybody, put your finger under the word **truck.** ✔
- What word? (Signal.) *Truck.*
- Is a truck in the class of vehicles, in the class of colors, or in the class of plants? (Signal.) *Vehicles.*
- Copy the word **vehicles** next to the word **truck.** (Observe children and give feedback.)
- Read what you wrote. (Signal.) *Vehicles.*

4. Everybody, put your finger under the next word. ✔
- What word? (Signal.) *Tree.*
- Is a tree in the class of vehicles, in the class of colors, or in the class of plants? (Signal.) *Plants.*
- Copy the word **plants** next to the word **tree.** (Observe children and give feedback.)
- Read what you wrote. (Signal.) *Plants.*
5. Everybody, put your finger under the next word. ✔
- What word? (Signal.) *Ship.*
- Is a ship in the class of vehicles, in the class of colors, or in the class of plants? (Signal.) *Vehicles.*
- Copy the word **vehicles** next to the word **ship.** (Observe children and give feedback.)
- Read what you wrote. (Signal.) *Vehicles.*
6. Everybody, put your finger under the word **green.** ✔
- What word? (Signal.) *Green.*
- Next word. What word? (Signal.) *Van.*
- Next word. What word? (Signal.) *Weed.*
- Next word. What word? (Signal.) *Pink.*
- Next word. What word? (Signal.) *Yellow.*
- Next word. What word? (Signal.) *Grass.*
- Last word. What word? (Signal.) *Red.*
7. (Repeat step 6 until firm.)
- Later you can write the class that goes with each word you just read.

EXERCISE 8 Map Reading

1. (Hold up workbook. Point to bottom half.) Everybody, touch the bird. ✔
2. This picture is a map of where the bird flew. You're going to color the arrows red and write the directions on the objects. Remember to start from the bird.
3. Everybody, color the first arrow red. Do it. ✔
- Now write the letter that shows the direction the bird flew. ✔
4. You'll do the rest of the arrows later.

Objectives

- Generate questions to find a word's definition. (Exercise 1)
- Name things that a statement does NOT tell. (Exercise 2)
- Replace a word in a sentence with a synonym. (Exercise 3)
- Identify a word based on its characteristics. (Exercise 4)
- Construct an if-then rule involving condition. (Exercise 5)
- **Discriminate between good and bad clues for identifying a story character.** (Exercise 6)
- Write sentences given picture cues. (Exercise 7)

EXERCISE 1 Questioning Skills

1. I'm going to tell a story. When you hear a word you don't know, say **stop.**
2. A woman was **somnolent.** (The children are to say *stop.*) Everybody, what word don't you know? (Signal.) *Somnolent.*
3. Ask the question about what the word somnolent means. Get ready. (Signal.) *What does the word somnolent mean?*
4. I'll tell you what somnolent means. Somnolent is a synonym for **sleepy.** What is somnolent a synonym for? (Signal.) *Sleepy.*
- If a woman was somnolent, she was . . . (Signal.) *sleepy.*
5. Here's more of the story.
6. So she said, "I will see you in the morning. Right now I will **retire.**" (The children are to say *stop.*) Everybody, what word don't you know? (Signal.) *Retire.*
7. Ask the question about what the word retire means. Get ready. (Signal.) *What does the word retire mean?*
8. I'll tell you what retire means. Retire is a synonym for **go to bed.** What is retire a synonym for? (Signal.) *Go to bed.*
- If a woman was somnolent and she retired, she was sleepy and she . . . (Signal.) *went to bed.*
9. Here's more of the story.
10. She slept on the **davenport.** (The children are to say *stop.*) Everybody, what word don't you know? (Signal.) *Davenport.*
11. Ask the question about what the word davenport means. Get ready. (Signal.) *What does the word davenport mean?*
12. I'll tell you what davenport means. Davenport is a synonym for **couch.** What is davenport a synonym for? (Signal.) *Couch.*

- So if a woman was somnolent and she retired and slept on the davenport, she was sleepy and went to bed and slept on the couch. Would you wake her up? (Children respond.)
- That's the end of the story.

EXERCISE 2 Statements

1. Listen to this statement.
2. The boys will jump over the flowerpots. Everybody, say that statement. (Signal.) *The boys will jump over the flowerpots.*
3. Does that statement tell how many flowerpots there are? (Signal.) *No.*
- Does that statement tell what the boys will do? (Signal.) *Yes.*
- Does that statement tell where the flowerpots are? (Signal.) *No.*
- Does that statement tell if the flowerpots are red? (Signal.) *No.*
- Does that statement tell what the boys are doing now? (Signal.) *No.*
4. The boys will jump over the flowerpots. Everybody, say that statement again. Get ready. (Signal.) *The boys will jump over the flowerpots.*
5. Name three things the statement does not tell you. (Call on individual children. Repeat three correct responses.)
6. You have named three things the statement does not tell us.
- Name the first thing. (Hold up one finger.) (The children give the first response.)
- Name the second thing. (Hold up two fingers.) (The children give the second response.)
- Name the third thing. (Hold up three fingers.) (The children give the third response.)

EXERCISE 3 Synonyms

1. We're going to make up statements that mean the same thing.
2. What do we call two words that mean the same thing? (Signal.) *Synonyms.*
3. Listen: The building is big. Say that. (Signal.) *The building is big.*
   - Say the statement with a synonym for **big.** Get ready. (Signal.) *The building is large.*
   - (Repeat step 3 until firm.)
4. The building is big. The building is large. Those statements mean the same thing, because big and large are synonyms.
5. Listen: The plants are the same. Say that. (Signal.) *The plants are the same.*
   - Say the statement with a synonym for the same. Get ready. (Signal.) *The plants are alike.*
   - (Repeat step 5 until firm.)
6. Listen: The work is hard. Say that. (Signal.) *The work is hard.*
   - Say the statement with a synonym for hard. Get ready. (Signal.) *The work is difficult.*
   - (Repeat step 6 until firm.)

EXERCISE 4 Description

1. I'm going to say two things about something you know. See if you can figure out what I'm talking about.
2. (Hold up one finger.) Mert is an action.
   - (Hold up two fingers.) After you chew your food, you mert it.
3. Everybody, tell me what you know about mert.
   - (Hold up one finger.) *Mert is an action.*
   - (Hold up two fingers.) *After you chew your food, you mert it.*
4. (Repeat step 3 until firm.)
5. Everybody, tell me what merting is. Get ready. (Signal.) *Swallowing.*
6. (Repeat steps 3 and 5 until firm.)
7. Here's another one.
8. (Hold up one finger.) A sloom is a place.
   - (Hold up two fingers.) You see animals, barns, and tractors at a sloom.

9. Everybody, tell me what you know about a sloom.
   - (Hold up one finger.) *A sloom is a place.*
   - (Hold up two fingers.) *You see animals, barns, and tractors at a sloom.*
10. (Repeat step 9 until firm.)
11. Everybody, tell me what a sloom is. Get ready. (Signal.) *A farm.*
12. (Repeat steps 9 and 11 until firm.)

EXERCISE 5 If—Then

1. You're going to make up if-then statements.
2. Listen: Does a person get more work done when the person works hard or when the person doesn't work hard? (Signal.) *When the person works hard.*
3. Start with the words "If a person works hard," and say the whole statement. Get ready. (Signal.) *If a person works hard, the person gets more work done.*
4. (Repeat steps 2 and 3 until firm.)
5. Listen: When will the vacuum cleaner work, when it is plugged in or when it is not plugged in? (Signal.) *When it is plugged in.*
6. Start with the words "If a vacuum cleaner is plugged in," and say the whole statement. Get ready. (Signal.) *If a vacuum cleaner is plugged in, it will work.*
7. (Repeat steps 5 and 6 until firm.)
8. Let's do those statements again.
9. Say the statement that tells about a person who works hard. Get ready. (Signal.) *If a person works hard, the person gets more work done.*
10. Say the statement that tells about a vacuum cleaner that is plugged in. Get ready. (Signal.) *If a vacuum cleaner is plugged in, it will work.*
11. (Repeat steps 9 and 10 until firm.)

EXERCISE 6 Extrapolation

Identifying Good Clues

1. _____

    a.   true   false

    b.   true   false

    c.   true   false

2. _____

    a.   true   false

    b.   true   false

    c.   true   false

3. _____

    a.   true   false

    b.   true   false

    c.   true   false

4. _____

    a.   true   false

    b.   true   false

    c.   true   false

1. Everybody, open your workbook to Lesson 118. Write your name. ✔
- Here are some pictures of characters you know. I'm going to give you three clues about the characters. But one of those clues is a bad one. It doesn't **really** tell about the right character at all.
- Here's what you'll do: You'll listen to the clues. You won't say anything. Then you'll copy the name of the character that clue tells about. Remember, don't say anything.
2. Touch number 1. ✔
- Here are the three clues for character 1.
- Listen: This character is a person.
- This character loves words that begin with a certain letter.
- This character fixes up spilled paint by using rags and doing a lot of scrubbing.
- Everybody, write the name of the character those clues are supposed to tell about. Write the name on line 1. Raise your hand when you're finished.
  (Observe children and give feedback.)
- Everybody, whose name did you write for number 1? **(Signal.)** *Paul.*
- Yes, the clues are supposed to tell about Paul.

3. I'm going to say the clues one more time. You'll circle **true** if that clue tells about Paul. You'll circle **false** if that clue does not tell about Paul.
- Touch A, just below the name Paul. ✔
- Here's clue A: This character is a person. Circle **true** if that clue tells about Paul. Circle **false** if it does not tell about Paul. Raise your hand when you're finished. ✔
- Touch B. ✔
- Here's clue B: This character loves words that begin with a certain letter. Circle **true** or **false** for clue B. Raise your hand when you're finished. ✔
- Touch C. ✔
- Here's clue C: This character fixes up spilled paint by using rags and doing a lot of scrubbing. Circle **true** or **false** for clue C. Raise your hand when you're finished. ✔
4. Everybody, one of the clues is bad. That's the clue that's false. Which clue is false, clue A, clue B or clue C? **(Signal.)** *Clue C.*
- Raise your hand if you know how to change that clue so it really tells about Paul. Listen to clue C one more time: This character fixes up spilled paint by using rags and doing a lot of scrubbing.
- Tell me a good clue C. **(Call on a child. Praise idea: *This character fixes up spilled paint by painting.*)**
5. Everybody, touch number 2. ✔
- Here are the three clues for character 2. Listen: This character has made many inventions.
  This character is a cow.
  This character's inventions always have a problem.
- Everybody, write the name of the character those clues are supposed to tell about. Write the name on line 2. Raise your hand when you're finished.
  (Observe children and give feedback.)
- Everybody, whose name did you write for number 2? **(Signal.)** *Molly.*
  Yes, the clues are supposed to tell about Molly.

6. I'm going to say the clues one more time. You'll circle **true** if that clue tells about Molly. You'll circle **false** if that clue does not tell about Molly.
- Touch A, just below the name Molly. ✔
- Here's clue A: This character has made many inventions. Circle **true** or **false** for clue A. Raise your hand when you're finished. ✔
- Touch B. ✔
- Here's clue B: This character is a cow. Circle **true** or **false** for clue B. Raise your hand when you're finished. ✔
- Touch C. ✔
- Here's clue C: This character's inventions always have a problem. Circle **true** or **false** for clue C. Raise your hand when you're finished. ✔

7. Everybody, one of the clues is bad. That's the clue that's false. Which clue is false, clue A, clue B or clue C? (Signal.) *Clue B.*
- Raise your hand if you know how to change that clue so it really tells about Molly. Listen to clue B one more time: This character is a cow.
- Tell me a good clue B. (Call on a child. Praise idea: *This character is a person.*)

8. Everybody, touch number 3. ✔
- Here are the three clues for character 3.
- Listen: This character is an animal.
- This character loves to do what other animals and people do.
- This character doesn't weigh any more than Sweetie weighs.
- Everybody, write the name of the character those clues are supposed to tell about. Write the name on line 3. Raise your hand when you're finished.
  (Observe children and give feedback.)
- Everybody, whose name did you write for number 3? (Signal.) *Clarabelle.*
  Yes, the clues are supposed to tell about Clarabelle.

9. I'm going to say the clues one more time. You'll circle **true** if that clue tells about Clarabelle. You'll circle **false** if that clue does not tell about Clarabelle. ✔
- Touch A, just below the name Clarabelle. Here's clue A: This character is an animal. Circle **true** or **false** for clue A. Raise your hand when you're finished. ✔
- Touch B. ✔
- Here's clue B: This character loves to do what other animals and people do. Circle **true** or **false** for clue B. Raise your hand when you're finished. ✔
- Touch C. ✔
  Here's clue C: This character doesn't weigh any more than Sweetie weighs. Circle **true** or **false** for clue C. Raise your hand when you're finished. ✔

10. Everybody, one of the clues is bad. That's the clue that's false. Which clue is false, clue A, clue B or clue C? (Signal.) *Clue C.*
- Raise your hand if you know how to change that clue so it really tells about Clarabelle. Listen to clue C one more time: This character doesn't weigh any more than Sweetie weighs.
- Tell me a good clue C. (Call on a child. Praise idea: *This character is very heavy.*)

11. Everybody, touch number 4. ✔
- Here are the three clues for character 4.
- Listen: This character is gray and has a long tail.
- This character gets along very well with everybody.
- This character has spent a lot of time in a maze.

- Everybody, write the name of the character those clues are supposed to tell about. Write the name on line 4. Raise your hand when you're finished.
  (Observe children and give feedback.)
- Everybody, whose name did you write for number 4? **(Signal.)** *Bragging rat.*
  Yes, the clues are supposed to tell about a bragging rat.
12. I'm going to say the clues one more time. You'll circle **true** if that clue tells about the bragging rat. You'll circle **false** if that clue does not tell about the bragging rat.
- Touch A, just below the words bragging rat. ✔
- Here's clue A: This character is gray and has a long tail. Circle **true** or **false** for clue A. Raise your hand when you're finished. ✔
- Touch B. ✔
- Here's clue B: This character gets along very well with everybody. Circle **true** or **false** for clue B. Raise your hand when you're finished. ✔
- Touch C. ✔
- Here's clue C: This character has spent a lot of time in a maze. Circle **true** or **false** for clue C. Raise your hand when you're finished. ✔
13. Everybody, one of the clues is bad. That's the clue that's false. Which clue is false, clue A, clue B or clue C? **(Signal.)** *Clue B.*
- Raise your hand if you know how to change that clue so it really tells about the bragging rat. Listen to clue B one more time: This character gets along very well with everybody.
- Tell me a good clue B. **(Call on a child. Praise idea:** *This character argues a lot.***)**
14. You really know a lot about these characters.

EXERCISE 7 **Sentence Writing**

| hole   mouse |

_____
_____
_____
_____

1. Everybody, find the next page. ✔
- You're going to write sentences that do not rhyme.
- Touch the picture of the dog and the mouse. ✔
- The picture shows what the dog was in and what the mouse was in. What was the dog in? **(Signal.)** *A bed.* Yes, a **bed.**
- What was the mouse in? **(Signal.)** *A hole.* Yes, a **hole.**
2. Say the sentence for what the dog was in. Get ready. **(Signal.)** *The dog was in a bed.*
- Say the sentence for what the mouse was in. Get ready. **(Signal.)** *The mouse was in a hole.*
3. **(Repeat step 2 until firm.)**
4. The word box shows how to spell the words **hole** and **mouse.** You can figure out how to spell the other words.
5. Write the sentence for what the dog was in. Pencils down when you're finished. ✔
- Now go to the next line and write the sentence for what the mouse was in. Pencils down when you're finished. ✔
6. **(Call on individual children to read both their sentences.)**

Objectives

- Replace a word in a sentence with an opposite. (Exercise 1)
- **Identify and generate sentences involving past, present and future tense.** (Exercise 2)
- Replace a word in a sentence with a synonym. (Exercise 3)
- Identify words based on characteristics. (Exercise 4 & 5)
- Construct an if-then rule involving condition. (Exercise 6)
- Write rhyming sentences given picture cues. (Exercise 7)
- Follow coloring rules involving classes and subclasses. (Exercise 8)
- Construct verbal analogies. (Exercise 9)

EXERCISE 1   Opposites

1. Let's make up the statements with the opposite word.
2. Listen: The mirror is shiny. Say the statement. (Signal.) *The mirror is shiny.*
3. Now say a statement with the opposite of shiny. Get ready. (Signal.) *The mirror is dull.*
- (Repeat step 3 until firm.)
4. Listen: The runner is fast. Say the statement. (Signal.) *The runner is fast.*
5. Now say a statement with the opposite of fast. Get ready. (Signal.) *The runner is slow.*
- (Repeat step 5 until firm.)

EXERCISE 2   Verb Tense

1. Listen: The frog swam.
   What does that statement tell? (Signal.) *What the frog did.*
   Yes, it tells what the frog did. What did he do? (Signal.) *Swam.*
2. Listen: The man will run.
   What does that statement tell? (Signal.) *What the man will do.*
   Yes, it tells what the man will do. What will he do? (Signal.) *Run.*
3. Listen: The bear is sitting.
   What does that statement tell? (Signal.) *What the bear is doing.*
   Yes, it tells what the bear is doing. What is he doing? (Signal.) *Sitting.*
4. Listen: The deer is eating.
   What does that statement tell? (Signal.) *What the deer is doing.*
   Yes, it tells what the deer is doing. What is he doing. (Signal.) *Eating.*

5. Listen: The bear laughed.
   What does the statement tell? (Signal.) *What the bear did.*
   Yes, it tells what the bear did. What did he do? (Signal.) *Laughed.*
6. Let's play a statement game.
7. Everybody, say the statement that tells what the bear did. Get ready. (Signal.) *The bear laughed.*
8. My turn to say the statement that tells what the bear is doing: The bear is laughing.
9. Now I'll say the statement that tells what the bear will do: The bear will laugh.
10. Your turn. Say the statement that tells what the bear did. Get ready. (Signal.) *The bear laughed.*
11. Now say the statement that tells what the bear is doing. Get ready. (Signal.) *The bear is laughing.*
12. Now say the statement that tells what the bear will do. Get ready. (Signal.) *The bear will laugh.*
13. (Repeat steps 10 through 12 until firm.)
14. Let's play another statement game.
15. Listen: The deer ate. What does that statement tell? (Signal.) *What the deer did.*
16. Say the statement. Get ready. (Signal.) *The deer ate.*
17. Now make up a statement that tells what the deer is doing. Get ready. (Signal.) *The deer is eating.*
18. Now make up a statement that tells what the deer will do. Get ready. (Signal.) *The deer will eat.*
19. (Repeat steps 15 through 18, calling on individual children.)

EXERCISE 3 Synonyms

1. What do we call two words that mean the same thing? (Signal.) *Synonyms.*
2. Listen: The class will end at noon. Say that. (Signal.) *The class will end at noon.*
- Say that statement using a synonym for **end.** Get ready. (Signal.) *The class will finish at noon.*
- The class will end at noon. The class will finish at noon. Those statements mean the same thing, because **end** and **finish** are synonyms.
3. Listen: The house is near town. Say that. (Signal.) *The house is near town.*
- Say that statement using a synonym for **near.** Get ready. (Signal.) *The house is close to town.*
- (Repeat step 3 until firm.)
4. Listen: The ring is bright. Say that. (Signal.) *The ring is bright.*
- Say that statement using a synonym for **bright.** Get ready. (Signal.) *The ring is shiny.*
- The ring is bright. The ring is shiny. Those statements mean the same thing, because bright and shiny are synonyms.

EXERCISE 4 Description

1. I'm going to say two things about something you know. See if you can figure out what I'm talking about.
2. (Hold up one finger.) An oom is a place.
- (Hold up two fingers.) You see airplanes, baggage carts, and buildings at an oom.
3. Everybody, tell me what you know about an oom.
- (Hold up one finger.) *An oom is a place.*
- (Hold up two fingers.) *You see airplanes, baggage carts, and buildings at an oom.*
4. (Repeat step 3 until firm.)
5. Everybody, tell me what an oom is. Get ready. (Signal.) *An airport.*
6. (Repeat steps 3 and 5 until firm.)
7. Here's another one.
8. (Hold up one finger.) Gart is an action.
- (Hold up two fingers.) You move up and down on one foot when you gart.

9. Everybody, tell me what you know about gart. Get ready.
- (Hold up one finger.) *Gart is an action.*
- (Hold up two fingers.) *You move up and down on one foot when you gart.*
10. (Repeat step 6 until firm.)
11. Everybody, tell me what garting is. Get ready. (Signal.) *Hopping.*
12. (Repeat steps 9 and 11 until firm.)

EXERCISE 5 Description

1. I'm going to say two things about something you know. See if you can figure out what I'm talking about.
2. (Hold up one finger.) A pame is made of glass.
- (Hold up two fingers.) You can see yourself in a pame.
3. Everybody, tell me what you know about a pame.
- (Hold up one finger.) *A pame is made of glass.*
- (Hold up two fingers.) *You can see yourself in a pame.*
4. (Repeat step 3 until firm.)
5. Everybody, tell me what a pame is. Get ready. (Signal.) *A mirror.*
6. (Repeat steps 3 and 5 until firm.)
7. Here's another one.
8. (Hold up one finger.) Yorn is a season.
- (Hold up two fingers.) Yorn always comes after summer.
9. Everybody, tell me what you know about yorn.
- (Hold up one finger.) *Yorn is a season.*
- (Hold up two fingers.) *Yorn always comes after summer.*
10. (Repeat step 9 until firm.)
11. Everybody, tell me what yorn is. Get ready. (Signal.) *Fall.*
12. (Repeat steps 9 and 11 until firm.)

EXERCISE 6   If—Then

1. You're going to make up if-then statements.
2. Listen: Which ice would melt, ice that is in a freezer or ice that is on a table? (Signal.) *Ice that is on a table.*
3. Start with the words "If ice is," and say the whole statement. Get ready. (Signal.) *If ice is on the table, it will melt.*
4. (Repeat steps 2 and 3 until firm.)
5. Listen: Which door will not open, a door that is locked or a door that is unlocked? (Signal.) *A door that is locked.*
6. Start with the words, "If a door is locked," and say the whole statement. Get ready. (Signal.) *If a door is locked, it will not open.*
7. (Repeat steps 5 and 6 until firm.)
8. Let's do those statements again.
9. Say the statement that tells about ice that is on the table. Get ready. (Signal.) *If ice is on the table, it will melt.*
10. Say the statement that tells about a door that is locked. Get ready. (Signal.) *If a door is locked, it will not open.*
11. (Repeat steps 9 and 10 until firm.)

EXERCISE 7   Sentence Writing

| will | stick | turn |

_____

_____

_____

_____

1. Everybody, open your workbook to Lesson 119. Write your name. ✔
- You're going to write sentences that rhyme.
- Touch the picture of the cat and the stick. ✔
- The picture shows what the cat will do and what the stick will do. What will the cat do? (Signal.) *Turn.*
- What will the stick do? (Signal.) *Burn.*
2. Say the sentence for what the cat will do. Get ready. (Signal.) *The cat will turn.*
- Say the sentence for what the stick will do. Get ready. (Signal.) *The stick will burn.*
3. (Repeat step 2 until firm.)
4. The word box shows how to spell the words **will, stick** and **turn.** You can figure out how to spell the other words.
5. Write the sentence for what the cat will do. Pencils down when you're finished. ✔
- Now go to the next line and write the sentence for what the stick will do. Pencils down when you're finished. ✔
6. (Call on individual children to read both their sentences.)

EXERCISE 8 Classification

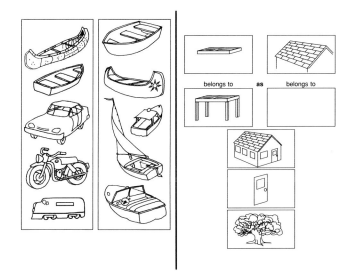

1. Everybody, find the next page. ✔
• (Hold up workbook. Point to first half.) Touch the picture of the **smaller** class. ✔
• What kind of thing is that in the picture? (Signal.) *Boats.*
2. Everybody, circle the picture that shows the **larger** class. ✔
• Everybody, what's the name of the larger class? (Signal.) *Vehicles.*
3. Everybody, touch the picture of the class that is **smaller.** ✔
• The boats in that picture of the **smaller** class should be blue and yellow. What colors? (Signal.) *Blue and yellow.*
• Mark a boat in that picture. ✔
4. Touch the picture that shows the **larger** class. ✔
• The boats in that picture should be yellow and red. What colors? (Signal.) *Yellow and red.*
• Mark a boat in that picture. ✔

EXERCISE 9 Analogies

1. (Hold up workbook. Point to second half.)
• The pictures show parts and the objects that have those parts.
2. Touch the top of something. ✔
• The picture that's right below shows what it belongs to. Everybody, what does a top belong to? (Signal.) *A table.*
• Tell me about a top. Get ready. (Signal.) *A top belongs to a table.*
3. Touch the roof. ✔
• Touch the picture that shows what a roof belongs to. ✔
• Everybody, what does a roof belong to? (Signal.) *A house.*
• Tell me about a roof. Get ready. (Signal.) *A roof belongs to a house.*
4. Tell me about a top. Get ready. (Signal.) *A top belongs to a table.*
• Tell me about a roof. Get ready. (Signal.) *A roof belongs to a house.*
5. Say the whole analogy about a top and a roof. Get ready. (Signal.) *A top belongs to a table as a roof belongs to a house.*
6. (Repeat step 5 until firm.)
7. Draw a line from the roof to the object it belongs to.
(Observe children and give feedback.)

LESSON 120

Objectives

- Listen to a short story and answer questions involving "who," "when," "why," "where" and "what". (Exercise 1)
- Identify absurdities. (Exercise 2)
- **Replace words in a sentence with appropriate contractions.** (Exercise 3)
- Replace a word in a sentence with an opposite. (Exercise 4)
- Identify a word based on its characteristics. (Exercise 5)
- Write sentences identifying sequence given picture cues. (Exercise 6)
- Ask questions to figure out the "mystery" picture. (Exercise 7)

EXERCISE 1   Who—What—When—Where—Why

1. Listen to this story.
- Mrs. Graham worked in a factory. She was very tired because she worked very hard. When it was five o'clock, she went home and took a nap.
- (Repeat the story.)
2. Tell who worked in a factory. (Signal.) *Mrs. Graham.*
- Tell why Mrs. Graham was very tired. (Signal.) *Because she worked very hard.*
- Tell where Mrs. Graham worked. (Signal.) *In a factory.*
- Tell what Mrs. Graham did when she got home. (Signal.) *Took a nap.*
- Tell when Mrs. Graham went home. (Signal.) *At five o'clock.*
3. (Repeat step 2 until firm.)

EXERCISE 2   Absurdity

1. Listen to this story and tell me what's absurd about it.
2. A man washed a plate in the clothes washer. Where did the man wash the plate? (Signal.) *In the clothes washer.*
3. Then he dried the plate with the electric mixer. What did he do with the plate? (Signal.) *Dried it with the electric mixer.*
4. Now tell me some things that are absurd about that story. (Call on two or three individual children. Ask the first child:) What's one thing that's absurd? (After the child responds, ask other children:) What's another thing that's absurd? (Praise all appropriate responses.)

EXERCISE 3   Contractions

1. It's time for some statements.
2. I'll say a statement about a boy. (Point to a boy.) He **does not** have wings. Now I'll say it a new way. He **doesn't** have wings.
3. Everybody, say the statement the **new** way. Get ready. (Signal.) *He doesn't have wings.*
- (Repeat step 3 until firm.)
4. Listen: You do not have wings. Now I'll say it a new way. You **don't** have wings.
5. Everybody, say the statement the **new** way. Get ready. (Signal.) *You don't have wings.*
- (Repeat step 5 until firm.)
6. Listen: She does not have wings. Now I'll say it a **new** way. She **doesn't** have wings.
7. Everybody, say the statement the **new** way. Get ready. (Signal.) *She doesn't have wings.*
- (Repeat step 7 until firm.)
8. Listen: They **do not** have wings. Now I'll say it a **new** way. They **don't** have wings.
9. Everybody, say the statement the **new** way. Get ready. (Signal.) *They don't have wings.*
- (Repeat step 9 until firm.)
10. Now let's see how fast you can go.
11. (Point to a boy.) Does he have wings? (Signal.) *No.*
- Say the statement the new way. Get ready. (Signal.) *He doesn't have wings.*
12. (Point to two boys.) Do they have wings? (Signal.) *No.*
- Say the statement the new way. Get ready. (Signal.) *They don't have wings.*
13. (Point to a girl.) Does she have wings? (Signal.) *No.*
- Say the statement the new way. Get ready. (Signal.) *She doesn't have wings.*
14. (Repeat steps 11 through 13 until firm.)

EXERCISE 4   Opposites

1. Let's make up statements with the opposite word.
2. Listen: The ocean is far. Say that statement. (Signal.) *The ocean is far.*
3. Now say a statement with the opposite of far. Get ready. (Signal.) *The ocean is near.*
4. (Repeat steps 2 and 3 until firm.)
5. Listen: The band is quiet. Say that statement. (Signal.) *The band is quiet.*
6. Now say a statement with the opposite of quiet. Get ready. (Signal.) *The band is noisy.*
7. (Repeat steps 5 and 6 until firm.)

EXERCISE 5   Description

1. I'm going to say two things about something you know. See if you can figure out what I'm talking about.
2. (Hold up one finger.) Forn is a season.
• (Hold up two fingers.) Forn always comes after spring.
3. Everybody, tell me what you know about forn.
• (Hold up one finger.) *Forn is a season.*
• (Hold up two fingers.) *Forn always comes after spring.*
4. (Repeat step 3 until firm.)
5. Everybody, tell me what forn is. Get ready. (Signal.) *Summer.*
6. (Repeat steps 3 and 5 until firm.)

WORKBOOK

EXERCISE 6   Sequence Sentence Writing

Clarabelle	little	chair	broke

1. Everybody, open your workbook to Lesson 120. Write your name. ✔

• You're going to write a sentence about each picture. The word box shows some of the words you may want to use in your sentences. Follow along as I read the words: **Clarabelle, little, chair, broke.**
2. Touch picture 1. ✔
• That shows what Clarabelle did. What did she do? (Call on a child. Ideas: *Sat on a little chair; Clarabelle sat down on a child's chair.*)
• Start with the name **Clarabelle** and say a sentence for picture 1. (Call on a child. Idea: *Clarabelle sat on a little chair.*)
• Everybody, write your sentence for picture 1. Pencils down when you're finished. (Observe children and give feedback.)
• (Call on individual children to read their sentence for picture 1.)
3. Touch picture 2. ✔
• That picture shows what happened to the chair. Start with the words **the chair** and tell what it did. (Call on a child. Ideas: *The chair fell apart. The chair broke.*)
• Write your sentence for picture 2. Start with the words **the chair.** Pencils down when you're finished. (Observe children and give feedback.)
• (Call on individual children to read their sentence for picture 2.)

EXERCISE 7   Questioning

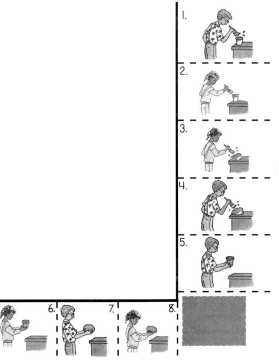

1. Everybody, find the next page. ✔
• We're going to play a question game with teams again. (Divide the class into four teams.)

2. Make a flap out of each picture. Cut carefully. Raise your hand when you're finished. (Observe children and give feedback.)

3. Now let's play the tough question game again. We'll see which teams can do it. Remember, if you're **really** smart, your team can find the mystery picture by asking only **three** questions. But they have to be **super** questions. You're working in teams. So your team has to agree on each question before the team asks it. Everybody on a team figures out which questions your team will ask. When your team has your first question, raise your hands and I'll come over. You'll whisper the question to me, so that none of the other teams can hear the question. I'll whisper the answer, and you'll fold over the pictures that could **not** be the mystery picture.

4. (**Key:** Target picture is 1—Paul painting a pot.)
   - You know your **first** question is good if you can fold over **four** pictures after I answer your first question. Remember, you're trying to find the mystery picture in only **three** questions. Raise your hand when your team has a good question.

   Answers:
   (Who is doing something?) Paul.
   (What is he doing?) Painting.
   (What is he painting?) A pot.
   (Do **not** combine answers, such as: **Painting** a **pot**.)

5. (After you answer each team's question, tell the team to fold over the pictures that could **not** be the mystery picture. Then ask them if that was a good question. Remind them by saying:) For a good first question, you can fold over four pictures.
   - (Then direct each team to agree on the next question. Tell them:) If it's a good question, you can fold over two pictures.
   - (Repeat the procedure for the third question:) If it's a good question, you'll know which picture is the mystery picture.

6. (After any team has found the mystery picture by asking only three questions, tell the class:) We have a winner. We have a team that found the mystery picture by asking only **three** questions.
   - (Call on a team member to say the three questions. Do not accept "combined" questions.)

7. Everybody, what's the number of the mystery picture? (Signal.) *One.*
   - Who is in that picture? (Signal.) *Paul.*
   - Listen: Paul is painting. What is Paul doing? (Signal.) *Painting.*
   - What is Paul painting? (Signal.) *A pot.*

8. (**Key:** The target picture is 8—Roxie holding a rock.)
   - We'll play the game again. Unfold each flap. This time I'm thinking of a different picture. Remember, here's how you know if your **first** question is good. If you can fold over **four** pictures after I answer your first question, it's a good question. If you can fold over only **one** picture, it's **not** a super good question. Remember, you're trying to find the mystery picture in only **three** questions. Raise your hands when your team has a good question.

9. (After any team has found the mystery picture by asking only three questions, tell the class:) We have a winner. We have a team that found the mystery picture by asking only **three** questions.
   - (Call on a team member to say the three questions. Do not accept "combined" questions.)

10. Everybody, what's the number of the mystery picture? (Signal.) *Eight.*
    - Who is in the picture? (Signal.) *Roxie.*
    - Roxie is holding something. That's what she is doing. Holding something. What is Roxie doing? (Signal.) *Holding something.*
    - What is she holding? (Signal.) *A rock.*

11. You figured out the mystery picture by working together and asking really good questions.

Objectives

- **Generate a sentence with past tense.** (Exercise 1)
- Generate questions to find a word's definition. (Exercise 2)
- Replace a word in a sentence with an opposite. (Exercise 3)
- Replace words in a sentence with appropriate contractions. (Exercise 4)
- Write sentences given picture cues. (Exercise 5)
- Read a word and write the opposite of that word. (Exercise 6)
- Construct verbal analogies. (Exercise 7)

EXERCISE 1   Verb Tense

1. I'll make a statement about a fire hydrant.
2. Listen: Next year the fire hydrant will be here. Everybody, say that statement. (Signal.) *Next year the fire hydrant will be here.*
3. Now make a statement about the fire hydrant last year. Get ready. (Signal.) *Last year the fire hydrant was here.*

EXERCISE 2   Questioning Skills

1. I'm going to tell a story. When you hear a word you don't know, say **stop.**
2. The man was very **fatigued.** (The children are to say *stop.*) Everybody, what word don't you know? (Signal.) *Fatigued.*
3. Ask the question about what the word fatigued means. Get ready. (Signal.) *What does the word fatigued mean?*
4. I'll tell you what fatigued means. Fatigued is a synonym for **tired.** What is fatigued a synonym for? (Signal.) *Tired.*
- If the man was fatigued, he was . . . (Signal.) *Tired.*
5. Here's more of the story.
6. So he decided to **recline.** (The children are to say *stop.*) Everybody, what word don't you know? (Signal.) *Recline.*
7. Ask the question about what the word recline means. Get ready. (Signal.) *What does the word recline mean?*
8. I'll tell you what recline means. Recline is a synonym for **lie down.** What is recline a synonym for? (Signal.) *Lie down.*
9. If the man was fatigued and decided to recline, he was tired and he decided to . . . (Signal.) *lie down.*
10. Here's more of the story.

11. But his bed **collapsed.** (The children are to say *stop.*) Everybody, what word don't you know? (Signal.) *Collapsed.*
12. Ask the question about what the word collapsed means. Get ready. (Signal.) *What does the word collapsed mean?*
13. I'll tell you what collapsed means. Collapsed is a synonym for **fell apart.** What is collapsed a synonym for? (Signal.) *Fell apart.*
14. If the man was fatigued and decided to recline, but his bed collapsed, he was tired and decided to lie down, but his bed . . . (Signal.) *fell apart.*
15. That's the end of the story.

EXERCISE 3   Opposites

1. I'm going to tell you a story. You have to know your opposites to follow this story.
2. There was a girl. Her stomach was the opposite of full. Everybody, what do you know about that girl's stomach? (Signal.) *It was empty.*
   Yes, the girl's stomach was empty.
3. The girl decided to eat some potatoes. The potatoes were the opposite of cooked. Everybody, what do you know about those potatoes? (Signal.) *They were raw.*
   Yes, the potatoes were raw.
4. The girl didn't like eating the raw potatoes. They tasted the opposite of good. Everybody, how did the raw potatoes taste? (Signal.) *Bad.*
   Yes, the raw potatoes tasted bad.
5. The girl kept eating the raw potatoes. She ate the opposite of fast. Everybody, what do you know about how the girl ate? (Signal.) *She ate slowly.*
   Yes, the girl ate slowly.
6. (Repeat steps 2 through 5 until firm.)

EXERCISE 4   Contractions

1. (Point to a boy.)
- Everybody, is he a boy? (Signal.) *Yes.*
- My turn to say the statement the new way. **He's a boy.**
- Everybody, say the statement the new way. Get ready. (Signal.) *He's a boy.*
2. It's time for some questions and statements.
- (Point to a girl.)
- Everybody, does she have three arms? (Signal.) *No.*
- My turn to say the statement the new way. She **doesn't** have three arms.
- Everybody, say the statement the new way. Get ready. (Signal.) *She doesn't have three arms.*
3. (Point to several children.)
- Everybody, do they have three arms? (Signal.) *No.*
- My turn to say the statement the new way. They **don't** have three arms.
- Everybody, say the statement the new way. Get ready. (Signal.) *They don't have three arms.*
4. Now let's see how fast you can go.
- (Point to a girl.)
- Does she have three arms? (Signal.) *No.*
- Say the statement the new way. Get ready. (Signal.) *She doesn't have three arms.*
5. (Point to several children.)
- Do they have three arms? (Signal.) *No.*
- Say the statement the new way. Get ready. (Signal.) *They don't have three arms.*
6. (Point to a boy.)
- Does he have three arms? (Signal.) *No.*
- Say the statement the new way. Get ready. (Signal.) *He doesn't have three arms.*

EXERCISE 5   Sentence Writing

near   cop

_____
_____
_____
_____

1. Everybody, open your workbook to Lesson 121. Write your name. ✔
- You're going to write sentences.
- Touch the picture of the fox and the rat. ✔
- The picture shows what the fox was near and what the rat was near. What was the fox near? (Signal.) *A cop.*
- What was the rat near? (Signal.) *A mop.*
2. Say the sentence for the fox. Get ready. (Signal.) *The fox was near a cop.*
- Say the sentence for the rat. Get ready. (Signal.) *The rat was near a mop.*
3. (Repeat step 2 until firm.)

4. The word box shows how to spell the words **near** and **cop.** You can figure out how to spell the other words.

5. Write the sentence for the fox. Pencils down when you're finished. ✔

• Now go to the next line and write the sentence for the rat. Pencils down when you're finished. ✔

6. (Call on individual children to read both their sentences.)

EXERCISE 6   Opposites

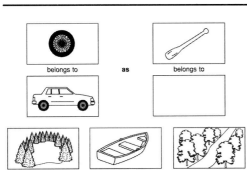

| quiet | shallow | cooked | short |

1. long _____
2. deep _____
3. loud _____
4. raw   _____

1. Everybody, find the next page. ✔
   (Hold up workbook. Point to top half.)
   Find the words in the box. ✔

• I'll read those words. Touch and follow along: **quiet, shallow, cooked, short.** ✔

2. Your turn. Touch the first word. ✔
   That word is **quiet.** What word? (Signal.) *Quiet.*

• Next word. ✔
   What word? (Signal.) *Shallow.*

• Next word. ✔
   What word? (Signal.) *Cooked.*

• Last word. ✔
   What word? (Signal.) *Short.*

• (Repeat step 2 until firm.)

3. You're going to write words that tell the opposite.

• Touch word 1. ✔

• That word is **long.** What word? (Signal.) *Long.*

• Everybody, what's the opposite of **long?** (Signal.) *Short.*

4. The word **short** is in the word box. Copy that word right after the word **long.** (Observe children and give feedback.)

5. (Repeat step 3 for word 2: **deep.**)
   (Repeat step 4 for **shallow.**)

6. (Repeat step 3 for word 3: **loud.**)
   (Repeat step 4 for **quiet.**)

7. (Repeat step 3 for word 4: **raw.**)
   (Repeat step 4 for **cooked.**)

EXERCISE 7   Analogies

1. (Hold up workbook. Point to bottom half.)

• The pictures show parts and the objects that have those parts.

2. Touch the wheel. ✔

• The picture that's right below shows what it belongs to. Everybody, what does a wheel belong to? (Signal.) *A car.*

• Tell me about a wheel. Get ready. (Signal.) *A wheel belongs to a car.*

3. Touch the oar. ✔

• Touch the picture that shows what it belongs to. ✔

• Everybody, what does an oar belong to? (Signal.) *A boat.*

• Tell me about an oar. Get ready. (Signal.) *An oar belongs to a boat.*

4. Tell me about a wheel. Get ready. (Signal.) *A wheel belongs to a car.*

• Tell me about an oar. Get ready. (Signal.) *An oar belongs to a boat.*

5. Say the whole analogy about a wheel and an oar. Get ready. (Signal.) *A wheel belongs to a car as an oar belongs to a boat.*

6. (Repeat step 5 until firm.)

7. Draw a line from the oar to the object it belongs to.
   (Observe children and give feedback.)

LESSON 122

EXERCISE 1 Synonyms/Opposites

1. Tell me if I name synonyms or opposites. Think big.
2. Listen: Laugh. Cry. Say those words. (Signal.) *Laugh. Cry.*
   - Do **laugh** and **cry** mean the same thing? (Signal.) *No.*
   - So are they synonyms or opposites? (Signal.) *Opposites.*
   - (Repeat step 2 until firm.)
3. Listen: Rough. Smooth. Say those words. (Signal.) *Rough. Smooth.*
   - Do **rough** and **smooth** mean the same thing? (Signal.) *No.*
   - So are they synonyms or opposites? (Signal.) *Opposites.*
   - (Repeat step 3 until firm.)
4. Listen: Fast. Quick. Say those words. (Signal.) *Fast. Quick.*
   - Do **fast** and **quick** mean the same thing? (Signal.) *Yes.*
   - So are they synonyms or opposites? (Signal.) *Synonyms.*
   - (Repeat step 4 until firm.)
5. (Repeat steps 2 through 4 until firm.)

EXERCISE 2 Verb Tense

1. Let's play a statement game.
2. This statement tells what the frog will do. Listen: The frog will jump.
   - What does that statement tell? Get ready. (Signal.) *What the frog will do.* Yes, what the frog will do.
   - (Repeat step 2 until firm.)

3. Everybody, say the statement that tells what the frog will do. Get ready. (Signal.) *The frog will jump.*
4. Now make up a statement that tells what the frog did. Get ready. (Signal.) *The frog jumped.*
5. Now make up a statement that tells what the frog is doing. Get ready. (Signal.) *The frog is jumping.*
6. (Repeat steps 3 through 5 until firm.)
7. Let's do one more.
8. This statement tells what the boy did. The boy walked.
   What does that statement tell? Get ready. (Signal.) *What the boy did.*
   Yes, what the boy did.
   - (Repeat step 8 until firm.)
9. Everybody, say the statement that tells what the boy did. Get ready. (Signal.) *The boy walked.*
10. Now make up a statement that tells what the boy will do. Get ready. (Signal.) *The boy will walk.*
11. Now make up a statement that tells what the boy is doing. Get ready. (Signal.) *The boy is walking.*
12. (Repeat steps 9 through 11 until firm.)

EXERCISE 3 Statements

1. Listen to this statement.
2. Yesterday Marsha climbed to the top of the tree. Everybody, say that statement. (Signal.) *Yesterday Marsha climbed to the top of the tree.*
3. Does that statement tell what Marsha did yesterday? (Signal.) *Yes.*
   - Does that statement tell if the tree is tall? (Signal.) *No.*

- Does that statement tell what Marsha will do tomorrow? (Signal.) *No.*
- Does that statement tell what Marsha is doing now? (Signal.) *No.*
- Does that statement tell if Marsha is wearing shoes? (Signal.) *No.*

4. Yesterday Marsha climbed to the top of the tree. Everybody, say that statement again. (Signal.) *Yesterday Marsha climbed to the top of the tree.*

5. Name three things the statement does not tell you. (Call on individual children. Repeat three correct responses.)

6. You have named three things the statement does not tell us.
- Name the first thing. (Hold up one finger.) (The children give the first response.)
- Name the second thing. (Hold up two fingers.) (The children give the second response.)
- Name the third thing. (Hold up three fingers.) (The children give the third response.)

EXERCISE 4   Opposites

1. I'm going to tell you a story. You have to know your opposites to follow this story.

2. There was a horse. It was the opposite of clean. Everybody, what do you know about that horse? (Signal.) *It was dirty.*
Yes, it was dirty.

3. This dirty horse met a dog. The dog was the opposite of slow. Everybody, what do you know about that dog? (Signal.) *It was fast.*
Yes, the dog was fast.

4. The fast dog started to chase the horse. It chased the horse to a stream that was the opposite of near. Everybody, what do you know about that stream? (Signal.) *It was far.*
Yes, that stream was far.

5. The dirty horse jumped over the stream but the dog didn't. The stream was the opposite of narrow. Everybody, what else do you know about that stream? (Signal.) *It was wide.*
Yes, the stream was wide.

6. (Repeat steps 2 through 5 until firm.)

7. Let's see what you remember about that story.

8. Everybody, tell me about the horse. (Signal.) *It was dirty.*
- Tell me about the dog. (Signal.) *It was fast.*
- Tell me where the stream was. (Signal.) *It was far.*
- Tell me how the stream looked. (Signal.) *It was wide.*
- (Repeat step 8 until firm.)

EXERCISE 5   Contractions

1. Listen: Some words are called contractions because they are really two words made into one.

2. Listen: Is not. The contraction is **isn't.**
Listen: Does not. The contraction is **doesn't.**
Listen: Cannot. The contraction is **can't.**
Listen: Are not. The contraction is **aren't.**
Listen: Did not. The contraction is **didn't.**
Listen: Do not. The contraction is **don't.**

3. You'll say sentences that don't have contractions and then say the same sentences with contractions.

4. Listen: They are not happy. Say it. (Signal.) *They are not happy.*
- Now say the statement with the contraction for **are not.** Get ready. (Signal.) *They aren't happy.*

5. Listen: They do not have money. Say that. (Signal.) *They do not have money.*
- Now say the statement with the contraction for **do not.** Get ready. (Signal.) *They don't have money.*

6. Listen: She cannot go with us. Say that. (Signal.) *She cannot go with us.*
- Now say the statement with the contraction for **cannot.** Get ready. (Signal.) *She can't go with us.*

7. (Repeat steps 4 through 6 until firm.)

EXERCISE 6 Sentence Writing

balls black boat white

1. Everybody, open your workbook to Lesson 122. Write your name. ✔
- You're going to write sentences.
- Touch the picture of the balls. ✔
- The picture shows what the black balls were in and what the white balls were in. What were the black balls in? (Signal.) *A van.*
- What were the white balls in? (Signal.) *A boat.*
2. Say the sentence for the black balls. Get ready. (Signal.) *The black balls were in a van.*
- Say the sentence for the white balls. Get ready. (Signal.) *The white balls were in a boat.*
3. (Repeat step 2 until firm.)
4. The word box shows how to spell the words **balls, black, boat** and **white.** You can figure out how to spell the other words.
5. Write the sentence for the black balls. Pencils down when you're finished. ✔
- Now go to the next line and write the sentence for the white balls. Pencils down when you're finished. ✔
6. (Call on individual children to read both their sentences.)

EXERCISE 7 Classification

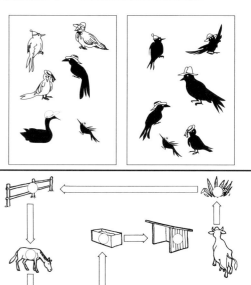

1. Everybody, find the next page. ✔ (Hold up workbook. Point to top half.) Touch the picture of the **smaller** class. ✔
- What kind of thing is that in the picture? (Call on a child. Accept *blackbirds* or *blackbirds with hats.*)
2. Everybody, circle the picture that shows the **larger** class. ✔
- What's the name of the larger class? (Call on a child. Accept *birds* or *birds with hats.*)
3. Everybody, touch the picture of the class that is **smaller.** ✔
- Each blackbird in that picture of the **smaller** class should be wearing a red hat. What color? (Signal.) *Red.*
- Mark a blackbird in that picture. ✔
4. Touch the picture that shows the **larger** class. ✔
- Each blackbird in that picture should be wearing a yellow hat. What color? (Signal.) *Yellow.*
- Mark a blackbird in that picture. ✔

EXERCISE 8 Map Reading

1. (Hold up workbook. Point to bottom half.) Everybody, touch the cow. ✔
2. This picture is a map of where the cow walked. You're going to color the arrows red and write the directions on the objects. Remember to start from the cow.
3. Everybody, color the first arrow red. Do it. ✔
- Now write the letter that shows the direction the cow walked. ✔
4. You'll do the rest of the arrows later.

Objectives

- **Generate sentences with past and future tense.** (Exercise 1)
- Identify a word based on its characteristics. (Exercise 2)
- Replace a word in a sentence with a synonym. (Exercise 3)
- Replace words in a sentence with appropriate contractions. (Exercise 4)
- Replace a word in a sentence with an opposite. (Exercise 5)
- **Use clues to identify objects referred to in familiar stories, and identify the character described in each clue.** (Exercise 6 & 7)

EXERCISE 1 Verb Tense

1. Let's play a statement game.
2. This statement tells what the airplane is doing. Listen: The airplane is moving. What does that statement tell? Get ready. (Signal.) *What the airplane is doing.* Yes, what the airplane is doing.
   - (Repeat step 2 until firm.)
3. Everybody, say the statement that tells what the airplane is doing. Get ready. (Signal.) *The airplane is moving.*
4. Now make up a statement that tells what the airplane did. Get ready. (Signal.) *The airplane moved.*
5. Now make up a statement that tells what the airplane will do. (Signal.) *The airplane will move.*
6. (Repeat steps 3 through 5 until firm.)
7. Let's do one more.
8. This statement tells what the kittens will do. Listen: The kittens will play. What does that statement tell? Get ready. (Signal.) *What the kittens will do.* Yes, what the kittens will do.
   - (Repeat step 8 until firm.)
9. Everybody, say the statement that tells what the kittens will do. Get ready. (Signal.) *The kittens will play.*
10. Now make up a statement that tells what the kittens did. Get ready. (Signal.) *The kittens played.*
11. Now make up a statement that tells what the kittens are doing. Get ready. (Signal.) *The kittens are playing.*
12. (Repeat steps 9 through 11 until firm.)

EXERCISE 2 Description

1. I'm going to say two things about something you know. See if you can figure out what I'm talking about.

2. (Hold up one finger.) Merlz is a word.
   - (Hold up two fingers.) Merlz is a synonym for feeling well.
3. Everybody, tell me what you know about merlz.
   - (Hold up one finger.) *Merlz is a word.*
   - (Hold up two fingers.) *Merlz is a synonym for feeling well.*
4. (Repeat step 3 until firm.)
5. Everybody, tell me what merlz is. Get ready. (Signal.) *Healthy.*
6. (Repeat steps 3 and 5 until firm.)
7. Here's another one.
8. (Hold up one finger.) A zast is a tool.
   - (Hold up two fingers.) A zast is made of wood, graphite, and rubber.
9. Everybody, tell me what you know about a zast.
   - (Hold up one finger.) *A zast is a tool.*
   - (Hold up two fingers.) *A zast is made of wood, graphite, and rubber.*
10. (Repeat step 9 until firm.)
11. Everybody, tell me what a zast is. Get ready. (Signal.) *A pencil.*
12. (Repeat steps 9 and 11 until firm.)

EXERCISE 3 Synonyms

1. What do we call two words that mean the same thing? (Signal.) *Synonyms.*
2. Listen: The class will finish at noon. Say that. (Signal.) *The class will finish at noon.*
   - Say that statement using a synonym for **finish.** Get ready. (Signal.) *The class will end at noon.*
   - (Repeat step 2 until firm.)

3. The class will finish at noon. The class will end at noon. Those statements mean the same thing because **finish** and **end** are synonyms.

4. Listen: The house is near town. Say that. (Signal.) *The house is near town.*
• Say that statement using a synonym for **near.** Get ready. (Signal.) *The house is close to town.*
• (Repeat step 4 until firm.)

5. Listen: The ring is bright. Say that. (Signal.) *The ring is bright.*
• Say that statement using a synonym for **bright.** Get ready. (Signal.) *The ring is shiny.*
• (Repeat step 5 until firm.)

EXERCISE 4 Contractions

1. You'll say statements with no contractions and then say the same statements with contractions.

2. Listen: They are not listening. Say that. (Signal.) *They are not listening.*
• Now say the statement with a contraction for **are not.** Get ready. (Signal.) *They aren't listening.*

3. Listen: I did not say anything. Say that. (Signal.) *I did not say anything.*
• Now say the statement with a contraction for **did not.** Get ready. (Signal.) *I didn't say anything.*

4. Listen: She is not going with us. Say that. (Signal.) *She is not going with us.*
• Now say the statement with a contraction for **is not.** Get ready. (Signal.) *She isn't going with us.*

5. (Repeat steps 2 through 4 until firm.)

EXERCISE 5 Opposites

1. Let's make up statements with the opposite word.

2. Listen: The baby is crying. Say that statement. (Signal.) *The baby is crying.*
• What's the opposite of crying? (Signal.) *Laughing.*

3. Now say a statement with the opposite of crying. Get ready. (Signal.) *The baby is laughing.*

4. (Repeat steps 2 and 3 until firm.)

5. Now let's make up some more statements.

6. Listen: The pond is deep. Say that statement. (Signal.) *The pond is deep.*
• What's the opposite of deep? (Signal.) *Shallow.*

7. Now say a statement with the opposite of deep. Get ready. (Signal.) *The pond is shallow.*

8. (Repeat steps 6 and 7 until firm.)

EXERCISE 6 Sentence Construction

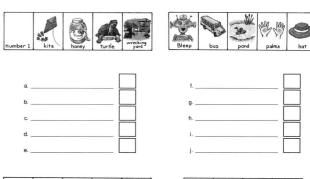

1. Everybody, open your workbook to Lesson 123. Write your name. ✔

2. We're going to do something very tricky today. I'll give you clues about different characters. You'll write the last word of each clue.

3. The boxes in the **top** row show all the answers. Touch the **top** row. ✔
• I'll read what it says for each box.
• Touch the first box. ✔
• The words are **number one.**
• Next box. The word is **kite.**
• Next box. The word is **honey.**
• Next box. The word is **turtle.**
• Next box. The words are **wrecking yard.**
• Next box. The word is **Bleep.**
• Next box. The word is **bus.**
• Next box. The word is **pond.**
• Next box. The word is **palms.**
• Last box. The word is **hat.**

4. Now you're going to write the **ending** of clue A. Touch line A. ✔
• Here's clue A: This character once went hunting for red butterflies, but ended up grabbing the tail of a **blank.**
• Write the name of **what** the character grabbed on line A. Don't write the name of the character. Raise your hand when you're finished.
(Observe children and give feedback.)

5. Here's clue B: This character once was puzzled when a bird moved his **blank.**
- Write the ending of that clue on line B. Raise your hand when you're finished. (Observe children but don't give feedback.)
6. Here's clue C: This character once told two women to go to a restaurant that wasn't really a restaurant at all, but was really a **blank.**
- Write the ending of that clue on line C. Raise your hand when you're finished. (Observe children.)
7. Here's clue D: A couple of times, this character went after little fish but ended up getting bitten by a **blank.**
- Write the ending of that clue on line D. Raise your hand when you're finished. (Observe children.)
8. Here's clue E: Once, this character was in a great race, but he didn't win the race. He ended up in a **blank.**
- Write the ending of that clue on line E. Raise your hand when you're finished. (Observe children.)
9. Here's clue F: People were always surprised because this character looked so mean but was really as sweet as **blank.**
- Write the ending of that clue on line F. Raise your hand when you're finished. (Observe children.)
10. Here's clue G: This character was very upset because she thought she was in last place and she went faster so she could be **blank.**
- Write the ending of that clue on line G. Raise your hand when you're finished. (Observe children.)
11. Here's clue H: This character once tried to go to school, but everybody was very unhappy when this character sat at the back of a **blank.**
- Write the ending of that clue on line H. Raise your hand when you're finished. (Observe children.)
12. Here's clue I: Once, this character invented a robot named **blank.**
- Write the ending of that clue on line I. Raise your hand when you're finished. (Observe children.)
13. Here's clue J: Once, this character figured out who picked the purple plums by seeing who had pink paint on their **blank.**
- Write the ending of that clue on line J. Raise your hand when you're finished. (Observe children.)

14. Now you're going to show which **character** each clue tells about.
- Touch the **box** at the end of line A. ✔
- We'll do this one together.
- I'll read clue A again. Listen: This character went hunting for red butterflies but ended up grabbing the tail of something. Everybody, which character did that? (Signal.) *Sweetie.*
- Look at Sweetie's picture at the **bottom** of the page. That picture has a number. Raise your hand when you've found the number in Sweetie's picture. ✔
- Everybody, what number is Sweetie? (Signal.) *Four.*
- So you write number **4** in the box at the end of line A. Do it. Raise your hand when you're finished. (Observe children and give feedback.)
15. Touch the box at the end of line B. ✔
- Here's clue B again: This character once was puzzled when a bird moved something of his.
- Find the character who was puzzled when a bird moved something of his. Look at the number of that character. Write the number in the box at the end of line B. Raise your hand when you're finished. (Observe children but don't give feedback.)
16. Touch the box at the end of line C. ✔
- Here's clue C again: This character once told two women to go to a restaurant that wasn't really a restaurant.
- Find the character who told two women to go to a restaurant that wasn't really a restaurant. Look at the number of that character. Write the number in the box at the end of line C. Raise your hand when you're finished. (Observe children.)
17. Touch the box at the end of line D. ✔
- Here's clue D again: A couple of times, this character went after little fish but ended up getting bitten by something that wasn't a fish.
- Find the character who went after little fish but ended up getting bitten by something that wasn't a fish. Look at the number of that character. Write the number in the box at the end of line D. Raise your hand when you're finished. (Observe children.)
18. Touch the box at the end of line E. ✔
- Here's clue E again: Once, this character was in a great race, but he didn't win the race. He ended up in something.

- Find the character who didn't win the race but ended up in something. Look at the number of that character. Write the number in the box at the end of line E. Raise your hand when you're finished.
  (Observe children.)

19. Touch the box at the end of line F. ✔
- Here's clue F again: People were always surprised because this character looked so mean but was really as sweet as something.
- Find the character who looked so mean but was really as sweet as something. Look at the number of that character. Write the number in the box at the end of line F. Raise your hand when you're finished.
  (Observe children.)

20. Touch the box at the end of line G. ✔
- Here's clue G again: This character was very upset because she thought she was in last place and she went faster so she could be something.
- Find the character who was upset because she thought she was in last place. Look at the number of that character. Write the number in the box at the end of line G. Raise your hand when you're finished.
  (Observe children.)

21. Touch the box at the end of line H. ✔
- Here's clue H again: This character once tried to go to school but made everybody unhappy when this character sat at the back of something.
- Find the character who tried to go to school. Look at the number of that character. Write the number in the box at the end of line H. Raise your hand when you're finished.
  (Observe children.)

22. Touch the box at the end of line I. ✔
- Here's clue I again: Once, this character invented a robot named something.
- Find the character who invented a robot. Look at the number of that character. Write the number in the box at the end of line I. Raise your hand when you're finished.
  (Observe children.)

23. Touch the box at the end of line J. ✔
  Here's clue J again: Once, this character figured out who picked the purple plums by seeing who had pink paint on their something.
- Find the character who figured out who picked the purple plums. Look at the number of that character. Write the number in the box at the end of line J. Raise your hand when you're finished.
  (Observe children.)

EXERCISE 7 Correcting Work

1. Now let's check our work. First you'll tell me the ending for a clue. Then you'll tell me the name and number for the character the clue tells about.

2. (Reread each clue. Ask the children to tell you the ending for the clue and the name and number for the character the clue tells about.)

Key:

Objectives

• Replace words in a sentence with appropriate contractions. (Exercise 1)
• **Generate sentences with past, present and future tense.** (Exercise 2)
• Identify a word based on its characteristics. (Exercise 3)
• Answer questions involving previously learned calendar facts. (Exercise 4)
• Write sentences given picture cues. (Exercise 5)
• Follow coloring rules involving classes and subclasses. (Exercise 6)
• Construct verbal analogies. (Exercise 7)

EXERCISE 1 Contractions

1. Here are some more contractions:
• We are. The contraction is we're.
• You are. The contraction is you're.
• She is. The contraction is she's.
• I will. The contraction is I'll.
• They are. The contraction is they're.
• I am. The contraction is I'm.
2. What's the contraction for I will? (Signal.) *I'll.*
3. What's the contraction for she is? (Signal.) *She's.*
4. What's the contraction for he is? (Signal.) *He's.*
5. What's the contraction for they are? (Signal.) *They're.*
6. What's the contraction for I am? (Signal.) *I'm.*
7. (Repeat steps 2 through 6 until firm.)
8. You're going to say sentences.
9. Listen: I am happy. Say that. (Signal.) *I am happy.*
• Now say the statement with a contraction for **I am.** Get ready. (Signal.) *I'm happy.*
10. Listen: It is nice outside. Say that. (Signal.) *It is nice outside.*
• Now say the statement with a contraction for **it is.** Get ready. (Signal.) *It's nice outside.*
11. Listen: You are not working. Say that. (Signal.) *You are not working.*
• Now say the statement with a contraction for **you are.** Get ready. (Signal.) *You're not working.*
12. Listen: They do not live here. Say that. (Signal.) *They do not live here.*
• Now say the statement with a contraction for **do not.** Get ready. (Signal.) *They don't live here.*

EXERCISE 2 Verb Tense

1. Let's play a statement game.
2. This statement tells what the trees did. Listen: The trees grew. What does that statement tell? (Signal.) *What the trees did.* Yes, what the trees did.
• (Repeat step 2 until firm.)
3. Everybody, say the statement that tells what the trees did. Get ready. (Signal.) *The trees grew.*
4. Now make up a statement that tells what the trees will do. Get ready. (Signal.) *The trees will grow.*
5. Now make up a statement that tells what the trees are doing. Get ready. (Signal.) *The trees are growing.*
6. (Repeat steps 3 through 5 until firm.)
7. Let's do one more.
8. This statement tells what the car is doing. The car is starting. What does that statement tell? (Signal.) *What the car is doing.* Yes, what the car is doing.
• (Repeat step 8 until firm.)
9. Everybody, say the statement that tells what the car is doing. Get ready. (Signal.) *The car is starting.*
10. Now make up a statement that tells what the car did. Get ready. (Signal.) *The car started.*
11. Now make up a statement that tells what the car will do. Get ready. (Signal.) *The car will start.*
12. (Repeat steps 9 through 11 until firm.)

EXERCISE 3   Description

1. I'm going to say two things about something you know. See if you can figure out what I'm talking about.
2. (Hold up one finger.) Garf is a word.
- (Hold up two fingers.) Garf is the opposite of noisy.
3. Everybody, tell me what you know about garf.
- (Hold up one finger.) *Garf is a word.*
- (Hold up two fingers.) *Garf is the opposite of noisy.*
4. (Repeat step 3 until firm.)
5. Everybody, tell me what garf is. Get ready. (Signal.) *Quiet.*
6. (Repeat step 3 and 5 until firm.)
7. Here's another one.
8. (Hold up one finger.) A chock is a tool that is made of wood.
- (Hold up two fingers.) A chock is used to measure how long something is.
9. Everybody, tell me what you know about a chock.
- (Hold up one finger.) *A chock is a tool that is made of wood.*
- (Hold up two fingers.) *A chock is used to measure how long something is.*
10. (Repeat step 9 until firm.)
11. Everybody, tell me what a chock is. Get ready. (Signal.) *A ruler.*
12. (Repeat steps 9 and 11 until firm.)

EXERCISE 4   Calendar Facts

1. It's time for calendar facts.

2. How many months are in a year? (Signal.) *12.*
- Name the 12 months of the year. Get ready. (Signal.) *January, February, March, April, May, June, July, August, September, October, November, December.*
3. How many seasons are in a year? (Signal.) *Four.*
- Say the seasons of the year. Get ready. (Signal.) *Winter, spring, summer, fall.*
4. How many days does February usually have? Get ready. (Signal.) *Twenty-eight.*
5. How many days are there in a week? (Signal.) *Seven.*
- Name the days of the week. Get ready. (Signal.) *Sunday, Monday, Tuesday, Wednesday, Thursday, Friday, Saturday.*
6. How many weeks are in a year? (Signal.) *52.*
7. How many days do most months have? (Signal.) *Thirty-one.*
8. How many days are there in a year? (Signal.) *365.*
9. Tell me what day it is today. Get ready. (Signal.)
- Tell me what day it was yesterday. Get ready. (Signal.)
- Tell me what day it will be tomorrow. Get ready. (Signal.)
10. (Repeat steps 2 through 9 until firm.)

WORKBOOK

EXERCISE 5   Sentence Writing

1. Everybody, open your workbook to Lesson 124. Write your name. ✔
- You're going to write sentences about this picture.
- Touch the picture of the cat and the cow. ✔
- The picture shows what the cat licked and what the cow licked. What did the cat lick? (Signal.) *A hand.*
- What did the cow lick? (Signal.) *An ear.*

2. Say the sentence for the cat. Get ready. (Signal.) *The cat licked a hand.*
- Say the sentence for the cow. Get ready. (Signal.) *The cow licked an ear.*
3. (Repeat step 2 until firm.)
4. The word box shows how to spell the words **licked, ear** and **cow.** You can figure out how to spell the other words.
5. Write the sentence for the cat. Pencils down when you're finished. ✔
- Now go to the next line and write the sentence for the cow. Pencils down when you're finished. ✔
6. (Call on individual children to read both their sentences.)

EXERCISE 6 Classification

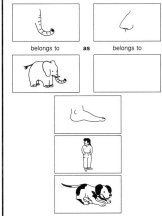

1. Everybody, find the next page. ✔
- (Hold up workbook. Point to first half.) Touch the picture of the **smaller** class. ✔
- What kind of thing is that in the picture? (Signal.) *Giraffes.*
2. Everybody, circle the picture that shows the **larger** class. ✔
- Everybody, what's the name of the **larger** class? (Signal.) *Living things.*

3. Everybody, touch the picture of the class that is **smaller.** ✔
- The giraffes in that picture of the **smaller** class should be orange and black. What colors? (Signal.) *Orange and black.*
- Mark a giraffe in that picture. ✔
4. Touch the picture that shows the **larger** class. ✔
- The giraffes in that picture should be yellow and black. What colors? (Signal.) *Yellow and black.*
- Mark a giraffe in that picture. ✔

EXERCISE 7 Analogies

1. (Hold up workbook. Point to second half.)
- The pictures show parts and the objects that have those parts.
2. Touch the trunk. ✔
- The picture that's right below shows what it belongs to. Everybody, what does a trunk belong to? (Signal.) *An elephant.*
- Tell me about a trunk. Get ready. (Signal.) *A trunk belongs to an elephant.*
3. Touch the nose. ✔
- Touch the picture that shows what a nose belongs to. ✔
- Everybody, what does a nose belong to? (Signal.) *A person.*
- Tell me about a nose. Get ready. (Signal.) *A nose belongs to a person.*
4. Tell me about a trunk. Get ready. (Signal.) *A trunk belongs to an elephant.*
- Tell me about a nose. Get ready. (Signal.) *A nose belongs to a person.*
5. Say the whole analogy about a trunk and a nose. Get ready. (Signal.) *A trunk belongs to an elephant as a nose belongs to a person.*
6. (Repeat step 5 until firm.)
7. Draw a line from the nose to the object it belongs to.
   (Observe children and give feedback.)

LESSON 125

Objectives

- Name things that a statement does NOT tell. (Exercise 1)
- Identify words based on characteristics. (Exercise 2)
- Replace a word in a sentence with an opposite. (Exercise 3)
- Identify absurdities. (Exercise 4)
- Write sequence sentences given picture cues. (Exercise 5)
- Read a word and write the opposite of that word. (Exercise 6)
- Write class names next to members of the class. (Exercise 7)

EXERCISE 1 Statements

1. Listen to this statement.
2. The boy has peanut butter on his chin. Everybody, say that statement. (Signal.) *The boy has peanut butter on his chin.*
3. Does that statement tell what the boy has on his chin? (Signal.) *Yes.*
- Does that statement tell what the boy will have on his chin tomorrow? (Signal.) *No.*
- Does that statement tell if the boy is wearing gloves? (Signal.) *No.*
- Does that statement tell if the boy likes peanut butter? (Signal.) *No.*
4. The boy has peanut butter on his chin. Say that statement again. (Signal.) *The boy has peanut butter on his chin.*
5. Name three things the statement does not tell you. (Call on individual children. Repeat three correct responses.)
6. You have named three things the statement does not tell us.
- Name the first thing. (Hold up one finger.) (The children give the first response.)
- Name the second thing. (Hold up two fingers.) (The children give the second response.)
- Name the third thing. (Hold up three fingers.) (The children give the third response.)
- (Repeat step 6 until all children can name the three things in order.)

EXERCISE 2 Description

1. I'm going to say two things about something you know. See if you can figure out what I'm talking about.
2. (Hold up one finger.) Sloom is the name of a class.
- (Hold up two fingers.) You put on sloom every morning.
3. Everybody, tell me what you know about sloom.
- (Hold up one finger.) *Sloom is the name of a class.*
- (Hold up two fingers.) *You put on sloom every morning.*
4. (Repeat step 3 until firm.)
5. Everybody, tell me what sloom is. Get ready. (Signal.) *Clothing.*
6. (Repeat steps 3 and 5 until firm.)

EXERCISE 3 Opposites

1. I'm going to tell you a story. You have to know your opposites to follow this story.
2. There was a boy. He was the opposite of clean. Everybody, what do you know about that boy? (Signal.) *He was dirty.* Yes, the boy was dirty.
3. Some other boys always bothered the dirty boy. Those other boys were the opposite of quiet. What do you know about the other boys? (Call on a child. Accept *loud,* but use: *They were noisy.*) Yes, the other boys were noisy.
4. The dirty boy always fought with the noisy boys. He would always do the opposite of win. Everybody, what do you know about what the dirty boy would do? (Signal.) *He would lose.* Yes, the dirty boy would lose.
5. One day the dirty boy saw the noisy boys playing in the mud. He did the opposite of cry. Everybody, what did the dirty boy do? (Signal.) *He laughed.* Yes, the dirty boy laughed.
6. He laughed because those boys were the opposite of clean. Everybody, what do you know about those boys? (Signal.) *They were dirty.* Yes, they were dirty.
7. (Repeat steps 2 through 6 until firm.)

8. Let's see what you remember about that story.

9. Everybody, tell me how the boy looked. (Signal.) *Dirty.*

- Tell me what the dirty boy would do when the boys fought. (Signal.) *Lose.*

- Tell me what the dirty boy did when he saw the noisy boys in the mud. (Signal.) *Laughed.*

- Tell me how the noisy boys looked. (Signal.) *Dirty.*

- (Repeat step 9 until firm.)

EXERCISE 4 Absurdity

1. Listen to this story and tell me what's absurd about it.

2. The shortest girl in the family is taller than her sister. Say the statement. Get ready. (Signal.) *The shortest girl in the family is taller than her sister.*

3. What's absurd about that statement? (Call on a child.) (Praise all reasonable responses; then say:) Yes, the shortest girl in the family can't be taller than her sister.

4. Here's another absurd statement.

5. Listen: Figure out what's absurd about this one. The slowest runner won the race. Say the statement. (Signal.) *The slowest runner won the race.*

6. What's absurd about that statement? (Call on a child.) (Praise all reasonable responses; then say:) Yes, the slowest runner can't win the race.

EXERCISE 5 Sequence Sentence Writing

| Sweetie | Andrea | Honey | bit | chased |

1. Everybody, open your workbook to Lesson 125. Write your name. ✔

- These pictures show what Sweetie did and what Honey did. You're going to write a sentence about each picture. The word box shows some of the words you may want to use in your sentences. Follow along as I read the words: **Sweetie, Andrea, Honey, bit, chased.**

2. Touch picture 1. ✔

- That shows what Sweetie did. What did he do? (Call on a child. Idea: *Chased Andrea.*)

- Start with the name **Sweetie** and say a sentence for picture 1. (Call on a child. Idea: *Sweetie chased Andrea.*)

- Everybody, write your sentence for picture 1. Pencils down when you're finished. (Observe children and give feedback.)

- (Call on individual children to read their sentence for picture 1.)

3. Touch picture 2. ✔

- The picture shows what Honey did. What did she do? (Call on a child. Idea: *Bit Sweetie's tail.*)

- Start with the name **Honey** and tell what she did. (Call on a child. Idea: *Honey bit Sweetie's tail.*)

- Write your sentence for picture 2. Start with the words **So Honey** and tell what she did. Pencils down when you're finished. (Observe children and give feedback.)

- (Call on individual children to read their sentence for picture 2. Idea: *So Honey bit Sweetie's tail.*)

EXERCISE 6 Opposites

wide	shiny	pull	short	long

1. tall _____

2. push _____

3. narrow _____

4. dull _____

5. short _____

---

containers	numbers	tools

jar _____	six _____
saw _____	bag _____
ten _____	rake _____
cup _____	three _____
mop _____	nine _____

1. Everybody, find the next page.
   (Hold up workbook. Point to top half.) Find the words in the box at the top of your worksheet. ✔
   • I'll read those words. Touch and follow along: **wide, shiny, pull, short, long.** ✔
2. Your turn. Touch the first word. ✔
   • What word? (Signal.) *Wide.*
   • Next word. ✔
   • What word? (Signal.) *Shiny.*
   • Next word. ✔
   • What word? (Signal.) *Pull.*
   • Next word. ✔
   • What word? (Signal.) *Short.*
   • Last word. ✔
   • What word? (Signal.) *Long.*
   • (Repeat step 2 until firm.)

3. You're going to write words that tell the opposite.
   • Touch word 1. ✔
   • That word is **tall.** What word? (Signal.) *Tall.*
   • Everybody, what's the opposite of **tall?** (Signal.) *Short.*
4. The word **short** is in the word box. Copy that word right after the word **tall.** (Observe children and give feedback.)
5. (Repeat step 3 for word 2: **push.**)
   • (Repeat step 4 for **pull.**)
6. (Repeat step 3 for word 3: **narrow.**)
   • (Repeat step 4 for **wide.**)
7. (Repeat step 3 for word 4: **dull.**)
   • (Repeat step 4 for **shiny.**)
8. (Repeat step 3 for word 5: **short.**)
   • Which word in the box is the opposite of **short?** (Signal.) *Long.*
   • Copy that word right after the word **short.**

EXERCISE 7 Classification

1. (Hold up workbook. Point to bottom half.) Everybody, I'll read the words in the box for the bottom part. You touch the words.
   • First word: containers. ✔
   • Next word: numbers. ✔
   • Last word: tools. ✔
2. Your turn to read the words in the box.
   • First word. What word? (Signal.) *Containers.*
   • Next word. What word? (Signal.) *Numbers.*
   • Last word. What word? (Signal.) *Tools.*
   • Yes, containers, numbers, and tools.
3. Everybody, put your finger under the word **jar.** ✔
   • What word? (Signal.) *Jar.*
   • Is a **jar** in the class of containers, in the class of numbers, or in the class of tools? (Signal.) *Containers.*

- Copy the word **containers** next to the word **jar.**
  (Observe children and give feedback.)
- Read what you wrote. (Signal.) *Containers.*
4. Everybody, put your finger under the next word. ✔
- That word is **saw.** What word? (Signal.) *Saw.*
- Is a **saw** in the class of containers, in the class of numbers, or in the class of tools? (Signal.) *Tools.*
- Copy the word **tools** next to the word **saw.**
  (Observe children and give feedback.)
- Read what you wrote. (Signal.) *Tools.*
5. Everybody, put your finger under the next word. ✔
- What word? (Signal.) *Ten.*
- Is **ten** in the class of containers, in the class of numbers, or in the class of tools? (Signal.) *Numbers.*

- Copy the word **numbers** next to the word **ten.**
  (Observe children and give feedback.)
- Read what you wrote. (Signal.) *Numbers.*
6. Everybody, put your finger under the word **cup.** ✔
- What word? (Signal.) *Cup.*
- Next word. What word? (Signal.) *Mop.*
- Next word. What word? (Signal.) *Six.*
- Next word. What word? (Signal.) *Bag.*
- Next word. What word? (Signal.) *Rake.*
- Next word. What word? (Signal.) *Three.*
- Next word. What word? (Signal.) *Nine.*
7. (Repeat step 6 until firm.)
8. Later you can write the class that goes with each word you just read.

Objectives

- **Generate sentences with contractions.** (Exercise 1)
- Follow directions involving if-then. (Exercise 2)
- Identify a word based on its characteristics. (Exercise 3)
- Apply narrowing criteria to guess a mystery object. (Exercise 4)
- Write sentences given picture cues. (Exercise 5)
- Read a word and write the opposite of that word. (Exercise 6)
- Label cardinal directions on a map. (Exercise 7)

EXERCISE 1 Contractions

1. You're going to make up statements that have contractions.
2. (Point to a boy.)
- Everybody, is he wearing a mask? (Signal.) *No.*
- Say the statement with a contraction for **is not.** Get ready. (Signal.) *He isn't wearing a mask.*
3. (Point to several children.)
- Are they wearing masks? (Signal.) *No.*
- Say the statement with a contraction for **are not.** Get ready. (Signal.) *They aren't wearing masks.*
4. (Point to two boys.)
- Are they wearing masks? (Signal.) *No.*
- Say the statement with a contraction for **are not.** Get ready. (Signal.) *They aren't wearing masks.*
5. (Point to one girl.)
- Is she wearing a mask? (Signal.) *No.*
- Say the statement with a contraction for **is not.** Get ready. (Signal.) *She isn't wearing a mask.*
6. (Point to everybody.)
- Are we wearing masks? (Signal.) *No.*
- Say the statement with a contraction for **are not.** Get ready. (Signal.) *We aren't wearing masks.*
7. (Repeat steps 2 through 6 until firm.)

EXERCISE 2 Actions

1. We're going to play an action game.

2. Listen to this rule. If the teacher claps and stamps a foot, stand up. Listen again. If the teacher claps and stamps a foot, stand up.
- Everybody, say the rule with me. Get ready. (Signal.) *If the teacher claps and stamps a foot, stand up.*
  All by yourselves. Get ready. (Signal.) *If the teacher claps and stamps a foot, stand up.*
- (Repeat step 2 until firm.)
3. What's the rule? (Signal.) *If the teacher claps and stamps a foot, stand up.*
- Tell me, what are you going to do if the teacher claps and stamps a foot? (Signal.) *Stand up.*
4. Are you going to stand up if the teacher claps? (Signal.) *No.*
- Are you going to stand up if the teacher stamps a foot? (Signal.) *No.*
- Are you going to stand up if the teacher claps and stamps a foot? (Signal.) *Yes.*
5. What's the rule? (Signal.) *If the teacher claps and stamps a foot, stand up.*
6. Let's see if I can fool you. Get ready. (Pause, stand up.) (Signal.) (The children should not do anything.) (Sit down.)
7. See if I can fool you. Get ready. (Pause, clap and stamp your foot.) (Signal.) (Every child should stand up.)
- Good, sit down.
8. See if I can fool you this time. Get ready. (Pause, stamp your foot.) (Signal.) (The children should not do anything.)
9. (Repeat steps 6 through 8 until firm.)

EXERCISE 3   Description

1. I'm going to say two things about something you know. See if you can figure out what I'm talking about.
2. (Hold up one finger.) Tast is a day of the week.
- (Hold up two fingers.) Tast always comes after Wednesday.
3. Everybody, tell me what you know about Tast.
- (Hold up one finger.) *Tast is a day of the week.*
- (Hold up two fingers.) *Tast always comes after Wednesday.*
4. (Repeat step 3 until firm.)
5. Everybody, tell me what Tast is. Get ready. (Signal.) *Thursday.*
6. (Repeat steps 3 and 5 until firm.)
7. Here's another one.
8. (Hold up one finger.) Proot is a word.
- (Hold up two fingers.) Proot is the opposite of fat.
9. Everybody, tell me what you know about proot.
- (Hold up one finger.) *Proot is a word.*
- (Hold up two fingers.) *Proot is the opposite of fat.*
10. (Repeat step 9 until firm.)
11. Everybody, tell me what proot is. Get ready. (Signal.) *Skinny.*
12. (Repeat steps 9 and 11 until firm.)

EXERCISE 4   Description

1. Get ready to play detective and find out what object I'm thinking of. I'll give you two clues.
2. (Hold up one finger.) It's an animal.
   (Hold up two fingers.) It's a pet.
3. Say the two things we know about the object.
   (Hold up one finger.) *It's an animal.*
   (Hold up two fingers.) *It's a pet.*
- (Repeat step 3 until firm.)
4. Those clues don't tell you enough to find the right animal. They could tell you about a lot of animals. See how many animals you can name that are pets. (Call on individual children. The group is to name at least three animals that are pets, such as *a cat, a dog,* and *a bird.*)
5. Here's another clue for finding the right object.
6. Listen: It sharpens its claws on your furniture. Everybody, say that. (Signal.) *It sharpens its claws on your furniture.*

7. Now here are the three things we know about the object.
   (Hold up one finger.) It's an animal.
   (Hold up two fingers.) It's a pet.
   (Hold up three fingers.) It sharpens its claws on your furniture.
8. Everybody, say all the things we know.
   (Hold up one finger.) *It's an animal.*
   (Hold up two fingers.) *It's a pet.*
   (Hold up three fingers.) *It sharpens its claws on your furniture.*
9. Everybody, tell me what animal I am thinking of. Get ready. (Signal.) *A cat.*
   Yes, a cat.

EXERCISE 5   Sentence Writing

black   white

_____

_____

_____

_____

1. Everybody, open your workbook to Lesson 126. Write your name. ✔
- You're going to write sentences about this picture.
- Touch the picture of the toad and the bird. ✔
- The picture shows what will go in the white car and what will go in the black car. What will go in the white car? (Signal.) *A toad.*
- What will go in the black car? (Signal.) *A bird.*
2. Say the sentence that tells what will go in the white car. Get ready. (Signal.) *The toad will go in the white car.*
- Say the sentence that tells what will go in the black car. Get ready. (Signal.) *The bird will go in the black car.*
3. (Repeat step 2 until firm.)

4. The word box shows how to spell the words **black** and **white.** You can figure out how to spell the other words.

5. Write the sentence for the toad. Pencils down when you're finished. ✔
   • Now go to the next line and write the sentence for the bird. Pencils down when you're finished. ✔

6. (Call on individual children to read both their sentences.)

EXERCISE 6 **Opposites**

cry	short	difficult	wide	dark

1. easy _____
2. laugh _____
3. light _____
4. narrow _____
5. tall _____

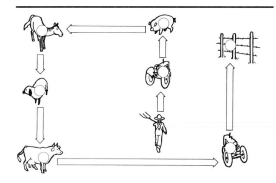

1. Everybody, find the next page. ✔
   (Hold up workbook. Point to top half.)
   • Find the words in the box. ✔
   • I'll read those words. Touch and follow along: **cry, short, difficult, wide, dark.** ✔

2. Your turn. Touch the first word. ✔
   What word? (Signal.) *Cry.*
   • Next word. ✔
   What word? (Signal.) *Short.*
   • Next word. ✔
   What word? (Signal.) *Difficult.*
   • Next word. ✔
   What word? (Signal.) *Wide.*
   • Last word. ✔
   What word? (Signal.) *Dark.*
   • (Repeat step 2 until firm.)

3. You're going to write words that tell the opposite.

4. Touch word 1. ✔
   • That word is **easy.** What word? (Signal.) *Easy.*
   • Everybody, what word in the box is the opposite of **easy?** (Signal.) *Difficult.*

5. Copy the word **difficult** right after the word **easy.**
   (Observe children and give feedback.)

6. (Repeat step 4 for word 2: **laugh.**)
   • (Repeat step 5 for **cry.**)

7. (Repeat step 4 for word 3: **light.**)
   • (Repeat step 5 for **dark.**)

8. (Repeat step 4 for word 4: **narrow.**)
   • (Repeat step 5 for **wide.**)

9. (Repeat step 4 for word 5: **tall.**)
   • (Repeat step 5 for **short.**)

EXERCISE 7 **Map Reading**

1. (Hold up workbook. Point to bottom half.)
   Everybody, touch the farmer. ✔

2. This picture is a map of where the farmer walked. You're going to color the arrows blue and write the directions on the objects. Remember to start from the farmer.

3. Everybody, color the first arrow blue. Do it. ✔
   • Now write the letter that shows the direction the farmer walked. ✔

4. You'll do the rest of the arrows later.

Objectives

- Generate sentences with contractions. (Exercise 1)
- Identify words based on characteristics. (Exercise 2)
- Generate questions to find a word's definition. (Exercise 3)
- Listen to a short story and answer questions involving "who," "when," "why," "where" and "what". (Exercise 4)
- Identify absurdities. (Exercise 5)
- Cooperatively generate an ending for a story. (Exercise 6)
- Draw pictures to retell a story. (Exercise 7)

EXERCISE 1 Contractions

1. It's time for some questions and statements.
2. (Point to three windows.)
- Do they have feet? (Signal.) *No.*
- Say the statement with a contraction. Get ready. (Signal.) *They don't have feet.*
3. (Point to a window.)
- Does a window have feet? (Signal.) *No.*
- Say the statement. Get ready. (Signal.) *A window doesn't have feet.*
4. (Point to a door.)
- Does a door have feet? (Signal.) *No.*
- Say the statement. Get ready. (Signal.) *A door doesn't have feet.*
5. (Point to a girl.)
- Is she washing her hair? (Signal.) *No.*
- Say the statement with a contraction for **is not.** Get ready. (Signal.) *She isn't washing her hair.*
6. (Point to yourself.)
- Am I washing my hair? (Signal.) *No.*
- Say the statement with a contraction. Get ready. (Signal.) *You aren't washing your hair.*
7. (Point to two girls.)
- Are they washing their hair? (Signal.) *No.*
- Say the statement with a contraction for **are not.** Get ready. (Signal.) *They aren't washing their hair.*
8. (Point to everybody.)
- Are we washing our hair? (Signal.) *No.*
- Say the statement with a contraction for **are not.** Get ready. (Signal.) *We aren't washing our hair.*
9. (Point to a boy.)
- Is he washing his hair? (Signal.) *No.*
- Say the statement with a contraction for **is not.** Get ready. (Signal.) *He isn't washing his hair.*
10. (Repeat steps 6 through 9 until firm.)

EXERCISE 2 Description

1. I'm going to say two things about something you know. See if you can figure out what I'm talking about.
2. (Hold up one finger.) Bafe is a holiday.
- (Hold up two fingers.) There are parades and fireworks on Bafe.
3. Everybody, tell me what you know about Bafe.
- (Hold up one finger.) *Bafe is a holiday.*
- (Hold up two fingers.) *There are parades and fireworks on Bafe.*
4. (Repeat step 3 until firm.)
5. Tell me what Bafe is. Get ready. (Call on a child. Idea: *the Fourth of July.*)
6. (Repeat steps 3 and 5 until firm.)
7. Here's another one.
8. (Hold up one finger.) A dast is found in a house.
- (Hold up two fingers.) A dast is used to sweep the floor.
9. Everybody, tell me what you know about a dast.
- (Hold up one finger.) *A dast is found in a house.*
- (Hold up two fingers.) *A dast is used to sweep the floor.*
10. (Repeat step 9 until firm.)
11. Everybody, tell me what a dast is. Get ready. (Signal.) *A broom.*
12. (Repeat steps 9 and 11 until firm.)

EXERCISE 3 Questioning Skills

1. I'm going to tell a story. When you hear a word you don't know, say **stop.**
2. In front of the school there was a **banner.** (The children are to say *stop.*) Everybody, what word don't you know? (Signal.) *Banner.*
3. Ask the question about what the word banner means. Get ready. (Signal.) *What does the word banner mean?*
4. I'll tell you what banner means. Banner is a synonym for **flag.** What is banner a synonym for? (Signal.) *Flag.*
• If in front of the school there was a banner, there was a . . . (Signal.) *flag.*
5. Here's more of the story.
6. The banner was **ancient.** (The children are to say *stop.*) Everybody, what word don't you know? (Signal.) *Ancient.*
7. Ask the question about what the word ancient means. Get ready. (Signal.) *What does the word ancient mean?*
8. I'll tell you what ancient means. Ancient is a synonym for **old.** What is ancient a synonym for? (Signal.) *Old.*
9. If in front of the school there was a banner and the banner was ancient, there was a flag and it was . . . (Signal.) *old.*
10. Here's more of the story.
11. But its colors were still **vivid.** (The children are to say *stop.*) Everybody, what word don't you know? (Signal.) *Vivid.*
12. Ask the question about what the word vivid means. Get ready. (Signal.) *What does the word vivid mean?*
13. I'll tell you what vivid means. Vivid is a synonym for **bright.** What is vivid a synonym for? (Signal.) *Bright.*
14. If there was a banner and the banner was ancient but its colors were still vivid, then there was a flag and the flag was old but its colors were still . . . (Signal.) *bright.*
15. That's the end of the story.

EXERCISE 4 Who—What—When—Where—Why

1. Listen to this story.
• It was early in the morning. The frog jumped into the pond. The water was cold, so he jumped out. Then he saw a turtle. The turtle said, "I like cold water."
• (Repeat the story.)
2. Tell where the frog jumped first. (Signal.) *Into the pond.*
• Tell when the frog jumped into the pond. (Signal.) *Early in the morning.*
• Tell why the frog jumped out of the pond. (Signal.) *The water was cold.*
• Tell what the frog saw. (Signal.) *A turtle.*
• Tell what the turtle said. (Signal.) *"I like cold water."*
• (Repeat step 2 until firm.)

EXERCISE 5 Absurdity

1. Listen to this statement and figure out what is absurd about it.
2. A boy was three years older than his mother. Say the statement. (Signal.) *A boy was three years older than his mother.*
3. What's absurd about that statement? (Call on one child.) (Praise all reasonable responses; then say:) Yes, a boy can't be older than his mother.
4. Here's another absurd statement.
5. Listen: Figure out what's absurd about this one. The oldest person in my family is almost as old as my grandfather. Say the statement. (Signal.) *The oldest person in my family is almost as old as my grandfather.*
6. What's absurd about that statement? (Call on one child.) (Praise all reasonable responses; then say:) Yes, the oldest person in my family can't be younger than my grandfather.

EXERCISE 6   The Mystery Of Roger's Favorite Hat

Story Completion

1. You're going to work in teams again and figure out the ending to a story. I'll tell the first part. Then your team will figure out a good ending. (Assign children to teams.)

• Here's an important clue about the ending: This story is about why Roger couldn't find his very favorite hat. Remember, that's what this story is about. So your ending will have to explain why Roger couldn't find his very favorite hat.

2. Here's the story:

> Roger had many favorite hats. But his most favorite was a big black hat. One day, he put on that hat and went out for a walk. The day was very hot and Roger started to sweat.
>
> Roger didn't want to sweat all over his very favorite hat. So he took off his hat and put it under a bench that was next to a house. Roger planned to finish his walk without his hat, come back to the bench, pick up his black hat and go back home.
>
> What Roger didn't know was that the bench was next to Paul's house, and that Paul planned to paint that bench pink. Roger also didn't know that when Paul painted things, he plopped paint on things that were nearby.
>
> So, while Roger was on his walk, Paul came out and . . .

• And that's as far as the story goes.

3. Listen: Make up a good ending. Now remember, this story is about why Roger couldn't find his very favorite hat. So you'll have to explain that with your ending.

• Talk about your ending with your teammates, but remember to whisper. Don't let the members of the other teams hear what you're saying. Raise your hands when your team has a really good ending. (Observe children and give feedback.)

4. (Call on a team member from each team to tell their ending. Praise appropriate endings.)

EXERCISE 7   Workbook Activity

> 1. Roger had many favorite hats. But his most favorite was a big black hat. One day, he put on that hat and went out for a walk. The day was very hot and Roger started to sweat.
>
> 2. Roger didn't want to sweat all over his very favorite hat. So he took off his hat and put it under a bench that was next to a house. Roger planned to finish his walk without his hat, come back to the bench, pick up his black hat and go back home.
>
> 3. What Roger didn't know was that the bench was next to Paul's house and that Paul planned to paint that bench pink. Roger also didn't know that when Paul painted things, he plopped paint on things that were nearby.
>
> 4. So, while Roger was on his walk, Paul came out and

1. Everybody, open your workbook to Lesson 127. Write your name. ✔

• Here's the whole story I just read.

2. The first part of the story tells what you'll draw in box 1. Listen to that part and remember what you're going to draw in box 1.

• Touch the first word of the story and follow along. ✔

• (Read paragraph 1 at a reasonably slow pace:)

> Roger had many favorite hats. But his most favorite was a big black hat. One day, he put on that hat and went out for a walk. The day was very hot and Roger started to sweat.

• So for picture 1, you'll show that part of the story: Roger taking a walk, wearing his favorite big black hat and starting to sweat.

3. The next part of the story tells what you'll draw in box 2.

• Touch the first word after the number 2. ✔

• (Read paragraph 2 at a reasonably slow pace:)

> Roger didn't want to sweat all over his very favorite hat. So he took off his hat and put it under a bench that was next to a house. Roger planned to finish his walk without his hat, come back to the bench, pick up his black hat and go back home.

- So for picture 2, you'll show that part of the story: Roger putting his black hat under a bench.
4. The next part of the story tells what you'll draw in box 3.
- Touch the first word after the number 3. ✔
- (Read paragraph 3 at a reasonably slow pace:)

> What Roger didn't know was that the bench was next to Paul's house, and that Paul planned to paint that bench pink. Roger also didn't know that when Paul painted things, he plopped paint on things that were nearby.

- So for picture 3, you'll show that part of the story: The bench Roger's hat was under was next to Paul's house and you might want to show Paul getting his painting supplies ready.
5. Remember, you'll show Roger taking a walk, wearing his favorite big black hat and starting to sweat in picture 1. You'll show Roger putting his favorite hat under a bench in picture 2. You'll show that bench was next to Paul's house in picture 3 and that Paul was getting his painting supplies ready.

6. Everybody, touch the first word after the number 4. ✔
- All it says for number 4 is: **So, while Roger was on his walk, Paul came out and . . .** You're going to tell me what to write. I'll write it on the board. Then you'll copy it and draw a picture to show the ending.
- (Write on the board:)

   So, while Roger was on his walk, Paul came out and

- That's the part that's already written. Tell me the first thing to write: **So, while Roger was on his walk, Paul came out and . . .** what?
   (Call on several children. Write the story ending that the children dictate on the board. Prompt endings that express these ideas: *Paul started to paint the bench pink. Pink paint plopped on Roger's hat. Paul decided to fix the hat by painting it pink. Roger came back and couldn't find his black hat under the bench. A pink hat was there instead.*)
7. (After the story is completed, say:) Your turn. Copy the whole story ending. Don't copy the words that are already written, but copy everything else. Write carefully. Raise your hand when you're finished.
   (Observe children and give feedback.)
8. Later you can draw the pictures to tell about each part of the story.

Objectives

- Generate sentences with past, present and future tense. (Exercise 1)
- Identify words based on characteristics. (Exercise 2)
- Generate sentences with contractions. (Exercise 3)
- Identify absurdities. (Exercise 4)
- Name things that a statement does NOT tell. (Exercise 5)
- Write sentences given picture cues. (Exercise 6)
- Read a word and write the opposite of the word. (Exercise 7)
- Label cardinal directions on a map. (Exercise 8)

EXERCISE 1   Verb Tense

1. Let's play a statement game.
2. Listen: The teacher will talk. What does that statement tell? (Signal.) *What the teacher will do.*
3. Everybody, say the statement that tells what the teacher will do. Get ready. (Signal.) *The teacher will talk.*
4. Now make up a statement that tells what the teacher did. Get ready. (Signal.) *The teacher talked.*
5. Now make up a statement that tells what the teacher is doing. Get ready. (Signal.) *The teacher is talking.*
- (Repeat steps 2 through 5 until firm.)
6. Let's do one more.
7. Listen: The cars are stopping. What does that statement tell? (Signal.) *What the cars are doing.*
8. Everybody, say the statement that tells what the cars are doing. Get ready. (Signal.) *The cars are stopping.*
9. Now make up a statement that tells what the cars will do. Get ready. (Signal.) *The cars will stop.*
10. Now make up a statement that tells what the cars did. Get ready. (Signal.) *The cars stopped.*
- (Repeat steps 7 through 10 until firm.)

EXERCISE 2   Description

1. I'm going to say two things about something you know. See if you can figure out what I'm talking about.
2. (Hold up one finger.) A glot is a person.
- (Hold up two fingers.) A glot delivers mail to people's houses.

3. Everybody, tell me what you know about a glot.
- (Hold up one finger.) *A glot is a person.*
- (Hold up two fingers.) *A glot delivers mail to people's houses.*
4. (Repeat step 3 until firm.)
5. Everybody, tell me what a glot is. Get ready. (Signal.) *A mail carrier.*
6. (Repeat steps 3 and 5 until firm.)
7. Here's another one.
8. (Hold up one finger.) Katting is a word.
- (Hold up two fingers.) Katting is a synonym for weeping.
9. Everybody, tell me what you know about katting.
- (Hold up one finger.) *Katting is a word.*
- (Hold up two fingers.) *Katting is a synonym for weeping.*
10. (Repeat step 9 until firm.)
11. Everybody, tell me what katting is. Get ready. (Signal.) *Crying.*
12. (Repeat steps 9 and 11 until firm.)

EXERCISE 3   Contractions

Note: You will need books and a box.

1. It's time for some questions and statements.
2. (Point to a book.)
- Does a book have roots? (Signal.) *No.*
- Say the statement with a contraction. Get ready. (Signal.) *A book doesn't have roots.*
3. (Point to several books.)
- Do books have roots? (Signal.) *No.*
- Say the statement. Get ready. (Signal.) *Books don't have roots.*

4. (Point to three girls.)
- Do girls have roots? (Signal.) *No.*
- Say the statement. Get ready. (Signal.) *Girls don't have roots.*
5. (Point to a box.)
- Does a box have roots? (Signal.) *No.*
- Say the statement. Get ready. (Signal.) *A box doesn't have roots.*
6. Are we eating a wastebasket? (Signal.) *No.*
- Say the statement with a contraction for **are not.** Get ready. (Signal.) *We aren't eating a wastebasket.*
7. (Point to several girls.)
- Are they eating a wastebasket? (Signal.) *No.*
- Say the statement with a contraction for **are not.** Get ready. (Signal.) *They aren't eating a wastebasket.*
8. (Point to yourself.)
- Am I eating a wastebasket? (Signal.) *No.*
- Say the statement with a contraction for **are not.** Get ready. (Signal.) *You aren't eating a wastebasket.*
9. (Point to a boy.)
- Is he eating a wastebasket? (Signal.) *No.*
- Say the statement with a contraction for **is not.** Get ready. (Signal.) *He isn't eating a wastebasket.*
10. (Repeat steps 6 through 9 until firm.)

EXERCISE 4 Absurdity

1. Listen to this text and tell me what's absurd about it.
2. A girl used a pencil to sew a button on her glove. What did the girl do with the pencil? (Signal.) *Used it to sew a button on her glove.*
3. Then she put the glove on her foot. Where did she put the glove? (Signal.) *On her foot.*
4. Now tell me some things that are absurd about that text. (Call on two or three individual children.) (Ask the first child:) What's one thing that's absurd? (After the child's response, ask other children:) What's another thing that's absurd? (Praise all appropriate responses.)

EXERCISE 5 Statements

1. Listen to this statement.
2. The girl smiled because she was happy. Everybody, say that statement. Get ready. (Signal.) *The girl smiled because she was happy.*
3. Does that statement tell where the girl was? (Signal.) *No.*
- Does that statement tell if the girl was standing? (Signal.) *No.*
- Does that statement tell why the girl smiled? (Signal.) *Yes.*
- Does that statement tell what the girl is doing now? (Signal.) *No.*
- Does that statement tell why the girl is happy? (Signal.) *No.*
4. The girl smiled because she was happy. Everybody, say that statement again. (Signal.) *The girl smiled because she was happy.*
5. Name three things the statement does not tell you. (Call on individual children. Repeat three correct responses.)
6. You have named three things the statement does not tell us.
- Name the first thing. (Hold up one finger.) (The children give the first response.)
- Name the second thing. (Hold up two fingers.) (The children give the second response.)
- Name the third thing. (Hold up three fingers.) (The children give the third response.)

WORKBOOK

EXERCISE 6 Sentence Writing

| front | of | back |

———————————————————
———————————————————
———————————————————
———————————————————

1. Everybody, open your workbook to Lesson 128. Write your name. ✔
- You're going to write sentences about this picture.
- Touch the picture of the goat and the snake. ✔
- The picture shows who is in front of the car and who is in back of the car. Who is in front of the car? (Signal.) *A goat.*
- Who is in back of the car? (Signal.) *A snake.*
2. Say the sentence that tells who is in front of the car. Get ready. (Signal.) *The goat is in front of the car.*
- Say the sentence that tells who is in back of the car. Get ready. (Signal.) *The snake is in back of the car.*
3. (Repeat step 2 until firm.)
4. The word box shows how to spell the words **front, of** and **back.** You can figure out how to spell the other words.
5. Write the sentence for the goat. Pencils down when you're finished. ✔
- Now go to the next line and write the sentence for the snake. Pencils down when you're finished. ✔
6. (Call on individual children to read both their sentences.)

EXERCISE 7 **Opposites**

sad	clean	push	near	dirty

1. dirty _____

2. clean _____

3. far _____

4. happy _____

5. pull _____

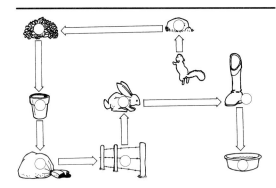

1. Everybody, find the next page. ✔
- (Hold up workbook. Point to top half.) Find the words in the box. ✔
- I'll read those words. Touch and follow along: **sad, clean, push, near, dirty.** ✔

2. Your turn. Touch the first word. ✔
- What word? (Signal.) *Sad.*
- Next word. ✔
- What word? (Signal.) *Clean.*
- Next word. ✔
- What word? (Signal.) *Push.*
- Next word. ✔
- What word? (Signal.) *Near.*
- Last word. ✔
- What word? (Signal.) *Dirty.*
- (Repeat step 2 until firm.)
3. You're going to write words that tell the opposite.
- Touch word 1. ✔
- That word is **dirty.** What word? (Signal.) *Dirty.*
- Everybody, what's the opposite of dirty? (Signal.) *Clean.*
4. The word **clean** is in the word box. Copy that word right after the word **dirty.** (Observe children and give feedback.)
5. (Repeat step 3 for word 2: **clean.**) (Repeat step 4 for **dirty.**)
6. (Repeat step 3 for word 3: **far.**) (Repeat step 4 for **near.**)
7. (Repeat step 3 for word 4: **happy.**) (Repeat step 4 for **sad.**)
8. (Repeat step 3 for word 5: **pull.**) (Repeat step 4 for **push.**)

EXERCISE 8 **Map Reading**

1. (Hold up workbook. Point to bottom half.) Everybody, touch the squirrel. ✔
2. This picture is a map of where the squirrel ran. You're going to color the arrows purple and write the directions on the objects.
3. Everybody, color the first arrow purple. ✔
- Remember to start from the squirrel. Then write the letter that shows the direction the squirrel went. ✔
4. You'll do the rest of the arrows later.

Objectives

- Name things that a statement does NOT tell. (Exercise 1)
- Identify absurdities. (Exercise 2)
- Discriminate between synonyms and opposites. (Exercise 3)
- Identify words based on characteristics. (Exercise 4)
- Generate sentences with contractions. (Exercise 5)
- Write sentences given picture cues. (Exercise 6)
- Construct verbal analogies. (Exercise 7)
- Write class names next to members of the class. (Exercise 8)

EXERCISE 1   Statements

1. Listen to this statement.
2. The boys laughed because the joke was funny. Everybody, say that statement. (Signal.) *The boys laughed because the joke was funny.*
3. Does that statement tell what the boys will do? (Signal.) *No.*
- Does that statement tell who laughed? (Signal.) *Yes.*
- Does that statement tell what the boys did? (Signal.) *Yes.*
- Does that statement tell who told the joke? (Signal.) *No.*
- Does that statement tell why the boys laughed? (Signal.) *Yes.*
4. The boys laughed because the joke was funny. Everybody, say that statement again. (Signal.) *The boys laughed because the joke was funny.*
5. Name three things the statement does not tell you. (Call on individual children. Repeat three correct responses.)
6. You have named three things the statement does not tell us.
- Name the first thing. (Hold up one finger.) (The children give the first response.)
- Name the second thing. (Hold up two fingers.) (The children give the second response.)
- Name the third thing. (Hold up three fingers.) (The children give the third response.)

EXERCISE 2   Absurdity

1. Listen to this text and tell me what's absurd about it.
2. A woman used some dirt to clean a table. What did the woman do with the dirt? (Signal.) *Cleaned a table.*

3. Then she put a rug on the table. What did she put on the table? (Signal.) *A rug.*
4. Now tell me some things that are absurd about the text. (Call on two or three individual children. Ask the first child:) What's one thing that's absurd? (After the child's response, ask other children:) What's another thing that's absurd? (Praise all appropriate responses.)

EXERCISE 3   Synonyms/Opposites

1. Tell me if I name synonyms or opposites. Think big.
2. Listen: Near. Close. Say those words. (Signal.) *Near. Close.*
- Do near and close mean the same thing? (Signal.) *Yes.*
- So are they synonyms or opposites? (Signal.) *Synonyms.*
- (Repeat step 2 until firm.)
3. Listen: Small. Little. Say those words. (Signal.) *Small. Little.*
- Do small and little mean the same thing? (Signal.) *Yes.*
- So are they synonyms or opposites? (Signal.) *Synonyms.*
- (Repeat step 3 until firm.)
4. Listen: Shiny. Dull. Say those words. (Signal.) *Shiny. Dull.*
- Do shiny and dull mean the same thing? (Signal.) *No.*
- So are they synonyms or opposites? (Signal.) *Opposites.*
5. (Repeat steps 2 through 4 until firm.)

EXERCISE 4   Description

1. I'm going to say two things about something you know. See if you can figure out what I'm talking about.
2. (Hold up one finger.) A chuke is a place.
   - (Hold up two fingers.) You buy food to cook at home at a chuke.
3. Everybody, tell me what you know about a chuke.
   - (Hold up one finger.) *A chuke is a place.*
   - (Hold up two fingers.) *You buy food to cook at home at a chuke.*
4. (Repeat step 3 until firm.)
5. Everybody, tell me what a chuke is. Get ready. (Signal.) *A grocery store.*
6. (Repeat steps 3 and 5 until firm.)
7. Here's another one.
8. (Hold up one finger.) Garg is a month of the year.
   - (Hold up two fingers.) Garg comes after November.
9. Everybody, tell me what you know about Garg.
   - (Hold up one finger.) *Garg is a month of the year.*
   - (Hold up two fingers.) *Garg comes after November.*
10. (Repeat step 9 until firm.)
11. Everybody, tell me what Garg is. Get ready. (Signal.) *December.*
12. (Repeat steps 9 and 11 until firm.)

EXERCISE 5   Contractions

1. You're going to say statements with contractions.
2. (Point to everyone.)
   - Were we walking on the ceiling? (Signal.) *No.*
   - Here's the statement with a contraction: We weren't walking on the ceiling. Everybody, say the statement. (Signal.) *We weren't walking on the ceiling.*
3. (Point to two boys.)
   - Were they walking on the ceiling? (Signal.) *No.*
   - Say the statement. Get ready. (Signal.) *They weren't walking on the ceiling.*
4. (Point to one boy.)
   - Was he walking on the ceiling? (Signal.) *No.*
   - Say the statement. Get ready. (Signal.) *He wasn't walking on the ceiling.*
5. (Point to yourself.)
   - Was I walking on the ceiling? (Signal.) *No.*
   - Say the statement. Get ready. (Signal.) *You weren't walking on the ceiling.*
6. (Point to a girl.)
   - Was she walking on the ceiling? (Signal.) *No.*
   - Say the statement. Get ready. (Signal.) *She wasn't walking on the ceiling.*
7. (Repeat steps 2 through 7 until firm.)
8. Here are some more.
9. (Point to a girl. Use the girl's name in sentences.)
   - Is _____ flying out the window? (Signal.) *No.*
   - Say the statement about _____. Get ready. (Signal.) *_____ isn't flying out the window.*
10. (Point to everyone.)
    - Are we flying out the window? (Signal.) *No.*
    - Say the statement. Get ready. (Signal.) *We aren't flying out the window.*
11. (Point to three children.)
    - Are they flying out the window? (Signal.) *No.*
    - Say the statement. Get ready. (Signal.) *They aren't flying out the window.*
12. (Point to a boy.)
    - Is he flying out the window? (Signal.) *No.*
    - Say the statement. Get ready. (Signal.) *He isn't flying out the window.*
13. (Repeat steps 9 through 12 until firm.)

EXERCISE 6 Sentence Writing

tiger   front   of
eagle   back

1. Everybody, open your workbook to Lesson 129. Write your name. ✔
•   You're going to write sentences about this picture.
•   Touch the picture of the tiger and the eagle. ✔
•   The picture shows who is in front of the tree and who is in back of the tree. Who is in front of the tree? (Signal.) *An eagle.*
•   Who is in back of the tree? (Signal.) *A tiger.*
2. Say the sentence that tells who is in front of the tree. Get ready. (Signal.) *The eagle is in front of the tree.*
•   Say the sentence that tells who is in back of the tree. Get ready. (Signal.) *The tiger is in back of the tree.*
3. (Repeat step 2 until firm.)
4. The word box shows how to spell the words **tiger, front, of, eagle,** and **back.** You can figure out how to spell the other words.
5. Write the sentence for the eagle. Pencils down when you're finished. ✔
•   Now go to the next line and write the sentence for the tiger. Pencils down when you're finished. ✔
6. (Call on individual children to read both their sentences.)

EXERCISE 7 Analogies

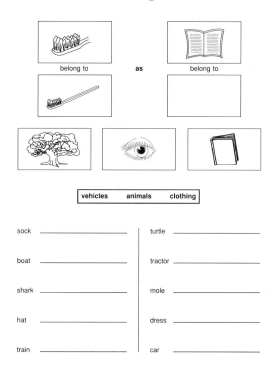

belong to   as   belong to

vehicles   animals   clothing

sock	_____	turtle	_____
boat	_____	tractor	_____
shark	_____	mole	_____
hat	_____	dress	_____
train	_____	car	_____

1. Everybody, find the next page. ✔
•   (Hold up workbook. Point to top half.)
•   The pictures show parts and the objects that have those parts.
2. Touch the bristles. ✔
•   The picture that's right below shows what they belong to. Everybody, what do bristles belong to? (Signal.) *A toothbrush.*
•   Tell me about bristles. Get ready. (Signal.) *Bristles belong to a toothbrush.*
3. Touch the pages. ✔
•   Touch the picture that shows what pages belong to. ✔
•   Everybody, what do pages belong to? (Signal.) *A book.*
•   Tell me about pages. Get ready. (Signal.) *Pages belong to a book.*
4. Tell me about bristles. Get ready. (Signal.) *Bristles belong to a toothbrush.*
•   Tell me about pages. Get ready. (Signal.) *Pages belong to a book.*
5. Say the whole analogy about bristles and pages. Get ready. (Signal.) *Bristles belong to a toothbrush as pages belong to a book.*
6. (Repeat step 5 until firm.)
7. Draw a line from the pages to the object they belong to.
    (Observe children and give feedback.)

EXERCISE 8 Classification

1. (Hold up workbook. Point to bottom half.) Everybody, I'll read the words in the box. You touch the words.
- First word: vehicles. ✔
- Next word: animals. ✔
- Last word: clothing. ✔
2. Your turn to read the words in the box.
- First word. What word? (Signal.) *Vehicles.*
- Next word. What word? (Signal.) *Animals.*
- Last word. What word? (Signal.) *Clothing.* Yes, vehicles, animals, and clothing.
3. Everybody, put your finger under the word **sock.** ✔
- What word? (Signal.) *Sock.*
- Is a **sock** in the class of vehicles, in the class of animals, or in the class of clothing? (Signal.) *Clothing.*
- Copy the word **clothing** next to the word **sock.** ✔
- Read what you wrote. (Signal.) *Clothing.*
4. Everybody, put your finger under the next word. ✔
- What word? (Signal.) *Boat.*
- Is a **boat** in the class of vehicles, in the class of animals, or in the class of clothing? (Signal.) *Vehicles.*
- Copy the word **vehicles** next to the word **boat.** ✔
- Read what you wrote. (Signal.) *Vehicles.*
5. Everybody, put your finger under the next word. ✔
- What word? (Signal.) *Shark.*
- Is a **shark** in the class of vehicles, in the class of animals, or in the class of clothing? (Signal.) *Animals.*
- Copy the word **animals** next to the word **shark.** ✔
- Read what you wrote. (Signal.) *Animals.*
6. Everybody, put your finger under the word **hat.** ✔
- What word? (Signal.) *Hat.*
- Next word. What word? (Signal.) *Train.*
- Next word. What word? (Signal.) *Turtle.*
- Next word. What word? (Signal.) *Tractor.*
- Next word. What word? (Signal.) *Mole.*
- Next word. What word? (Signal.) *Dress.*
- Last word. What word? (Signal.) *Car.*
7. (Repeat step 6 until firm.)
8. Later you can write the class that goes with each word you just read.

LESSON 130

EXERCISE 1 Contractions

1. It's time for some questions and statements.
2. (Point to a girl.)
- Does she have gloves on her feet? (Signal.) *No.*
- Say the statement with a contraction. Get ready. (Signal.) *She doesn't have gloves on her feet.*
3. (Point to several girls.)
- Do they have gloves on their feet? (Signal.) *No.*
- Say the statement. Get ready. (Signal.) *They don't have gloves on their feet.*
4. (Point to yourself.)
- Do I have gloves on my feet? (Signal.) *No.*
- Say the statement. Get ready. (Signal.) *You don't have gloves on your feet.*
5. (Point to everyone.)
- Do we have gloves on our feet? (Signal.) *No.*
- Say the statement. Get ready. (Signal.) *We don't have gloves on our feet.*
6. (Repeat steps 2 through 5 until firm.)
7. Here are some more.

8. (Point to several children.)
- Were they washing an elephant? (Signal.) *No.*
- Say the statement with a contraction. Get ready. (Signal.) *They weren't washing an elephant.*
9. (Point to a chair.)
- Was it washing an elephant? (Signal.) *No.*
- Say the statement. Get ready. (Signal.) *It wasn't washing an elephant.*
10. (Point to a boy.)
- Was he washing an elephant? (Signal.) *No.*
- Say the statement. Get ready. (Signal.) *He wasn't washing an elephant.*
11. (Point to two boys.)
- Were they washing an elephant? (Signal.) *No.*
- Say the statement. Get ready. (Signal.) *They weren't washing an elephant.*
12. (Point to three chairs.)
- Were they washing an elephant? (Signal.) *No.*
- Say the statement. Get ready. (Signal.) *They weren't washing an elephant.*
13. (Repeat steps 8 through 12 until firm.)

EXERCISE 2 Actions

1. We're going to play an action game.
2. Listen to this rule. If the teacher stands up **and** waves, say **stop.**
Listen again. If the teacher stands up and waves, say **stop.**
- Everybody, say the rule with me. Get ready. (Signal.) *If the teacher stands up and waves, say **stop.***
- All by yourselves. Get ready. (Signal.) *If the teacher stands up and waves, say stop.*
- (Repeat step 2 until firm.)

3. What's the rule? (Signal.) *If the teacher stands up and waves, say stop.*
* Tell me, what are you going to do if the teacher stands up and waves? (Signal.) *Say stop.*
4. Are you going to say **stop** if the teacher stands up and waves? (Signal.) *Yes.*
* Are you going to say **stop** if the teacher waves? (Signal.) *No.*
* Are you going to say **stop** if the teacher stands up? (Signal.) *No.*
5. Now we're going to play the game.
6. What's the rule? (Signal.) *If the teacher stands up and waves, say stop.*
7. Let's see if I can fool you. Get ready. (Pause. Wave.) (Signal.) (The children should not do anything.)
8. See if I can fool you. Get ready. (Pause. Stand up.) (Signal.) (The children should not do anything.)
9. See if I can fool you this time. Get ready. (Pause. Stand up and wave.) (Signal.) (The children should say *stop.*)
10. (Repeat steps 7 through 9 until firm.)

EXERCISE 3 Verb Tense

1. Let's play a statement game.
2. Listen: The girls are trying. What does that statement tell? (Signal.) *What the girls are doing.*
   Yes, what the girls are doing.
3. Everybody, say the statement that tells what the girls are doing. Get ready. (Signal.) *The girls are trying.*
4. Now make up a statement that tells what the girls will do. Get ready. (Signal.) *The girls will try.*
5. Now make up a statement that tells what the girls did. Get ready. (Signal.) *The girls tried.*
6. (Repeat steps 2 through 5 until firm.)

7. Let's do one more.
8. Listen: The monkey climbed. What does that statement tell? (Signal.) *What the monkey did.*
9. Everybody, say the statement that tells what the monkey did. Get ready. (Signal.) *The monkey climbed.*
10. Now make up a statement that tells what the monkey is doing. Get ready. (Signal.) *The monkey is climbing.*
11. Now make up a statement that tells what the monkey will do. Get ready. (Signal.) *The monkey will climb.*
12. (Repeat steps 8 through 11 until firm.)

EXERCISE 4 Opposites

1. Listen: an opposite of strong is weak. What's an opposite of strong? (Signal.) *Weak.*
* Listen: an opposite of dark is light.
* What's an opposite of dark? (Signal.) *Light.*
2. We're going to play a word game.
3. Everybody, think of a chicken that is not cooked. It is the opposite of cooked. What's the opposite of cooked? (Signal.) *Raw.*
* So a chicken that is the opposite of cooked is . . . (Signal.) *raw.*
4. Everybody, think of a song that is not happy. It is the opposite of happy. What's the opposite of happy? (Signal.) *Sad.*
* So a song that is the opposite of happy is . . . (Signal.) *sad.*
5. Everybody, think of an elephant that is not strong. It is the opposite of strong. What's the opposite of strong? (Signal.) *Weak.*
* So an elephant that is the opposite of strong is . . . (Signal.) *weak.*

6. Everybody, think of a theater that is not dark. It is the opposite of dark. What's the opposite of dark? (Signal.) *Light.*
- So a theater that is the opposite of dark is . . . (Signal.) *light.*
7. Everybody, think of a dish that is not dirty. It is the opposite of dirty. What's the opposite of dirty? (Signal.) *Clean.*
- So a dish that is the opposite of dirty is . . . (Signal.) *clean.*

EXERCISE 5   Description

1. I'm going to say two things about something you know. See if you can figure out what I'm talking about.
2. (Hold up one finger.) A bome is a building.
- (Hold up two fingers.) You find teachers and students in a bome.
3. Everybody, tell me what you know about a bome.
- (Hold up one finger.) *A bome is a building.*
- (Hold up two fingers.) *You find teachers and students in a bome.*
4. (Repeat step 3 until firm.)
5. Everybody, tell me what a bome is. Get ready. (Signal.) *A school.*
6. (Repeat steps 3 and 5 until firm.)
7. Here's another one.
8. (Hold up one finger.) A regturb is a tool.
- (Hold up two fingers.) You use a regturb to take your temperature.
9. Everybody, tell me what you know about a regturb.
- (Hold up one finger.) *A regturb is a tool.*
- (Hold up two fingers.) *You use a regturb to take your temperature.*
10. (Repeat step 9 until firm.)
11. Everybody, tell me what a regturb is. Get ready. (Signal.) *A thermometer.*
12. (Repeat steps 9 and 11 until firm.)

EXERCISE 6   Writing Stories About Characters

☐ Paul   ☐ Sweetie   ☐ Bleep and Molly

☐ Rolla   ☐ Roger   ☐ Clarabelle

☐ Honey   ☐ Roxie   ☐ Bragging Rats

1. We don't have any more lessons in this program. But we need some more stories for our library, so you're going to write them.
- First we have to figure out which characters we're going to write about.
2. Everybody, open your workbook to Lesson 130. Write your name. ✔
- Those are pictures of the characters you've read about. You have to pick your three favorite characters. Those are the characters you'd like to write about most.
- Here's how you do that: You make a check in the box by your three favorite characters. Remember, you can make only three check marks. So look over the characters carefully. Select the three you'd like to write about most and put check marks for those three characters. Remember, only three characters. Do it now.
(Observe children and give feedback.)

3. Let's see who the all-time favorites are. (Write on the board:)

Paul

- Raise your hand if you made a check for Paul. ✔
(Count children's raised hands. Write the number after Paul.)
- (Repeat step 3 for the rest of the characters:) (Write to show)

Paul ☐
Sweetie ☐
Bleep and Molly ☐
Rolla ☐
Roger ☐
Clarabelle ☐
Honey ☐
Roxie ☐
Bragging Rats ☐

4. (Announce the three winning characters.)
5. (Assign children to four teams.)
We'll work in teams to make up one good story today. Each team should get together and decide which of the three characters they want to tell about today.
- Talk to your teammates and agree on one of the three winning characters. Raise your hands when you're finished. ✔
- (Ask each team which character they want to tell about.)

6. Now each team is going to work together to make up a good story about the character you chose. Remember, the stories you make up must be the right kind of story for the character. So work out the details. Then each team will tell their story to me. I'll write it. We'll see if each team can come up with a great story.
(Observe teams and give feedback. Praise teams that consider different ideas. Praise cute ideas.)

Note: The rest of the lesson may be spread out over several days.

---

7. (Direct each team to dictate a story. Write it on the board or on a piece of butcher paper. You may wish to type up the stories and duplicate them so that each child will have their own booklet to illustrate.)
8. (For later assignments:
a. teams can make up a story for one of the other characters;
b. children can individually copy and illustrate one or more of the stories;
c. teams can make up a story based on a made-up character not introduced in the program.)

Scope
and
Sequence

Grade 1

	Phonics/ Vocabulary	Comprehension	Grammar/ Usage/ Mechanics	Writing/ Composition/ Speaking	Study Skills
Lesson 1	Opposites: 2	Classification: 1, 3, 4, 8 Listening Comprehension: 5 Recalling Details: 6 Following Directions: 7			
Lesson 2	Where: 2 Days Of Weeks: 3, 6 Opposites: 5	Classification: 1, 4, 10 Listening Comprehension: 7 Recalling Details: 8 Following Directions: 9			
Lesson 3	Where: 2 Days Of Week: 3, 6 Opposites: 5	Classification: 1, 4, 10 Listening Comprehension: 7 Recalling Details: 8 Following Directions: 9			
Lesson 4	Where: 2 Months Of Year: 3 Opposites: 5 Days Of Week: 6 Part/Whole: 9	Classification: 1, 4 Listening Comprehension: 7 Recalling Details: 8 Following Directions: 10			
Lesson 5	Actions: 1 Where/When: 3 Days Of The Week: 4 Months Of The Year: 4 Seasons: 4 Opposites: 5 Yesterday/Today: 6 Part/Whole: 9	Classification: 2, 10 Listening Comprehension: 7 Recalling Details: 8			
Lesson 6	Where: 2 Days Of The Week: 3 Seasons: 3 Months Of The Year: 3 Where/When: 4 Opposites: 6 Yesterday/Today: 7	Classification: 1, 5 Listening Comprehension: 8 Recalling Details: 9			
Lesson 7	Where: 1 Where/When: 2 Occupations: 3 Days Of The Week: 4 Seasons: 4 Months Of The Year: 4 Opposites: 5 Yesterday/Today: 6 Part/Whole: 8	Listening Comprehension: 7 Sequencing: 7 Classification: 9			
Lesson 8	Actions: 1 Where/When: 2 Days Of The Week: 3 Months Of The Year: 3 Seasons: 3 Same/Different: 4 Yesterday/Today: 6	Classification: 5, 9 Recalling Details: 7 Sequencing: 8 Following Directions: 10			
Lesson 9	Actions: 1 Where/When: 3 Opposites: 4 Days Of The Week: 5 Months Of The Year: 5 Seasons: 5 Same/Different: 6 Yesterday/Today: 8 Part/Whole: 11 Location: 12	Classification: 2 Reasoning: 7 Listening Comprehension: 9 Sequencing: 10			
Lesson 10	Actions: 1 Opposites: 3 Days Of The Week: 4 Months Of The Year: 4 Seasons: 4 Same/Different: 5 Yesterday/Today: 6 Location: 9	Classification: 2 Listening Comprehension: 7 Following Directions: 8			

	Phonics/ Vocabulary	Comprehension	Grammar/ Usage/ Mechanics	Writing/ Composition/ Speaking	Study Skills
Lesson 11	Actions: 1 Where: 3 Opposites: 4 Months Of The Year: 5 Days Of The Week: 5 Seasons: 6 Same/Different: 6 Yesterday/Today: 7 Location: 10	Classification: 2, 9 Sequencing: 8			
Lesson 12	All/Some/None: 1 Where: 3 Opposites: 4 Days Of The Week: 5 Months Of The Year: 5 Seasons: 5 Same/Different: 6 Yesterday/Today: 7 Part/Whole: 10 Location: 11	Classification: 2 Listening Comprehension: 8 Recalling Details: 9			
Lesson 13	All/Some/None: 1 Opposites: 3 Same/Different: 5 Months Of The Year: 6 Days Of The Week: 6 Seasons: 5 Today/Yesterday: 7 Part/Whole: 9	Classification: 2, 10 Reasoning: 4 Sequencing: 8			
Lesson 14	Actions: 1 Days Of The Week: 2 Months Of The Year: 2 Seasons: 2 Same/Different: 4 When/Where: 6 Location: 9	Sequencing: 3, 7 True/False: 5 Classification: 8			
Lesson 15	Actions: 1 Calendars: 3 Yesterday/Today: 4 Same/Different: 5	True/False: 2 Sequencing: 6 Listening Comprehension: 7 Recalling Details: 8			
Lesson 16	Actions: 1 Same/Different: 3 Materials: 4, 5 Calendars: 7 Yesterday/Today: 8 Part/Whole: 10 Location: 11	Sequencing: 2, 9 True/False: 6			
Lesson 17	Actions: 1 When: 2 Materials: 4, 5 Same/Different: 6 Opposites: 7 Calendars: 10 Part/Whole: 13	Reasoning: 3 Sequencing: 8, 11 True/False: 9 Character Extrapolation: 12 Following Directions: 14			
Lesson 18	Actions: 1 Materials: 2 Opposites: 3 When: 4 Calendars: 6 Location: 10	Only: 5 Sequencing: 7, 8 Listening Comprehension: 8 Asking Questions: 9			
Lesson 19	Actions: 1 Materials: 2 Opposites: 3 Yesterday/Today: 6 Calendars: 7	Only: 4 Sequencing: 5, 8 Listening Comprehension: 8			
Lesson 20	Actions: 1 Materials: 2 When: 3 Opposites: 4 Calendars: 5, 7 Who/Where/When: 6 Part/Whole: 10	Sequencing: 8 Asking Questions: 9			
Lesson 21	Actions: 1 Materials: 4 Opposites: 5 Who/Where/When: 7 Calendars: 8 Part/Whole: 12	Reasoning: 2 Only: 3 Classification: 6 Listening Comprehension: 9 Recalling Details: 10 Asking Questions: 11			

	Phonics/ Vocabulary	Comprehension	Grammar/ Usage/ Mechanics	Writing/ Composition/ Speaking	Study Skills
Lesson 22	All/Some/None: 1 When: 2 Calendars: 4 Materials: 6 Opposites: 7 Part/Whole: 11	Classification: 3 Only: 5 Listening Comprehension: 8 Sequencing: 9 Asking Questions: 10			
Lesson 23	Actions: 1 Opposites: 3 Calendars: 6 Yesterday/Today: 7 Location: 10	Only: 2 Reasoning: 4 Classification: 5 Sequencing: 8 Asking Questions: 9			
Lesson 24	Materials: 1, 6 Calendars: 2 Opposites: 4	Classification: 3 Who/Where/When: 5 Sequencing: 7			
Lesson 25	Opposites: 4 Calendars: 6 Location: 10	Asking Questions: 1 Only: 2 Who/Where/When: 3 Classification: 5 Listening Comprehension: 7 Recalling Details: 8 Asking Questions: 9			
Lesson 26	Calendars: 2 Yesterday/Today/ Tomorrow: 3 Opposites: 6 Part/Whole: 9	Only: 1 Asking Questions: 4, 8 Classification: 5 Sequencing: 7			
Lesson 27	Actions: 1 Calendars: 3 Opposites: 6 Yesterday/Today/ Tomorrow: 7 Location: 10	Only: 2 Who/Where/When/What: 4 Asking Questions: 5, 9 Sequencing: 8			
Lesson 28	Actions: 1 Calendars: 3 Opposites: 4 Yesterday/Today/ Tomorrow: 6 Asking Questions: 9 Classification: 10	Who/Where/When/What: 2 Classification: 5 Listening Comprehension: 7 Recalling Details: 8	Verb Tense: 1		
Lesson 29	Actions: 1 Calendars: 2 Opposites: 4 Yesterday/Today/ Tomorrow: 7	Classification: 3 Sequencing: 5, 8 Only: 6 Asking Questions: 9 Classification: 10	Verb Tense: 1		
Lesson 30	Actions: 1 Materials: 2 Opposites: 3 Today/Tomorrow/ Future: 4 Part/Whole: 9	Classification: 5 Asking Questions: 6, 8 Recalling Details: 7			
Lesson 31	Today/Tomorrow/ Future: 3 Part/Whole: 9	Classification: 1, 5 Opposites: 2 Who/When/What/Why: 4 Recalling Details: 6 Sequencing: 7 Asking Questions: 8			
Lesson 32	Today/Tomorrow/ Future: 3 From/To: 8 Location: 9	Classification: 1, 2, 5 Who/When/Why: 4 Asking Questions: 6 Sequencing: 7			
Lesson 33	Today/Tomorrow/ Future: 5	Classification: 1, 4 Who/What/Why: 2 Asking Questions: 3 Listening Comprehension: 6 Sequencing: 7			
Lesson 34	Today/Tomorrow/ Future: 3 Actions: 5 From/To: 7 Part/Whole: 8	Classification: 1, 2 What/Where/Why: 4 Sequencing: 5 Listening Comprehension: 6 Recalling Details: 6			
Lesson 35	Actions: 1 Today/Tomorrow/ Future: 2 Materials: 5 From/To: 7	Sequencing: 1, 6 Who/What/Why: 3 Classification: 4 Asking Questions: 8			

	Phonics/ Vocabulary	Comprehension	Grammar/ Usage/ Mechanics	Writing/ Composition/ Speaking	Study Skills
Lesson 36	Calendar: 3 Materials: 5 Today/Tomorrow/ Future: 7 From/To: 9	Classification: 1 Who/How/Why: 2 Classification: 4 Why/When/Where: 6 Sequencing: 8 Asking Questions: 10			
Lesson 37	Actions: 1 From/To: 2 Calendar: 4 Opposites: 5 Today/Tomorrow/ Future: 7	Why/When/Where: 3 Who/How/Why/Where: 6 Sequencing: 8			
Lesson 38	Calendars: 4 Today/Tomorrow/ Future: 7 Materials: 10	Classification: 1, 11 When/Where: 2 Deduction: 3, 5 Asking Questions: 6 Listening Comprehension: 8 Sequencing: 9 All/Some: 11			
Lesson 39	Opposites: 3 Today/Tomorrow/ Future: 4 From/To: 7 Materials: 8	Classification: 1 Deduction: 2 Sequencing: 5		Dramatic Activity: 6	
Lesson 40	Opposites: 4 Today/Tomorrow/ Future: 6 From/To: 8	Classification: 1, 7 Deduction: 2 Who/How/Why: 3 Why/Where: 5		Dramatic Activity: 9	
Lesson 41	Definitions: 1 From/To: 2 Things/Actions: 3 Today/ Tomorrow/ Future: 5 Part/Whole: 10	Classification: 1, 4, 9 True/False: 6 Recalling Details: 7 Sequencing: 8			

Lesson 42	Actions: 1
	Definitions: 2
	Today/Tomorrow/
	  Future: 4
	From/To: 5
	Things/Actions: 6, 7
		Classification: 2, 3
		True/False: 8
					Data
					  Collection: 9

Lesson 43	Actions: 1 Definitions: 2 Today/Tomorrow/ Future: 3 From/To: 10	Classification: 2, 6, 9 True/False: 4 Listening Comprehension: 7 Recalling Details: 8	Verb Tense: 5 Address: 8		
Lesson 44	Actions: 1 Today/Tomorrow/ Future: 3 From/To: 4, 9 Things/Actions: 5 Part/Whole: 10	Classification: 2 True/False: 6 Listening Comprehension: 7 Recalling Details: 8			

Lesson 45	Actions: 1
	Things/Actions: 2, 6
	Today/Tomorrow/
	  Future: 4
		Who/What/When/Where/
		  Why: 3
		Classification: 5, 10
		True/False: 7
		Listening Comprehension: 8
		Recalling Details: 9
		Following Directions: 11			

Lesson 46	Today/Tomorrow/
	  Future: 2
	Things/Actions: 4
	Opposites: 6
		Classification: 3
		Who/What/When/Where/
		  Why: 5
		Sequencing: 8
			Verb Tense: 1		Maps: 7
					Cardinal
					  Directions: 7

Lesson 47	Actions: 1
	Today/Tomorrow/
	  Future: 2
	Description: 4
	Things/Actions: 7, 8
	From/To: 12
	Materials: 13
		Classification: 3
		Who/What/When/Where/
		  Why: 5
		Reasoning: 6
		Listening Comprehension: 10
		Recalling Details: 10
		Sequencing: 11
					Maps: 9
					Cardinal
					  Directions: 9

Lesson 48	Actions: 1
	From/To: 2
	Today/Tomorrow/
	  Future: 4
	Things/Actions: 5, 6
	Description: 8
	Materials: 13
		Classification: 7, 12
		Who/What/When/Where/
		  Why: 9
		Sequencing: 11
			Verb Tense: 3		Maps: 10
					Cardinal
					  Directions:
					  10

	Phonics/ Vocabulary	Comprehension	Grammar/ Usage/ Mechanics	Writing/ Composition/ Speaking	Study Skills
Lesson 49	Actions: 1 Today/Tomorrow/ Future: 3 Description: 4 Things/Actions: 5 Materials: 6 Analogies: 11 Locations: 12	Classification: 2 True/False: 7 Listening Comprehension: 9 Recalling Details: 10 Following Directions: 12			Maps: 8 Cardinal Directions: 8
Lesson 50	Actions: 1 Things/Actions: 3 Description: 4 Materials: 5, 11 Opposites: 6 Today/Tomorrow/ Future: 7 Analogies: 10	Classification: 2			Maps: 8 Cardinal Directions: 8 Data Collection: 9
Lesson 51	Actions: 1 Description: 2 Materials: 3, 4 Today/Tomorrow/ Future: 5		Verb Tense: 6	Sentences: 8	Maps: 7 Cardinal Directions: 7
Lesson 52	Actions: 1 Description: 3 Things/Actions: 4 Today/Tomorrow/ Future: 5 Analogies: 10	Classification: 2, 9 Listening Comprehension: 7 Recalling Details: 8			Maps: 6 Cardinal Directions: 6
Lesson 53	Actions: 1 Things/Actions: 2 Materials: 3 Today/Tomorrow/ Future: 6	True/False: 4 Classification: 5		Sentences: 8	Maps: 7 Cardinal Directions: 7
Lesson 54	Actions: 1 Materials: 2 Things/Actions: 3 Today/Tomorrow/ Future: 4 Materials: 8	Listening Comprehension: 5 Recalling Details: 6			Maps: 7 Cardinal Directions: 7
Lesson 55	Things/Actions: 1 Materials: 3 Opposites: 4 Today/Tomorrow/ Future: 5	Classification: 2		Sentences: 6	
Lesson 56	Things/Actions: 1 Opposites: 2 Calendars: 3 Materials: 5 Today/Tomorrow/ Future: 6 Locations: 9	True/False: 4 Listening Comprehension: 7			Maps: 8 Cardinal Directions: 8
Lesson 57	Description: 1 Opposites: 3 Calendars: 4 Things/Actions: 5 Materials: 6 Analogies: 9	True/False: 2 Character Extrapolation: 7 Classification: 8			
Lesson 58	Things/Actions: 1 Description: 2, 5 Opposites: 3 Calendars: 4 Locations: 9	Listening Comprehension: 6		Days Of The Week: 7	Maps: 8 Cardinal Direction: 8
Lesson 59	Things/Actions: 1 Actions: 3 Description: 5 Calendars: 6 Opposites: 7	Main Ideas: 4 Listening Comprehension: 8	Verb Tense: 2	Days Of The Week: 9	
Lesson 60	Description: 1, 3 Opposites: 4 Calendars: 5	Classification: 2 Listening Comprehension: 6		Dramatic Activity: 7 Days Of The Week: 8	
Lesson 61	Description: 1 Opposites: 4 Calendars: 5 Analogies: 8	True/False: 2 Who/What/Where/When/ Why: 3 Classification: 7		Sentences: 6	

	Phonics/ Vocabulary	Comprehension	Grammar/ Usage/ Mechanics	Writing/ Composition/ Speaking	Study Skills
Lesson 62	Things/Actions: 1 Description: 2 Opposites: 4 Calendars: 5 Analogies: 9	Who/What/Where/When/ Why: 3 Listening Comprehension: 6 Story Completion: 6 Recalling Details: 7			Maps: 8 Cardinal Directions: 8
Lesson 63	Actions: 1 Description: 3 Opposites: 4 Calendars: 5 Part/Whole: 8	Main Ideas: 2 Listening Comprehension: 6 Story Completion: 6 Classification: 7			
Lesson 64	Opposites: 2 Description: 3, 4 Calendars: 5	Classification: 1		Sentences: 6	
Lesson 65	Opposites: 1 Description: 3 Calendars: 5 Analogies: 6 Materials: 10	Main Ideas: 2 Classification: 4 Listening Comprehension: 7		Months Of The Year: 8	Maps: 9 Cardinal Directions: 9
Lesson 66	Description: 1 Analogies: 2 Opposites: 3 Calendars: 4	Listening Comprehension: 5 Recalling Details: 5		Months Of The Year: 6	
Lesson 67	Opposites: 1 Description: 2 Calendars: 3 Analogies: 5	Main Ideas: 4 Sequencing: 6		Dramatic Activity: 7	
Lesson 68	Opposites: 1, 3 Things/Actions: 2 Calendars: 4 Analogies: 5, 9	Listening Comprehension: 6 Classification: 8		Months Of The Year: 7	
Lesson 69	Actions: 1 Things/Actions: 2 Calendars: 3 Opposites: 4 Description: 5 Analogies: 6	Sequencing: 1 Recalling Details: 8		Dramatic Activity: 7	
Lesson 70	Analogies: 1, 8 Opposites: 3 Calendars: 4 Actions: 5	Main Ideas: 2 Character Extrapolation: 6 Classification: 7			
Lesson 71	Analogies: 1 Calendars: 2 Description: 3, 4 Materials: 8	Classification: 5 Sequencing: 6			Maps: 7 Cardinal Directions: 7
Lesson 72	Analogies: 1 Opposites: 2 Calendars: 3 Description: 4 Things/Actions: 6 Materials: 9	Why/When/Where: 5 Character Extrapolation: 7 Classification: 8			
Lesson 73	Description: 1 Analogies: 2 Calendars: 3 Things/Actions: 4	Classification: 5		Sentences: 6	
Lesson 74	Analogies: 1 Calendars: 3 Actions: 4 Things/Actions: 5 Materials: 9	True/False: 2 Who/What/When/Where/ Why: 6 Classification: 8		Sentences: 7	
Lesson 75	Analogies: 1 Calendars: 4, 6 Description: 5 Part/Whole: 9	Classification: 2, 8 True/False: 3		Sentences: 7	
Lesson 76	Calendars: 3 Description: 4 Analogies: 5, 10 Materials: 6	True/False: 1 Who/What/When/Where/ Why: 2 Reasoning: 7 Classification: 9		Sentences: 8	
Lesson 77	Materials: 1 Synonyms: 2, 6 Calendars: 3 Analogies: 4 Same/Different: 5 Description: 7	True/False: 8 Listening Comprehension: 9 Story Completion: 9 Recalling Details: 11		Dramatic Activity: 10	

	Phonics/ Vocabulary	Comprehension	Grammar/ Usage/ Mechanics	Writing/ Composition/ Speaking	Study Skills
Lesson 78	Things/Actions: 1 Calendars: 2 Analogies: 3 Synonyms: 4 Same/Different: 5 Description: 7	True/False: 6		Sentences: 8	
Lesson 79	Analogies: 1 Calendars: 2 Description: 3 Synonyms: 4 Materials: 5 Same/Different: 6	Classification: 7 Reasoning: 8 Listening Comprehension: 9 Sequencing: 11		Dramatic Activity: 10	
Lesson 80	Analogies: 1 Description: 2 Calendars: 3 Synonyms: 4 Materials: 5 Analogies: 9	Reasoning: 6 Classification: 8		Sentences: 7	
Lesson 81	Description: 1, 7 Analogies: 2, 10 Calendars: 4 Things/Actions: 5 Synonyms: 6	Reasoning: 3 Classification: 9		Sentences: 8	
Lesson 82	Analogies: 1, 5 Calendars: 2 Description: 4	Listening Comprehension: 6 Recalling Details: 6 Classification: 7			Maps: 3 Cardinal Directions: 3
Lesson 83	Analogies: 1, 10 Calendars: 3, 7 Synonyms: 5 Things/Actions: 6	Asking Questions: 2 Classification: 9		Sentences: 8	Maps: 4 Cardinal Directions: 4
Lesson 84	Calendars: 1, 2 Analogies: 3 Synonyms: 4	Classification: 7		Sentences: 5	Maps: 6 Cardinal Directions: 6
Lesson 85	Synonyms: 1 Description: 2 Calendars: 3	Who/What/When/Where/Why: 5, 7 Asking Questions: 6 Reasoning: 8 Classification: 9 Listening Comprehension: 10 Sequencing: 10			Maps: 4 Cardinal Directions: 4
Lesson 86	Analogies: 1 Calendars: 2 Things/Actions: 3 Synonyms: 4 Synonyms/Opposites: 5 Description: 7 Materials: 11	Asking Questions: 5 Who/What/When/Where/Why: 8 Classification: 10		Sentences: 9	
Lesson 87	Analogies: 1 Description: 2 Calendars: 3 Synonyms: 5	Asking Questions: 4		Sentences: 6	Data Collection: 7
Lesson 88	Analogies: 1 Calendars: 3 Description: 4 Synonyms: 5	Classification: 2, 7		Sentences: 6	
Lesson 89	Description: 2 Synonyms: 3 Calendars: 4 Materials: 6 Analogies: 9	Classification: 1, 10 Who/What/When/Where/Why: 5 Reasoning: 7		Sentences: 8	
Lesson 90	Synonyms: 1 Description: 2 Analogies: 4 Calendars: 5	Asking Questions: 3 Classification: 8		Sentences: 6	Maps: 7 Cardinal Directions: 7
Lesson 91	Synonyms/Opposites: 1 Description: 2 Synonyms: 3 Analogies: 4 Calendars: 6	Who/What/When/Where/Why: 5 Asking Questions: 8		Sentences: 7	
Lesson 92	Calendars: 3 Description: 4 Synonyms: 5	Who/What/When/Where/Why: 1 Asking Questions: 2, 7		Sentences: 6	
Lesson 93	Analogies: 1, 4 Calendars: 2 Descriptions: 3, 5	Classification: 8		Sentences: 6	Maps: 7 Cardinal Directions: 7

	Phonics/ Vocabulary	Comprehension	Grammar/ Usage/ Mechanics	Writing/ Composition/ Speaking	Study Skills
Lesson 94	Description: 1 Synonyms: 2 Analogies: 4	Asking Questions: 3 Who/What/When/Where/ Why: 5 If-Then: 6		Sentences: 7	
Lesson 95	Analogies: 1 Description: 2 Synonyms/Opposites: 5 Materials: 8	Main Ideas: 3 Who/What/When/Where/ Why: 4 If-Then: 6 Classification: 7			
Lesson 96	Analogies: 1 Description: 2, 6 Synonyms/Opposites: 3	Main Ideas: 4 Asking Questions: 5 Character Extrapolation: 8		Sentences: 7	
Lesson 97	Synonyms: 1 Description: 3 Synonyms/Opposites: 4 Analogies: 5	Reasoning: 2 Asking Questions: 6 Classification: 7			
Lesson 98	Synonyms/Opposites: 1 Opposites: 3 Analogies: 4, 9 Description: 6	Main Ideas: 2	Verb Tense: 5	Sentences: 7	Maps: 8 Cardinal Directions: 8
Lesson 99	Description: 1 Synonyms: 2 Calendars: 3 Analogies: 4	Asking Questions: 5 Who/What/When/Where/ Why: 6 If-Then: 7		Sentences: 8	
Lesson 100	Opposites: 1 Analogies: 2 Description: 3 Synonyms: 4	Reasoning: 5 If-Then: 6		Sentences: 7	
Lesson 101	Analogies: 1 Opposites: 2 Description: 4 Synonyms: 5	Reasoning: 6 Classification: 9	Verb Tense: 3	Sentences: 7	Maps: 8 Cardinal Directions: 8
Lesson 102	Analogies: 1 Opposite: 2 Synonyms: 3 Materials: 4	Classification: 7	Verb Tense: 5	Sentences: 6	Maps: 8 Cardinal Directions: 8
Lesson 103	Analogies: 1, 7 Opposites: 2 Description: 4 Synonyms: 5	Classification: 3, 8		Sentences: 6	

Lesson 104	Analogies: 2
	Opposites: 3
		Who/What/When/Where/
		Why: 4
		Classification: 5, 8
				Sentences: 6	Maps: 1, 7
					Cardinal
					  Directions:
					  1, 7

Lesson 105	Analogies: 1 Description: 4 Synonyms: 5	Main Ideas: 2 Classification: 3 Asking Questions: 7		Sentences: 6	
Lesson 106	Analogies: 1, 7 Opposites: 2 Description: 3 Synonyms/Opposites: 4 Calendars: 5 Materials: 8			Sentences: 6	
Lesson 107	Description: 2 Opposites: 3 Synonyms/Opposites: 5 Analogies: 7	Classification: 1, 8 Asking Questions: 4		Sentences: 6	
Lesson 108	Analogies: 1 Materials: 2 Description: 3 Opposites: 5	Reasoning: 4 Classification: 8		Sentences: 6	Maps: 7 Cardinal Directions: 7
Lesson 109	Analogies: 1 Opposites: 2 Description: 5	Asking Questions: 4 If-Then: 6	Verb Tenses: 3	Sentences: 7	
Lesson 110	Synonyms: 1 Description: 4 Analogies: 5	Reasoning: 2 Classification: 7	Verb Tenses: 3	Sentences: 6	Maps: 8 Cardinal Directions: 8
Lesson 111	Synonyms: 1, 2 Calendars: 3 Opposites: 4 Analogies: 8	Reasoning: 5 Classification: 7		Sentences: 6	

	Phonics/ Vocabulary	Comprehension	Grammar/ Usage/ Mechanics	Writing/ Composition/ Speaking	Study Skills
Lesson 112	Synonyms: 1 Description: 3, 5 Opposites: 7	Who/What/When/Where/ Why: 2 Classification: 8	Verb Tenses: 4	Sentences: 6	
Lesson 113	Opposites: 1, 3, 8 Actions: 2 Synonyms: 5 Analogies: 7	Asking Questions: 4		Sentences: 6	
Lesson 114	Synonyms: 1 Materials: 2 Description: 3 Calendars: 5	Main Ideas: 4 If-Then: 6		Sentences: 7	
Lesson 115	Opposites: 1 Synonyms: 3 Description: 4	Reasoning: 2 Listening Comprehension: 5 Recalling Details: 5			
Lesson 116	Opposites: 2, 8 Description: 3 Synonyms: 4, 5	If-Then: 1 Classification: 7		Sentences: 6	
Lesson 117	Synonyms: 2 Description: 3 Opposites: 4 Calendars: 5	If-Then: 1 Classification: 7		Sentences: 6	Maps: 8 Cardinal Directions: 8
Lesson 118	Synonyms: 3 Description: 4	Asking Questions: 1 Main Ideas: 2 If-Then: 5 Character Extrapolation: 6		Sentences: 7	
Lesson 119	Opposites: 1 Synonyms: 3 Description: 4, 5 Analogies: 9	If-Then: 6 Classification: 8	Verb Tenses: 2	Sentences: 7	
Lesson 120	Contractions: 3 Opposites: 4 Description: 5	Who/What/When/Where/ Why: 1 Reasoning: 2 Asking Questions: 7	Contractions: 3	Sentences: 6	
Lesson 121	Opposites: 3, 6 Contractions: 4 Analogies: 7	Asking Questions: 2	Verb Tenses: 1	Sentences: 5	
Lesson 122	Synonyms/Opposites: 1 Opposites: 4 Contractions: 5	Main Ideas: 3 Classification: 7	Verb Tenses: 2 Contractions: 5	Sentences: 6	Maps: 8 Cardinal Directions: 8
Lesson 123	Description: 2 Synonyms: 3 Contractions: 4 Opposites: 5	Character Extrapolation: 7	Verb Tenses: 1 Contractions: 4	Sentences: 6	
Lesson 124	Contractions: 1 Description: 3 Calendars: 4 Analogies: 7	Classification: 6	Contractions: 1 Verb Tenses: 2	Sentences: 5	
Lesson 125	Description: 2 Opposites: 3, 6	Main Ideas: 1 Reasoning: 4 Classification: 7		Sentences: 5	
Lesson 126	Contractions: 1 Actions: 2 Description: 3, 4 Opposites: 6		Contractions: 1	Sentences: 5	Maps: 7 Cardinal Directions: 7
Lesson 127	Contractions: 1 Description: 2	Asking Questions: 3 Who/What/When/Where/ Why: 4 Reasoning: 5 Listening Comprehension: 6 Story Completion: 6, 7 Recalling Details: 7	Contractions: 1		
Lesson 128	Description: 2 Contractions: 3 Opposites: 7	Reasoning: 4 Main Ideas: 5	Verb Tenses: 1 Contractions: 3	Sentences: 6	Maps: 8 Cardinal Directions: 8
Lesson 129	Synonyms/Opposites: 3 Description: 4 Contractions: 5 Analogies: 7	Main Ideas: 1 Reasoning: 2 Classification: 8	Contractions: 5	Sentences: 6	
Lesson 130	Contractions: 1 Actions: 2 Opposites: 4 Descriptions: 5		Contractions: 1 Verb Tenses: 3	Writing Stories About Characters: 6	